OPPORTUNITIES IN CLOTHING

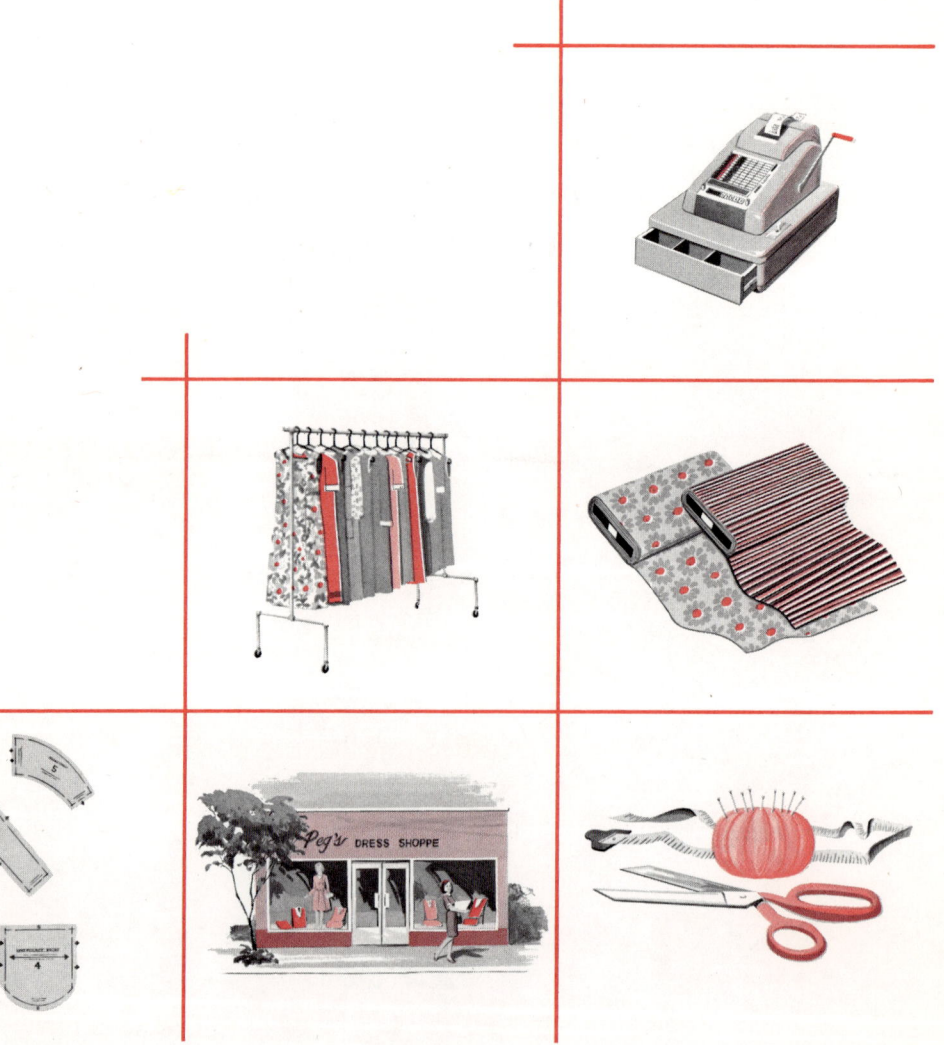

Opportunities in clothing

FASHION • MERCHANDISING

IRENE E. McDERMOTT, author of home economics textbooks

and

JEANNE L. NORRIS, High School home economics teacher, Pittsburgh Public Schools, Pittsburgh, Pennsylvania

CHAS. A. BENNETT CO., INC., PEORIA, ILLINOIS

Copyright 1968, 1972

By
IRENE E. MCDERMOTT and JEANNE L. NORRIS
All rights reserved
Library of Congress Catalog No. 68–10288
PRINTED IN THE UNITED STATES OF AMERICA
ISBN 87002–140–0
75 K 5 4 3 2

Preface

In today's automated, rapidly changing world there is a major emphasis on education and the need for better preparation to cope with a more complicated tomorrow. There is a growing competition for employment, and an ever-decreasing need for unskilled and untrained workers. It becomes increasingly important for those students who plan no further education beyond high school to acquire some vocational skill *before* high school graduation. A good basic education, plus the acquisition of a skill, may open the door to an interesting and satisfying job, good wages, and steady employment. This textbook is designed to meet the needs of any who will soon be faced with taking their places in the working world.

The selection of a life's work is a very serious decision. Vocational planning deserves a great deal of time and thought. There isn't space in a book of this nature, however, to explore your interests and abilities, to investigate vocational opportunities and classify them, and then to help you decide what job best suits you. It is assumed that you have already given serious thought to all important preliminary steps and have decided that your interests and abilities point to the field of clothing.

Perhaps you still are not certain about the exact job you want. You may wish to explore the types of jobs available in greater detail (See Chapter 2). However, you do know that you want to work with some aspect of clothing.

With this decision already made, you are concerned with acquiring the necessary information and skills to prepare yourself for the clothing industry, obtaining the job, taking your place in the working world, and being successful on the job. This book is concerned with these areas. Its aim is to prepare you broadly for your chosen occupation—employment in the clothing field. It is intended to provide you with the necessary information and concepts, plus give you an opportunity for practical experience so that you will be qualified for employment in some particular area. Possibilities include: salesperson (in either wearing apparel or fabrics), stock clerk, alterations (in a store, shop, or as a business at home), clothing repair (in a laundry or dry-cleaning establishment), home dressmaking, or garment manufacturing. Included is a complete study in the following areas: fabrics; color, line, and design; industrial sewing; basic clothing construction skills; fitting and alteration; retailing policies and procedures; selling techniques; and merchandise know-how.

CONTENTS...

	Page
PREFACE	5

Chapter 1. YOU IN THE WORLD OF WORK 9

Getting the Job, 10; Sample Resumés, 12, 13; Sample Application Form, 16, 17; Sample Applicant's Health Form, 18; Simple Applications, What Can You Expect from the Job?, 20; What Does the Employer Expect from You?, 26; For the Real Career Girl, 27; Review Questions, Further Discussions, To Gain Experience, 29.

Chapter 2. A PLACE FOR YOU IN THE CLOTHING FIELD . . 30

Merchandising, Salesperson, 30; Stock Clerk, 34; Comparison Shopper, 36; Industrial Sewing, Sewing Machine Operator, 37; Sewing Services, Dressmaking, 39.

Chapter 3. THE COLOR, LINE, AND DESIGN STORY IN FASHION 43

Color, 46; The Language of Color, 49; What Color Can Do, 50; How Colors Affect Each Other, 52; Principles in Using Color Effectively, 54; Selecting Colors for an Individual, 57; The Power of Color, 59; Line, 60; The Power of Line, 65; Using Line Effectively in Clothing, 67; Principles of Design, 72; Proportion, 74; Rhythm, 76; Emphasis, 78; Hints for Selecting Flattering Fashions, 79; Review Questions, Further Discussion, To Gain Experience, 61, 71, 82.

Chapter 4. THE FABRIC STORY TODAY AND TOMORROW . . 83

Sewing, Clothing Maintenance, 83; Selling, 84; Labeling Controlled by Law, 86; Generic Names, 87; The Natural Fibers, Cotton, 88; Linen, 92; Wool, 95; Silk, 103; The Man-made Fibers, 109; Rayon, 111; Acetate, 115; Nylon, 119; Acrylic Fibers, 121; Polyester Fibers, 123; How Cloth Is Made, 126; Fabric Finishes, 142; Review Questions, 108, 126, 143, 150.

Chapter 5. MERCHANDISING CLOTHING—A FASCINATING BUSINESS 151

Distribution or Marketing, 151; Work of Salesperson, 152; The Store, 153; Sound Selling Techniques, 163; Mechanics of Selling, 174; Samples: Cash Register Receipt, Sales Slips, 177–179; Stock Card, 190; Inventory Sheet, 191; Knowing Your Merchandise, 193; Ready-to-Wear, 195; Coats, 201; Suits, 202, Separates, Skirts, 204; Blouses, 205;

Contents

Page

Sweaters, 207; Sportswear, 209; Swim Wear, 210; Foundation Garments, Girdles, 212; Bras, 214; Lingerie, 217; Panties, Sleepwear, Lounge Wear, 218; Hosiery, 219; Shoes, 221; Gloves, 223; Yard Goods, 225; Review Questions, Further Discussion, 162, 173, 192, 229, 230; To Gain Experience, 173, 192, 230.

Chapter 6. INDUSTRIAL SEWING **231**

Machines for Industrial Sewing, 233; Dress, Posture, Self Care at Machines, 234; Control of Power-Driven Machines, 235; Straight Stitching, 236; Turning Corners, 237; Stitching Curves, Parts of a Power-Driven Lockstitch Machine, Threading the Machine, 239–241; Winding the Bobbin, Under Threading Directions, 242; Length of Stitch, Thread Tensions, 244; Simple Machine Adjustments, 245; Adjusting Bobbin Winder, Knee Press Lever, 247; Adjusting the Foot Treadle, Care of the Machine, Cleaning and Oiling the Machine, 248; Time-Saving Stitching Techniques, 249; To Backstitch, Stitching Without Pinning or Basting, 250; Ripping Properly, 251; Production Chart, 253; Inspection Chart, 254; Safety Tips, 234, 236, 237, 239, 241, 243, 246–249, 251; Helpful Hints, 242, 245, 250; Review Questions, 257.

Chapter 7. BASIC SKILLS FOR CLOTHING CONSTRUCTION . . **258**

The Materials You Work With, Fabric, 259; Thread, 260; Tools and Equipment, 261, Scissors, 262, 263; Measuring Gauges, 264; Tools for Marking, 264; Needles, 265; Pressing Equipment, 266–268; The Language of Sewing, 268; Taking Measurements, 272; Charts: Pattern Sizes, Teen, Junior, Misses', 274, Women's, Junior Petite, Half-Size, 275; Using a Commercial Pattern, 276; Pattern Markings, 277; The Cutting Process, 279; Assembling a Garment, 286; Construction Techniques, 287; Seams, 287–291; Darts, 291; Tucks, Pleats, 292; Gathers, 293; Shirring, Easing, Facing and Interfacings, 294, 295; Bias Facings, 296; Bindings, 297; Collars, 298–300; Sleeves, 300, 301; Plackets, 301; Slide Fasteners, 302–304; Hems, 304–306.

Chapter 8. FITTING AND ALTERATION, A HIGHLY SPECIALIZED BUSINESS **307**

Skill and Understanding Required, Judging What Can Be Done, 308; "How-to" Points, 309; To Mark with Chalk, Thread, 311; Fitting Techniques, Skirt Alterations, Guidelines for Proper Fit, Correcting Fitting Problems, 312–321; Bodice Alterations, 321–336; To Gain Experience, 336.

BIBLIOGRAPHY **337**

INDEX **345**

LIST OF COLOR ILLUSTRATIONS

A rainbow, 47

The color wheel, 49

New fibers, novelty yarns and weaves, interesting finishes—make available the wide range of fabrics on the market today, 84

Sample fabric swatches of plain weave and its variations, 132

A punch card system automatically controls the weaving of intricate patterns on a modern Jacquard loom, 136

A tailored shirt dress, jacketed sheath dress ensemble, and the separates shown are all color coordinated, 194

A shift and skimmer, 195

Dress stylings: Princess line skimmer, Blouson, Baby doll, and Coat dress, 196

The coat—a basic piece around which to build a wardrobe, 201

Suit stylings: Tailored, Dressmaker, Cardigan, Pants suit, Ensemble—dress and jacket, 203

Separates: Skirts, jacket, blouses, pullovers, shells; Sportswear: Slacks, skirts, pants toppers, pullovers, and skimmers, 205

Chapter 1

You in the World of Work

THE CHANGING role of women is shown in many ways, particularly in statistics on our nation's work force. Not long ago women worked only when there was economic necessity for them to do so; now it is the custom for a girl to work, regardless of need. Approximately 40% of the entire population is working, and more than one-third of these workers—over 27 million—are women. According to the U. S. Department of Labor, 45% of all women over 16 are working, and 56% of women between the ages of 20 and 24 are employed. The proportion of women who work is expected to continue to rise. Viewed another way, girls born today have a life expectancy of about 73 years; it is expected that 8 out of 10 of them will work at least 30 years during their lifetime.

No longer do women feel they must choose between marriage and a career; they can have both. In part this is because there is less work to do in the modern home. Most goods are produced outside the home. Also, with time-saving modern conveniences and labor-saving equipment, household chores require considerably less time. Homemakers thus find more time available for other activities, so that many of them—including your own mother, perhaps—seek gainful employment, assuming the dual role of homemaker and career woman.

According to studies of the United States Bureau of Labor Statistics, approximately 60% of all working women are married; one out of every three married women is working. This proportion is expected to rise steadily.

Most girls who finish high school can look forward to a life pattern that fits somewhere in the following, unless they go on to college:

17–18	start working
18–22	get married
19–25	first child
26–29+	last child
24–35	youngest child ready for school
17–65	25 to 30 years to work (not continuously)

Some girls will stop working when they get married, but the majority

9

continue to work. With the first baby coming, the majority of young mothers stop working and remain home until the youngest child is ready for school. A few mothers with preschool children (1 in 5) do continue to work, however, usually because of need. When all the children are in school, the trend is for mother to go back to work. She is approaching her middle thirties, has been a non-wage earner for approximately 10 years, and has 20–25 productive years ahead of her. Although she may not work continuously until she is 65, she will no doubt spend a substantial part of those years in the working world.

However, the girl who starts to work when she is 18 may work for as many as 44 years, if she remains single. Also, the married woman who remains childless may work as many as 35 years, perhaps more; and we have seen that even the woman with children may spend 25–30 years in the working world. Like any other average, these are not necessarily what *you* will do. Figures do imply that you may be working for the greater part of your life.

About half of your waking hours will be devoted to working. Whether or not you will be happy and satisfied or discontented and unhappy will depend primarily upon whether or not *you are doing the kind of work that you enjoy, that brings good returns, that others appreciate, and that best suits you*. It will also depend to a large extent upon your *attitude* toward your job. Why are you working? What do you expect from your job? What are your obligations to your job? To your employer? To your co-workers? Day after day, whether or not you are successful in your work depends not as much on luck or "pull" or getting the breaks, as on your ability to do the job, your interest in the job, and your attitude.

"What do I want to do?" is a very serious question for a person to ask. It deserves a great deal of time and thought. It is assumed that you have already given serious thought to this important question and have decided that your interests and abilities point to some particular area in the field of clothing. You know you are *needed;* you know you will be in the great world of *fashion,* whatever the job may be. With your decision already made, you are concerned with (1) acquiring the necessary information and skills, (2) obtaining the job, and (3) being successful on the job.

GETTING THE JOB

Finding a job can be compared to selling, only in this case you are both the salesman and the "product" that is for sale! Your "customers" are prospective employers. The employer has a job opening; you are interested in getting that job. You will succeed in being hired—when others are applying also—if the employer feels that you are the best possible choice.

How can you accomplish this? First, think about the type of work in which you are interested. Have you studied subjects in school that will help you toward your goal? Have you acquired the basic information about

Getting the Job

the subject matter (such as garment construction) necessary to understand and perform the job? Have you any practical experience? (Vocational-technical courses in the secondary schools may have helped you obtain this experience by providing on-the-job training while in school. Such training enables anyone to progress more quickly and naturally from school to the business world.) Knowing what you want and what you think you can do, plus some practical experience (such as summer or Christmas work you have had), you will then be qualified for employment. Alert people with the right training in a particular skill usually have no difficulty obtaining employment in the clothing-fashion world. Also there are many opportunities for those with a desire and willingness to *work and learn.*

Next, plan your *approach to job-hunting* carefully. To sell a product, it is helpful to learn all you can about that product. In like manner, if you want to impress another person, you must know yourself. • What are the pertinent facts about you that make you suitable for employment? • What evidence is there that you are qualified for this particular job? Identify your *special skills* and *talents,* enumerate your personal qualifications, and organize all the information about you that may be of interest to a prospective employer. Concentrate on your education, background, and experiences that are pertinent to the kind of work you hope to do. List your *activities* and *interests* that are relevant. Have you received any *honors* or *awards;* made any significant contributions or accomplishments; or distinguished yourself in any other way?

Remember, you will find good things about yourself if you try, even though you have never thought of your special interests—and have never won any prizes.

Special requirements:

There are also special requirements that must be met before you start to work. • You must register for *Social Security* and receive a card and identifying number. If you do not have a card yet, you can get one by applying at your district office of the Social Security Administration. (Inquire at the post office.) • If you are under 18 years of age, you will need a *Work Certificate,* which verifies your age. This paper can be obtained at school by presenting your birth certificate and having your parents appear to sign for you. • Anticipate having to furnish your prospective employer with *personal references.* Determine the people you feel will be able to recommend you—your school principal or counselor, a teacher, a former employer, your rabbi, minister, or priest, etc.—and ask permission to use their names. • Take time to organize all the pertinent information about yourself and prepare a *data sheet* or *résumé.* There are several advantages to putting the information in writing: (1) You organize everything clearly in your own mind and are less likely to forget something. (2) The information is at your fingertips, all thought out beforehand, ready to present clearly and concisely when needed. There is no hesitation or stammering; you can talk convincingly and to the point about your qualifications. Incomplete or inaccurate information may result in failure to get a particular job.

(3) It is a businesslike procedure—and creates a favorable impression—to include such a summary sheet with a letter of application or to hand it to a prospective employer at the interview. At a glance, the interviewer can find out what he needs to know about you. (4) Every point is clearly set down. In this regard, always *type* the résumé, limiting it to one page if possible. For general information, a good copy is satisfactory (except for carbons, which smudge). But also present the original of a typed letter, so that it becomes more personal.

Applying through an agency:

The employment agency will ask for copies of your references. You will be told about other conditions—such as your record of grades and cost of the service.

A SAMPLE RÉSUMÉ

<u>Name</u>: Jane Doe

<u>Address</u>: 1001 Main Street, Anytown, U.S.A.

<u>Telephone</u>: 765-4321

<u>Personal Information</u>:
  Date of Birth: January 5, 19___

  Birthplace: Anytown, U.S.A.

  Height: 5' 5"

  Weight: 110 lbs.

  Health: Excellent (perfect attendance this year) Problems (if at all serious, describe frankly)

  Marital Status: Single

<u>Educational Information</u>:
  Will be graduated June 5, 19___ from North High School.

  Class standing: Upper third (or other position in standing)

  Major: Home Economics, including Merchandise-Clothing

  Related Subjects: Personal Development; Fabrics; Color, Line, and Design; Merchandising; Clothing Construction (or other subjects)

Getting the Job

    Activities: Honor society; cheerleader; class play costume committee; senior class social chairman; treasurer, travel club; church activities, or others

    Hobbies: Swimming, skiing, sewing, photography, or others

<u>Work Experience</u>:

    Part-time selling, sportswear, The Townhouse Department Store

    Member of Teen Fashion Board, The Townhouse

    Taught sewing at Day Camp (2 summers)

    Cashier, Neighborhood Theater (evenings and Saturday, 2 years)

    Others

<u>References</u>:

    Mr. John Smith, counselor
        North High School   2004 North St., Anytown   765-1224

    Mrs. T. L. Brown, director
        Anytown Day Camp   151 Glen St., Anytown   765-2413

    Miss Helen Green, sportswear supervisor
        The Townhouse Department Store   450 First St., Anytown   765-2000 Ext. 245

    The Reverend Frank M. Robbins
        Anytown Church   1250 Main St., Anytown   765-2212

    Others

SIMPLER FORM

For a job as salesperson or stock checking, gift wrapping, clothing construction, and others, a written application may not be expected. However, *have all information* on your grades, references, and previous work *with you* when you interview, so that you can fill out the application form properly.

Deciding where to apply:

Now you are ready, but how do you find job openings? You are looking for a job—and, in like manner, an employer with an opening is looking for applicants. The two of you can get together in a number of ways:

To contact a small business, the approach may be as informal as seeing a sign in the window—"Salesperson Wanted." In applying at larger retailers, distributors, or manufacturers, perhaps by word-of-mouth you hear of a soon-to-be-available opening where a friend works. *Let as many people as possible know that you are looking for work.* Then you have a good chance of hearing about possible openings. In addition, you may see in the newspaper that a company is planning to expand, or a store is planning to open a new branch. In these cases there will be new employment opportunities. If you find a promising lead, follow it through promptly. For out-of-town jobs, write a letter. Locally, call—in person or by telephone—to request an interview.

Employers make use of several methods to locate workers. You can easily use these when you apply. Large companies have their own personnel offices that are responsible for hiring new employees. These offices usually welcome new applicants. If you are interested in employment with a company, visit the personnel department and fill in an application blank. If nothing is available at the time, your application will be on file when an opening comes.

Some companies look for their prospective employees at the schools that train the kind of workers they need, especially when the job requires a special skill but not necessarily previous experience. Your school may operate a placement bureau or at least have a vocational counselor or coordinator who helps graduates find employment. There are definite advantages for you in making use of the school facilities. The school takes a personal interest in you and seeks to place you in a job for which you are well suited. Many also investigate the requests and accept only those that are desirable and reputable. There is no charge for this service.

A business with job openings often places an advertisement in the *Help Wanted* section of the newspaper. Check these ads for leads, if interested answer promptly, but don't depend upon them. In any city there are many jobs available that are never advertised in this way. The employer depends upon other methods to find employees. NOTE: Ask questions before answering "blind ads" in the newspaper, which do not describe the job. Although the great majority are legitimate, some may not be. Secure all the information you can before arranging an interview. Check with the Better Business Bureau if you are not familiar with the business or its reputation. **Caution:** Be wary of making telephone interview arrangements, to take place at unusual spots such as in a hotel or at unusual times such as after closing hours or weekends.

Many firms seek the help of *employment agencies* to find prospective employees and will register their openings with such an agency. State Employment Offices, in addition to giving an applicant job "leads," also operate counseling and testing services in an attempt to place the applicant in a job for which he is best suited. The State Employment Service makes no charge for either the employer or the applicant.

Private employment agencies offer assistance to those seeking employment. Those that specialize in certain types of employment may have exclusive access to the so-called "better jobs." Most of the private agencies are reliable, but unfortunately there are a few that are not. A check with the Better Business Bureau again will confirm an agency's reputation. All of the private agencies charge for their services. In some rare cases the employer pays the fee, but the usual practice is to charge the applicant. The fee is based on the beginning salary—perhaps the first week's or a percentage of the salary for a specified number of weeks. **Caution:** If you avail yourself of an agency's services, be sure you clearly understand the terms involved.

Employers' techniques with applicants:

If you have had a part-time or a summer job while you are in school, you have had some experience with employment techniques. Employers are seeking the one they feel is the best person of all the applicants to fill a position, and they make use of different methods to arrive at this conclusion. Requesting letters of application, application blanks, interviews, performance tests, and written tests of various types are all devices used to screen applicants. Whatever the procedure required, you must put your best foot forward to stand out from all the other applicants. The prospective employer probably has never seen you before and has comparatively few clues to the type of person you are. On such a basis he must reach a decision about you. Little things become very important, especially when you are being compared with others; they can mean the difference between being hired and not.

A busy employer may not have time to interview all the applicants for a job. The *letter of application,* therefore, is one way to eliminate those applicants who are obviously not suitable. Your letter can tell a prospective employer a great deal about you. Obviously, the information you include must tell him what he wants to know—why you are *interested* in the position for which you are applying and why you feel *qualified* for the position. The way the letter looks, the form used, spelling, grammar, neatness are also very revealing. **Remember,** be sure to follow the accepted form for writing a business letter. If you are not sure, check the instructions in an English or business textbook.

Your letter reflects your work habits. To create a favorable impression, follow these suggestions:

- Type the letter.
- Address it to a specific person, not just the company in general.
- Be brief and to the point.
- Indicate what type of work you are applying for, explain why you are applying for this particular job, and how you heard of the opening.
- If there is no particular opening that you know of—you are filing a general application—indicate the type of work you are interested in and why with this particular company.
- Include your personal résumé.
- Request an interview.
- Proofread the letter before sending it. Be sure *spelling is correct* and the letter *looks neat.*

You in the World of Work

A SAMPLE OF APPLICATION

> 1001 Main Street
> Anytown, U. S. A.
> May 18, 19___
>
> Mr. Gregg B. Russell, Personnel Manager
> Main Department Store
> Bigtown, U. S. A.
>
> Dear Mr. Russell:
>
> I wish to apply for the selling position advertised in this morning's Bigtown News.
>
> I shall be graduated from North High School on June 5 and am available for employment immediately. Selling is the type of work in which I am most interested and for which I believe I am well qualified.
>
> The enclosed resumé provides you with some of the information you may want concerning me. My favorite school subject was merchandising and I enjoy working with people. My counselor tells me I have a special aptitude for sales and my supervisor at the Townhouse Department Store, where I have worked on a part-time basis for the last two years, commended me on my sales ability and manner of dealing with customers. With my background and training I am confident I can meet your requirements.
>
> I can come for an interview any school day after four o'clock or I can come on a Saturday if you prefer. My home telephone number is 765-4321.
>
> Respectfully yours,
>
> *Jane Doe*
>
> (Miss) Jane Doe

Many companies require you to fill in an *application form*. Even though you provide a résumé, they prefer to have information regarding a certain set of details. Again, little things are important. The way in which you fill in the form provides a clue to your work habits and creates an impression of you in the eyes of the prospective employer. • Take time to fill in the form neatly and accurately. • Have your own pen with you in case the one that is provided doesn't write well. • *Read the directions* before

Getting the Job

KAUFMANN DEPARTMENT STORES
PITTSBURGH, PENNSYLVANIA
APPLICATION FOR EMPLOYMENT

L11W

PLEASE PRINT

Answer All Questions on Both Sides

NAME — LAST | FIRST | MIDDLE INITIAL | MAIDEN NAME
Date
Position Desired

ADDRESS — NO. | STREET | CITY | ZONE | PHONE NUMBER

AGE | BIRTH DATE — MONTH | DAY | YEAR | HUSBAND'S (WIFE'S) NAME
Social Security Number

How Long Lived at Present Address | List Previous Addresses

RMA

Mark X in Proper Space:
- ☐ Citizen
- ☐ Alien
- ☐ Intend to Become Citizen
- ☐ Married
- ☐ Single
- ☐ Widowed
- ☐ Separated
- ☐ Divorced
- ☐ Live with Parents
- ☐ Live with Relatives
- ☐ Own Home
- ☐ Rent
- ☐ Rooming
- ☐ No. of Dependents
- Relationship to you:

Inquiry | Checked

Education — Fill in Spaces | Grade Completed | Year | Graduated Yes / No | Last School Attended: Name ... City ... State ...
- Grade School
- High School
- Bus. College
- College or University

Inquiry | Checked

Service Record — Branch of Service | Date entered ... | Type of discharge ... | Date discharged ... | Serial Number ...

Have You Ever Applied To Kaufmann's for a Position? ☐ No ☐ Yes
Were You Ever in Kaufmann's Employ? ☐ No ☐ Yes
If so, When? ... What Dept? ...

IF PREVIOUSLY EMPLOYED GIVE NAMES AND ADDRESSES OF FORMER EMPLOYERS, STARTING WITH *LAST* ONE

Inquiry | Checked

1. NAME AND ADDRESS OF FIRM | Employed from Month/Year To Month/Year
   POSITION HELD | SALARY $ | IF SALESPERSON, WHAT DID YOU SELL? | WHY DID YOU LEAVE?

2. NAME AND ADDRESS OF FIRM | Employed from Month/Year To Month/Year
   POSITION HELD | SALARY $ | IF SALESPERSON, WHAT DID YOU SELL? | WHY DID YOU LEAVE?

3. NAME AND ADDRESS OF FIRM | Employed from Month/Year To Month/Year
   POSITION HELD | SALARY $ | IF SALESPERSON, WHAT DID YOU SELL? | WHY DID YOU LEAVE?

Remarks

Give Names of Two Persons, Neither Relatives Nor Former Employers, Who Have Known You for Over One Year and Can Vouch for Your Character and Habits
Inquiry | Checked

NAME | ADDRESS | CITY | OCCUPATION
NAME | ADDRESS | CITY | OCCUPATION

Service Card | Location Card

Give Names of Relatives or Friends Employed by Kaufmann's
NAME | RELATIONSHIP | DEPARTMENT
NAME | RELATIONSHIP | DEPARTMENT

Age Cert. applied for
Rec'd.
Ret'd.

ANSWER QUESTIONS ON OTHER SIDE—DO NOT WRITE BELOW THIS LINE

Date to Start Work | Department | Salary | Work Schedule | Position

Signature | Employed By | Date

Kaufmann's, Pittsburgh   *A sample application form.*   17

You in the World of Work

STATEMENT OF APPLICANT'S HEALTH

Height:............ft...............in. Weight..................lbs. Has your weight changed in the past year?

Gained................lbs. Lost..................lbs.

Answer "Yes" or "No" to each of the following questions:

1. Is condition of your health good? ....

   Do you have full use of:

   Both hands?................ Both feet?................. Sight of both eyes?...............

   If answer is "No" to any of the above questions, give details:..

   ....

2. Is an operation contemplated or has one been recommended by a physician?..................

3. Have you ever had trouble with any ailment or disease affecting your:

   Heart?............... Stomach?................ Brain or nervous system?...............

   Lungs?............... Back?.................... Kidneys?..................................

4. Is there an existing rupture or hernia?............... Tumor?..................

5. Have you had treatment or a surgical operation by any Physician or Practitioner within the past three years?............... If yes give details:..

   ....

6. Have you ever been declined for Life or Health Insurance?..................

7. Have you ever been arrested or convicted of any crime?..................

8. Name person you wish to be notified in case of accident or emergency:

   Name.................... Address.................... Phone Number....................

I hereby certify that all the statements and answers on both sides of this application form are complete and true; and I understand that if employed, and, subsequently, should any of the above statements be found false, Kaufmann's may terminate my employment.

....
Signature

```
Do not write in this block
T
A
P
Ex
Int.
Sp. Sk.
Rem.
```

Reverse side of application for employment.

you start. An erasure or cross-out detracts from the appearance and will give an unfavorable impression. If you make a mistake, perhaps you can have another form, but the fact that you needed another one could be detrimental to you. • Bring your own résumé with you to refer to so that the information is accurate and complete.

A *personal interview* usually follows the letter of application and filling out of the application form. The employer has all the factual information about you, but he can learn a great deal more "face to face." He is admittedly looking you over and you have only this one opportunity to give a favorable impression. Whether or not you get the job may depend upon what happens at this time. Many things affect the impression you make—your *appearance,* your *attitude,* your *personality,* your *interest,* your *personal manner,* as well as your qualifications and preparation for the job.

Appearance:

The interviewer forms an opinion about you the instant he sees you. Your appearance—neatness, good grooming, and appropriate dress—rate high or low. Pay particular attention to these points so as to score your best. How you dress depends in part upon the type of job for which you are applying. Wear clothing appropriate to the job—neither too dressy nor too casual, but remember that on some jobs you may dress more casually than usually seen outside. For example, some garment manufacturers permit their employees to wear slacks to work. Even so, slacks are not the appropriate attire when applying for the job. Put the school blouse and skirt, sox and flats away also—you are in an adult world. Dress simply; the cocktail dress is just as out of place as sports clothes. Your best choice is a basic, tailored, conservative dress or suit. Go easy on the eye make-up or dressy hair-do; avoid dangly jewelry; wear stockings; no loafers or casual shoes; be sure your clothing is spotlessly clean, in good repair, neat, and well-pressed. Again, little things are important. Is your *hair* neat, clean, and attractively styled but conservative? Are your *hands* and *nails* clean and well-groomed?

Answering questions:

The interviewer's main concern is how well you qualify for the job. All the questions he will ask are aimed in this direction; all of your answers should be carefully stated. *Let the interviewer lead all the talking.* Keep in mind he isn't trying to trick you or trap you, merely to find out all he thinks he should know about you. Answer his questions and nothing more; keep your comments brief and to the point. This is not a social conversation and "small-talk" is not appropriate. Still, certain special questions are inevitable; such as, "Tell me about yourself," or, "Why are you interested in this type of work?" Anticipate questions of this type and be prepared to answer them, emphasizing the information about yourself that *applies to the job.* (Refer to your résumé, perhaps giving the interviewer a copy at this time if he does not have one.)

The interviewer may ask if you have any questions. You will score higher if you ask about your responsibilities, the duties on the job, etc., rather than expressing an interest in coffee breaks, vacations, or fringe benefits. If you are hired, such information will be given you, whereupon you may turn down the job if you wish. *At this time,* such an interest doesn't indicate a serious attitude about work. Show simply that you are genuinely interested—if you are—and in what ways you have prepared for it.

Personal manner and actions:

Your personal manner is as important as what you say. Be courteous and alert. Speak distinctly in a pleasant tone of voice. Avoid nervous mannerisms, such as making lots of gestures with your hands, playing with jewelry, or fidgeting with your clothing, your hair, or your fingers. Practice good posture—sit straight, well back in the chair, hands in your lap, both feet on the floor, legs crossed at the ankles. Try to look calm and poised. A little nervousness can't be helped, but try to relax.

Here are some additional suggestions to help you put your best foot forward:
- Arrive on time.
- If you cannot keep your appointment, notify the interviewer ahead of time.
- Go by yourself.
- Introduce yourself.
- Call the interviewer by name, if possible.
- Stand until asked to be seated.
- Act in a businesslike way.
- Thank the interviewer at the close of the interview.
- Follow this up with a very brief "thank-you" letter.

SIMPLE APPLICATIONS

No matter where you apply, you probably will fill out an application form; you will have an interview. But you will not have to write a letter or go through formal steps of application. **Remember,** though, to dress well but simply, answer questions briefly and truthfully. Wait till offered the job before asking questions about extra things. You can always phone back if you find something better.

WHAT CAN YOU EXPECT FROM THE JOB?

Most people work to earn money to pay for the things they need and want for themselves and their families. It is natural to expect an adequate income. But if one has no experience and no special training or skill, it is reasonable that one will receive only a minimum wage. Then, with increased experience and further training or higher education, higher earnings can be expected. (Note that Federal law requires *equal pay* for work requiring *equal skill,* effort, and responsibility, prohibiting wage differential based only on sex.)

Starting salary alone, however, does not give the overall salary picture. In some cases, especially in your first job, although the starting salary may look big to you, some jobs never

Simple Applications

pay much more. You should know under what conditions and to what extent you can expect your earnings to increase. Are raises automatic according to years of employment, cost of living, or some such pre-arranged system; or are they based on employee performance and merit? If so, is the base salary just minimum; will there be more total pay dependent upon *sales* or *how much you produce?* Is the work *seasonal*, paying high wages during times of peak production and "laying-off" employees during the slack season?

The actual money in the pay envelope doesn't give the complete present earning picture either. Other benefits that employers offer often add considerably to your real income. Some of these "fringe benefits" include:

- **Group life insurance**—available to employees at reduced rates (payment deducted regularly from wages), or may be paid in full or in part by the company.
- **Group hospital insurance,** and/or *health and accident insurance,* and/or *major medical insurance*—may all be available to employees at lower rates (payment deducted from wages), or may be paid in full or in part by the company.
- **Pension plan**—a plan by which an employee may receive an income upon retirement after working a specified number of years, upon reaching a certain age, or both. Contribution to such a plan may be made entirely by the company or on a mutual basis, by which the employee contributes so much and the company matches his contribution. Upon termination of employment before retirement age, in most cases the employee receives the amount he has contributed plus interest, but not the employer's contribution.
- **Bonus**—a monetary "thank-you" that some employers give their employees at the end of the company's fiscal year or perhaps at Christmas, depending on profits or other considerations.
- **Profit-sharing**—a certain percentage of the company's profit is distributed to the employees in the form of cash or stock in the company.
- **Vacations with pay**—the amount of time depends upon the years of service and the company policy.
- **Paid holidays**—certain days each year—for example, Christmas, New Year's, Thanksgiving, Fourth of July, Memorial Day, and Labor Day—for which employees are paid although they do not work.
- **Sick leave**—an employee is permitted absence for illness without loss of pay. Company policy determines the number of days and whether or not they are cumulative from year to year.
- **Discount privileges**—opportunity to buy company products or other merchandise at a reduced price.
- **Credit union**—operated by employees, for employees only, offering the opportunity to save money, often at higher interest rates than other savings institutions, and to borrow money, usually at lower interest rates than available elsewhere.
- **Medical department**—medical attention available for accidents and illnesses while working.
- **Cafeteria**—lunch, snacks available to employees at comparatively low prices.

You in the World of Work

Let's take time to examine the *pay check* in more detail. As we mentioned, your beginning pay may sound large to you—more money than you have ever had at one time before. As you know, you don't "take home" all you earned, however. There are certain payroll deductions, some voluntary (your own choice), such as the insurance plans noted above, and some mandatory (required by law)—withholding tax and Social Security, for example. Your *total earnings before deductions* make up your *gross income*. Your *actual take-home pay* after deductions is *net income*.

Withholding tax:

The federal government, as well as many states, imposes an income tax on wage earners. You will probably pay this through an involuntary deduction—that is, a certain amount of money will be withheld from each paycheck. Thus you pay part of your tax each time you are paid, rather than having to pay it all in a lump sum. The amount of withholding depends on how much you earn, whether you are married or single, and how many exemptions you claim. (Basically you can claim one exemption for yourself and one for each person who depends on you for financial support.) Your employer gives you a statement each year showing what your total wages and withholding have been. You may still owe the government some money, if not enough was withheld, or you may be entitled to a refund.

Local wage tax:

Many local communities levy a wage tax, often 1 or 1½% of your salary. Some communities collect head taxes or an occupation tax which are flat rates—everyone pays the same amount regardless of earnings. These taxes may be deducted from your pay if your taxes go to the same community in which you are employed. If you do not live in the same community, you are responsible for paying direct.

Social Security:

The official name is Federal Old-Age and Survivors Insurance, a savings insurance plan which provides monthly payments when you retire or if you are permanently disabled, hospital benefits when you reach 65, or payments to your family in case of your death. The employee and employer share the cost by paying taxes. Deductions are made from your wages according to a definite tax rate. (For the current tax table, check with the area office of the Social Security Administration.) The employer contributes at the same rate, paying a matching amount for you. The employer is also responsible for reporting your wages and turning in your Social Security taxes every three months.

Almost all gainful employment is now covered by Social Security. The Social Security Administration keeps a record for each individual worker under his name and Social Security number. Before you start to work, you must register for Social Security and receive a card and identifying number. This number, good as long as you live, is used extensively for identification. You use it when you file your income tax; banks, Blue Cross, and any company that pays you dividends

Simple Applications

or interest, all require it for identification. Keep the card in a safe place where you can always find it. Have your number with you for convenient use.

Job security:

Along with a reasonable income, you are no doubt interested in job security. If you do not measure up to the job, or do not satisfactorily perform the duties for which you were hired, it is natural to expect some action to be taken on the part of your employer—either a warning or dismissal. If you accept part-time or seasonal work, you may expect lay-offs or periods when you will not be working. Cut-backs in production because of unexpected economic conditions and business set-backs also result in loss of employment, perhaps only temporarily.

- **Unemployment compensation** is a joint federal-state program designed to protect wage earners from total loss of income when they are out of work. The system provides them with a weekly income to carry them over until they are working again. In all but a few states, employees make no contributions to this insurance plan. The funds are obtained by taxing the employer, with each state setting its own tax rate. The federal government also provides some funds. The amount of benefits and the length of time the benefits are paid vary from state to state. For information on this program in your state contact the local public employment office.

In order to be eligible for unemployment compensation, the person must have worked a *specified minimum period of time* in a job covered by unemployment compensation. In general, the law covers workers in factories, mills, mines, shops, stores, offices, restaurants, laundries, banks, and other private industries. It *does not* cover such occupations as domestics and farm workers, state and municipal employees, or those employed in non-profit educational, religious, or charitable organizations. In addition, a person must be out of work through no fault of his own and must be willing and able to work. Then, to receive payments, the individual must register and report once a week at the local state employment office.

- **Workmen's Compensation** is another state-operated income protection program. Payments are made in case of loss of pay due to occupational illness, injury, or fatality. This insurance system is financed by the employer in the same way as the unemployment compensation program.

Working standards:

Working conditions are also of great importance to the employee. Some are controlled by law—minimum wage, equal pay, maximum hours, and overtime, for example.

- The Federal Wage and Hour Law sets the minimum wage, the maximum hours, and the pay for overtime work for all employees covered by the act. This includes any business involved in interstate commerce or the production of goods for interstate commerce. All workers covered must be paid a certain amount per hour (can change with Congressional action) and time-and-a-half for overtime (at present, any hours beyond 40 in any week). The law does not necessarily apply to part-time workers, apprentices, or full-time students employed after school hours.

Thirty-four states have also enacted minimum wage laws covering local trade and service industries.

- **The Fair Labor Standards Act** outlines *child-labor* standards and places limitations on the type of work women are permitted to do. No one under 18 years of age can be employed in occupations found to be hazardous or detrimental to health or well-being. Included in these occupations is the operation of certain power-driven machinery. The regulations also prohibit the employment of *women* in certain occupations or under conditions that are considered dangerous to health or safety.
- **The Equal Pay Act** applies to all employees covered by the Fair Labor Standards Act. It requires an employer to pay equal wages to both men and women for equal work on jobs that require the same skill, effort, and responsibility and that are performed under similar working conditions. There can be no differential in pay based on sex alone; the rate of pay must be based on the job, not the sex of the worker.
- **Equal Employment Opportunity** provides that employees are treated equally in all phases of the employment relationship, regardless of race, creed, color, or national origin.

Special laws for women—Forty-six states have laws governing the hours women are permitted to work. The maximum hours, both daily and weekly, vary in different states from 8 *to 10 hours a day* and 48 to 60 hours a week.

Twenty-three states have restricted women to a maximum *6 day work week*. The majority of the remaining states have made some provision to limit the work week—either prohibiting Sunday employment or requiring time-and-a-half for work on the seventh day or Sunday. In this way they discourage a 7 day work week.

Twenty-five states provide that women be allowed a *meal period*, varying from 20 minutes to an hour. Twelve states also require a *rest period*—in addition to the meal period—for women workers. Most provide for *two 10 minute breaks*, one before and one after lunch.

A number of states have set up standards for *plant facilities for women employees,* including seating, lounges, dressing rooms, lunch rooms, and toilet facilities.

For the employment regulations and provisions *in your particular state*, refer to the latest copy of the *Handbook on Women Workers* published periodically by the Women's Bureau of the U. S. Department of Labor.

Some working conditions, characteristic of the job or place of employment, must be accepted as part of the job. For example, in discount or department store *retailing*, the hours may be irregular. You can rarely expect to have Saturday off because that is one of the busiest days in the retailing business. You may even be scheduled six days a week. You can also expect to work some night hours. In the garment *manufacturing* industry, on the other hand, the hours are regular—usually eight hours a day, five days a week.

Other work standards—Some conditions are the result of rules and reg-

Simple Applications

ulations either set up by the employer or through mutual agreement between the employer and the employee—work hours, coffee breaks, lunch hours, dress regulations, etc. There are working rules that are concerned with day-to-day conduct on the job—operations, safety, hygiene, records, etc.

Most states have inspection laws governing *unsanitary or hazardous working conditions,* dangerous to the health and safety of employees. The "sweat shop" of yesteryear is a thing of the past. Today's modern manufacturing plants are light, colorful, cheerful, clean, usually air conditioned, and may even have piped-in music for the workers' enjoyment. However, not only are they usually noisy from the whirr of perhaps hundreds of machines all in one large room, there is always a risk involved in working around power machinery.

Unions—Union organization is extensive, especially among workers in manufacturing industries. Some examples include: The Amalgamated Clothing Workers of America, International Ladies Garment Workers' Union, and United Garment Workers of America in the apparel industry and clothing service areas; Retail Clerks International Association and Retail, Wholesale, and Department Store Union, in the retail trade.

The labor union is an outgrowth of and protest against the "sweat shop" era of production when workers were plentiful, wages were low, hours were long, working conditions were poor, and the employer's attitude was "take it or leave it." By organizing, workers were able to command attention and accomplish much more as a group than they could alone. Today the union acts as a spokesman for the employees—representatives of labor (the employees) meet with representatives of management (the employer) to discuss problems and reach an agreement.

Many employers welcome union organization and encourage union membership among their employees. They feel it is easier and more efficient to deal with one representative than with each employee individually. Other employers are opposed to unions and discourage their organization in their companies. Also there have been instances of unscrupulous union leaders who have done more harm than good for the people they represent and unreasonable union demands have been more detrimental than beneficial. In general, however, the unions deserve a great deal of credit for the contributions they have made over the years toward improving working conditions. Worthwhile accomplishments can result when both union and management have a sense of obligation and are willing to accept responsibility, and when there is mutual understanding and respect.

Status and prestige:

Some people seek status from their jobs. Selling in the most exclusive, "better-dress" salon carries more prestige for them than selling in the "bargain basement" or even in the regular dress department. In a like manner they feel that a person who "dresses for the job" (the salesperson) commands more respect than one who wears casual or work clothing to work (the machine operator). In reverse, many believe that what they term

You in the World of Work

"better jobs" also mean better pay. *These ideas do not always hold true.*

For example, let's compare the salesperson with the machine operator. Neither job is more important than the other—rather, each is dependent upon the other. The one who sews probably requires more training and greater ability to acquire the technical skill and generally makes more money than the one who sells at the counter. Very often, so-called job prestige is a misconception and merely a figment of the imagination. Any necessary job is worthwhile and important.

Perhaps the most important gain from your job is *personal satisfaction.* Many people have left higher paying positions because they felt something missing—they were unhappy or dissatisfied with the work they were doing. To them, money was not the most important factor. They placed a greater value on happiness, contentment, and an inner sense of accomplishment. When so many hours of the day are spent on the job, it is important that you are a real part of what you are doing—to feel that what you are doing is important—that you belong—that you make friends with other workers—and that you are making a worthwhile contribution, no matter how small it may be. You can be successful in your work and as a result both you and the job will benefit.

WHAT DOES THE EMPLOYER EXPECT FROM YOU?

In the business world, where profit is essential, you represent a cash investment to your employer. Because he invests money in you he expects a fair return. He has the right to expect efficiency and cooperation on the part of his employees. His main concern must be getting the job done well, or he fails; so he expects "a day's work for a day's pay." It is true that he may favor a member of the family in the business. *But so would you in his place.* In school, everywhere, you find some favoritism. But if you are a person who has to work hard—because of your nature—you just won't be happy if you worry about those who seem to get by without doing their share. *Generally you will be treated fairly* in American business.

Many companies check their employees regularly on their general efficiency and performance. Then they base their raises and promotions, and perhaps even transfers or dismissals, on these ratings. A look at the items taken into consideration on a typical rating form clearly reveals what an employer expects of his employees.

You will be expected to have the knowledge necessary to perform your job and be able to perform it without always being told what to do and how to do it. Yet, even though you have prepared for a job, you won't be expected to be an expert from the very beginning. In fact, any employer would rather that you would ask questions instead of proceeding with something you do not understand and do it incorrectly.

You will be expected to learn all

What Does the Employer Expect From You?

aspects of your job quickly. There will probably be a period of on-the-job training. The person who learns to understand and follow instructions, who listens and learns, and who has the ability to figure things out for himself and works individually without constant supervision will advance faster.

You will be expected to do your work well. Your appearance and personality were perhaps influential in helping you get a job and are still important factors, but now you must produce to keep the job. **Remember,** if you display a desire to learn, an enthusiasm and interest in your work, you are off to a good start. An employer is interested in both how much work you do and how well you do it. Your work habits can be either a help or hindrance to you.

- Are you *well organized?*
- Do you plan your work and tackle important tasks first?
- Can you stick with a job—even though rather tedious—until it is completed, or are you easily distracted?

An orderly, well-organized person wastes less time and accomplishes a great deal more than one who is not well organized. A reliable person can be counted on to get the work done, even under pressure, and to follow a job through until it is completed.

- Are you *neat and accurate* about your work? Careless, inferior work is not acceptable and, since it must often be done over, it is also costly. Business cannot afford careless workers. You will be expected to turn out an adequate volume of work that meets certain quality standards.
- As you know, you must be *regular in attendance.* Frequent absence and tardiness are as bad in business as at school. Also, absence of any employee can upset the routine or cause a lag in production or affect the efficient operation of the business. Except for illness, a person should be on the job and should report for work on time.

In case of absence, an employer should be notified ahead of time. Each company has a specific procedure to be followed. Find it out and be conscientious in following it.

FOR THE REAL CAREER GIRL

Every business has certain *rules and regulations* that it expects its employees to follow. Learn these right away and abide by them. *Things will go smoother for you.* If you are entitled to a twenty minute break, not before ten o'clock nor after three o'clock, don't leave the floor at five minutes to ten and stretch the break to twenty-five minutes. If you are to start to work at nine o'clock, be on the job at nine o'clock—not in the ladies' room or the employees' lounge. If you work until 5:30, don't spend the last half hour getting ready to walk out on the dot of 5:30. Tardiness, clock watching, and wasting time are a form of cheating along with bending the rules and label you as "least likely to succeed."

An employer expects you to utilize working hours to best advantage—

with work. Working hours belong to the company and you owe it to them to give your job your full attention. Gab sessions with fellow workers, personal phone calls, and personal errands should not be conducted on company time. Even personal problems should be put aside during working hours.

Your attitude toward your job is important. Are you merely interested in collecting your pay? Do you try to get out of doing things? Do you do the very least you can to get by? Or are you sincerely interested in doing your job to the best of your ability —not merely putting in time? Do you look at your job as a worthwhile contribution worthy of your best efforts? Every job has some dull, routine tasks. Do you accept them in good spirit? If your attitude is right, you will do well on the job and the job will mean more than "eight hours a day at so much per hour."

Honesty—An employer expects employees to display certain personal characteristics. Honesty seems almost too obvious to mention. Of course you aren't going to steal from your employer—but will you? Wasting time and supplies is a form of stealing. How about that personal call on the company phone? or the pencil in your purse? or that little fib about not having time to finish a task? All of these are minor, it is true, but all are dishonest just the same.

Dependability rates high with employers. The person who can be depended upon to be on the job, to carry out any assignment given him and do it graciously and well, to work without supervision, to take on "that little extra" when necessary, to assume his share, will get ahead. Dependable workers are the ones singled out for promotion. They also are less miserable, have less trouble, and really lead the easier life! Do you understand why?

As an employee you owe your superior respect. You may disagree with his ideas, judgment, and methods or perhaps even secretly resent some of his requests and actions. However, he is your superior and as such, "he is the boss"—entitled to your respect just because of his position, if for no other reason. Why *invent* reasons for finding fault or complaining? Why not comply graciously with his wishes and carry out your assignment to the best of your ability? Such an attitude reflects favorably on both you and your work. Even when there are conditions you don't like, give them a fair chance before complaining; they may work out. Business demands respect for authority, or nothing will function right.

Loyalty to both your employer, your company, and your co-workers is really as valuable as gold. Make it a habit never to run down your employer or criticize him to your fellow workers. Be genuinely concerned with the welfare of the company, if for no other reason than a selfish one—the company's welfare has a direct effect on you and your welfare. You and your co-workers are a team—all of you dependent upon the others. Your working hours will be more pleasant and productive if you are cooperative and get along well together. It isn't necessary to become "close friends" with all the people with whom you work—in fact there are many dangers in becoming too close—but it is necessary to work well together and to respect them as individuals. If you possess a sense of loyalty, you will cooperate and work well together.

It is said that more people lose—or hate—their jobs because of their inability to get along with people than for any other reason, including inability to do the job. Desirable personal characteristics are essential for success and happiness in all your daily contacts—with superiors and co-workers alike. A desirable social attitude requires that you be fair, cooperative, and courteous. Always put yourself in the other person's place: How would you want to be treated? Do you *try* to be considerate? helpful? tactful? pleasant? agreeable? tolerant? kind? Do you *try* to behave in a mature manner? Trying, really trying, is an essential quality for success in any endeavor.

In review:

How do you find job leads?

Why is job hunting compared to selling?

What purpose does a résumé serve? What information is included?

What purpose does an interview serve?

What personal values can be gained from employment?

What is the difference between gross income, net income, and real income?

Do you know the meaning of these words: base salary, bonus, commission, withholding?

In what way can fringe benefits be considered earnings?

What payroll deductions are mandatory?

For further discussion:

The preliminary steps to job hunting.

Employment agencies—how they operate and your obligations.

Factors to consider in selecting references.

Union membership.

Legislation governing employment in your particular area.

Your obligations to the job.

Keys to success on the job. Barriers to success.

To gain experience:

Check the Help Wanted ads in the newspaper for job openings in which you are interested and for which you qualify.

Write a sample letter of application in answer to one of the ads.

Prepare a personal data sheet.

Obtain permission to use three names for references.

Fill in a sample application blank.

Rehearse oral answers to the questions: "Tell me something about yourself." and "Why are you interested in this job?"

Practice being interviewed for a job. Dress appropriately and role-play the entire interview with a classmate.

Write a sample follow-up letter after an interview.

Obtain a social security card.

Fill in a Federal Income Tax form.

Chapter 2

A Place for You in the Clothing Field

Your interests and abilities point to employment in the field of clothing. What are the opportunities and what specific openings are available to you? Perhaps you dream of being a famous designer or a buyer who travels to the glamorous fashion markets of the world. It takes more than dreams. You are to be admired if you set your sights high, but bear in mind that it is necessary to prepare yourself—to acquire the knowledge and skill needed to attain your goals. In addition, it is usually necessary to start at the bottom, gain experience, and work your way up the ladder step by step.

Are you interested in the merchandising field? You may start as a stock clerk or a salesperson with opportunities for advancement. Do you like to sew? There are opportunities for you in the garment manufacturing industry as a sewing machine operator, hand sewer, or sample maker. In addition to the apparel industry, machine operators are needed wherever sewing is a part of manufacturing—for example; home furnishings such as draperies, slip covers, bedspreads, etc.; household linens and accessories; travel accessories; etc. Sewing service occupations offer many employment opportunities, perhaps in alterations (in a department or clothing store), in clothing repair (in a laundry or dry cleaning establishment), or in free lance dressmaking and/or alterations in your own home or small shop. Let us examine each of these occupations in greater detail.

MERCHANDISING

Salesperson

Duties:

A salesperson's duties and responsibilities differ according to the type of merchandise sold and the type of store. In general, the duties can be grouped into three categories:

Selling:
Serve the customer.
Record the sale.

What's New in Home Economics

The salesperson represents the store to the customer. Manner and skill are responsible for both sales and satisfied customers.

Receive payment.
Wrap the merchandise.

Stock control:
Check in merchandise.
Prepare merchandise for sale.
Arrange merchandise.
Keep merchandise in order.
Keep work area neat and clean.
Take stock counts and inventories.
Help with ordering merchandise.

Promotional:
Prepare displays.
Plan and execute sales promotions.

In some situations, the salesperson may be involved with nothing but direct selling duties. In a small, independently owned store, however, a salesperson may be responsible in all areas.

Education and training requirements:

High school graduates are preferred. Subjects that provide a good background for selling include salesmanship, merchandising, business mathematics, and home economics with emphasis on fabrics, color-line-design, fashion, and clothing construction.

• Some specific background helpful in selling *ready-to-wear*:
An awareness of fashion, color, design.

What's New in Home Economics

These students are members of a school-store cooperative training program. In the classroom they gain the background knowledge and theory that they will have a chance to practice in work-experience training at the store.

A knowledge of style and color for the individual.

An understanding of clothing construction.

Fabric knowledge—fabric content, qualities of the fabric.

• Some specific background helpful in selling *yard goods:*

An awareness of fashion, color, design.

Fabric knowledge—trade names, fabric description, fiber content, qualities of the fabrics.

Ability to advise concerning style for the individual and type of fabric suitable for the pattern.

Ability to determine pattern size and yardage requirements.

Knowledge of all sewing accessories—thread, zipper, interfacings, linings, etc.

Basic knowledge of sewing—it is an advantage for top-flight fabric salespeople to wear clothes that they have made.

A cooperative *school-work experience program* provides a person an opportunity to get supervised, practical experience. This may lead to immediate full-time employment. Then most stores give new employees some instructions before they start to work—perhaps informally or in an extensive training program, depending upon the type and size of the store. On-the-job training is necessary to acquaint them with store procedures and policies. NOTE: Part-time experience is helpful, but not a requirement for employment.

Personal qualifications:

Has neat, attractive appearance; dresses appropriately, becomingly,

Merchandising

and fashionably; has pleasing personality; likes people; is congenial; has a pleasant voice; can express oneself easily and correctly about what is for sale; in good health; doesn't tire easily; is alert; has a sense of humor; is industrious; has a good memory. (Having good sense and a good disposition are the main requirements.)

Pay and working conditions:

A salesperson may be paid on a straight salary basis or a base pay plus commission (a percentage of the total sales made). Beginning salaries are moderate—often the minimum wage required by law—and part-time workers are often paid less than the minimum wage. With experience, and in sales positions involving more than "merely waiting on" customers, where sales skill and knowledge are necessary, salaries increase accordingly. Fringe benefits usually include the privilege of buying merchandise at a discount, usually 10 to 20% off the regular price.

Full-time salespersons may work a 5 day 40 hour week; usually the hours are not regular. In most stores, employees are scheduled to work at least one evening a week—more in stores that are open every evening. Saturday is a busy day, so salespeople usually work that day and have some other day off during the week. During peak seasons—Christmas, pre-Easter, anniversaries, and special sales—hours may be longer than usual. During inventory it isn't unusual to work until midnight—for which you are paid and you might have fun doing it because it is different, informal, and more relaxed.

Salespeople work in pleasant surroundings. The physical surroundings must be pleasant to appeal to the customers—well-lighted, colorful, clean, often carpeted and tastefully furnished, and usually air-conditioned. The work can be physically tiring if you try to do everything at once—a salesperson spends her day on her feet—and some days may be mentally trying. Dealing with people demands courtesy and tact, even at the end of a long, hard day. In return, you will find that time goes fast when you are busy. If you like people, you will find sales most interesting.

Opportunities for employment:

Retailing is a growing field. Sales jobs are available in almost every community in all sections of the country, wherever clothing is sold—in department stores, in specialty shops, and even by direct selling. Naturally, most openings are found in the large cities and the rapidly growing suburban areas, but every community has stores. Job openings occur regularly, both new jobs and job replacements. The turnover in sales is rapid as women leave to get married and rear families and as young people gain experience and move on to another job. It is expected that the need for salespersons will steadily increase as population increases and communities grow rapidly. New communities and more people mean new shopping areas, more stores, and more sales jobs. The self-service trend in retailing indicates that there will be little demand for people without skill or training to fill routine sales jobs. Sales employment is expected to increase, but the demand will be for people who are skilled in sales ability and

A Place for You in the Clothing Field

have a real knowledge of the merchandise they sell.

Opportunities for advancement:

In small stores, the opportunities are limited by the fact that changes are very slow. In large stores, executive positions are frequently filled by college graduates. As trainees, they may participate in an "executive training program" in which they gain experience in all aspects of retailing in preparation for promotion. However, it is possible for an employee without a college degree to advance to an executive position if he displays initiative and ability. Some stores operate a "junior executive" training program for promising employees. A salesperson may be promoted to supervisor, section manager, assistant buyer, and perhaps eventually buyer. Sales experience is the means of reaching these positions.

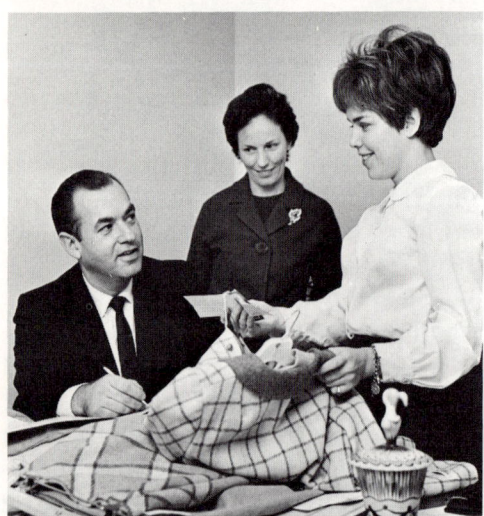

What's New in Home Economics

Work experience is a valuable part of training. This young lady is gaining practical experience in all aspects of retailing. Here she is working with the buyer, helping to order new merchandise.

Stock Clerk

Duties:

The store's receiving department is responsible for merchandise from the time it arrives at the store until it reaches the selling floor. The activities of a clerk in this department are many:

Receive merchandise:

Open and sort.

Unpack and place on hangers (in the case of ready-to-wear outer clothing).

Check accuracy of order—compare original order with the merchandise received and with the manufacturer's or shipper's invoice. (The *invoice* is the shipper's "bill.")

Check the condition of the merchandise as received.

File reports of damaged or lost merchandise.

"Enter" merchandise:

Prepare stock control forms (lists of quantities).

On these forms, record merchandise received.

Prepare merchandise for sale:

Print price tags or tickets.

Attach tags to the merchandise.

Distribute merchandise to the proper departments:

• Instead of going directly to the selling floor, merchandise may be kept in reserve in a stock room, usually located close to the selling department for convenience. Here *stock duties* include storing the merchandise in a logical manner and keeping it arranged in proper order.

Department Store Journal
Here in the receiving department these garments have been sorted, ticketed, and are awaiting transfer to the selling department. The receiving clerk, at the desk in the background, is working on the records necessary for entering the merchandise.

• Stock work may also include the transfer of merchandise (from one store to another branch store, or back to the main store, or back to the manufacturer) and the record keeping involved in transferring, plus filling special merchandise orders.

Education and training requirements:

High school graduates are preferred, with a background in mathematics and typing. On-the-job training is given new employees to acquaint them with store procedures, records, and forms. Special skills and careful handling of clothing are required to prevent soiling and damage.

Personal qualifications:

Is dependable, industrious, accurate, neat, a legible writer, doesn't tire easily.

Working conditions:

Pay is on an hourly wage basis, with beginners starting at a moderate minimum. As a store employee, discount privileges usually are extended

A Place for You in the Clothing Field

the same as to all others. Hours are regular—usually 40 hours a week for full-time employees.

Whereas the selling floors are made attractive to appeal to the customers, the stock rooms and receiving rooms are storage and work rooms behind the scenes. As such they are plainer. They are often large open areas resembling warehouses. Some work is exposed to weather, as when unloading trucks. This is an advantage on a nice day. Since merchandise can stack up in peak seasons, a great deal of physical activity may be involved. On quieter days, stock clerks arrange stock, clean up, mark shelves, and do other maintenance work. Limited opportunity for girls.

Opportunities for employment:

Wherever there is a retail store, there is stock work. In the small stores, however, there probably will not be stock clerks hired as such—salespeople often do the stock work. The larger department stores, where duties are specialized, offer more opportunities. They hire employees specifically as receiving clerks, stock clerks, etc. to work in separate receiving and stock departments. With increased efficiency and automation both in record keeping and in handling merchandise, more work can be done with fewer workers. This means that the need for employees in this area of retailing may not increase in proportion to the need for sales personnel as the retailing field grows. There is expected to be a gradual increase, however. Competition for employment may be high, since special training and skill are usually not required and there are generally many young applicants.

Opportunities for advancement:

Stock work may be classified as an "entry" job. It offers an excellent opportunity to learn the total merchandise picture. Duties give you contacts and experience with manufacturers, shippers, merchandise, the selling floor, buyers, and sales personnel. An ambitious, alert person may advance to selling or be promoted to assistant or head of the stock room, floor, or warehouse.

COMPARISON SHOPPER

Duties:

A limited opportunity, but competition is keen in retailing, and large department stores do hire people to "shop" the competition. Perhaps a customer complains that she has seen the same merchandise at a lower price in another store. Perhaps another store advertises merchandise at a lower price. Comparison shoppers check these leads. They compare specific items of merchandise in their store with the same items in another store, checking the quality, style, and price. If the other store is underselling, they determine whether or not the merchandise is identical in style, quality, etc. Perhaps they purchase the item for further comparison or study in the store's testing laboratory. They also note display methods, sales techniques, and any methods of operation of interest in the other competing store.

Some stores hire people for another kind of "shopping." In this case, the person merely does routine shopping in the store and then files a report on the service rendered by the salesperson—the way the customer was treated, the way the sale was transacted, and other pertinent information. This type of employment is usually part-time. A regular, full-time "shopper" would be recognized by the sales personnel.

Education and training requirements:

This work offers an interesting opportunity for the person who *knows merchandise,* but is generally limited to large department stores in cities with several stores. In most cases women with strong *sales* experience are hired.

INDUSTRIAL SEWING

Sewing Machine Operator

Duties:

As the name implies, the operator stitches on a machine. It may be on a conventional (regular) lock-stitch industrial machine, similar to the one at home, or it may be on a machine designed to do a special stitch (blind stitch, for example) or to perform a special function (sew on buttons, make buttonholes, or stitch rows of tucks). Depending upon the article being made and the procedure established by the manufacturer, an operator may perform only one operation (stitch shoulder seams, for example) or make only one part of a garment (sew collars). Then other operators assemble the pieces and sew them together, again each one doing one step—so the garment is thus completed step by step. In the case of higher priced, top quality custom clothing, one person may do all the sewing on a garment, but the usual procedure in garment manufacture is the "section" method as described.

Although we have referred to garment manufacturing and clothing in this discussion, the same information can apply to any area of industrial sewing, such as bedclothes, draperies, curtains, and outdoor fabrics. Specific duties will vary with each branch of the industry according to the article being made and the manufacturer's particular methods.

Education and training:

Thorough training in the use of the power-driven industrial machine is essential. Specific construction techniques required by the particular manufacturer may be learned on the job, but basic sewing knowledge and ability come before. The *length* of on-the-job training depends upon specific techniques being learned and the ability of the employee. A beginner usually learns to stitch simple straight seams until she displays the speed and ability the manufacturer desires. Although operators usually perform only one step of the construction process, a thorough knowledge of clothing construction and the ability to make every part of a garment are helpful, especially for the person interested in advancement.

Personal qualifications:

Finger dexterity, coordination, keen sense of touch, good eyesight, good judgment, cleanliness, neatness, ability to work at a steady, fast pace, ability to do routine work.

Working conditions:

Usually workers are paid according to their production on a piece work rate—the more pieces of work turned out, the better the pay. Actual earnings vary according to location and cost of living, and the type of garment produced (women's ready-to-wear pays better than work clothing). Generally earnings in the apparel industry compare favorably with those in clerical occupations, but are not as high as in other manufacturing industries.

Hours are regular, but if employed in the production of seasonal merchandise—bathing suits, for example—there may be lay-offs during the off-season.

Garment manufacturing plants in metropolitan areas may still be located in old warehouse-type buildings, often with undesirable surroundings, crowded conditions, and inadequate facilities. The trend, however, is toward locating new plants in small communities and rural areas. These new plants are attractive (inside and out), clean, light, air-conditioned. In general, they are very pleasant places to work.

The work itself is not strenuous—you sit to perform your job—but you work at a rapid pace, which may prove tiring. Your work may be repetitious and therefore monotonous to some people. For speed and efficiency, your work area will be very compact, perhaps even crowded, and you will be working close to others. There may be rows of machines in one open area. A large number of machines going at top speed means noise, also, although efforts are made to deaden the sound.

Opportunities for employment:

Over a million workers are engaged in the manufacture of clothing alone, not considering the other fabric construction industries. It is expected that the need for workers will increase steadily, with thousands of job openings occurring annually. In any field employing primarily women (about 80% of the workers in the apparel industry are women) there are always job openings occurring merely to replace those who leave each year to get married or to rear a family. In addition, several factors point to an *increasing demand* for clothing. The expected increase in *population* means more clothing is needed. *Young people* in their teens and twenties—the biggest clothing market—will increase in numbers steadily over several years. The trend is toward an increasing number of *white collar workers* who earn more money and "dress" for work; as a result, they buy more clothing. The number of women in the *working world* continues to increase and women require a different kind and greater quantity of clothing for the working world than they need if they remain at home. A steadily increasing average income and *higher standard* of living means more money can be spent for clothing. As a result of growing demand and an expanding industry, opportunities for employment can be expected to increase steadily.

Job experience is not necessary, so

Industrial Sewing

that beginners with a knowledge of sewing and training in machine operation have no difficulty obtaining employment.

New York City is still the center for women's fashions, with over half the plants specializing in women's clothing being located in the general New York-northern New Jersey area. Still, there are numerous plants located throughout the country; as said, the trend is toward small communities rather than centralized metropolitan areas.

Opportunities for advancement:

Promotion is usually restricted to the same field, from a simple sewing technique (straight seams) to a more complicated process requiring more skill (setting in sleeves or detail work on a special machine). The more skilled jobs naturally bring better pay. Also it is possible to advance to inspector, checker, forelady, or training supervisor instructing new employees, although the possibilities are limited.

A person with a great deal of talent, proven ability, and experience may become a *sample maker* who constructs the designer's sample garments, doing all the hand and machine sewing required. This position is only available in large manufacturing companies that have designing departments. The smaller companies do not have their own designers, but buy their designs and patterns.

Hand sewer—In mass production, speed is essential; for this reason, the sewing is done almost entirely by machine. In better quality, higher-priced garments, where greater attention is paid to fit, drapability, custom details, and higher standards of workmanship, an increasing amount of hand work is involved. Manufacturers who specialize in better quality merchandise employ people skilled in hand sewing, as well as machine operators. Like the machine operator, these hand sewers may specialize in one technique—perhaps attaching linings, the back of bound buttonholes, or hand "picking." This type of work commands a higher rate of pay, even though employment is limited to the manufacturers of better quality merchandise. Otherwise the information in the discussion of machine operators applies as well to the hand sewer.

Alterations—In the *apparel industry,* "alteration" means repairing defects and correcting mistakes made during the production of the garment. The inspector or checker may reject a garment because a part was not sewn correctly. If the mistake can be corrected, the alteration department is responsible for restoring these "seconds" to first quality merchandise. A person engaged in this type of work must be thoroughly familiar with all the construction techniques involved in making a garment and must be an expert sewer. NOTE: Repair work is more difficult, more tedious, and usually requires greater ability than the original construction.

SEWING SERVICES

DRESSMAKING

Tailors and dressmakers usually do custom sewing, making garments from start to finish for specific individuals. Many dressmakers also do alteration and repair work.

A person must be expert in all phases of clothing construction—cutting, fitting, pressing, finishing, as well as actual sewing techniques (both hand and machine). A knowledge of fitting is especially important, since many of the people who employ a dressmaker to make their clothes are those who have fitting problems and are unable to buy ready-to-wear garments that fit without major alterations. Therefore you will most likely be working with *problem figures.*

Another group of people that make use of a dressmaker's services are those who want something specific, have definite style ideas, and have been unable to find exactly what they want in ready-to-wear (either in style, fabric, or color). They turn to a dressmaker to create an *original* for them. An understanding of design is essential as well as the ability to translate a design, or picture, or perhaps just someone's idea into a finished garment.

A knowledge of *fabrics* is also essential. The characteristics of fabrics determine the choice of fabric for particular styles as well as the special sewing and pressing techniques necessary to insure proper handling during construction.

In the apparel industry, dressmakers may be employed as *sample makers* who create the entire garment either to interpret the designer's sketches or to establish the procedure and techniques to be used in production. However, employment in this area is very limited, as noted earlier.

The majority of dressmakers are self-employed, perhaps working in their own homes. They may alter old garments or make clothes, as best determined by the demand. The work offers an excellent opportunity for the married woman with a family to supplement the family income without leaving home. They may work on a part-time or full-time basis, the number of hours worked and the amount of work being entirely dependent upon the time the person wishes to devote to it. Many start out modestly—in their own neighborhoods, among their friends, passing the word along by mouth, or advertising in the classifieds of the local paper. It is usually true that before long they have as much—or more—business than they can handle and find it necessary to turn down work—if the quality is good and people recommend them. Some open their own shops, perhaps on an individual basis or in partnership with another person—perhaps a tailor, although this is becoming rare, as men's tailors are vanishing except in the luxury trade. When dressmakers become well-established and build up a clientele, they may even expand to the point of hiring a staff of workers and operating on a small-scale production basis, still maintaining the custom factor and individualized service for their customers.

The amount of money earned in dressmaking varies considerably, depending upon the amount of time the person devotes to working, and the type of work done. Individuals set their own prices, so much per type of garment. It is dangerous to quote prices because they change so rapidly and vary considerably with location. However, to give you an idea of the amount that can be earned, making a simple cotton dress may be under

Sewing Services

$25.00 and a lined wool dress $35.00 and up. Those people with a flair for design who specialize in luxury quality women's clothing—dresses, suits, and coats—command top prices and find the work quite profitable. This is also true of men's tailors.

Altering—A person specializing in altering clothing is concerned with changing an already completed garment in some way—usually to make it fit better, perhaps to restyle it.

It is necessary to be just as familiar with all the techniques of clothing construction as you would if you made clothing from start to finish. Alterations may vary from the very simple lengthening and shortening hemlines or letting out and taking in seams to the more complicated, major changes that are necessary when dealing with severe fitting problems. These may sometimes involve almost remaking a garment.

It is necessary to be an expert in *fitting* techniques as well as in sewing techniques. In addition, it is just as necessary to know whether or not an alteration *can even be made* as it is to know how to make it!

A person may enter this field on a home *basis*, similar to the dressmaker, under the same conditions noted in the dressmaker discussion. You may specialize in alterations alone, or combine alterations and dressmaking. Also, *department stores* offer alteration service as do many small shops that sell clothing. The small shop may have one person responsible for all fitting and sewing. As the store increases in size and volume of business, so does the alteration service. In the large department store, a person may specialize in a particular phase —fitting, sewing, women's clothing, men's clothing, etc. (Usually men do the work in men's departments—and these men are scarce.)

The amount of money earned depends partly upon whether or not you are self-employed or are working for someone else. In a store, the alteration people are paid an hourly wage. In free-lance work you set your own rates. Again, it is dangerous to quote prices, but you should investigate them so you can get an idea of the amount of money that can be earned.

Clothing repair—Laundries and dry cleaning establishments may employ people with sewing ability to make repairs on the articles of clothing they handle. The workers must be familiar with basic hand stitches and sewing techniques. They must be able to operate the sewing machine. (In most cases the industrial type, power-driven machine is used in preference to the home sewing machine because it is capable of doing heavy-duty as well as regular sewing.) They must also know how to perform the basic repair techniques. Included in these may be: stitching broken seams, ripped hemming stitches, etc.; replacing broken zippers; sewing on buttons, hooks and eyes, and snaps; making thread loops and belt carriers; tacking cuffs, facings, etc.; replacing pockets; replacing worn linings; reworking buttonholes; etc.

Related sewing—Although not connected with clothing, any discussion of job opportunities for people skilled in sewing would not be complete without including the making of household furnishings—curtains, draperies, and slip covers. There are

A Place for You in the Clothing Field

opportunities for employment in factories, similar to garment manufacturing plants in requirements and working conditions. Stores that sell fabric for these articles usually also offer to make them as an extra service to their customers. They may have a workroom, hiring their own personnel for this. Chain stores in the field may operate with a central plant similar to a garment manufacturing plant. Department stores often lease their work to a local, independently owned company that does the work for them. As in dressmaking and alterations, many people do this type of sewing on an individual basis. An interested person must be able to operate the sewing machine and learn the special techniques involved.

The home furnishings area opens a whole new field, offering more opportunities for the person who can sew.

To Gain Further Information

• Investigate all employment opportunities in your particular locality for a person skilled in sewing.

• Select an area of the clothing field in which you are particularly interested and investigate it in further detail. Consider the number of businesses in your area that employ people in the field, the types of positions open, the number of jobs available, hours, wages, and specific working conditions.

• Make arrangements to visit a clothing manufacturing plant.

• Invite people to class who are employed in the various areas to discuss the advantages and disadvantages of their jobs.

Chapter **3**

The Color, Line, and Design Story in Fashion

EVERY season the world's fashion designers introduce their "new" fashions. The current look may be soft and feminine, bulky and textured, or crisp and tailored. Colors may be bright, gay, and vibrant or pale, soft, and subdued. The hemline varies, the waistline wanders, jacket lengths change, the amount of fullness varies, and trimming details come and go. The word "fashion" refers to the current or prevailing style of dress, but it also means different things to different people. To some—the smartest designers and best-dressed among us—fashion is as much an art as painting a picture or creating a design; to others, fashion is a frivolous toy that is fun to experiment with. To some merchandisers, fashion is a serious business; to others, an exciting game; to still other persons—who care little for clothes—a necessary evil, perhaps even a nuisance.

The history of fashion is a fascinating story in itself. It is said that there is nothing new under the sun. Yet we speak of the "new look for fall or spring." We anxiously await the designers' showings to discover the new trends in fashion. If we are a part of fashion merchandising, we pore over the magazines and trade papers to learn how the new trends are interpreted in ready-to-wear. Are the styles actually new? If we closely examine fashions over the years, we can see how fashion repeats itself. There are variations, of course, and styles are adapted to suit current conditions, but we can find a counterpart in history to most of the so-called new styles. Look at the empire waistline as

The typical costume at the time of the French Empire featured a high waistline, short bodice, short puffed sleeves, and a straight, loose skirt. Today's "empire" is an adaptation of that popular style of the early 1800's.

Simplicity Pattern Co., Inc.

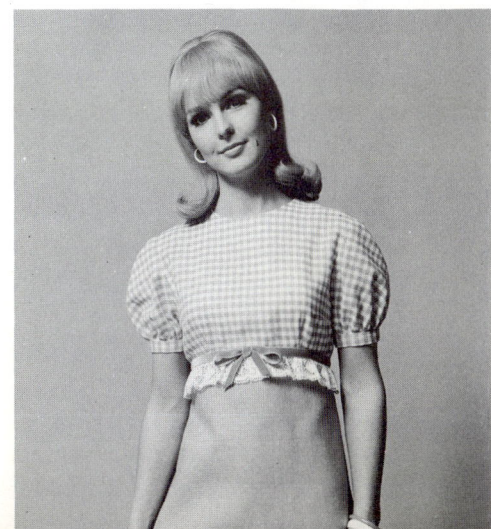

The Metropolitan Museum of Art, Gift of Mrs. John Innes Kane

Empire style, 1804.

an example. This high waistline was characteristic of the dress favored by Empress Josephine at the time of the French Empire (1804–1814). Another example is the chemise dress that was popular in the 1920's. In the 1950's, its revival as the "sack" was unsuccessful. In the 1960's, it gained wide acceptance again—this time as the "shift."

Fashion also reflects the times. The military influence upon clothes is very evident during an armed conflict—the Eisenhower jacket, the pea coat, bell-bottoms, braid, brass buttons, epaulets. Women's skirt lengths seem to indicate economic conditions—short skirts in prosperous times, long skirts in times of recession. Skirts were above the knees in the late 1920's, below the calf of the leg in

The chemise was a popular style in the early part of the 20th century. The shapeless, easy-fitting dress hung straight from the shoulder.

McCall's Patterns

The shift of the 60's got its inspiration from the chemise of the 20's. This modern adaptation has the same straight, easy-fitting lines—complete to the placement of the belt around the hipline.

Simplicity Pattern Co., Inc.

the 1930's, back up to the knee in the early 1940's, almost to the ankle in the late 1940's, up to the calf of the leg in the 1950's, and above the knee again by the mid 1960's. Can you recall from your study of history the economic conditions in these periods?

Fashion has a language all its own. Are you familiar with the meaning of these popularly used terms?

- CLASSIC: An item of wearing apparel that continues to be in style even though fashions change; for example—the shirtwaist dress.
- FAD: A temporary fashion, usually extreme or odd—a passing fancy.
- FASHION: The current or prevailing appearance or style of dress; especially striking features—as skirt length.
- FASHION CYCLE: The periodic return of a particular fashion; for example—short skirts.

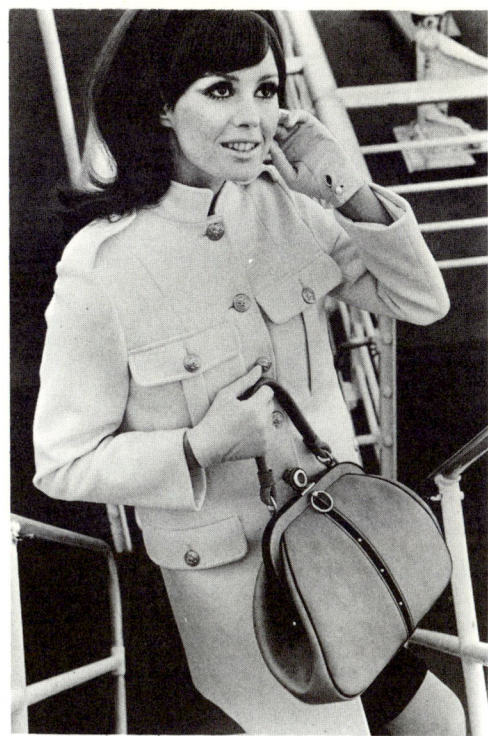

Jaclyn Handbags

The epaulets, stand-up collar, large patch pockets, and brass buttons all reflect the military influence.

Skirt lengths reflect the times. These short skirts are all popular styles from prosperous years: A: The late 20's; B: The early 40's; C: The early 70's.

McCall's Patterns   Bobbie Brooks

45

The Color, Line, and Design Story in Fashion

- **HIGH FASHION**: Very smart, successful, new.
- **MODE**: A synonym for fashion, but not as distinctive.
- **STYLE**: A particular design or type; for example—the *simple style* of a school coat or dress. A distinctive characteristic; for example—the *princess style*.

An approved fashion, implying good taste and complying with approved standards; for example—*a garment or a person has style*.

- **VOGUE**: A synonym for fashion—really new, riskier, might not last.

Some people have a quick sense about fashion—we might say they have a natural flair. In preparing for employment in the clothing field, however, you cannot afford to rely solely upon intuition, fashion sense, personal good taste, or likes and dislikes. You will be called upon to help people select clothing that expresses their personality, that conceals possible figure irregularities, and that accentuates their best features. *You must be able to visualize effects.* To do this, you need to become familiar with the components of fashion—color, line, design, and fabrics; to understand the principles—the reasons why—and learn to relate them to clothing. These can help you interpret fashion and use it to best advantage. As a result, you will be able to help others, as well as yourself, to dress with confidence.

COLOR

Color is perhaps the most important component of fashion. When you see a person, what is the first thing you notice about his clothing? Note the style, the fit, the structural details, the appropriateness of the costume. All of these are important to good appearance, of course. However, you automatically note first the predominent color the person is wearing. If someone asks "What did she wear?", you usually answer with a color: "She wore a blue suit." Most people usually think of a color first when selecting clothing. "I want a blue sweater," or a purple skirt, or a pink dress. In looking through the racks of clothing in the store, most people make tentative selections based on color. If the color appeals, then they examine the dress further for details of style. Color makes the first impression.

Some designers work closely with the textile manufacturers designing new fabrics and suggesting colors and textures for interest. Colors favored by the fashion designers are likely to be announced as the "new" colors for the season. Actually there is no such thing as a new color. There are hundreds of variations of each color, though the eye cannot readily distinguish all of them, they are so slight. The colors which are proclaimed as new colors have always existed but are popular for the season and differ from the popular colors of a preceding period.

There are many theories about color and the use of color, but all of them are based on certain fundamen-

A rainbow.

tal scientific principles. *Color is reflected light, and without light there is no color.* In turn, light is all colors. Sir Isaac Newton was the first to break light down into separate colors. He used a prism, which is a transparent, three-sided, solid object. When a light ray passes through the prism, it separates, revealing the major colors visible to the eye. A rainbow—that natural phenomenon in which raindrops act as prisms—reveals the same colors. In this band of colors—known as the spectrum—the colors always appear in the same order—violet, indigo, blue, green, yellow, orange, and red. If you could bend the spectrum, joining both ends to form a circle, you would create the color wheel used extensively in the study of color.

Why do we "see" different colors? Why is one item green and another blue? Each color, like a musical note, has a characteristic frequency (number of vibrations per second) and wave length (distance between crests of the wave by which it is transmitted). Red at one end of the spectrum has the lowest frequency and the longest wave length (like the deep sound of a low musical note). The colors in the spectrum are arranged in order according to their wave

Prism.

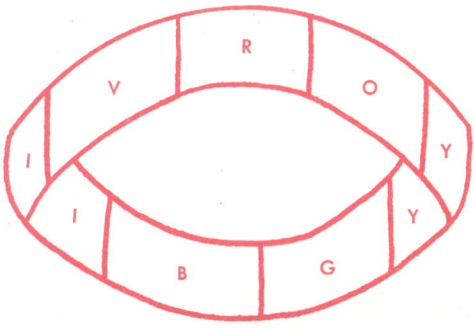

Bent spectrum.

47

The Color, Line, and Design Story in Fashion

lengths—from violet, the shortest, to red, the longest.

The color of a substance is determined by the wave length of the light it reflects. When light strikes an object that it cannot pass through, some of the light waves may be absorbed; some are reflected: (1) If all the wave lengths are reflected, we see all colors, so the object appears as white. (2) If none is reflected—all the light is absorbed—the object is black. (3) When all are absorbed except one wave length, that one is the visible color.

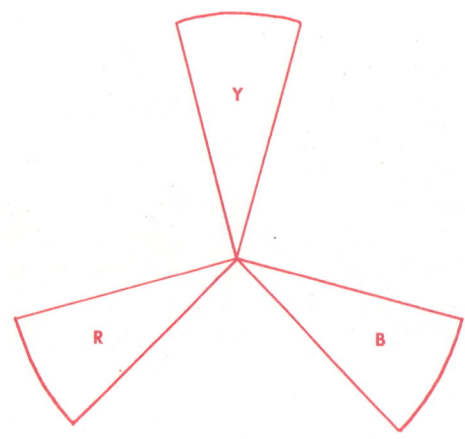

Primary colors.

Coloring matter, or pigment, is used to reproduce colors for practical uses. There are three pigments—red, yellow, and blue—which cannot be created from any other pigment, but from which all other colors can be produced. These are known as the *primary colors*.

If the two primary colors are mixed together in equal amounts, the result is a *secondary color*. Red and yellow produce orange; yellow and blue produce green; and blue and red produce purple.

There are still several gradations of color between the primary and the secondary colors. Mix a primary color (red) with an equal amount of a secondary color (orange) to produce an *intermediate color* (red-orange). Mix these *adjacent colors* in equal amounts and it is possible to produce a total of 24 separate colors, each of which is different enough to be distinguished promptly by the human eye.

The method of dividing colors into regular intervals and arranging them equidistant from each other around a circle aids in the identification of color. The color wheel also serves as a guide for using colors successfully to produce pleasing combinations. Like any other guide, however, it should be thought of as just that—not as a final "measuring" device that must be followed. Part of the fun of using color is to experiment with subtle, unusual combinations.

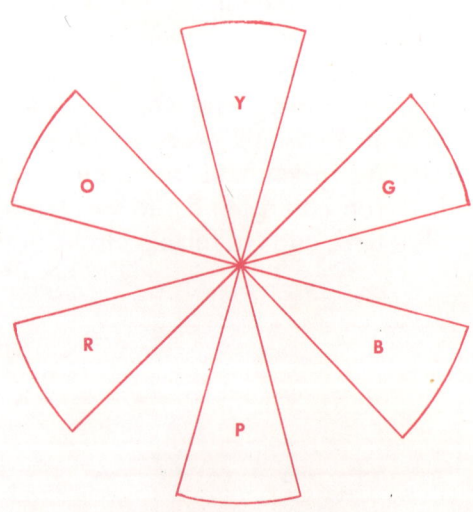

Secondary colors.

Color

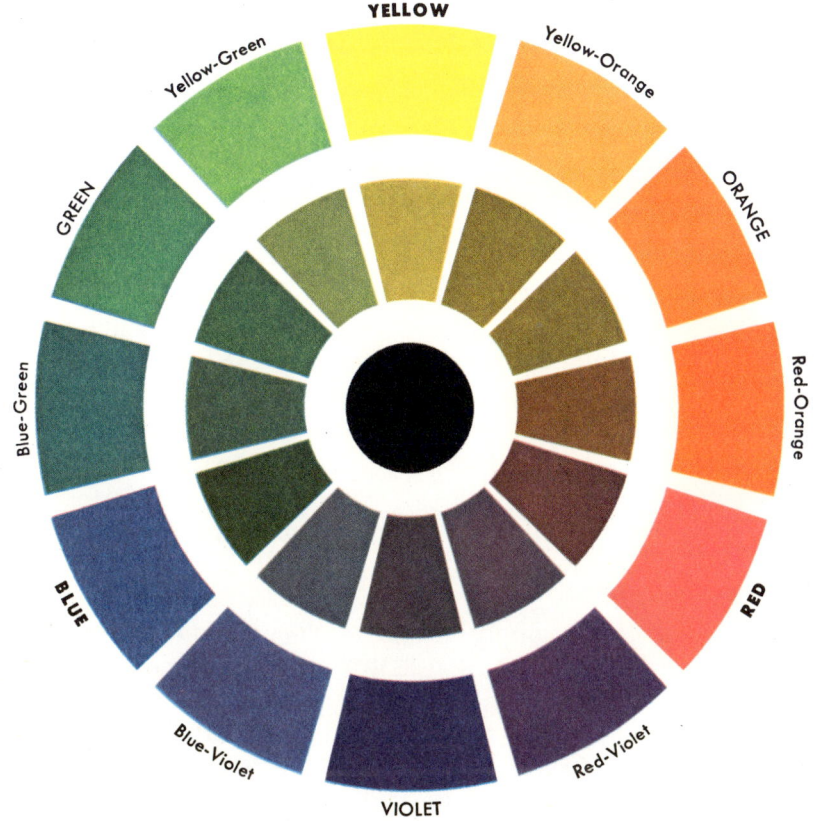

The outer circle shows the primary and secondary colors, separated by six intermediate colors. The inner circle shows darker colors obtained by mixing two colors that lie opposite each other in the outer circle.
Copyright 1968 Field Enterprises Educational Corp.

The color wheel.

The Language of Color

- **Hue**: The name of the color; for example, red is a hue.
- **Warm colors**: Those associated with the colors of heat, the fire, and the sun. Red, yellow, and orange are warm colors.
- **Cool colors**: Those associated with coolness—the color of a deep pool under a blue sky. Any tone predominantly blue is a cool color.
- **Value**: The quality of light (clear or pure) or dark (black added) in a color.
- **Tint**: White added to a color to make it lighter. "Ice blue" is a tint of blue. Pink is a tint of red.
- **Shade**: Add black to a color to make it darker in *value*. Navy is a shade of blue.
- **Intensity**: The quality of brightness or dullness in a color. Add some *complementary coloring* to dull or "gray" a color's intensity. The colors as they appear on the color wheel are full strength. Such intense colors are very striking as accent colors, but used on a large surface they can be

The Color, Line, and Design Story in Fashion

overpowering. The less intense colors are more interesting and easier to use. Because they are more subtle and easier on the eyes they can be used in larger amounts.

- CHROMA: Color—except white, which is *all* colors.
- ACHROMATIC: Without color. The so-called neutrals—white, black, and gray—are achromatic.
- MONOCHROMATIC: One color. A brown, tan, and orange combination is monochromatic because all of these colors are a form of orange. A black, red, and white scheme is also monochromatic. Red is the only color. (As said, black and white are achromatic.)
- COMPLEMENTARY: Colors opposite each other in wave length. Complementary colors represent the greatest contrast possible because they have nothing in common. Orange and blue are complementary colors. A small amount of a color mixed with its complement dulls it. As mentioned, mixing complementary colors in equal amounts produces gray.
- RELATED: Colors near each other on the color wheel. They are "related" because they have a color in common. Red-orange and yellow-orange are related colors. They both contain red.
- ANALAGOUS: Colors beside each other on the color wheel. They are also called *adjacent*. Red-orange, orange, and yellow-orange are analagous because they are next to each other. Analagous and adjacent colors are also *related*, because they have a color in common.

In creating the color wheel, came the possibility of twenty-four distinct colors. Using just these twenty-four we have the possibility of hundreds. Let's see how:

Suppose we allow nine different steps on the value scale for each color, from the very lightest (almost white) to the very darkest (almost black). Change the *intensity* of the color—for example, add blue to orange (its complement) to create a dull orange or rust. Then change the *value* of the rust from beige to dark brown—again nine steps. From one color—orange—you have created eighteen variations; eighteen variations possible with a total of twenty-four variations in hue—432 in all.

WHAT COLOR CAN DO

Colors give more than an illusion of warmth or coolness. If you take the temperature of the wave lengths of the colors in the spectrum (there is a sensitive instrument that can do just that), it is a scientific fact that the colors at the red end of the spectrum register a higher temperature than those at the blue end. A red dress is a good choice for a cold winter day because the color actually makes a person look and feel warmer. For the same reason, red is uncomfortable on a hot summer day.

Draw an imaginary line across the color wheel between red and green, dividing it in half. Notice that one half of the wheel is "cool," the other half "warm." Note that as yellow approaches green it loses some of its warmth. The same happens to red as it approaches purple.

Warm colors are stimulating and gay; cool colors are restful and perhaps even depressing or sad. Colors can set a mood—vibrant and exciting or calm and peaceful.

Color

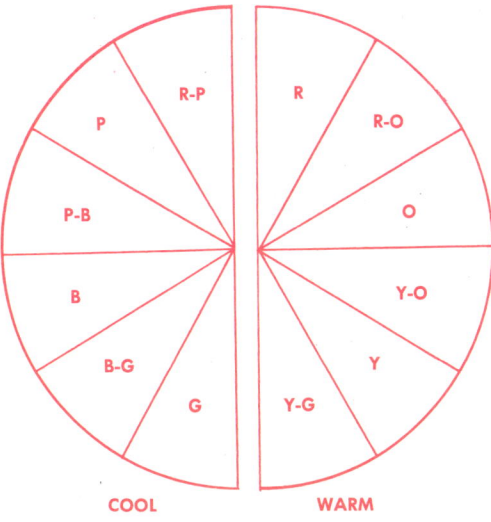

Warm and cool colors.

principle. This time make one light blue, the other navy blue. Which one looks larger? Put a white shoe on one foot and a black one on the other. Which foot looks larger?

Practical application in clothing: If you want the figure to look smaller, use dark colors.

Notice the figures below. They are actually the same size, but you can see that the girl in the white dress looks larger than the one in the dark dress. Use color value either to advance the figure, thus making it look larger, or to subdue it and make it look smaller.

Warm colors are also known as *advancing* colors—they "reach" toward you and attract your attention. They seemingly bring an object closer and in turn make it appear larger than it is. Cool colors are *receding*. They don't call attention to themselves. Instead they make an object seem to be moving farther away and, in so doing, decrease its size.

Try this experiment: Cut two rectangles exactly the same size—one red, the other blue. Use construction paper of the same value and intensity. Mount these on a neutral background. Which rectangle looks larger? Using dolls the same size—or paper figure silhouettes—dress one in red, the other in blue. Which figure looks larger?

Practical application in clothing: If you want the figure to look smaller, use cool colors.

Other properties of color can also influence the size of the figure. Light colors tend to make an object look larger; dark colors, smaller. Use the rectangle test again to illustrate this

Vogue Pattern Service
Dark versus light.

Light and dark colors also affect temperature. White reflects light; black absorbs it. Therefore light colors are actually cooler and more comfortable to wear in warm weather than dark colors. Because dark colors absorb light they also seem to drain color from the skin. White on the other hand reflects the light and enhances your coloring.

Practical application in clothing: Put a white collar on a black dress.

The gaze is drawn toward light colors, especially when contrasted with a

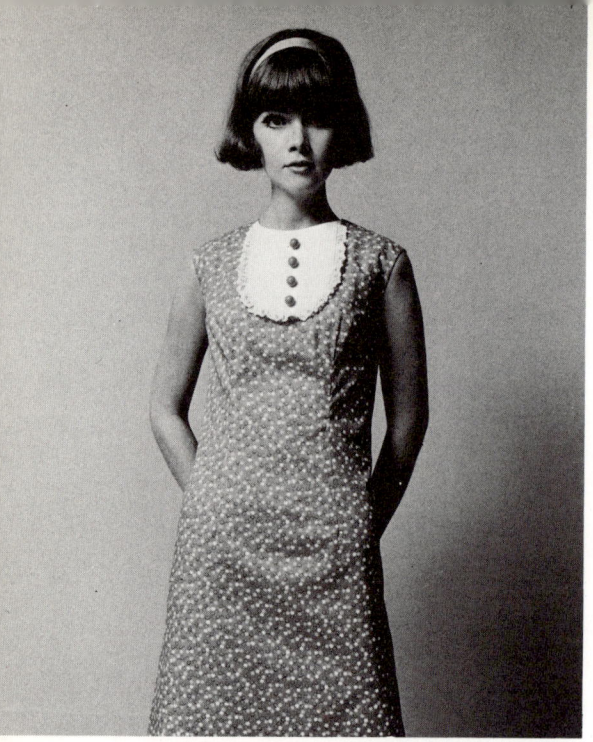

Simplicity Pattern Co., Inc.
Notice how the white "bib" draws the eye away from the hips toward the face.

darker background. This fact can be used to advantage to camouflage a figure problem by attracting the attention elsewhere with a light color. A colorful blouse can attract the gaze away from the hips, for instance, thus minimizing their size.

Intensity has the same ability as value to influence the size of the figure. Bright colors make an object look larger; dull colors, smaller. Repeat the rectangle test, using bright blue and teal blue this time. Which one looks larger?

Practical application in clothing: If you want the figure to look smaller, avoid allover bright colors.

Bright colors, like warm ones, are exciting and gay but difficult to use in clothing. They tend to be overpowering and only a person with strong personal coloring and a strong personality can wear so much color well. A person with delicate coloring looks "washed out." The garment becomes the main attraction, while the person fades into the background, defeating the purpose of attractive clothing—to enhance the individual. NOTE: Striking effects can be achieved by using intense colors in small amounts as accents with more subtle, subdued colors for the background and larger areas.

The *texture* of the fabric influences the brightness of the color. Compare a sample of kelly green satin with a sample of tweed the same color. The satin reflects light; the tweed absorbs it. The color appears much more intense in a smooth, shiny fabric than in one with a rough texture.

Wear a patent leather shoe on one foot and a suede shoe on the other. Even though both shoes are the same color, the foot will look larger in the shiny surface. Why?

How Colors Affect Each Other

Any color can be attractive by itself, but we don't see isolated colors. In combination with others—including personal coloring—care must be taken to create the effect desired. Colors influence each other; they even play tricks on each other. They can be emphasized or subdued; they can be made to appear more intense—or dull and lifeless; they can be made to look different or even seem to change completely. All this can be accomplished by combining them differently—by altering the background or placing them next to different colors—or by using them in different lights.

When contrasts are used together —either in hue, value, or intensity

—they emphasize each other. Dark colors look darker against light backgrounds; a dull color looks even more so when used next to a bright color; warm colors make cool colors seem even cooler. The opposite in each of these cases is also true. Strong contrasts are dramatic; no contrast at all can be monotonous; slight contrast variations can be interesting and pleasing.

Value contrasts.

Strong value contrasts attract attention. Look at the drawings above. In which one is the dividing band most noticeable? Least noticeable?

Practical application in clothing: Use contrasting values to emphasize a desirable feature; avoid them to make undesirable features less noticeable.

Complementary colors when used together will both seem brighter than when used alone. They intensify each other. In fact, if used in full intensity, they almost scream. Because they are so overpowering they are difficult to handle, but used correctly, they can create interesting effects. To subdue one color, use it with a slightly different shade or intensity from its complements. Very intense red and green used together can be displeasing to the eye, but green and dusky pink or red and gray-green are subtle, attractive combinations.

A color can also be made to look more intense by placing it next to a less intense shade of the same color. Pure blue, for example, seems to drain the blue from a duller shade of blue. The dull color looks even duller, whereas the pure blue looks brighter and bluer.

A color has the power of "forcing" its complement on a neutral or white background. The *after-image* is an example of this phenomenon. Stare steadily at a red circle for a count of ten. Then close your eyes or switch your glance quickly to a white background. A green circle the same size as the red one will appear. The eye becomes fatigued with the green ray and when the green spot is removed the eye sees its complement.

This factor can be applied in selecting colors to flatter the complexion: green "forces" red into the skin; purple "forces" yellow, etc.

This after-image factor affects the color of neutrals used in combination with intense colors. If gray and red are used together, the gray picks up the color of the complement (green), not the color itself, and has a green cast.

Two *primary* colors used together create the same illusion; they bring out the complementary color in each. Red used with blue looks a little orange, while the blue has a green cast.

Any two *adjacent* colors used together seem to draw apart. The primary color drains its own hue from the other. For example, combine blue and green and the blue looks bluer, whereas the green seems to be more yellow than when by itself. Use yellow and orange and the orange seems to be redder, etc.

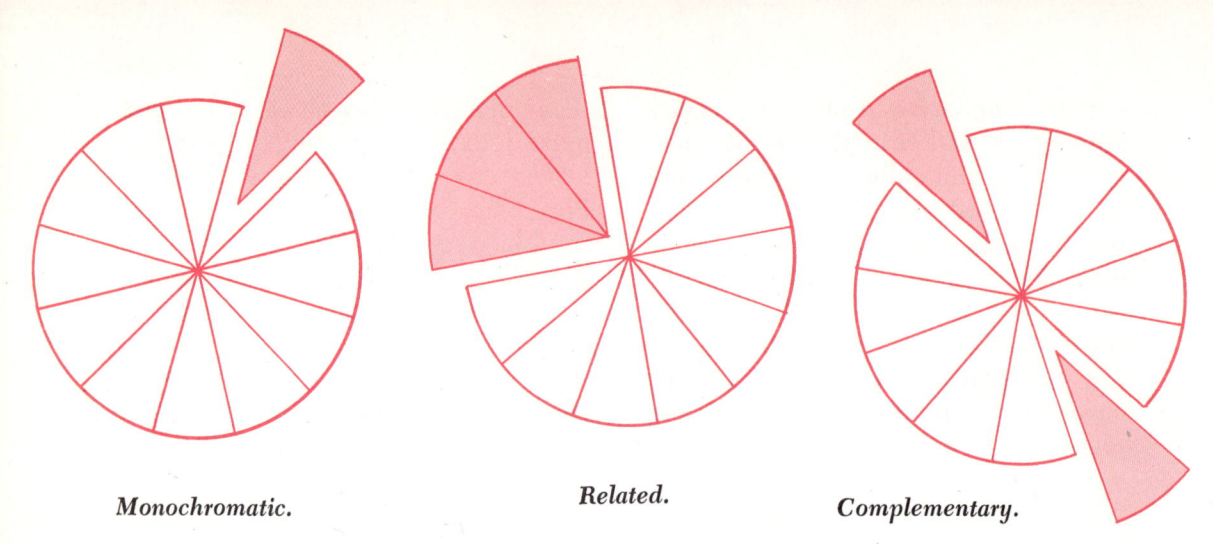

Monochromatic. *Related.* *Complementary.*

Principles in Using Color Effectively

All the tricks and illusions with color can serve as guides to help you combine colors effectively. In combining colors, the first principle to follow is that they should be in harmony—that is, they look as though they belong together and the end result is pleasing. No color should "fight" for attention. Neither should the colors be so much alike that the effect is monotonous.

There are certain generally accepted schemes for combining colors. We have already noted three of these basic combinations—monochromatic, related, and complementary. (See page 50 and above.) Others:

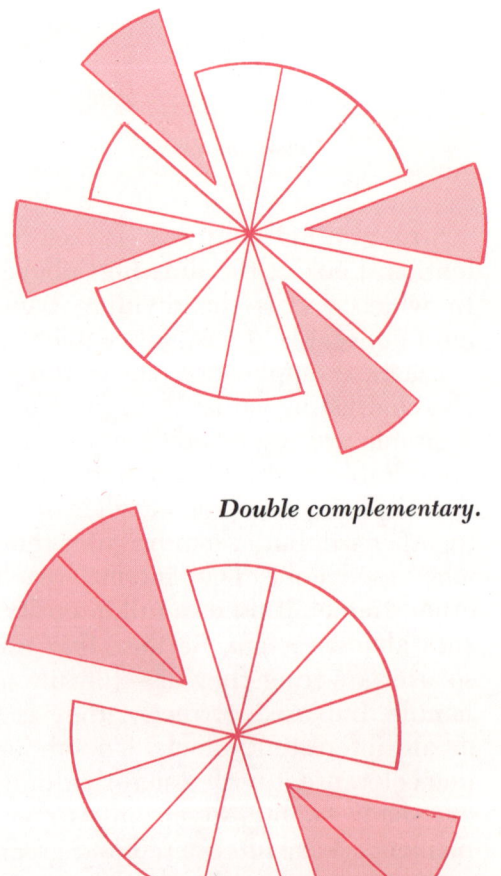

Double complementary.

- **Double complementary:** Four colors are used—the colors on each side of direct complementary colors (red-orange and purple-red, blue-green and yellow-green) or two adjacent colors and their complements (red and red-orange, green and blue-green). Such combinations are often found in plaids and prints.

- SPLIT COMPLEMENTARY: Any color (red) with the two colors on each side of its direct complement (blue-green and yellow-green).
- ADJACENT COMPLEMENTARY: Two adjacent colors (green and blue-green) with the complement of the dominant color (red).
- TRIAD: Any three colors that are an equal distance apart on the color wheel. Red, yellow, and blue—the primary colors form a triad. So do the secondary colors—orange, green, and purple.

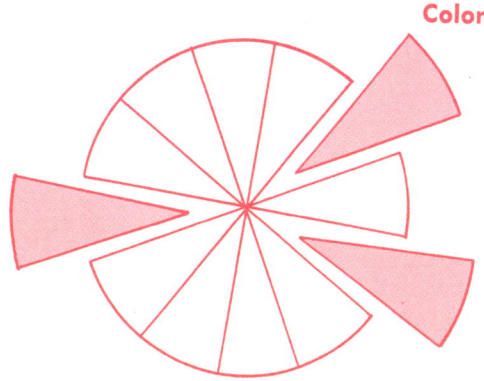

Split complementary.

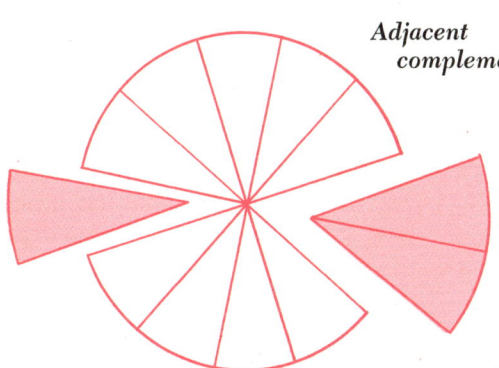

Adjacent complementary.

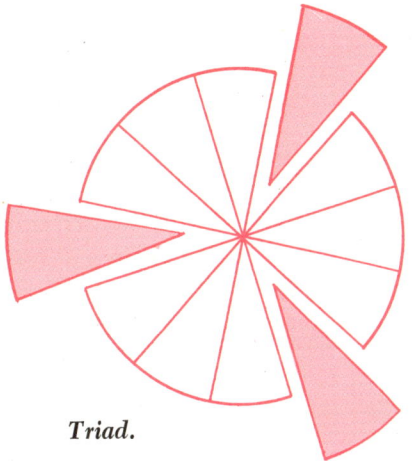

Triad.

By observation and analysis of color—in art, in your surroundings, in clothing—you can develop a more acute awareness and gain confidence in the correct use of color. These basic schemes are nothing more than guides to help you in the study of color. They should not be considered as prescribed formulas to be followed strictly in selecting and using color. Even discord can prove effective; cleverly used, it can mean the difference between the commonplace and the outstanding. It is fun to experiment, always keeping in mind the influence colors have on each other when used together.

Any combination is more interesting when there are variations in value, intensity, and texture. As already noted, intense red and green used together create a harsh effect, but certain shades of these same colors are quite pleasing when combined. Pure colors, as they appear in the spectrum are difficult to handle in clothing. Intermediate tints and shades are generally much more flattering. The colors used to illustrate the different color schemes above were pure, directly based on the color wheel. Look again at the double complementary—red-orange, purple-red, blue-green, and yellow-green. In

The Color, Line, and Design Story in Fashion

practical application this combination may be a small plaid of wine, aqua, and chartreuse on a beige background with a pink cast. Learn to think of each color in terms of eighteen different variations (see page 50), *not as a single pure hue.* Then the possibilities are endless.

The colors in the spectrum move from light to dark in a specific order. Starting with yellow (the lightest), they get progressively darker in both directions (yellow to orange to red, or yellow to green to blue) toward purple (the darkest). **Remember:** A combination that follows this natural order is more pleasing than one that upsets the order. For example, a pale chartreuse with purple is attractive, but *dark brown* with purple upsets the order and adds nothing.

Here are some additional guides to help you. Experiment with them to see the results.

- TINTS are attractive in combination with other tints, intense spectrum colors, intermediate colors, and shades. Try pink with light purple; bright green; teal blue; maroon. All are attractive combinations.

- SHADES are attractive in combination with tints, achromatic colors, and intermediate colors, but not with spectrum colors. Try wine with light green; gray; blue-green. All are attractive. However, combine wine with bright blue and see the difference.

In the same way, intermediate colors do not combine well with intense spectrum colors. Try dusty rose with red.

Colors can be distributed in such a way as to create a feeling of *balance.* Without balance, things seem to come apart. Bright colors "carry more weight" than those of less intensity. Therefore a lesser amount of a bright color is needed to balance a subdued color. A good rule to follow: the larger the area, the more subdued the color; the smaller the area, the more intense the color can be. **Remember:** Avoid large areas of an intense color. Bright colors are more attractive in small amounts.

Too many colors in combination create confusion. Generally three is the maximum number that can be handled attractively in clothing. A guide to follow: one dark, one light, one bright. You may ask, what about the color schemes that are based on four colors? These are reserved mainly for prints and plaids.

In coordinating colors for a costume, one color should be dominant. Equal amounts of several colors can create confusion. Emphasize one color; use the others as subordinates or accents. Remember the rule concerning the relationship between the size of the area and the intensity of the color.

One way *to emphasize a color* is by using it for the largest area. Another is by repetition. By repeating a color the gaze can also be made to move from one area to another, following the color. If the color is cleverly placed and used in the proper amount, the gaze seems to glide over the costume.

Improperly used, repetition becomes spotty—and too much repetition is monotonous. For instance, red hat, shoes, purse, and gloves create too much repetition. The gaze jumps from one to the other and the overall effect is displeasing.

Selecting Colors for an Individual

The colors a person wears are very important to general appearance. No matter how fine the fabric, or how good the style is for you, if the color is not becoming the outfit is not right. It is said that everyone can wear every color; it is just a matter of finding the right shade or tint. The goal is to create a true harmony. **Remember:** You have a color to start with—your personal coloring. The colors of clothing should harmonize with this. It is a matter of analyzing a person's coloring, putting to work all your knowledge about what color can do, then selecting the ones that will do the most for the person. (An individual can usually do this for himself by the process of trying and rejecting.) You must learn to visualize the end result, so that you are able to make suggestions with confidence that they will produce a pleasing effect.

The usual way of describing a girl's coloring is to say that she is a blonde or a brunette, a redhead, or perhaps an in-between or intermediate type. This is not enough. There are many variations: The color of the eyes and especially the skin must be taken into consideration. The colors a person wears should complement the hair of course and, if possible, accent the color of the eyes. However, a color must be flattering to the complexion, or the whole effect is weakened.

A white person's skin coloring is basically some tone of red or yellow—warm skins having yellow undertones and cool skins, pink. To be most flattering, the colors a person wears should "play down" the prominence of either of these colors in the complexion. We have already noted that colors can be emphasized by contrast. Green forces red in the face, and should be avoided if the face is already ruddy. In the same way, purple forces yellow, so it should be avoided if the skin is sallow.

Repetition also emphasizes the skin color of a person with light complexion, usually the wrong way! It produces an unpleasant effect. If yellow dominates the skin tone, the major use of colors in the yellow range will be unattractive because they will make the skin look more sallow. For the same reason, avoid red with ruddy complexions.

There are times, however, when it may be desirable to force the pink in the cheeks—if the person has very delicate, clear, light skin, for instance. Wearing just the right tint of red will cause a pink flush to appear.

Colors are "forced" by repetition in two ways. (1) The repetition of the colors makes it more noticeable and (2) therefore you become more conscious of it, as in the case of yellow emphasizing a sallow skin. Repetition of a color in the face, however, is sometimes produced by reflection. Try the following experiment. Take two sheets of drawing paper—a white one and a red one. Clip them together at one end so as to make a folder. Holding it so that daylight will shine inside, open the other end of the folder slightly. As you look inside, you will see that the red color is reflected on the surface of the white sheet of paper. In the same way, a red

The Color, Line, and Design Story in Fashion

dress may reflect color onto the neck or lower part of the face. NOTE: Some skins pick up color reflections more readily than others.

To emphasize the color of hair or eyes, follow the same principle—repeat the color or contrast it. The right shade of blue enhances blue eyes and makes them appear more blue. Dark eyes contrast beautifully with light colors. Black and dark brown hair look darker with light colors and dark colors emphasize light hair.

You can understand why the method of forcing a desirable color in personal coloring is helpful in the selection of becoming colors. It isn't entirely possible to prescribe colors that will be flattering, but here are some suggestions that will be helpful:

One *blonde* may have very light hair and skin, and light blue eyes. Another blonde may have more yellowish, tawny hair, a warmer, pale, honey-colored skin, and darker blue eyes. So the same colors will not be the best choices for both types. The white-skinned girl is likely to look best in pastel tints, pale blue, orchid, and delicate pinks. The blonde with warmer coloring will find warm browns, ivory, and dull greens more flattering. NOTE: Both of these types should avoid harsh, bright colors. They are too overpowering.

Brunettes vary in coloring from vivid, dramatic types with very black hair to those with dark brown hair and complexions varying from pale white through sallow, ruddy, and warm olive. It is the vivid type that can best wear bright colors because the personal coloring is not overwhelmed by the bright colors of the clothing. Delicate, pastel tones may emphasize the sallow or ruddy tones of the skin too much. Dramatize with clear tones.

Perhaps you have heard that *redheads* should avoid wearing red and pink because these colors have a tendency to clash with the hair. This is not necessarily true. There are varieties of red ranging from blue-reds on through to orange-reds. If she is clever in her selection, the redhead may find a red tone that is quite flattering. With fair skin she may find coral and golden pinks becoming. If she looks well in blue, she should select a red with a tinge of blue in it. Browns, tans, greens (not too bright), aqua, and blue-green tones are generally becoming to redheads. Play up the natural coloring.

The *intermediate types* can wear many colors but should not choose the intense tones which are likely to make the personal coloring look drab. This does not mean that they should choose only grayed, subdued colors either. On the other hand they should avoid drab colors and select interesting and pleasing colors which bring out the best points in their personal color schemes. For example, a girl with medium brown hair, blue eyes, and a slightly sallow skin should not choose yellow, chartreuse, or strong blue because these colors are almost sure to make her skin seem more sallow or "washed out." She will find peach, pale blue-green (aqua), navy blue, brown, and dull pinks more becoming.

If you are a Negro, your skin may be classified in three basic complexion groups: the very dark, the medium brown, or the very light. Those in the first group have very dark brown hair and eyes. The skin is a warm brown containing very rich tones of orange. Never select colors so dark that they are uninteresting, nor so light that they clash harshly, as do the traditional colors of Halloween. Deep, rich, warm "jewel" colors are a wise choice: ruby red, sapphire blue, pearl gray, or emerald green.

Those with medium brown skin will look well in the neutral tones of beige or tan. They wear colors well that are in between the very bright and the very dark. Nature displays the best examples during autumn in most of the U. S. just before the trees shed their leaves: shades of red, green, brown, orange, and yellow.

The very light complexions have a wide range of color to choose from. Strawberry, lemon, lime, peach, and orange are all bright, light, and attractive for this group. Coral pink and light blue are most flattering. Quiet colors are preferred because extremely bright, vivid colors tend to "fade" the sallow hues of the face.

White is considered becoming to most people regardless of skin coloring because it brings out the best of their own natural tones, even though it usually holds true that people with pale coloring look better in pastel tones. Brilliant colors make them look faded. Just the opposite holds true for those with vivid coloring; they look better in brilliants than in pale pastels. *Great contrast, although dramatic, is often displeasing*.

Keep your figure in mind also when selecting colors. **Remember:** Dark, subdued, cool colors make the figure look smaller, whereas light, bright, warm colors make it look larger. A

Solid versus contrast.

Vogue Pattern Service

one-color outfit gives the illusion of height, whereas contrasting colors, as in the drawing, divide the figure into definite parts. If a short person wears a dark skirt and a contrasting top, she will look even shorter because she has divided her figure into two distinct parts. A tall person, however, can wear contrasting colors very nicely.

Analyze your figure for any irregularities. Then put color to work to minimize them by employing the tricks you have learned. **Remember:** A dark skirt minimizes the size of the hips; a strong detail of the blouse draws the gaze away from the hipline. If there is a particularly good color for a person, but the figure says "No!"—red, for example—use a small amount of this color close to the face—perhaps a scarf or necklace.

The Power of Color

Did you know that you may feel lively, vivacious, glamorous, feminine, or demure partly because of color? Color can influence our moods. We have already noted that warm colors are full of life, are vibrant and cheerful; they have the power to refresh and stimulate a person. Other hues are quiet and peaceful; they can soothe or even depress. Pastels tend

The Color, Line, and Design Story in Fashion

to make a woman feel very feminine; bright colors, adventuresome; dull colors, drab; red, daring; and black, sophisticated or dressy.

Color causes an emotional experience. People react to it, have definite attitudes toward it. They can be attracted to it or repelled by it. Very few people are neutral in their feelings about colors; their personal preferences often reveal their personalities. For instance, those who prefer red tend toward being fun-loving and dynamic; blue—cautious and conservative; green—are agreeable and steady; purple—charming, self-satisfied, and often impractical; yellow, the least popular color—intellectual or a "loner."

Color is symbolic of our feelings and emotions. Aren't all of these expressions familiar? *Feel blue; see red; in the pink; a black rage; green with envy?* We also associate color with certain personal characteristics—"yellow," "true blue," "green." All of these are commonly recognized descriptions. We have built up associations with color; each one has connotations:

Black:	sorrow, gloom, death
Red:	danger
White:	innocence, purity
Green:	immaturity, freshness, spring
Blue:	sadness, serenity, fidelity
Gray:	old age
Purple:	royalty, passion
Yellow:	cowardice

Also a color preference can be the result of some personal association. An unhappy home life, or connection with pleasant times (as certain flowers in the spring), usually means dislike and vice versa. No matter what the rules say about how becoming or flattering a color should be, a person must first of all like a color to wear it and enjoy it!

LINE

Whatever a person's connection with fashion—whether as a designer, a buyer, or a salesperson; as a fitter or machine operator; as a teacher; or working in promotion, advertising, or display—an understanding of line is essential. Line serves many purposes: it gives direction, outlines shape, divides space, connects parts, suggests movement, and creates a feeling of rhythm. Like color, it is an important element of design that can be used to create impressions and moods as well as illusions. It can be put to work to conceal figure irregularities or to accentuate good features, and to increase or decrease appearance as desired. Understanding what line can do will increase your ability to help people dress with confidence.

Basically there are two kinds of line—straight and curved.

Straight lines are severe, but they suggest dignity and formality. You are perhaps familiar with the expressions "—like soldiers in a row" or

Straight line—gentle curve—full curve.

In review:

What is the difference between fashion, fad, and style?

What is color?

Why does the eye see different colors?

Explain: primary colors, secondary colors, intermediate colors.

Do you know the meaning of: hue, value, tint, shade, intensity?

What is meant by advancing colors? receding colors? What effects do they have on an object?

What properties of color influence the size of the figure? In what way?

How can you emphasize a color? subdue it?

What is meant by harmony? How can harmony be achieved in combining colors?

For further discussion:

Fashion repeats itself.

Fashion reflects the times.

Color causes an emotional experience.

The power of color.

Color symbolism.

To gain experience:

Find counterparts in history for today's popular styles.

Examine the major fashion changes from 1900 to the current time and relate clothing to the conditions prevalent at each period.

Examine light as it passes through a prism.

Using water colors, create a color wheel; a value scale; an intensity scale.

In fashion magazines, find examples of each of the color schemes.

Try color samples on individuals to determine the effects on their coloring.

Experiment with using color to de-emphasize figure irregularities.

"—straight as a ramrod." Both of these suggest the stiff, tense, rigid impression created by straightness.

Curves on the other hand are soft and graceful; they seemingly flow along gently and smoothly. They may vary from very gentle, to almost straight, to very deep. The stronger the curve, the more powerful the line, because it seems to move more. In clothing, straight lines suggest the severe, tailored look; they give an impression of dignity and stiffness. On the other hand curved lines seem more informal and soft, creating a gayer, more feminine look. Yet the exclusive use of curves in any design can be monotonous. The presence of some straight lines as a steadying influence is desirable.

On the other hand, straight lines alone, though dignified, are also stiff and cold and need to be relieved with some curved line. However, the total picture is more pleasing if the lines in the garment are mainly straight or curved, not a balanced combination of the two.

Because the gaze follows a line, it gives direction—vertical, horizontal,

Vertical—horizontal—diagonal lines.

Simplicity Pattern Co., Inc.

A gaily printed scarf around the neck relieves the plainness of the basic dress. The soft folds of the scarf are in pleasing contrast to the straight lines of the dress.

and diagonal. If the line goes up (vertically) the gaze follows it up. Therefore the vertical lines suggest height ("stand tall"), strength, and dignity. If the line moves horizontally, the eye also moves from side to side. As a result, horizontal lines suggest width. They also suggest quiet and rest ("lie down" or "stretch out"). The third direction—diagonal—usually carries the eye vertically. However, as the slant approaches the horizontal, the gaze also moves more toward the horizontal. Because they lean, diagonal lines seem insecure and need support.

The degree of slant determines how the diagonal line carries the eye.

Oppositional and transitional lines.

Used alone they give the impression of falling over. (Think of a leaning fence.) In clothing, vertical lines obviously add height, making the figure look taller, and horizontal lines suggest width, making the figure look shorter and heavier. (There are other more subtle reactions to these lines. Vertical lines also suggest a feeling of sophistication; horizontal lines, gentleness.) The diagonal line, being a combination of the two, modifies the severity of the vertical, and the result is a more relaxed feeling.

- OPPOSITIONAL LINES are straight lines that meet each other at right angles.
- TRANSITIONAL LINES, on the other hand, are modified, as with a curve that leads the gaze gradually from one plane to another.

Line suggests *movement,* again because the gaze follows it. The way lines are combined, or the characteristic of the line itself, creates the sense of movement. A line that moves upward is exhilarating and stimulating. It is forceful and therefore suggests courage and inspiration. On the other hand, lines that move downward tend to reject and depress. The drawings illustrate movement through the use of line. An unbroken line carries the eye along smoothly and directly. If the line changes direction abruptly, as in the case of a zigzag line, the movement is jumpy

Line

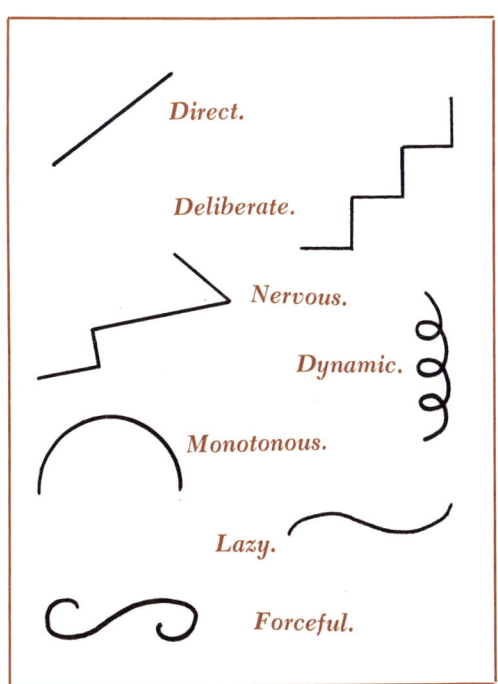

Direct.
Deliberate.
Nervous.
Dynamic.
Monotonous.
Lazy.
Forceful.

and erratic. On the other hand the movement may be slow and lazy if the line rambles.

Line suggests rhythm as it leads the gaze through the parts of a design. Long, sweeping curves, as in the first drawing, carry the gaze smoothly and pleasantly. Weak, disorganized curves, as in drawing B, wander in an aimless fashion and can hardly be called rhythmic. The transitions expressed in the third example, on the other hand, have a strong rhythmic movement. (See below.)

As a line moves throughout an area, it also connects parts into a unit. The *eye* will even *connect separate objects,* forming a line as it passes from one to the other. Think of the shapes the stars produce. The Big Dipper, as

The Color, Line, and Design Story in Fashion

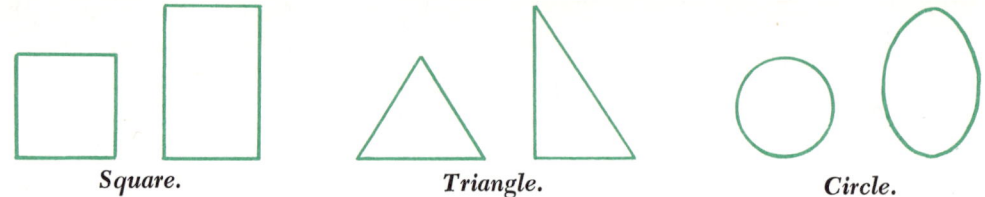

Square. *Triangle.* *Circle.*

an example, is a group of separate stars, connected only by the eye. In clothing, a series of buttons or rows of trimming, although disconnected objects, form a line as the eye moves from one to the other.

Lines *combine* in different directions to outline the shape of an object, creating form. Basically there are three shapes—the square or rectangle, the triangle, and the circle or oval. All others are variations of these three. In fashion there are also basically three shapes—the straight or tubular (rectangle), the full or bouffant (oval or triangle), and the bustle with fullness in the back (triangle). When encompassing shapes or contours, known as the silhouette, these are perhaps the most important lines of a garment because the outline is the first thing you notice about a design. As someone approaches you from a distance, you may not be able to make out the details of the outfit, but you can see its general shape or outline. From it you get an impression of size and figure qualities.

Generally the straight silhouette gives an impression of slimness, while the full silhouette appears to add pounds to the figure. Compare the two dresses in the illustration. Notice which silhouette makes the figure look larger.

The modern skyscraper is a sample of vertical lines at work, carrying your eye up and up.

Alcoa

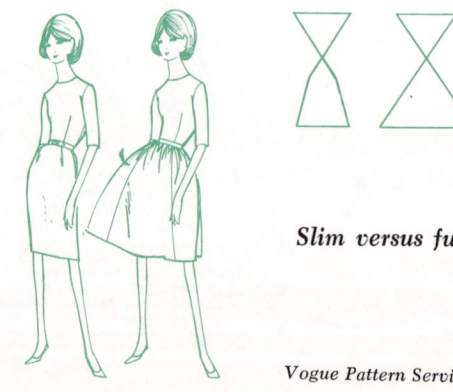

Slim versus full

Vogue Pattern Service

Line is also used to *divide space* into various smaller areas, each of which has a definite shape of its own. In clothing, there are two types of lines that divide the silhouette into individual parts—construction or structural lines (neckline, sleeve line, waistline, hemline, and other seam lines) and trimming lines (pockets, bands, borders, bows, belts, buttons, and other trimmings). The placement of each line creates the design of the garment. If carefully considered, these lines can also be used effectively to flatter the figure.

THE POWER OF LINE

Can your eyes always believe what they see? Through the clever use of optical illusion it is possible to deceive the eye. There are many illustrations of this fool-the-eye magic. Here are some of the more familiar.

Which line is longer? Of course, the lines are the same length, but the optical illusion makes you think otherwise. Deflecting the gaze downward in A seems to shorten the line. Extending the line as in B makes the line seem longer.

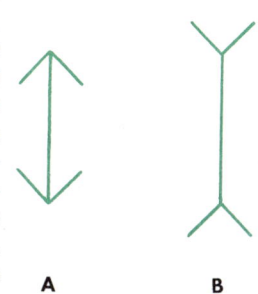

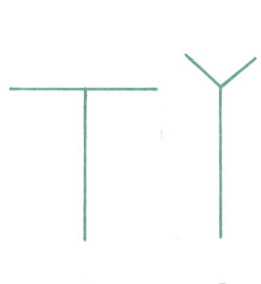

Which line is longer? When the eye is stopped as in A, it follows the horizontal line, making A look shorter than it really is. In B, the eye continues to follow the diagonal lines upward, seemingly increasing the length of the line.

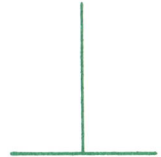

Which line is longer? Again, they are the same length, but because the vertical line carries the gaze upward it appears longer.

Which line is longer, A or B. Both are the same length, but A seems to be longer because the line above it is the same length. A longer line or added width at the top, diminishes the size of the lower line.

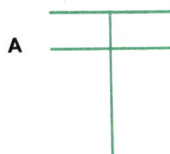 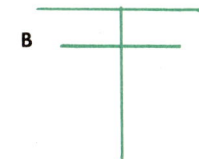

Is A longer than B? No, but the longer line under B makes B look shorter.

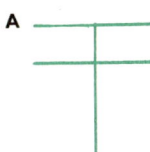 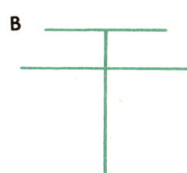

Do the vertical lines bulge in the center? Although it would appear so, this is merely an optical illusion. The lines are parallel, but the many lines that converge upon one point call attention to that area, making it appear wider.

Are the vertical lines parallel? Yes. The zig-zag of the opposing lines only makes them appear to waver.

The Color, Line, and Design Story in Fashion

We have seen that, as a general rule, vertical lines carry the gaze upward, whereas horizontal lines carry it from side to side. This statement does not always hold true, however. A lone vertical line will carry the gaze upward. Two vertical lines placed close together also carry it upward. But move the two vertical lines farther apart and the vertical illusion no longer holds. The gaze tends to move from one line to the other, creating a horizontal effect because the eye is now moving from side to side instead of up and down. The vertical effect of the lines in this case is dominated by the space between the lines.

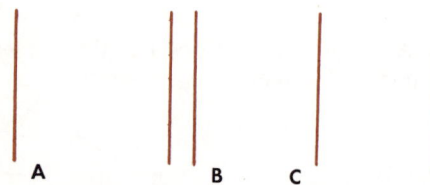

When lines are used in a series, their width and the space between them determine the illusion created. If the lines are all the same width and evenly spaced, the gaze is inclined to move from line to line, changing the original direction perhaps intended. Examine the two illustrations and notice how the vertical lines carry the gaze from side to side, whereas the horizontal lines carry it up and down. An effect has been created that is just the opposite of what is expected —the figure looks wider in the vertical stripes.

Spaces, as noted, can play tricks. The way in which an area is divided into parts affects the size and appearance of the whole. Perhaps you have seen these familiar illustrations:

Which rectangle is narrower? They are both the same, but the one divided horizontally looks shorter and wider than the one divided vertically. The two long, narrow rectangles make the entire area look smaller than two squares.

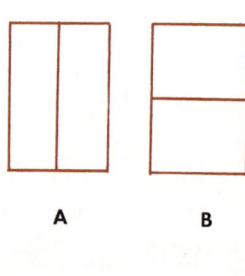

Which rectangle is narrower? Again, both are the same, but the one divided into three equal parts looks spaced out and therefore wider than the one with the narrow strip down the middle.

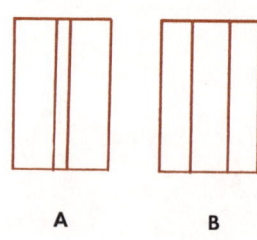

Which rectangle is narrower? The longer, narrow division of A makes the whole rectangle look narrower than B, which is divided in a manner approaching the horizontal, resulting in wider portions.

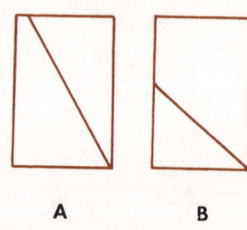

Vogue Pattern Service

Horizontal versus vertical lines.

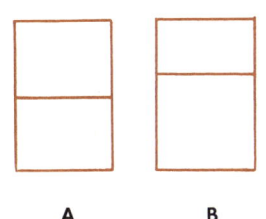

Which rectangle is narrower? Although both are divided horizontally, B looks longer and not as wide as A. The lower portion of B gives an illusion of total length not present in the two equal parts of A.

USING LINE EFFECTIVELY IN CLOTHING

Line, like color, is a most important factor in dress design. When used correctly, lines can create a pleasing appearance. They can be used to call attention to figure assets or, through illusion, they can cleverly hide liabilities. Thus the "optical-illusion power" of line can be used to advantage in clothing.

We have seen how the gaze follows the direction of lines. If verticals predominate in a garment, the eye naturally follows them up and down, creating the feeling of height; as a result, the figure appears taller. The following establish *vertical lines:*

- Straight silhouette.
- Narrow vertical stripes and narrow center panels.
- Vertical trimming, rows of buttons, and braid.
- Full length closings, diagonal surplice closings.
- Princess lines, full length unbroken seams, unbroken sheath.
- No belt or narrow, self-fabric belt.
- Long, straight sleeves.
- V or U neckline.
- Tuxedo, shawl, and long narrow collars.
- Full length coats, short jackets, straight skirts.

Simplicity Pattern Co., Inc.

A. The contrasting colored buttons and rows of trimming create vertical lines on this dress.

B. The horizontal stripes, wide belt, and contrasting skirt and bodice create strong horizontal lines that carry the gaze from side to side.

Strong horizontal lines carry the eye from side to side and make the figure appear wider and therefore heavier. The following design details establish *horizontal lines:*

- Full or bouffant silhouette.
- Wide vertical stripes, pleats, tucks, and panels.
- Horizontal stripes or trimming.
- Short sleeves, contrasting color sleeves with jumpers, wide sleeves, full sleeves, sleeves with cuffs, no sleeves.
- Contrasting belts and midriffs.
- Wide belts and cummerbunds.
- Contrasting colored separates.
- Full skirts, overskirts.
- Suits, two-piece dresses, capes, short coats or jackets.
- Yokes, peplums, tunics.
- Wide bows, collars; round, bateau, and square necklines.
- Pockets or flaps on each side of the garment.

The Color, Line, and Design Story in Fashion

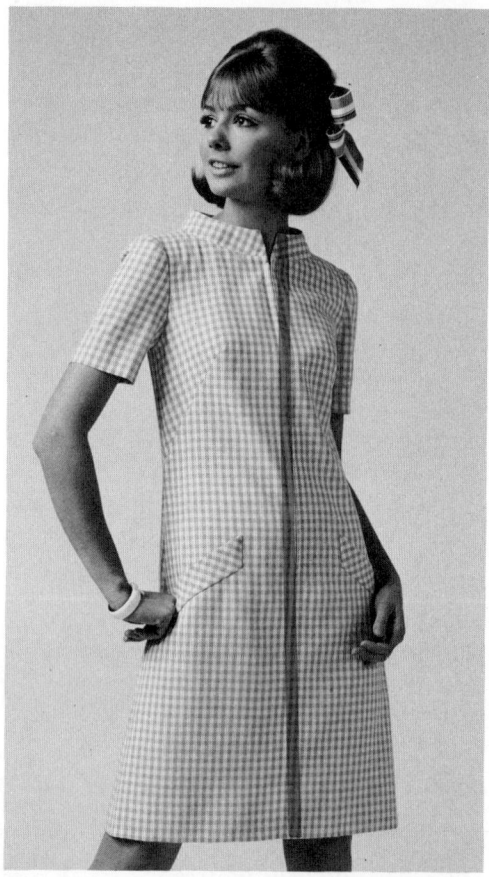

McCall's Patterns

The I Line—a strong, vertical line that carries the gaze upward, making the figure look taller and more slender.

figure, balancing the extra width below, making it less conspicuous.

Line can be used to flatter the face as well as the figure. The neckline of a garment frames the face and should complement it. Although an *oval face* takes any neckline, if the face is *round*, avoid a neckline that repeats the curve. A more vertical neckline, such as the V, makes the face appear longer. If the face is *long*, avoid a neckline that continues the long line of the face. A neck opening with a horizontal look, such as the high round jewel neckline, is more flattering because it counteracts the length of the face.

The T Line—a horizontal line that stops the upward movement of the gaze, cutting height and creating an effect of width.
Simplicity Pattern Co., Inc.

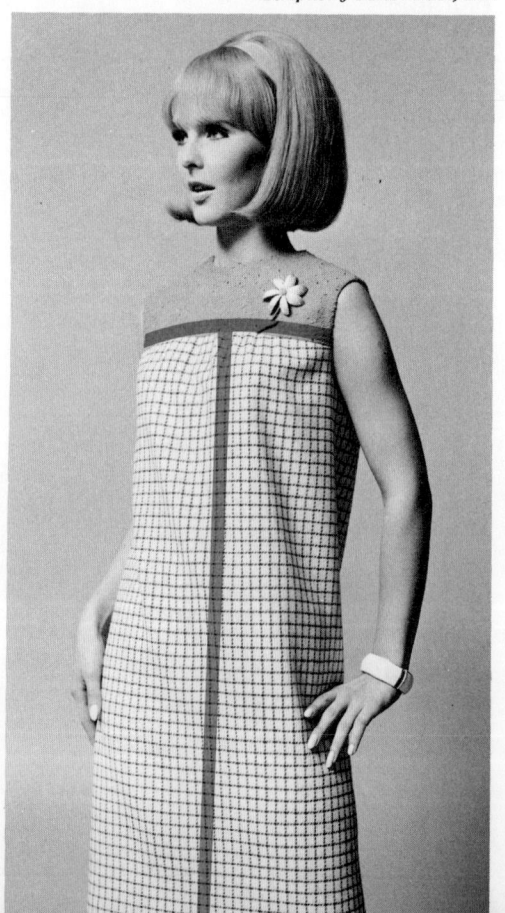

In most garments, we find several lines—horizontal and vertical. The dominant line—perhaps a strong cross stripe or just a decorative feature—catches the gaze. With this fact in mind, it is possible to attract the eye to a certain area and, at the same time, draw it away from another area. You can make use of this trick to emphasize good points and minimize weak ones. **Remember,** if the hips are large, attract attention to the neck and shoulder area. A large collar will seem to broaden the peak of the

Line

The Λ Line—an arrow line that deflects the gaze downward, cutting height.
<small>Simplicity Pattern Co., Inc.</small>

<small>McCall's Patterns</small>

The Y Line—a continuing line that makes the figure look taller and more slender.

This dress has a strong vertical line up the front, but the wide sleeves accented with white fringes carry the gaze across the figure, giving the impression of width. A design such as this is good for a person with large hips, since the impression of width at the top minimizes the width of the hips. The white beads also help by catching the eye and deflecting it from the hipline.
<small>Simplicity Pattern Co., Inc.</small>

The way the *lines of the garment divide the figure* also has an effect on size. Think of the garment as the rectangle divided by lines into smaller sections. Divided *vertically*, with a single line down the middle, the figure looks taller and slimmer. A narrow band or front panel still carries the gaze up and down, making the figure look taller and slimmer. A wide panel makes the figure look wider and, as a result, heavier. *Divided in half horizontally*, the figure looks shorter, wider, and as a result, heavier. *Divided horizontally about one-third of the way down* rather than across the middle, the figure again looks taller and not as wide. Short jackets and the high empire waistline are examples of this space division.

McCall's Patterns
A narrow front panel divides the figure vertically. The gaze still moves up and down, making the figure look taller and thinner.

An area divided in half vertically looks tall and thin. Divide the same area in half horizontally and it looks shorter and wider.
Simplicity Pattern Co., Inc.

A wide front panel, although it also divides the figure vertically, adds width because the gaze hops back and forth across the panel. The width of the panel is more noticeable than the vertical lines forming the panel.

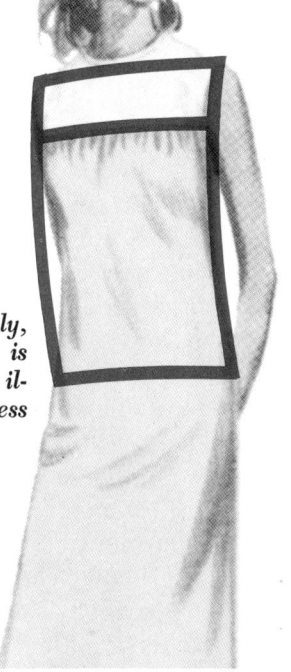

Divide an area horizontally, but above center so that it is not divided in half, and the illusion of height and slenderness is not destroyed.

Simplicity Pattern Co., Inc.

In review:

What purpose does line serve?

What are the two basic kinds of line? What impression does each suggest?

Name an example of a "stimulating" line; a "sad" line; a "lazy" line.

What are the three basic style shapes? Give an example of each.

What is meant by structural lines? decorative lines?

Cite examples that use vertical lines to carry the eye across instead of up and down?

Cite examples that use horizontal lines to carry the eye up and down instead of across.

What is meant by dominant line?

How can dominant line be used for figure flattery?

For further discussion:

Line creates mood.
Line plays tricks.
Spaces can play tricks.

To gain experience:

Experiment at home with optical illusion in clothing.

Find examples of clothing that will make the figure appear taller, shorter, heavier, and more slender.

Try neckline samples with various shaped faces of classmates and note the effect!

The Color, Line, and Design Story in Fashion

PRINCIPLES OF DESIGN

A design is a plan, a grouping, an arrangement, a scheme. We speak of the *design* of a dress, a car, or a building; a house *plan;* a flower or furniture *arrangement;* the *organization* of a decorative pattern or picture; a color *scheme*. All of these have one thing in common—they are a medium of expression. In each case the meaning is the same—a created effect involving both structure and appearance, organized so as to produce harmonious and unified results.

The elements of design—line, form, color—are those features that are combined and manipulated to create the design. There are basically three methods for combining them; repetition, harmony, and discord. The drawings show very simple examples—not really "designed." In repetition, items identical in size, shape, and color are used together. The only major variation is in the spacing between items. Discord is the opposite extreme of repetition. Completely different, unrelated items are used together. Discord makes use of the greatest contrast possible. Harmony lies somewhere between the two extremes. Items that are similar in one or more respects, but not identical, are used together. Exact repetition can be boring and monotonous. Complete discord can be jarring and displeasing.

Harmony, on the other hand, is usually the desired result of any design—enough variation to be interesting but not enough to displease. Harmony is achieved when all parts of the design give the feeling that they belong together. You will find many examples in nature—such as repetitive waves breaking against a rugged shore. Notice scenes that have harmonious "design" in your locality.

There are fundamental principles that, when successfully applied, serve as guides for both creating and evaluating good design. These principles are the same whether applied to a painting, a building, a room, a piece of furniture, or an article of clothing. The only problem is in the materials the designer uses to create his product and the limitations each of these materials presents. Balance, proportion, rhythm, and emphasis—the principles of design—all can be expressed as effectively with bricks, steel, or cloth as with the artist's pencil or brush.

BALANCE

Good designs are balanced. If you have ever played on a seesaw, you can understand the concept of bal-

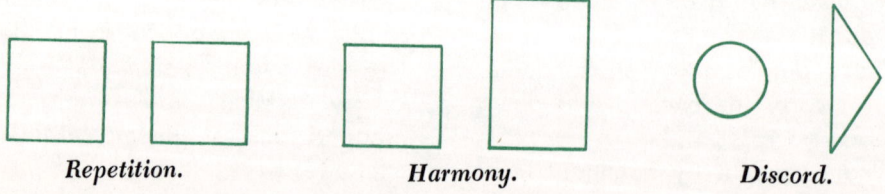

Repetition.　　　　Harmony.　　　　Discord.

Principles of Design

In balance—out of balance.

In *informal balance,* the objects on either side of the central point are not alike, but they have been arranged in such a manner as to achieve balance. Think again about the seesaw example. Two people of equal weight balance the seesaw perfectly (formal balance). A third person comes along and jumps on one end and what happens? The end with only one person shoots up in the air and the other end with the two people comes down with a thud. However, if the two on one end should slide in toward the center, they would find a place which just balances the one person who sits at the end on the other side.

ance. You know that when two people of about equal weight are sitting at the ends of the seesaw, they balance each other so that the board is horizontal. If the two people are not equal in weight, however, the balance is lost. The end with the heavier person drops to the ground; the light end stays up in the air because it does not carry enough weight to balance or force the other end up. Good balance in design works in much the same way, only instead of balancing with pounds of weight, balance depends on the *appearance* of weight or bulk.

There are two kinds of balance—formal (symmetrical) and informal (asymmetrical). In formal balance, like objects are balanced on either side of a central point. Formal balance can also be managed by using non-identical objects at either side of the center. In such a case, it is necessary to use articles which appear to be approximately the same size and shape to secure a balanced effect.

Most clothing is designed with both sides alike; a dart on each side of the skirt; a flap on both sides of the jacket; a pocket on each side of a coat; buttons down the front with rows of tucks on each side of the blouse front, etc.

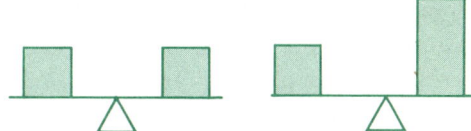

Formal balance—informal balance.

Clothing may be designed with an informal balance in which the two sides are not alike, but the whole effect is still in balance. A pocket, a decorative pin or button, a scarf, or some such other detail or accent can be used to balance a feature such as a side opening, side drape, or diagonal lap, etc. Dark or bright colors help such balance.

Formal balance, as the name implies, is dignified, formal in nature, and stiff looking. Because it is an obvious arrangement, it seems static and monotonous. Informal balance, on the other hand, is more subtle and therefore more interesting and dynamic. Casual in nature, it makes use of the unusual and the unexpected. Contemporary design depends greatly on

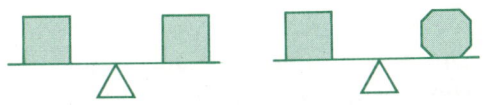

Formal balance.

The Color, Line, and Design Story in Fashion

informal balance. Yet the effect desired and the intended purpose determine the type of balance best suited. The human figure has formal balance. Therefore clothing is best designed to hang evenly on both sides—such as the neck opening, the waistline, and the hemline. You may decorate with simple, informal balance, but trouser legs are usually best when cut to equal lengths!

PROPORTION

The principle of proportion is concerned chiefly with spaces, sizes, and shapes within a design and their relationship to each other. As a line divides space into smaller areas, each area has a definite form and shape. These separate shapes and forms bear a relationship to each other and to the whole design. If carefully planned, the relationship results in a design that is interesting and pleasing to the eye.

To illustrate this principle, examine the rectangles. In both A and B the division of space is very obvious and therefore not as satisfying as C, which has a more subtle relationship. In

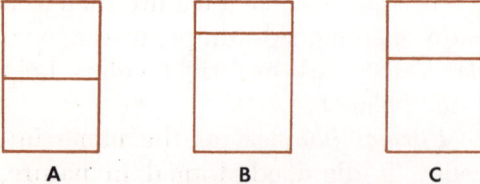

A   B   C

general, an uneven yet similar relationship is more interesting than either an even or completely dissimilar one. To be pleasing and in good proportion, the relationship should be neither too obvious nor too hard to see.

There are some laws of proportion that mathematically describe the best possible relationships between areas. These include:

- **Ratio of 1 to 1.618:** Ratio is a way of expressing a relationship between items, numerically describing how many times bigger the larger part is than the smaller. In the rectangles just shown, we saw that the 1 to 1 ratio (with parts the same size) in A and the 1 to 2 ratio (with the larger part twice as large as the smaller) in B are not pleasing because they are too obvious. The subtle, pleasing ratio of rectangle C approximates the 1 to 1.618 ratio.

- **Golden section:** A line or an area is divided so that the smaller part is the same percent of the larger part as the larger part is of the whole.

- **Summation series:** "The total of any two adjacent numbers gives the next number." This is also known as the ratio of successive numbers: 2—3—5, 3—5—8, 5—8—13. The proportion very closely resembles the golden section: the smaller part (3) is to the larger part (5) as the larger is to the total of both parts (8) or the whole.

It is true that pure proportion is based on mathematics, but in a practical sense it is a matter of feeling and judgment. You were able to sense fine proportion in the rectangle experiment. So it is possible to develop a feeling for all pleasing relationships. In good proportion, each segment of the design has individuality, but at the same time the total arrangement

Principles of Design

is unified. There is a variety in size, so as not to be monotonous, yet the parts are also harmonious in size. Good proportion in spacing and a pleasing relationship of sizes and shapes result in a design that is harmoniously related and unified. When the relationship is out of proportion, the effect is displeasing.

In clothing, the vertical figure is divided into different spaces by the neckline, the waistline, and the hemline. These spaces must bear a pleasing relationship to each other as well as to the entire figure. Proportion also enters the picture in each of the following situations:

- The width and placement of borders.
- The width of bands and the spacing between them.
- The width of collars, peplums, tiers, tunics, etc.
- The placement of the crosswise seams—yokes, waistlines, etc.
- The size and placement of pockets.
- The size and spacing of buttons.

Simplicity Pattern Co., Inc.

The location of the waistline divides the silhouette and creates a proportion relationship.

The Color, Line, and Design Story in Fashion

- The length of jackets in relation to length of skirt and height of the individual.
- The length of skirt in relation to the height of the individual.

As all of these examples divide the silhouette into separate parts, in turn they create a necessary relationship of sizes. Try the following experiment: Cut four figure silhouettes out of dark construction paper, all the same size. Using strips of light tape, place lines on the silhouette to represent a yoke, the empire waistline, a normal waistline, and a dropped waistline. Compare the relationship of the spaces created. The same experiment can be carried out with jacket lengths from bolero to walking suit, and with skirt lengths.

- **Scale,** which is very closely related to proportion, refers to a relationship of size also but, in this case, more the relationship of separate items to each other. As an example, picture a little boy in his father's hat or a little girl in her mother's shoes. The effect of both is ludicrous, because the sizes are wrong. That is all right because we can chuckle at youngsters dressed "out-of-scale," but picture a very heavy woman in strap sandals or a very small woman in a very large picture hat. Both present a strange picture because the scale is wrong. A feeling of rightness requires that there be not too much difference in size relationship.

Print fabrics present an excellent "scale situation." The size of the print should be scaled to the size of the individual. Small figures look best in small prints—large prints are out of scale and overpower the figure. Large

Small print versus large print.

Vogue Pattern Service

prints are for larger figures—small prints are the wrong scale for the large figure; they only draw attention to its size.

Other examples of "scale situations" in clothing include:
- The size of accessories in relation to the size of the individual. (Large handbags are not for a very small person.)
- The size of furs. (Long-haired, full, and fluffy furs are not for a very small person.)
- The texture of fabrics. (Very bulky fabrics are not for a very small person.)
- The size of individual parts of a garment. (Large pockets are not for a small person.)

RHYTHM

Rhythm helps to make a design more pleasing by giving it movement. It is expressed through lines, forms, and colors which lead the gaze smoothly and easily through the parts of a design. In one way, rhythm in design is like rhythm in music, although one comes to us through the sense of sight and the other through the sense of hearing. In both cases

Principles of Design

there is a repetition or movement of which we are conscious. A design without rhythm is confused; the subtle use of repetition to produce rhythm gives a design unity.

Rhythm creates a mood—steady, static, and monotonous; or smooth-flowing, slow, and restful; or gay, active, and lively; or bouncy, jumpy, and erratic—depending upon how the combination of lines, forms, colors, or spaces carry the eye.

Radiation.

The drawings on page 63 show how the movement of line creates rhythm! The strong, flowing lines carry the gaze easily, whereas the weak, erratic lines have little rhythmic movement. Radiation, in which lines emerge from a central point, also produces rhythm. The sunburst effect is an example.

Rhythm depends primarily upon repetition of line and shape. Simple repetition as in A and D is a form of rhythm, but not very interesting. The regular spacing without any variation is monotonous. A simple variation in the length of the lines, as in drawing B, makes the design more interesting. Slight curves, as in example C, help the gaze to glide along in a smooth, easy movement, making the rhythm still more pleasing.

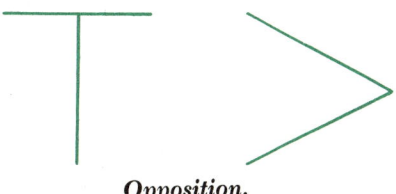
Opposition.

The principles of *opposition* and *gradation* also help to create rhythm in a design. Opposition involves lines going in different directions. Where they meet, they may be in direct contrast, as in the examples above, or they may be combined with transitional lines. These lines, usually

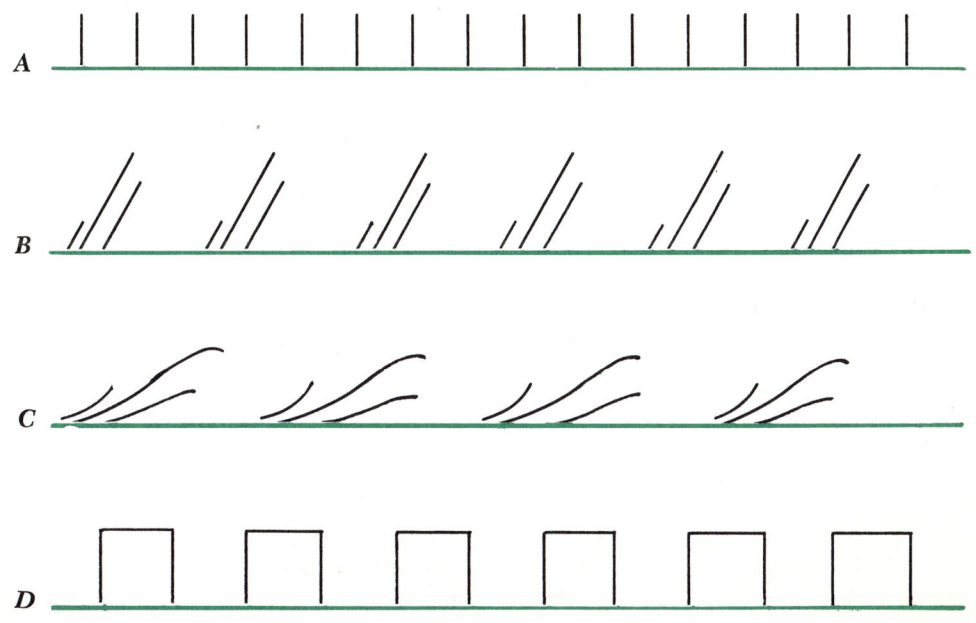

77

The Color, Line, and Design Story in Fashion

curved, modify the contrasting lines, resulting in a softer, more pleasing effect. As an example, think of the T as a yoke on a shirt. If the shirt is gathered to the yoke, the soft folds of the gathers serve as transitional lines to break the harsh contrast of the opposing lines.

Gradation involves a sequence of items that are similar but which progress, perhaps to an exact opposite, through a series of slightly different steps. The transition may be one of size (from small to large), of color (light to dark), of direction (from vertical to horizontal), of line (from straight to curved), of shape, or of a combination of these. Each step is similar to the one before, but the beginning and end may be in direct contrast. Although gradation thus provides the transition between opposites, it creates a smooth continuity along the way while giving a feeling of movement and change.

Remember, any design must be harmonious. There will be a pleasant, rhythmic feel about design if the parts give you the feeling that they belong together. If there is harmony, the gaze will move over the details smoothly, without a harsh, jarring clash. Without rhythmic harmony, just as in music, there will be confusion.

In clothing, rhythm is expressed the same way as in any other design—by lines, forms, and colors leading the gaze over the costume. Soft folds of fabric, sharply pressed pleats, rows of buttons, series of trimmings, progression of colors, and prints all contribute to a rhythmic feeling.

EMPHASIS

The principle of emphasis helps to give interest to a design. Every design—whether it is a picture, a furnished room, or an article of clothing—should have a center of interest. Without emphasis, a design is monotonous; to be effective, it must have a focal point—one part that is more important than all others—which attracts the gaze first.

One dominant center of interest is sufficient. If there are several equally forceful attention-getters, the effect is too busy, therefore undesirable. All points are shouting for attention. Instead of harmony, there is general confusion.

Emphasis may be created through the use of *contrast in color or texture*. We know the eye is drawn to light, bright colors, and shiny surfaces attract attention. Place a light area on a dark background and the eye is drawn to that area. That part of the design becomes the center of interest—that part of the design is emphasized.

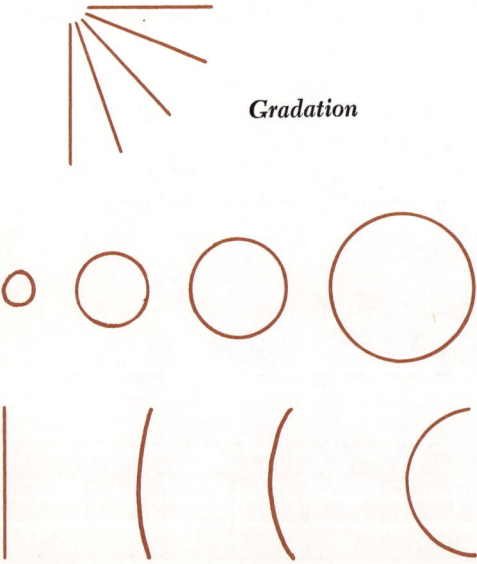

Gradation

Hints for Selecting Flattering Fashions

Line can be used to create a center of interest. Since the gaze follows line, it can be used to lead to the focal point. Unusual *shapes* or contrasting *design outlines* also attract the attention. Yet certain lines and shapes have more significance than others.

In example A, the lines are of equal length. Since there is no difference, neither line is dominant—they are of equal importance. In example B, however, the eye focuses on the longer line. It has more significance and, in contrast, the shorter line is subordinate.

Decorative details applied to the basic design can be used for emphasis. The center of interest can be achieved by one large item or by a group of small ones whose arrangement must create an interesting pattern.

In clothing, a center of interest can be created by using the same devices: contrasting colors and textures; contrasting lines and using unusual shapes—for scallops, yokes, belts, collars, etc.; and use of decorative details such as buttons, braid, trimmings, scarves, and jewelry. The center of interest, since it attracts the eye, can call attention to your good features and in turn diminish less desirable ones. **Remember,** by drawing attention away from a figure problem to another more desirable feature, the problem becomes subordinate and less noticeable.

HINTS FOR SELECTING FLATTERING FASHIONS

You see how the elements and principles of design can be applied to any creative expression; you know that in this discussion we are primarily interested in design as it applies to clothing. Because clothing should flatter the face and figure, selection of becoming designs requires some thought. Study fashion magazines and newspaper advertisements to help you become aware of what different designs will do for the figure. Thoughtful study and experience should help you select fashions wisely, for yourself and, in your work, for others.

For the Average Figure with Ideal Proportions: This person is indeed fortunate. She may wear what she likes. Suggest, however, that she avoid extreme fashions that distract from her fine figure. Simplicity of line and design will accent the figure and make her look outstanding.

For the Tall and Slender: This is the ideal figure for wearing clothes. Most styles will look attractive on her.

Can wear:

    Dramatic clothes.

    Sheath dresses (to accent the figure).

    Full skirts—gathered, full-flared, pleated (to add width).

    Bulky fabrics; bright, bold prints; plaids.

    Shirtwaist dresses; double breasted dresses, jackets, or coats.

The Color, Line, and Design Story in Fashion

Bold, contrasting separates.
Two-piece outfits.
High necklines (jewel, boatshaped, round, square).
Wide, flat collars.
Big sleeves.
Bloused tops, overblouses.
Long blouses or jackets.
Softly crushed cummerbunds or wide, contrasting belts.
Horizontal details.
Exaggerated details—large pockets, big buttons, etc.
Tucks, gathers, smocking.
Slightly shorter hem lengths.

Should avoid:
"Little girl" clothes.
Ruffles, frills.
Either tightly fitted or too loose clothes.
Close, vertical lines.
Straight, severe lines of any kind.
Sleeveless dresses.
Deep V necklines.
Too slim skirts.
Too short skirts.
Small accessories.

For the Tall and Heavy: Care must be taken in selecting clothing. Most lines that shorten also tend to add width.

Can wear:
Simply planned clothes.
Simply decorated clothes.
Vertical and diagonal lines.
"Gentle," soft lines.
Small prints.
Two-piece dresses.
Cardigan tops.
Loose-fitting jackets.
Neck details.
Soft flattering collars.
V necklines.
Set-in sleeves.
¾ length sleeves.
Dropped waistline.
Inconspicuous belts.
Front panels.
Eased straight, softly flared skirts.

Should avoid:
Anything skimpy.
Anything severe.
Youthful, "little girl" clothes.
Either too large or too dainty designs.
Plaids or checks.
Ruffles, frills.
Scallops.
Princess lines.
Deep, round necklines.
Sleeves cut in one with the bodice.
All-around pleated skirts.

For the Short and Slender: This is actually a small version of the perfect figure. If there is a desire to appear taller, make it only a little taller! Trying to add too many inches will just make a person look odd.

Can wear:
Feminine, casual clothes.
Simple lines and designs.
"Uncluttered" clothes.
Small prints and thin textured fabrics.
Crisp fabrics.
Small plaids, prints.
Princess line.
Straight sheath.
Softly tailored suits.
Short, stand-out jackets.
Full, gored, wide-pleated skirts. (Emphasize small, slim size.)
Knife-pleated skirts.
High, round neckline.

Hints for Selecting Flattering Fashions

Full sleeves.
High waistline.
Narrow self-belts.
Small trims, ruffles, collars.
Small-scale accessories.

Should avoid:
Overpowering colors.
Bold prints.
Too much decoration.
Horizontal lines.
Big hats or accessories.
Wide belts.
Very high heels.

For the Short and Heavy: Most lines that add height will also tend to make the figure look thinner.

Can wear:
Softly tailored styles.
Easy (slightly loose) fitting clothes.
Lightweight, smooth textured fabrics.
Muted or minute prints.
Vertical lines.
Soft, non-clinging lines.
One-piece outfits.
Cardigan tops.
Jackets that don't cling to the waistline.
Neck details.
Set-in sleeves.
¾ length sleeves.
Gently gored skirts.
Center pleats.
Slightly longer skirts.
Beltless styles or narrow self-belts.
Scarce and neat trimmings.

Should avoid:
Snug clothes.
Fussy clothes.
Bulky fabrics.
Princess line.
Pencil-slim sheath.
Sleeveless dresses.
Horizontal lines.
Oversize, loose sweaters.
Long jackets.
Round necks or circle designs.
Full skirts.
Box pleats.
Large trimmings.

Remember, perhaps there is some particular figure problem that a person would like to camouflage. Clothing can play a big part in concealing figure faults. Put to practice what you have learned about playing tricks with lines.

For a short, thick neck: Suggest the V-line. Long, narrow shirt collars and narrow shawl collars are becoming. Avoid choker beads, high round necklines, or any round line. Direct the gaze down to give the illusion of length.

For a long thin neck: Do just the opposite. Suggest round, wide designs to carry the eye across and, by illusion, cut the length.

For rounded shoulders: Suggest styles with fullness below the shoulders, set-in sleeves, and short, straight jackets. Avoid round collars, raglan or kimono sleeves, and princess styles.

For a small bust: Suggest clothes that add bulk above the waistline, such as full blouses, wide collars, shawl collars, jabots and ruffles, and horizontal tucks. Double-breasted styles are also good. Avoid snug-fitting bodices or sweaters and strict, plain styles.

For a large bust: Suggest simple, untrimmed bodices with soft fullness and V necklines. Dark colors above the waist help to minimize size.

Straight coats and jackets and full skirts give good proportion. Avoid bulky or shiny fabrics, tight belts or waistlines, narrow skirts, and fussy details.

For a thick waist and stomach: Suggest gently full or flared skirts and self-belts. Draw the gaze away from the waist with shoulder and neck interest. Avoid set-in midriffs, princess styles, very straight skirts, and large prints or patterns.

For large hips: Suggest clothes that draw the attention away from the hips. V necklines, yokes, big collars, and wide necklines are all good. Skirts with slight flare and easy fit will look better than straight, pleated, or full skirts. Avoid any details such as pockets or horizontal lines at the hipline. A tight belt only makes the hips seem larger. Long full sleeves and contrasting color gloves call attention to width at the hipline, also.

For small hips and waist: Bulkier but well-fitted skirts help to conceal thinness. Avoid the stiff and plain fabrics.

In review:
What is design?
What are the elements of design?
What are the three methods of combining the elements?
Explain the concept of balance. What is the difference between formal and informal balance?
What is meant by proportion? How is it achieved in clothing?
How does *scale* differ from *proportion*?
What does rhythm contribute to design? How is rhythm achieved in clothing?
What is meant by emphasis? How can it be achieved in clothing?

For further discussion:
Design is a form of expression.
Evaluation of design.
Application of design principles to art, architecture, decorating, as well as fashion.
Good design—a form of good taste.

To gain experience:
Find samples of clothing illustrating each of the following:

formal balance	rhythm
informal balance	emphasis
good proportion	

Experiment with the placement of the waistline seam and the length of jackets on identical silhouettes. Note the effects on the figure.

Analyze several garments and classify them as good and poor design, giving reasons for your decision.

Chapter 4

The Fabric Story Today and Tomorrow

The story of fabrics—from fiber to finished product—is a fascinating tale. It takes you all around the world to many far-distant lands and through the pages of history. Its beginning goes back even before recorded history, and there is no ending. We live in a dynamic world where improvement of existing products and introduction of new products are taking place every day. So it is with fabrics. The discovery of new fibers and new developments for familiar fibers make yesterday's facts and information outdated today. Changes take place so rapidly that it is difficult to keep up to date with the current information and facts. From month to month new fabrics appear, new processes are developed, new properties are made possible, new finishes are offered, new advantages are available, and often new problems occur.

Anyone who plans to enter the merchandising field or any business that deals in clothing and textiles—whether designing and making clothing, buying and selling yard goods or ready-to-wear, or working in the alteration or clothing maintenance area—needs a knowledge of fabrics.

Designers have to know how fabrics "behave." Will the fabric fall in a soft drape or stand out stiffly? Does it hold a crease well? Can it be shaped? Is it too bulky for gathers or too soft to hold a certain line? Only by knowing the fabric's characteristics can fabric and design be matched successfully in an attractive garment.

Sewing

Those who sew, whether in production or alteration of clothing, have to know how to handle fabric successfully. Does the fabric require special care in handling? Should the stitch on the machine be adjusted? Does the tension need adjustment? What kind of thread should be used? How should the fabric be pressed?

Clothing maintenance

Those working in clothing maintenance—laundry, pressing, spotting, dry cleaning—must have basic fabric knowledge. Can it be washed? Will it shrink? Does it stretch easily? Does it water spot? Will certain chemicals damage it? A garment may be damaged permanently because of improper treatment.

Simplicity Pattern Co., Inc.

There is an almost magical quality to the expanding world of fabrics. New fibers, novelty yarns and weaves, interesting finishes all contribute to making available the wide range of fabrics on the market today.

Selling

A successful salesperson is thoroughly familiar with merchandise. Customers want information about the fabric: what is it? how will it wear? how do you care for it? are there any precautions to take in using it or cleaning it? A salesperson with fabric knowledge background knows the selling points and can make recommendations. He or she can answer the customers' questions intelligently and give valuable information that will help the customer obtain satisfaction from her purchase. As a result, her sales increase and her customers are pleased.

There was a time when a person could identify fabric content by looking at it or feeling it. There were only four natural fibers—cotton, wool, linen, and silk—and each one differed from the other so markedly in appearance that recognition was easy. The discovery and increased use of more and more synthetic fibers, the improvement of the natural fibers, the blending of fibers, other new manufacturing processes, and the development of new finishes for fabrics make it almost impossible to identify positively the fiber content of a fabric just by appearance.

Can you identify the fiber content of the fabrics you are wearing?

Examine samples of many types of fabrics used for clothing. What can you tell about the fabric by looking at it? What should a wise shopper know about a fabric? Compare ideas in your class. How can this information be acquired?

The following discussion of textile fibers and their characteristics is intended to help you become familiar with the textile products on the market today—what they are, their characteristics, and what can be expected of them. Each major clothing fiber will be discussed in detail including the *origin and history* of the fiber, *identification,* and *properties,* as well as information concerning *recommended uses* of the fiber and the *handling and care* of fabrics made from the fiber. This basic textile information will be of value to you not only in your work but as a consumer. Everyone uses and wears a variety of fabrics. A study of textile fibers and their properties will help you judge the quality of fabrics, to select them wisely for specific purposes, and to care for them properly.

"Textiles" has a language all its own. First let us look at some of the terms we have already used in this introductory discussion.

The word *textile,* for instance, refers to fabric or a material suitable for making fabric. The terms *fabric* and *cloth* both refer to the finished consumer product and are interchangeable. According to the dictionary, fabric is a cloth woven or otherwise made from fibers, and cloth is defined as a fabric. *Material* is a very general term referring to the substance from which something is made. The word material is used freely in referring to fabric, as in dress material. Either the word fabric or cloth, however, is preferable because it is more exact.

Fibers are the strands from which threads or *yarns* are *spun.* Closely examine a sample of any woven fabric. Unravel it and note that it is made from threads. These threads are called yarns. Untwist a yarn and note that it separates into many individual strands. These strands are known as fibers.

Fibers vary one from another in a great many ways. Some are long, some are short. Some are curly, some are straight. Each fiber has its own distinctive markings and characteristics. These differences determine the properties of the resulting fabric. For instance, fabrics made from long fibers (*long-staple*) are usually very smooth and often lustrous in appearance, whereas those made from short fibers (*short-staple*) are soft and fuzzy. (The word staple, used in this manner, refers to the raw material or fiber.) As you study fibers in more detail, you will learn about their properties and the characteristics of the fabric made from these fibers.

The Fabric Story Today and Tomorrow

All fibers can be divided into three general groups:

Natural fibers:

Vegetable (cellulose)	Cotton
	Linen
Animal (protein)	Silk
	Wool

Man-made fibers:

Cellulose	Rayon
	Acetate
	Triacetate
Mineral	Glass
	Metallic

Synthetic fibers:

Nylon
Polyester
Acrylic, etc.

The natural fibers are those that are found in the fiber form in nature. Neither man-made nor synthetic fibers are found as fibers in nature—man must create them. By this definition, the terms man-made and synthetic are the same, but there is a difference. True, synthetic fibers are man-made—both are manufactured fibers. What is the distinction? *The term man-made is used for those fibers that are created from natural materials by merely changing their form.* For example, rayon is made from cellulose found in wood pulp and cotton linters. The cellulose is transformed into a liquid and then solidified into rayon fiber. *Synthetic fibers, on the other hand, are created in the test tube from chemicals.* No natural form of substance is used as in the case of the man-made fiber. The various elements—hydrogen, carbon, oxygen, and others—are the raw materials. There are many long and complicated chemical and manufacturing processes between the starting materials and the finished fiber.

The list of fibers in the chart, left, is not complete. For instance, there are many minor fibers of natural origin that were not listed—kapok, hemp, jute, cashmere, angora, mohair—to name a few. The list of synthetic fibers is also quite long, and the list increases as new fibers are discovered.

Look at the list of fibers again. The names of the natural and man-made fibers are no doubt familiar, but do you recognize the names used for the synthetic fibers? Perhaps you have seen the word *polyester* on a label, but what is it? The synthetic fibers are grouped together according to their chemical origin. Polyester is a generic (or family) name for a whole group of synthetic fibers that are produced from the same substances and that have the same general characteristics and properties. If we used the name Dacron, would you recognize it? Dacron is the trademarked name for the Du Pont polyester fiber. Other chemical companies also produce polyester fibers under their own trademarked names.

Labeling controlled by law

The Federal Trade Commission is a government agency charged with the responsibility of preventing unfair competition in trade between states and with foreign nations. Trade practice rules for many industries, as for unfair trade practices (misrepresentation of products in labeling or advertising), come under the authority of this Commission. Members of an

Generic Names

industry, in collaboration with the Federal Trade Commission, may propose trade practice rules in the interests of the industry and the purchasing public. After the proposed rules have undergone long deliberation and have been studied, modified, and finally presented to the Commission they may be approved and enacted into law. The Federal Trade Commission is then responsible for the interpretation and enforcement of the law.

One of these laws—the Textile Fiber Products Labeling Act of 1958, which became effective March 3, 1960—requires that all textile fiber products be labeled according to their fiber content. All fibers that constitute 5% or more of the content must be designated by generic name. The label may include the manufacturer's trademarked name for easy identification, but the trademark alone cannot be used. The generic name must appear—"Dacron Polyester Fiber," for example.

Generic Names

The Federal Trade Commission has established 16 generic groups of manufactured fibers and has defined the composition of each group. Although you will study only the more familiar groups used for clothing, you should be familiar with all the names. They are acrylic, modacrylic, polyester, rayon, acetate or triacetate, saran, azlon, nytril, nylon, rubber, spandex, vinal, olefin, vinyon, metallic, and glass. As new fibers are introduced provision is made for their addition.

The following table shows the grouping of the major manufactured fibers used for clothing.

Generic Name	Trade-marked Name	Manufacturer
Acrylic	Acrilan	Chemstrand Company
	Creslan	American Cyanamid Company
	Orlon	E. I. du Pont de Nemours & Co.
	Zefran	Dow Chemical Company
Modacrylic	Dynel	Union Carbide Corporation
	Verel	Eastman Kodak Company
Polyester	Dacron	E. I. du Pont de Nemours & Co.
	Fortrel	Fiber Industries, Inc.
	Kodel	Eastman Kodak Company
	Vycron	Beaunit Corporation
Rayon	American Bemberg	Beaunit Corporation
	Avril	FMC Corp. American Viscose Division
	Fortisan	Celanese Corporation of America
	Zantrel	American Enka Corporation
Acetate	Acele	E. I. du Pont de Nemours & Co.
	Avisco	FMC Corp. American Viscose Division
	Celanese	Celanese Corporation of America
	Chromspun	Eastman Kodak Company
	Estron	Eastman Kodak Company

(*continued on next page.*)

The Fabric Story Today and Tomorrow

Generic Name	Trade-marked Name	Manufacturer
Tri-acetate	Arnel	Celanese Corporation of America
Nylon	Caprolan	Allied Chemical Corporation
	Chemstrand	Chemstrand Company
	Antron	E. I. du Pont de Nemours & Co.
	Cantrece	E. I. du Pont de Nemours & Co.
	Du Pont	E. I. du Pont de Nemours & Co.
Spandex	Lycra	E. I. du Pont de Nemours & Co.
	C-Spandex	Chemstrand Company

In review:

In what ways will a knowledge of fabric benefit the following people:
    dress designer?
    dressmaker?
    clothing maintenance specialist?
    ready-to-wear salesperson?
    yardgoods salesperson?

Define the following terms:
    fabric   yarn
    fiber   staple

Name the natural fibers. Why are they called natural?

Explain the difference between man-made and synthetic fibers.

What is meant by generic name?

What are the provisions of the Textile Fiber Products Labeling Act.

THE NATURAL FIBERS

Cotton

Written records trace the use of cotton back as far as 3,000 years before Christ. Also, cotton fabrics have been found in prehistoric graves in Peru, in the ruins of ancient Indian cities, and in excavations of the southwestern United States, indicating their use before written records were kept.

India is given credit for having first used cotton for fabrics. The Chinese cultivated cotton merely as a garden flower. European travelers to ancient Asia told about seeing strange bushes whose fruit was "wool." Some actually spread the fantastic story that little lambs grew on bushes. Merchants brought cotton from Asia to western Europe in the 9th century. When Columbus arrived in America, cotton plants were growing and the people were wearing clothes which were made from cotton.

Cotton can be grown in some areas of all the continents of the world, but the four main cotton producing countries are the United States, Russia, China, and India. The United States alone produces approximately 32% of the world supply. The southern region of the United States stretching from Virginia to California is known as the Cotton Belt. Today Texas and California lead in production, with Texas raising about one third of our total.

There is such a demand for cotton goods that about 12 million people in the United States make their living

The Natural Fibers

Cotton boll.

by growing, processing, manufacturing, and selling cotton and its products. Since colonial days cotton has played such a vital role in the economy of the deep south that the fiber has been nicknamed King Cotton.

With the introduction of synthetic fibers and their easy-care advantages, cotton dropped in popularity during the 1950's. New processing, however, has since added desirable, easy-care properties and in some cases even changed the appearance of cotton. Instead of being replaced, cotton is gaining in popularity and use.

Cotton requires a warm climate and a long growing season. The cotton fiber makes its first appearance when the seed pods or bolls on the plant burst open and expose a mass of fleecy cotton lint. This lint is composed of the crinkly fibers that adhere to the seeds. Soon afterward the fields are snowy white and it is time for the cotton picking to begin. From the field, the cotton goes to the cotton gin where the seeds and other foreign materials are removed. The cotton fiber is then packed in large bales, ready for sale. Cotton buyers examine each bale carefully and judge the cotton according to color, length of fiber, and cleanness. This process is known as "classing." The class determines the selling price.

At the spinning mill the cotton is thoroughly cleaned, combed, and pulled until the fibers are smooth and lie straight and parallel. The whole process, known as combing, is done by machine. Perhaps you have heard the term "combed cotton." All cotton fibers are combed. Fibers used to produce high quality, fine cotton fabrics, however, receive extra combing.

Machinery simulating the old-fashioned spinning wheel technique twists the fibers into the yarns which are then woven or otherwise meshed into cloth.

Learn More About Cotton

Trace the history of cotton fabrics from ancient to modern times.

On a world map, mark the cotton producing countries.

Trace the development of the cotton industry in the United States.

Prepare reports on the following topics:
- *The steps in growing and harvesting cotton.*
- *The story of the cotton gin and its inventor.*
- *The story of the cotton fiber from cotton field to you.*
- *The products made from the seeds after the cotton lint has been removed.*

Collect samples of cotton fabric. Arrange an exhibit and discuss the differences in general appearance.

Learn the names of commonly used cotton fabrics. Can you identify them? How?

The Fabric Story Today and Tomorrow

Characteristics of cotton

The cotton fiber is a tiny, hairlike filament, slightly wavy in appearance, which varies in length from about ½ inch to 2½ inches. It is the shortest fiber of all.

Unravel one of the yarns from the edge of a cotton fabric; then untwist the yarn until it falls apart into separate fibers. You cannot see the structure of the cotton fiber with the naked eye, but if you look at it under a microscope you will see that it is flat, like a ribbon, and twisted. The picture below shows some cotton fibers, greatly enlarged, as you might see them under a microscope.

Testing for cotton

Examining a fiber under the *microscope* is the most accurate means of identification. The *burning test* can also help with identifying fibers because different fibers burn differently. Cotton ignites very quickly and burns with a blaze. There is an odor of burning paper and the residue is a light, feathery ash.

Feeling a fiber can be helpful, but it is not an accurate method of identification. The synthetic fibers can be made to look and even feel like other fibers; therefore the feeling test is of no help with them. Natural fibers, however, have a characteristic feel. Place your finger on a piece of cotton fabric. It will feel "cool," soft, and non-elastic.

What are the qualities of the cotton fiber which make cotton fabrics desirable for use? What are cotton's undesirable qualities? The properties of the fiber determine the qualities of the fabric.

Although cotton does not make a naturally lustrous fiber because it is so short and soft-surfaced, the better quality cottons made from the longest length fibers can be almost silky in appearance. Mercerizing—a simple chemical process—makes the cotton fiber stronger and more lustrous. In this process the cotton is immersed in caustic soda. After rinsing, it is then given a warm acid bath, rinsed again, and dried.

Cotton is such a versatile fiber that it can be spun and woven into many different fabric constructions—terry weave for bath towels, sheer organdy for dresses, or heavy canvas for awn-

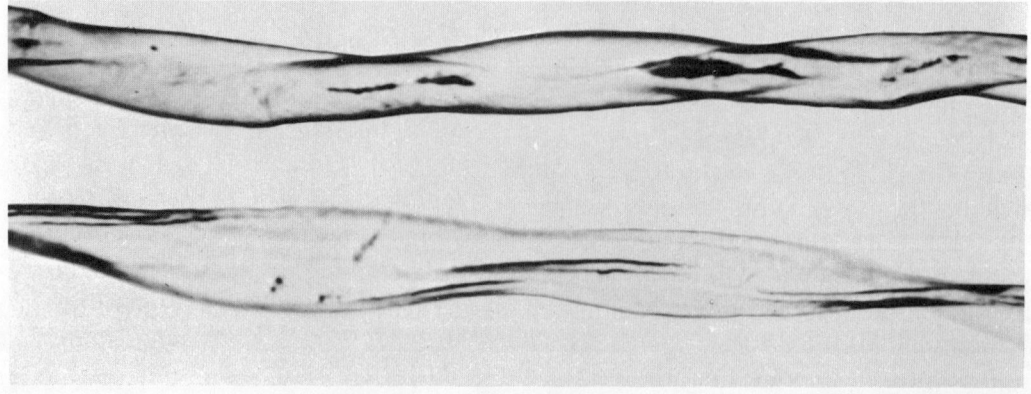

National Cotton Council

Cotton fiber.

The Natural Fibers

ings. The fiber can be treated to give the rough appearance of wool, the smoothness of silk, or the irregularity of linen.

The cotton fiber is fairly strong and good quality cotton fabrics are quite durable. Cotton is even stronger when wet and can be made permanently stronger by the mercerizing process.

Cotton has practically no elasticity. That is why the fabrics wrinkle so easily, although special finishing processes can be used to make the fabric wrinkle-resistant.

The lack of elasticity also means that the fiber does not stretch easily, so good quality cotton fabric holds its shape well.

Cotton absorbs moisture readily and dries fairly rapidly. (Mercerizing increases the fiber's absorbency.) Cotton is also a good conductor of heat. Cotton clothing is cool and comfortable for summer wear because it allows the heat to escape from the body and absorbs perspiration.

Because the cotton fiber is so short, its fabric has a rough surface that picks up dirt easily, but it can also be washed easily. Mercerized cottons are smoother and do not attract soil as readily. Cotton fabrics withstand rough handling and high temperatures without any damage. They can be laundered in very hot water—in fact, cotton can be sterilized—and can be ironed with a hot iron. Cotton can be bleached without any damage, but it becomes weaker and tends to turn yellow when exposed to sunlight.

Shrinkage labeling. Cotton shrinks, but pre-shrinking processes can reduce shrinkage considerably. The Federal Trade Commission approved trade practice rules in 1938 concerning the labeling of shrinkage in cotton goods. The use of such terms as "full shrunk," "shrinkproof," or "non-shrinkable" are prohibited unless there is absolutely no possibility of any shrinkage left in the fabric. The approved terms are "shrunk" or "pre-shrunk" used with a statement of the residual shrinkage. Perhaps you have seen labels stating that a fabric will not shrink more than 1 or 2 percent.

Strong acids will destroy cotton, but alkalies will not harm the cotton fiber. Therefore cotton can be washed with strong household soaps which are alkaline in composition.

The moth cannot digest cotton, so the fabric is naturally mothproof.

Cotton will mildew quickly when allowed to remain damp, but this difficulty can be eliminated by special finishing processes.

COTTON

Advantages	Disadvantages
Inexpensive	Wrinkles easily (unless treated)
Cool, comfortable	Requires ironing (unless treated)
Long wearing	
Holds its shape	Shrinks (unless treated)
Launders easily (machine washable)	Mildews (unless treated)
Can be bleached	Deteriorates in sunlight
Mothproof	

The Fabric Story Today and Tomorrow

Hints for handling cotton

- **Laundering:** Most cottons are machine washable. White and colorfast cottons can be laundered in hot water (140°) with heavy-duty soaps or detergents.

  Use warm water (100°–120°) and mild soap or detergent for non-colorfast fabrics, delicate sheers, or knits.

  Chlorine bleach is safe to use unless the fabric has a "wash-and-wear" or other resin finish.

  May be starched.

  Can be dried on the line or in the tumble dryer.

  Wash-and-wear cotton items require less pressing if permitted to drip dry. They should be removed from the washer while still wet and hung on a hanger to finish drying. The more wringing or spinning, the more wrinkles.

  "Automatic wash-and-wear," on the other hand, can go through the entire wash cycle and be dried in the dryer.

- **Pressing:** Cotton can be ironed with a hot iron, with or without moisture.

  Dry heat may be sufficient for touch-up pressing on lightweight cotton fabric. To remove wrinkles effectively and flatten seams or edges, however, moisture is needed.

  Cotton may be pressed on either the right or the wrong side, except for dark fabrics. These should be pressed on the wrong side to avoid a shine.

- **Sewing:** Use mercerized cotton thread.

  Cotton is generally considered easy to sew. No specific techniques are necessary unless a finishing process requires special handling. Such sewing hints are listed in the discussion of the finishing processes.

Linen

The linen fiber is probably the first vegetable fiber used for making cloth. Although the cotton fiber was used many hundreds of years B.C., it is thought that linen was known to man at a still earlier date. The first evidence available goes back 10,000 years to the Stone Age when the Neolithic Lake Dwellers used flax to make fishing nets. Fragments of linen cloth have been found in the tombs of the Egyptian pharaohs who lived 6,000 years ago. In these ancient times, linen was regarded as the ceremonial fabric. Mummies were wrapped in linen cloth as part of the preparation for burial. Through the ages, linen has been the luxury fiber of kings and merchants and still is regarded as the aristocrat of fibers.

Linen, like cotton, comes from a plant which is raised and cultivated for its fiber—the stem of flax. Flax requires a mild, damp climate. It is grown chiefly in Ireland, Scotland, Belgium, Holland, Russia, and France. Belgium has the reputation for best quality, Ireland the best workmanship. Most linen fabric is imported into the United States.

A limited amount of flax is grown in northern United States—North and South Dakota, Minnesota, Montana, and Oregon—but this is mostly for linseed oil which, of course, is obtained from the seeds of the plant. Products in which linseed oil is used include paints, varnishes, linoleum, oilcoth, imitation leather, and patent leather.

Flax plant.

A great many of the operations in growing and producing linen are so painstaking they still must be carried on by hand. It should first be noted that land will only yield a good flax crop every seven years. It takes six years to enrich the soil before it is in the proper condition for growing high quality flax. Not only must the soil be very right, the land must be level and there must be a plentiful soft water supply.

The seeds are sown by hand, weeding must be done by hand so as not to injure the delicate young plants, and harvesting is often done by hand also, since the plants must be pulled, not cut. Harvesting must be done at precisely the right time. If the plant is permitted to over-ripen, the linen fiber will be of inferior quality—neither lustrous nor soft.

After the flax is harvested, the fiber is loosened from the stem by soaking the plant in soft water until the woody part decomposes. This process, called *retting*, takes from seven days to four weeks. Insufficient retting makes it difficult to separate the fiber from the plant without damaging it. Too much retting weakens the fiber. There are mechanical and chemical methods of loosening the fiber so as to hasten the process, but these reduce the quality of the linen.

After retting, the stalks are spread in the field to dry before going to the mill where the woody parts are broken up and the fiber is separated from the plant—a process known as *scutching*. Contrast this complicated procedure with cotton, which goes directly from the field to the cotton gin.

The entire process of producing high quality linen is unique and cannot be hurried. Other fibers are cleaned and straightened by machine; fine linen is combed by hand. Through most of the production stages, the fibers and yarns must be kept moist. The yarns are passed through hot water in the spinning process. Weaving must be done in a moist atmosphere to keep the yarns from breaking.

Bleaching linen is another time-consuming process, since no chemical has yet been found to equal natural "grass-bleaching" for producing snowy-white fabrics. The extra time involved, the extra precautions that must be taken, and the amount of hand labor necessary in producing linen fabric explain in part why linen costs more than fabrics that can be produced more quickly and easily.

Labeling linen. Trade practice rules approved in 1941 by the Federal Trade Commission state that the use of the words "linen" and "flax" shall apply only to fibers obtained from the flax plant. Prohibited is the use of such syllables as "lin" or "lynn," and the use of such terms as "linen rayon" or "grass linen," which imply the presence of linen that is not there. The term "part linen" cannot be used

The Fabric Story Today and Tomorrow

unless true fiber content is stated. Deception as to the country or locality where the linen was produced is also prohibited.

Learn More About Linen

Trace the history of linen fabrics from ancient to modern times.

Trace the steps in growing and harvesting flax.

On a world map, mark the major flax producing countries, indicating whether for seed or for fiber.

Prepare reports on the following topics:

- *Production processes unique to linen.*
- *Story of linen production in Ireland, Belgium, and Russia. How do they differ?*
- *The products produced from flax seed.*

Collect samples of linen fabrics. Arrange an exhibit and discuss the differences in general appearance and usage.

Characteristics of linen

The linen fiber differs considerably in general characteristics from the cotton fiber. It is much longer, varying from 10 to 30 inches in length. Short-staple linen fibers and broken fibers combed out of the longer fibers as they are prepared for spinning are called *tow*. Yarns made from tow are irregular, and the fabric, although pure linen, is not top quality. Fine quality linen fabric is made from long staple, called *line*. One can sometimes detect the short fibers by careful examination of the fabric and by untwisting one of the yarns.

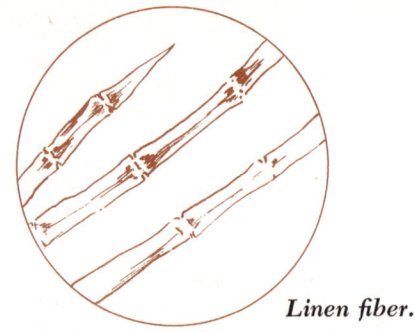

Linen fiber.

The linen fiber is smooth and straight with pointed ends. Under the microscope, as shown in the above drawing, it looks somewhat like a bamboo stalk, with joints at intervals and an inner canal. Considering the difference in structure of the cotton and the flax fibers, you would not expect linen and cotton fabric to have similar properties. Nevertheless, linen, like cotton, feels cool, but it is smooth and leathery.

Because linen is a vegetable fiber, it burns very much the same as cotton, except more slowly. There is an odor of burning paper and the residue is also a light, feathery ash. Burning, therefore, is not an accurate way of distinguishing linen from cotton.

Linen is smooth and more lustrous than cotton. Because the fiber is so long and smooth, there is no lint or fuzz from fiber ends on the surface of the fabric.

Linen is very strong and durable—much stronger than cotton. Among the natural fibers, it ranks next to silk in strength. The linen fiber is also stronger when wet than when dry.

The flax fiber has very little elasticity. For this reason linen fabrics hold their shape well, but linen also wrinkles very readily. Special finishing processes are now used to make the fabric crease-resistant.

Because the linen fiber is brittle, it may also break when creased repeatedly or ironed with a great deal of pressure.

Linen is very absorbent and dries quickly. These qualities, plus the fact that linen is lint free, make it excellent for both hand towels and kitchen towels.

Linen, unless treated, is cooler to wear than any other fiber. It permits the heat to escape from the body. Crease-resistant finishes, however, reduce the cooling effect.

Because the linen fiber is smooth and glossy, it resists soil better than cotton. Linen launders well, does not shrink, but is *weakened* by chemical bleaches. *No starching* is necessary. Because linen can withstand high temperatures without any damage, it can be laundered in very hot water or even boiled to sterilize it. It can be ironed at even higher temperature than cotton, and ironing increases its luster.

The fabric softens and improves with use.

Like cotton, linen is naturally mothproof, but will mildew. Strong acids will damage the fiber, but it is not affected by alkalies.

Linen does not absorb dyes readily. Therefore it is difficult to obtain colorfast quality.

Hints for handling linen

- LAUNDERING: Machine washable.

White linen fabrics should be washed in hot water (140°) with heavy duty soaps or detergents.

Colored fabrics should be washed in warm water (100°–120°).

Do not rub vigorously.

Do not use chemical bleaches.

Starching is not necessary. If desired, starch very lightly.

Linen may be dry cleaned, but washing is recommended.

- PRESSING: Linen must be very damp for ironing.

You may use a hot iron.

Iron on the wrong side to avoid a shine.

- SEWING: Use mercerized cotton thread.

Like cotton, linen is generally considered easy to sew.

WOOL

Like all other natural fibers, the story of wool reaches far back into prehistoric ages. It is not known which of the natural fibers was first used to make cloth, but wool is considered to be the oldest. Long before the days of recorded history there is evidence to show that man had learned to use sheep's wool for clothing because it was warmer than other animal skins. During the Stone Age,

LINEN

Advantages	Disadvantages
Long wearing	Expensive
Lint free	Wrinkles easily
Cool, comfortable	Requires ironing
Does not soil readily	Must be dampened for ironing
Launders easily	Mildews
Dries quickly	Breaks easily under pressure
Mothproof	
Retains natural crispness	

the sheep provided man with all the vital necessities of life—food, clothing, and shelter. Primitive hunters killed the sheep for food and then used the pelts to make clothing to cover them and skin tents to protect them. As the ancient tribes moved from Asia across Europe, they took their flocks with them.

Later man learned to spin and weave the wool into cloth. As early as 4,000 B.C. the Babylonians made wool garments. During the time of ancient Greek and Roman civilizations, the spinning and weaving of wool were skilled occupations. The Romans have received credit for establishing the woolen industry throughout Europe and in Britain. When their armies conquered a country, one of the first industries established was a textile plant. They introduced the art of textile manufacture to the Britons and from this beginning England gained world supremacy in the manufacture of wool. Even today wool products are a major British export.

Wool was even responsible, in part, for the discovery of America. During the first century A.D., Spanish sheep breeders developed the finest fleece-bearing sheep, known as the Merino. For centuries Spain was the only source of this strain of sheep. It helped Spain become immensely wealthy and powerful. Her great wealth made possible the voyages to far off lands which led to the establishment of the Spanish empire. One such voyage resulted in the discovery of America.

Today wool is grown all over the world, but because of temperate climates—best for sheep—Australia, New Zealand, South Africa, South America, and the United States lead all others in producing wool used for clothing. Wool is produced in almost every state in our country, but the great majority comes from the western states and Texas.

The production of finished fabric from wool fleece requires many steps. Shearing the sheep usually takes

Woolen yarn unraveled.

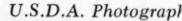
U.S.D.A. Photograph

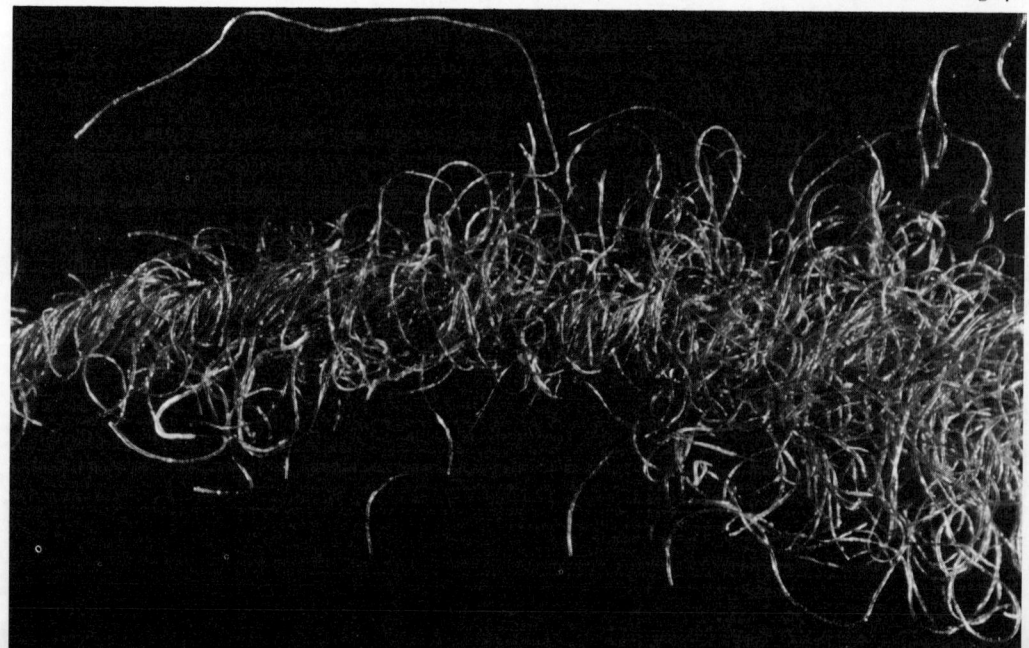

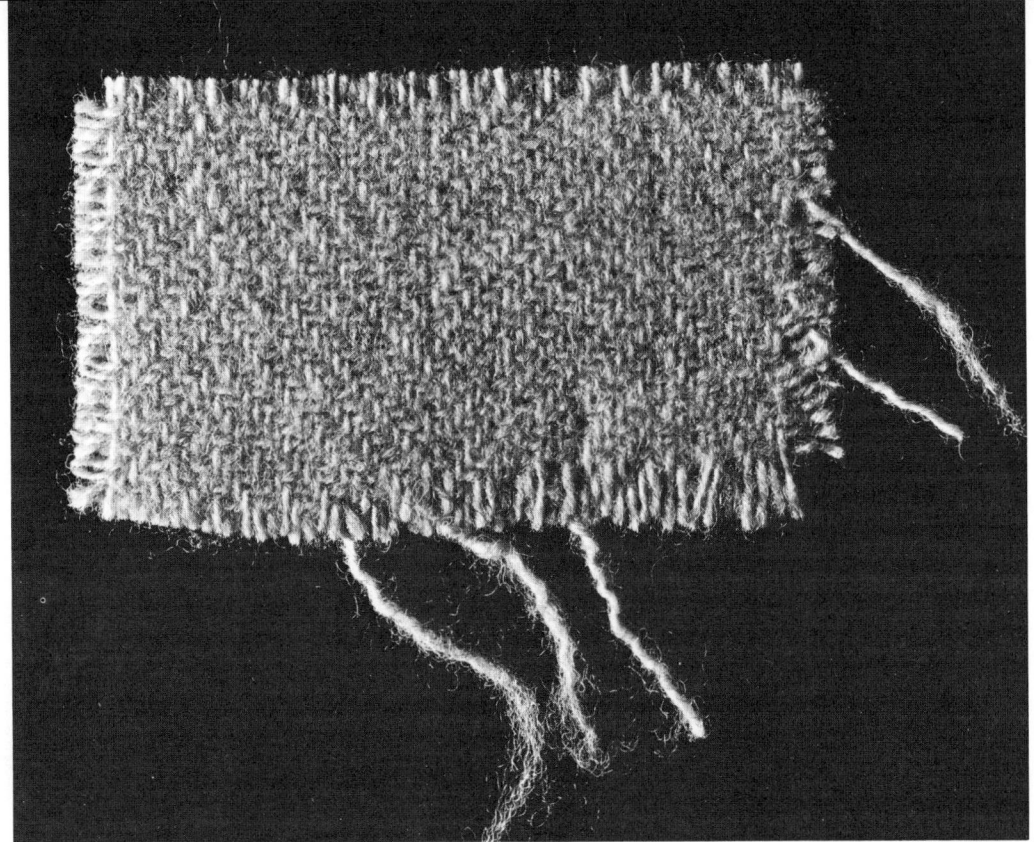

Fabric from woolen yarn.

U.S.D.A. Photograph

place in the spring of the year. In warmer climates it is necessary to shear them twice a year. Electric clippers remove the fleece in one piece. The fleece is then pulled apart by hand and the fibers sorted according to thickness and length.

After sorting, the wool is thoroughly washed to remove all grease and dirt. The process is called *scouring* and the grease that is removed is *lanolin*. You recognize that name as an ingredient in soaps, face creams, and other cosmetics.

The next step is *carding*. The wool passes between rollers faced with tiny wire teeth and the loose fibers are straightened and combed into single strands. These strands are then twisted together and spun into yarns which are woven or knit into cloth.

There are two kinds of wool yarns—*woolen* and *worsted* (pronounced wuhs-ted). Made from short fibers, woolen yarns are fuzzy in appearance. In the carding process, the fibers are brushed just enough to disentangle them. Then they are just placed at random and very loosely twisted together before being spun into yarn. The fabrics made from woolen yarns have a soft, "naplike" feel. Examples are tweed and flannel.

Worsteds are made from long, highly twisted fibers. After the fibers are disentangled in the carding process, they receive additional combing to remove short fibers and loose impurities. The fibers are straightened and made to lie as parallel as possible before spinning so the yarn will be smooth. The resulting fabric has a

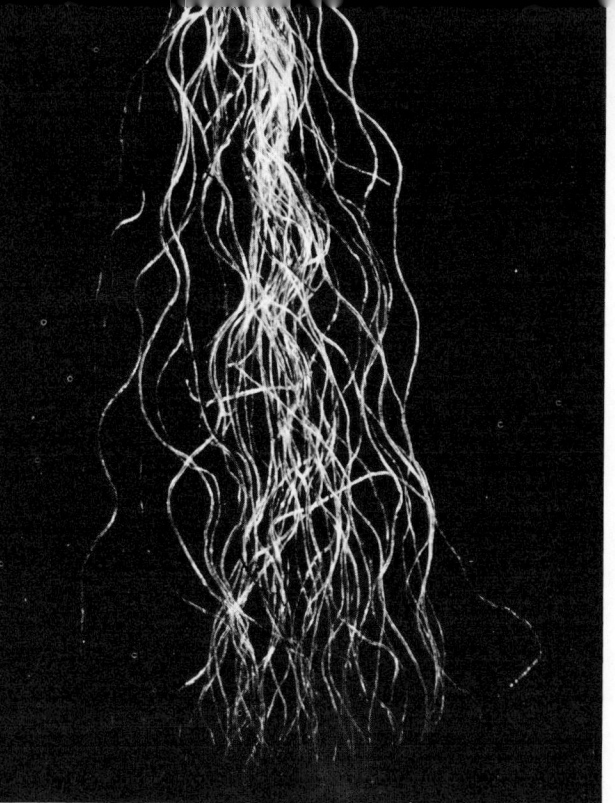
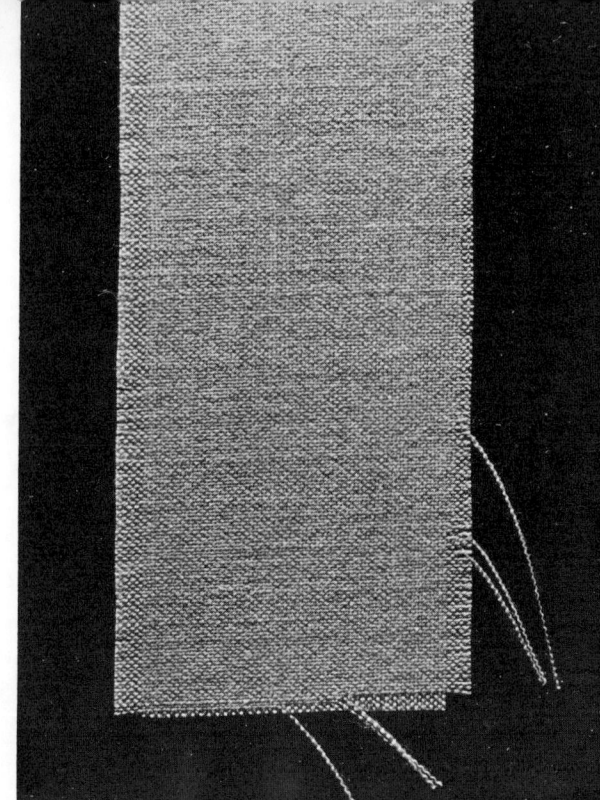

Worsted yarn unraveled.   U.S.D.A. Photograph   *Fabric from worsted yarn.*

firm, smooth appearance and is much stronger and more durable than woolen cloth. Some examples are gabardine and serge.

Wool cloth, after coming from the loom, goes through a finishing process peculiar to the material. The process, known as *fulling*, involves washing the cloth in warm, soapy water; pounding and twisting it; and then rinsing it in cold water. As a result the fabric shrinks and looks smoother, firmer, and more compact. After washing, drying, and a final pressing the cloth is finished, ready for use.

Wool refers only to the fleece of sheep. Other animal fibers, known as *hair fibers,* are also used for fabric. These differ from wool fibers in structure. They are straight and smoother than wool; however, their other qualities are the same as wool. They may be used alone or in combination with wool.

Camel's hair is popular for coat fabric because it insulates against cold very well but is lightweight. The hair from the two-humped camel found in all parts of Asia is very fine, soft, and a natural tan color. Once a year a camel's hair falls out in large clumps. These are gathered at this time and processed for use in fabric construction.

Cashmere is a very soft, luxurious fiber popular for coats and sweaters. It is warm, lightweight, and much finer than wool, but delicate and less durable. Cashmere goats are raised in the Himalaya region of India and China. Only the down, or underhair, is used to make fabric. When the goat is shedding, this down is combed from the animal.

Angora goats, which produce *mohair,* are native to the province of Angora, Turkey. They are also raised in Oregon, California, and Texas. Mohair is the strongest and stiffest of the hair fibers, used a great deal in upholstery and floor coverings. It does not shine or mat like wool.

The llama and the alpaca are very similar to the camel. Both animals are raised in the upper regions of the Andes Mountains in South America. The llama is primarily raised as a pack animal. *Llama hair* is rather coarse and is usually combined with other fibers in cloth. The alpaca on the other hand is raised primarily for its fleece. *Alpaca* is quite strong, but soft and silky in appearance.

The vicuna is a very rare animal found only in the highest, almost inaccessible regions of the Andes Mountains. It is also a very wild animal, making it difficult to capture. *Vicuna hair* fiber is very soft and delicate and makes the world's finest, most luxurious, and most expensive fabric.

Wool labeling

The Wool Products Labeling Act of 1939 requires that all products containing wool, with the exception of upholstery and floor coverings, must be labeled according to content. The label must state the percentage of wool and the amount of any other fibers that are present, as well as the type of wool fiber used. The law specifies three classifications: Wool, reprocessed wool, and re-used wool.

- WOOL: Wool fibers which have not been previously used in the manufacture of any woven or felted product. The fibers may have been partially processed. Perhaps they may have been spun into yarn, but they have never before been made into cloth.

"Virgin Wool" or "New Wool" refers to fibers that have never before been processed in any way.

"All Wool" indicates that the product is made entirely of wool fibers. Included may be fibers that have been previously spun into yarn, but none of the fibers has ever before been made into cloth.

According to the law, the word "wool" may also be used to refer to hair fibers.

- REPROCESSED WOOL: Wool fibers which have been previously woven or felted into cloth. The cloth has never been used by a consumer but has been reduced again to a fibrous state. For example, the woven or felted clippings and scraps of garment factories are reclaimed, reduced to fibers again, and rewoven or felted into new cloth.

- REUSED WOOL: Those wool or reprocessed wool fibers that have been previously spun, woven, knit, or felted in the manufacture of a finished product that has been used by a consumer. The product is subsequently cleaned and reduced again to the fibrous state for the manufacture of other wool products.

Generally a product made from "wool" is preferable to one made from reprocessed or reused wool because of the greater resilience and softness of the new fibers. Since it is doubtful that one can tell by feel or appearance whether an article is "wool" or not, labeling not only provides the consumer with valuable information but also protects him by preventing misrepresentation.

The Fabric Story Today and Tomorrow

Learn More About Wool

Trace the history of sheep raising from ancient to modern times.

Trace the story of wool as used by man.

On a world map, mark the wool producing countries.

Mark the countries where the animals raised for hair fibers are grown.

Prepare reports on the following topics:
- The breeds of sheep most important for producing wool.
- Other animal fibers used for fabrics.
- The production of wool from shearing to selling.
- Production processes unique to wool.

Prepare a display showing the steps in the production of wool from fleece to finished fabric.

Collect samples of wool fabrics. Arrange an exhibit and discuss the differences in general appearance.

Learn the names of the popular wool fabrics. Can you identify them?

Characteristics of wool

There is considerable variation in the length and fineness of wool fibers. They vary in length from approximately 1 inch to 15 inches. These variations depend upon the breed of sheep from which the fleece is produced. Woolen and worsted cloth are made from especially selected fibers suitable for each type of fabric. As you know, the woolen yarns and fabrics are made from shorter and sometimes coarser fibers. Worsted yarns and fabrics are made from fibers selected for their length and fineness.

Testing wool

If you look at wool under the microscope, you will see that the fiber is covered with a series of overlapping scales, arranged somewhat like fish scales or shingles on a roof. Over the entire fiber there is also a thin protective skin or membrane. There are minute pores in the outer covering which permit water vapor and air to pass through.

Under the microscope you can also see that the wool fiber is curly or wavy. Because of this natural crimp, wool springs back into shape after being compressed or after stretching, much as a spring does. This quality is known as resilience. Hold wool fabric between your fingers. It feels warm to the touch. Press it between your fingers and it feels elastic and springy. Crumple it in your hand. When you let go, it springs back to shape.

Because wool is an animal fiber it has a strong odor of burning hair or feathers when ignited. It burns very slowly and has a slow flickering flame which goes out as soon as the fire is withdrawn. The residue is a dark, crisp ash.

As noted before woolen fabrics are *soft* and *fuzzy,* whereas worsted fabrics are firm and flat. Any good quality wool, whether woolen or worsted, feels soft; poor quality wool is harsh and wiry to the touch.

Wool is the *weakest natural fiber,* although it usually wears well. When extra strength is necessary, synthetic fibers, such as nylon, are blended with the wool fibers.

We have already noted that the structure of the wool fiber makes it very *resilient.* Because of this elastic-

Wool

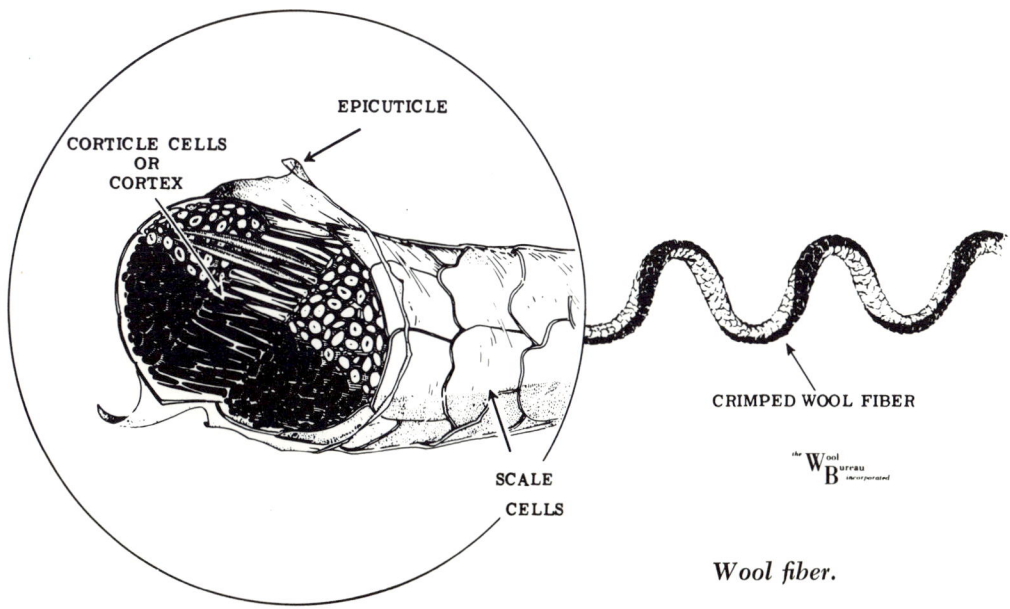

Wool fiber.

ity wool fabrics are crease resistant. They do not stay crushed and wrinkles hang or fall out easily.

Wool can *absorb* a great deal of *moisture* without becoming damp. Because of their porous structure, wool fibers can absorb as much as 30 percent of their own weight in moisture without feeling damp, and even more without becoming saturated. Wool dries very slowly and acts like a thermostat, guarding the body from rapid changes in temperature. It absorbs perspiration without feeling clammy or damp, and releases it slowly, and in this way helps to prevent chilling.

The readily absorbent quality of wool can be a detriment as well as an advantage. Wool *absorbs and retains odors* easily. This fact can prove very troublesome. A bonus factor, however, is the *lack of static electricity*. Wool's ability to absorb moisture from the air so readily prevents the build-up of static electricity. Therefore it does not cling or cause a spark.

Wool also has a great *affinity for dyes*. The inner core of the wool fiber is similar to a sponge and it absorbs dyes easily and completely.

Frequent cleaning is advisable, since the wool fiber absorbs odors readily and attracts and holds dirt particles. If wool becomes badly soiled, it is difficult to clean.

Reason for insulating quality

As the wool fibers are spun into yarn, the overlapping scales interlock and hold together. This creates numerous little air pockets between the enmeshed fibers. Since air is a poor conductor of heat or cold, a wool garment acts as a wall of insulation, preventing the escape of body heat and keeping the cold air from entering. Since body heat cannot escape and cold air cannot enter, wool is a warm fiber.

The Fabric Story Today and Tomorrow

Cleaning

Although wool fabric is washable, *dry cleaning* is recommended for most wool garments—dresses, suits, and coats—to hold the shape of the clothing. *Expert pressing* is needed for professional looking results. Small woolen articles, such as sweaters and socks, can be washed successfully. However, careful handling is necessary since high temperature and rubbing cause felting or matting and shrinking. Therefore cool or lukewarm water should be used, with as little agitation as possible. Often merely soaking a garment is sufficient to loosen the soil.

The moth problem. Unlike the vegetable fibers, wool is very susceptible to moths. A way has been found, however, to make wool permanently mothproof. If the fabric has not been chemically mothproofed, special care must be taken when storing wool garments to prevent moth damage. The most important precaution is: Be sure the garment is clean. Never store soiled garments.

They may be sprayed with a mothproofer or packed with moth crystals. Then they should be sealed in airtight bags or boxes for complete protection.

Also unlike vegetable fibers, alkalies damage the wool fiber. Therefore mild soaps and detergents must be used when laundering wool garments.

Hints for handling wool

- GENERAL CARE: Wool has the reputation of being very easy to care for. Little if any pressing is necessary between wearings. Ordinarily, if the garment is hung in an airy place after wearing, it will refresh itself. If wrinkles are persistent, steaming makes them disappear. Either press with a steam iron or hang the garment in the bathroom when taking a hot bath or shower.

- LAUNDERING: If the garment (such as a sweater) is washable, wash by hand. Some wool fabrics have received special finishes making them machine washable and dryable. All such wool will have a hang tag so indicating. Treated garments may be machine washed by the "soak method" or if the machine has a "very gentle agitation" speed.

Use lukewarm (100°) water, a water conditioner in hard water, mild soap or detergent, or cold water soap. Let soak or squeeze gently. Do not

WOOL

Advantages	Disadvantages
Warm	Susceptible to moths
Lightweight	Slow drying
Wrinkle resistant	Shrinks
Holds a press	Damaged by perspiration
Sheds soil and water	Weakened by hot water, alkalies
Non-flammable	Mats if improperly laundered
Static free	Becomes shiny if improperly pressed
Easy to care for	Singes or scorches easily
	Turns yellow, dissolves in chlorine bleach.

Wool

rub, twist, or wring. If washing by machine, agitate 1 to 3 minutes.

Rinse at least three times to remove all traces of soap. May use a fabric softener in last rinse.

Roll in a terry towel to remove excess moisture. Dry away from direct sunlight or heat. Garments of woven fabric may be hung on a well-padded hanger to drip dry or placed in the automatic dryer on low heat. Place several towels in the dryer with the wool garment to serve as buffers. Knit garments should be dried flat, shaping them to a predrawn pattern or form. Steam press.

- PRESSING: Use moist heat, either a steam iron or a dampened pressing cloth. Use warm, not hot iron.

Press on the wrong side. If necessary to press on the right side, use a piece of wool fabric between the garment and the moistened press cloth or steam iron. Wool against wool preserves the texture of the fabric and helps prevent a shine.

Press lightly by lowering and lifting the iron. Do not press completely dry. Let fabric air-dry to preserve the texture. After pressing, avoid handling until fabric is completely dry.

- SEWING: Easy to work with. Does not ravel. No difficulty with puckering, stretching, or slipping while being worked.

Can be "eased" and molded into shape. Tailors and drapes well.

Weight and type of fabric determine choice of thread. Mercerized cotton thread suitable for most types. Heavy duty cotton thread is stronger for heavy, bulky fabrics. Silk and dacron thread are both good because they are strong and elastic. Use less tension to prevent puckering.

Lightweight wool: Medium or fine machine needle; fine needle (#9 or 10) for hand sewing; small machine stitches (14 to 18 per inch).

Mediumweight: Medium machine needle; size No. 7 or 8 needle for hand sewing; 12 to 16 stitches per inch.

Heavyweight: Medium heavy machine needle; size No. 6 needle for hand sewing; 10 to 14 stitches per inch.

SILK

Silk, like wool, is an animal fiber, but from a very different source—the silkworm. It is believed that silk was discovered in China quite by accident almost 5,000 years ago. The story goes that a cocoon fell from a tree into a cup of hot tea the Empress was drinking in her garden. A very fine thread separated from the cocoon. The Empress pulled the thread to discover that the cocoon unwound itself into one long continuous filament. This was silk.

For years the Chinese were the only producers of silk. It wasn't until 500 A.D. that silk found its way to the Western world and only then because a supply of silkworm eggs was smuggled from China.

The Orient, particularly Japan, is still the world's leading silk producer. Italy and France also produce a large amount. Because of the high cost of labor, the United States has never produced an appreciable amount of silk, but it imports and uses more silk than any other country in the world.

To understand the characteristics of the silk fiber, it is helpful to know more about how it is produced. The life cycle of the silkworm is similar to that of the caterpillars we know. The worms hatch in the spring and attain full growth in five or six weeks, when they are ready to spin their cocoons.

The silkworm makes its own little house, or cocoon, out of self-created silk fiber. Two fine strands of sticky fluid are excreted through small openings on either side of the body. The strands come together in one flattened filament which hardens on contact with air. This filament is raw silk. Simultaneously, two other glands eject a gelatinous substance called silk gum or *sericin* which helps to cement the two filaments together. This gum has to be removed before the silk is made into thread.

The worm begins its cocoon by waving its head back and forth to spin the outer case. It then works inward until the whole body is entirely enmeshed in silk fiber. The whole process requires approximately 72 hours. The completed cocoon resembles a peanut shell both in size and shape.

The *chrysalis* (or *pupa*, as the worm also is called at this stage) develops into a moth in two or three weeks. If left alone, the moth cuts its way out of the cocoon, mates immediately, lays 500 to 600 eggs, and dies. When the eggs hatch into worms, the life cycle is repeated.

The rearing and keeping of silkworms for the production of silk is a specialized vocation called *sericulture*. The best silk is produced by a worm which feeds on the leaves of the white mulberry tree. Groves are established for this purpose. The moth eggs are kept carefully protected until spring when the mulberry leaves are ready. Then the eggs are placed in incubators where they will hatch into worms that will be supplied with mulberry leaves upon which they can feed.

Only those cocoons required for breeding are allowed to mature into moths because moths damage the silk fiber when they break through the cocoon. The cocoons to be used for the production of silk are placed in a 200° oven for 24 hours. The heat kills the chrysalis and evaporates the moisture. Then the cocoons are ready for the unwinding process.

When ready to be unwound the cocoons are placed in warm water to soften the sericin so that the filament can be unwound in one continuous thread—often between 1,000 and 2,000 feet long. In the unwinding process, called *reeling*, a great deal of

Reeled silk yarn.

U.S.D.A. Photograph

Doupioni silk yarn.
U.S.D.A. Photograph

skill is required to prevent breaking the fine thread. Indeed, since the strands are so fine, several cocoons are usually reeled together.

Reeled silk is twisted into silk yarn by a process called *throwing*. This is similar to the spinning of cotton, linen, or wool fibers into yarn. However, none of the preliminary steps necessary to produce a continuous yarn from the other fibers is required, because silk is already a continuous strand, hundreds of feet long. The strands are merely twisted the desired amount and wound on bobbins ready to be produced into fabric.

Spun silk, on the other hand, is made from short strands of silk fiber which are carded, combed, and spun together into yarn, the same as cotton fibers. Where do these short strands come from? When a moth breaks through the cocoon, it breaks the continuous filament. Sometimes silkworms spin their cocoons so close together that they are joined in a double cocoon. These double cocoons produce an uneven yarn, wider in diameter, known as *doupioni silk*. Any strands remaining on the cocoon after reeling, or any waste from the reeling or throwing process can also be used for spun silk.

Not all silk fiber is the result of sericulture. In Asia, uncultivated silkworms, hatched from a wild species of moth, grow wild, eat oak leaves instead of mulberry leaves, and produce a silk filament that is coarse, irregular in size, and a tan color. The silk from these uncultivated worms is known as *wild* or *Tussah* silk. Pongee and Shantung are examples of fabric made from wild silk.

Silk shantung fabric from doupioni yarn.
U.S.D.A. Photograph

U.S.D.A. Photograph
Fabric from wild silk.

A process unique to the production of silk fabric is *weighting*. Silk yarn still contains some sericin that must be removed before the fabric is woven. Eliminating all the sericin means a considerable weight loss in the finished fabric. To compensate for this loss, silk may be weighted with metallic substances during the dyeing or finishing process. Pure dye silk is a term used to describe a fabric which contains no metallic weighting substances. Weighting is an acceptable technique, but the Federal Trade Commission has ruled that weighted silk must be so labeled with the percentage of weighting clearly marked on the label.

Labeling. Other trade practice rules, approved in 1938, state that all products labeled "silk," "pure silk," or "pure dye silk" must contain silk and no other substances, except necessary dyeing and finishing materials not to exceed 10 per cent of the finished weight. Silk noil (short bits) or waste, if used, must be indicated on the label. Such terms as "silk linen" or "silk rayon" are prohibited.

Learn More About Silk

Trace the history of silk.
On a world map, mark the leading silk producing countries.
Make a chart illustrating the life cycle of the silkworm.
Prepare a display showing the steps in production of silk from cocoon to finished fabric.
Prepare reports on the following topics:
- The production of reeled silk; spun silk; wild silk
- Why sericulture is not a successful business in the United States.
- Factors influencing the use of silk in the United States.
- The Trade Practice Rules for the silk industry.
- The advantages and disadvantages of weighted silk; pure-dye silk.

Collect samples of silk fabrics. Arrange an exhibit and discuss the differences in general appearance.
Learn the names of the popular silk fabrics. Can you identify them?

Characteristics of silk

As noted, the silk fiber is by far the longest of the animal and vegetable fibers—often more than half a mile in length.

Silk

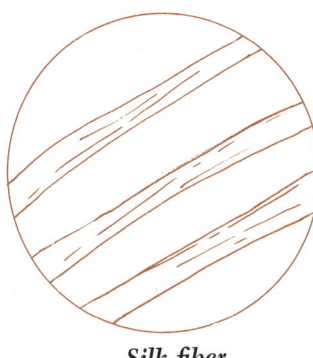
Silk fiber.

If you look at the raw silk fiber under the microscope it has an irregular, bumpy surface. If you look again after the sericin is removed, it looks like a smooth glass rod. Under the microscope, wild silk looks broad and coarse with wavy lines, whereas cultivated silk is narrow, smooth, and has no markings.

Because it is an animal fiber, silk *burns slowly* in very much the same way as wool. The odor of burning feathers is present, but not as strong as wool. The residue is in the form of shiny black beads unless the fabric has been weighted. Then the fabric merely chars but retains its shape because the metallic weighting does not burn.

Silk is sometimes called the aristocrat of textile fibers because of its handsome, *lustrous sheen*. The silk fiber is rich and lustrous in feel and appearance.

The silk fiber is *strong*, size for size the strongest of the natural fibers. Although it seems very fragile, it is actually stronger than a steel wire the same size. Silk retains most but not all of its strength when wet. *Weighted silk cracks* and splits readily even with little wear.

Silk is naturally *resilient* and therefore resistant to wrinkling and creasing. Weighted silk and spun silk fabrics do not possess this elasticity.

Silk, like wool, *can absorb a large amount of moisture* without feeling wet. This quality makes silk a comfortable fabric. Because it is absorbent, it also takes dye well.

Like wool, silk is a *poor conductor* of heat, making it a *warm fabric*. The presence of metallic weighting decreases the warmth quality because metal is a good conductor of heat.

Silk *wears well* and *sheds soil* easily because of its smooth surface. There are no short fiber ends to attract dirt. The silk fiber itself is washable. Like wool, however, *dry cleaning is usually recommended* to protect the fabric and style of the clothing. *If silk is laundered,* it should be hand washed with care. It is injured by high temperatures, so use lukewarm water and mild soap or detergent.

SILK

Advantages	*Disadvantages*
Luxurious feel and appearance	Expensive
	Water-spots
	Damaged by perspiration
Lightweight	Yellows with age
Comfortable	Damaged by heat and sunlight
Wrinkle resistant	Often not colorfast to washing
Holds shape	
Sheds soil	Splits or cracks
Strong	Weakened by both acid and alkali
Does not shrink	Yellows with chlorine bleach

The Fabric Story Today and Tomorrow

Exposure to *sunlight weakens silk* and turns white silk yellow. *Strong acids* also damage the fiber. In turn, *perspiration and deodorants* both damage silk. The fabric stains and actually deteriorates. Therefore it is important to wash or clean silk garments frequently.

Silk is *not affected by moths or mildew.*

Hints for handling silk

- GENERAL CARE: Like wool, silk garments require little if any pressing between wearings. Most wrinkles will fall out.

Spot cleaning silk garments requires professional skill. The fabric can be damaged by careless handling. It is usually safer to send the garment to a dry cleaner than attempt to remove spots and stains at home.

Wear dress shields in silk garments to protect the fabric from perspiration.

- LAUNDERING: Wash by hand. Use lukewarm (100°) water and mild soap suds. Handle gently. Squeeze, do not rub or twist. Rinse well. Roll in a terry towel to remove the excess moisture. Dry indoors away from direct heat. Iron when damp-dry.
- PRESSING: Use a warm, not hot iron and press on the wrong side. Use a press cloth if it is necessary to press on the right side. Use steam only if necessary. If using moist heat, place a dry press cloth between garment and moistened press cloth or steam iron to guard against water spotting.
- SEWING: Not a fabric for beginners. Slippery, delicate, requires care in handling, ravels.

Use sharp scissors and shears, fine pins and needles (hand sewing, size 8 or 9; machine sewing, size 11). Place pins in seam allowances, as they may leave marks or holes in the fabric.

Use hand basting. Machine stitches leave needle marks when removed. Avoid ripping. Use silk thread.

Use medium length machine stitch (10 to 12 stitches per inch for heavy fabrics, 12 to 15 for lightweight fabrics). Presser foot pressure should be light; loosen machine tension slightly. Support the fabric when stitching by holding both in front of and in back of the needle. Apply slight tension, but do not pull through the machine.

In review:

Outline the general steps in harvesting cotton and producing cloth.

What is mercerizing? What effect does it have on the fiber?

What characteristics of cotton make it suitable for infants' clothing? summer clothing? bed linens?

What are the advantages of cotton? disadvantages?

Outline the general care procedures for cotton.

Outline the general steps in harvesting linen and producing cloth.

Define tow, as applied to linen.

What characteristics of linen make it suitable for towels? handkerchiefs? summer clothing?

What are the advantages of linen? disadvantages?

Outline briefly the general care procedures for linen.

Outline briefly the steps in producing fabric from fleece.

What is the difference between woolen and worsted?

How do hair fibers differ from wool fibers? How are they similar?

Explain the three classifications of wool according to the Wool Products Labeling Act.

Describe the wool fiber as it appears under the microscope. What characteristics of wool are due to its appearance and structure?

What are the advantages of wool? disadvantages?

Outline the general care procedures for wool.

Outline the steps in processing silk fabric.

What is spun silk? thrown silk? douppioni silk? raw silk? wild silk?

Explain the difference between pure-dye silk and weighted silk.

What are the advantages of silk? the disadvantages?

Outline silk care procedures.

Of the natural fibers, which is the longest? the shortest? the strongest? the weakest? the least elastic? the most resilient? the most absorbent? the best heat conductor? a poor heat conductor?

THE MAN-MADE FIBERS

The twentieth century has seen the development of many man-made fibers with new and very different characteristics from the four natural fibers that have been used for thousands of years. Experimentation in the production of man-made fibers was attempted as long ago as 1710 when René A. de Réaumur suggested making a silklike fiber from gum and resin. It was not until 1855, however, that Count Hilaire de Chardonnet succeeded in making an imitation silk from the juice of mulberry leaves. This first man-made fiber was *rayon*.

Chardonnet, generally considered to be the father of man-made fibers, sparked a revolution in the textile industry. Although commercial production of rayon in the United States did not begin until 1911, there has been tremendous growth in the man-made fiber industry since that time. At present, there are over 240 man-made fibers. These fibers can be made to resemble the natural fibers so closely in feel and appearance that it is almost impossible to tell the difference between the "real thing" and the man-made. On the other hand, it is possible to control the manufacturing process of the fibers to produce desirable characteristics not present in the natural types.

Although the basic materials used may differ, the manufacturing process is the same for all man-made fibers. There are three main steps:

• The basic materials are transformed into a thick liquid or solution, often called "dope."

• The solution is forced through tiny holes in a spinneret—a perforated device resembling a shower nozzle except the holes are too small for the eye to see. The solution comes out of the spinneret in very fine liquid streams.

• The fine liquid streams harden into solid threads, called filaments.

109

Man-made fibers are produced in three forms: multifilament yarn, monofilament yarn, and staple strands. Multifilament yarn is made up of a number of tiny, almost endless strands twisted together into one yarn. Some yarns are more tightly twisted than others and the more the twist, the stronger the yarn. The size of the yarn —thin and delicate or coarse and heavy—depends upon the size of the individual strands and the number of strands twisted together. *Monofilament* yarn is made from a single strand of great strength and smoothness. *Staple* consists of many short, wavy strands (filament cut into short lengths) which are spun into soft, light yarns.

Fabrics made from continuous filament are very smooth and lustrous, much like silk. Fabrics from staple are thicker and rougher, much like cotton, linen, or wool.

The spinning solution is a clear, thick liquid that looks very much like honey.

FMC Corporation, American Viscose Division

A spinneret resembles a shower nozzle. There may be as many as 5,000 holes in a jet no larger than 2 inches wide.

The spinning solution is forced through the small holes in the spinneret, forming individual filaments.

RAYON

For many years rayon was thought of as nothing more than imitation silk, but since the first rayon fabrics appeared there has been constant research on how to improve rayon yarns and fabrics. Rayon fabrics today are far more beautiful and serviceable than those of fifty or sixty years ago. Rayon is no longer thought of as inferior or imitation. It is a fiber in its own right.

The basic substance from which rayon fibers are made is cellulose, from wood pulp and cotton linters. As you know from reading about the cotton fiber, cotton linters are the fibers left clinging to the seeds after the ginning process. Rayon is known as a *regenerated fiber* because it is created from natural materials that have been merely rearranged into a new form.

There are two types of rayon—viscose and cuprammonium. These words refer to the manufacturing process. It is not necessary to know the details of production, but in a

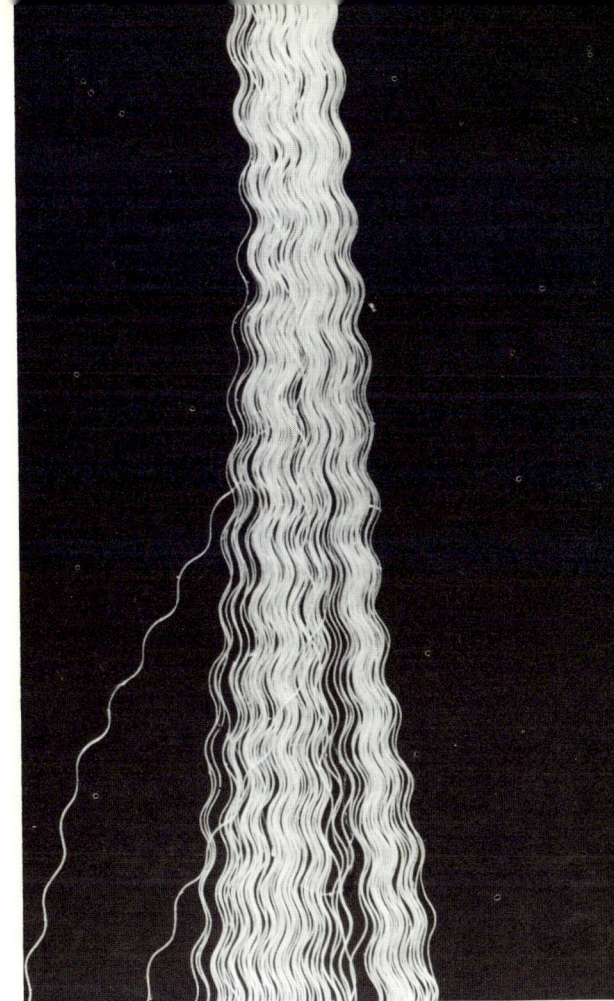

U.S.D.A. Photograph
Filament yarns.

U.S.D.A. Photograph

Fabric from filament yarns.

U.S.D.A. Photograph
Spun yarns unraveled.

general way here is the difference between the two: In the *viscose process*, the cellulose is dissolved in a solution of caustic soda and transformed into a viscous solution—hence "viscose." In the *cuprammonium* process the cellulose is dissolved in copper oxide and ammonia. The word cuprammonium is a combination of these two terms.

The cuprammonium process includes a special feature known as "stretch spinning" which produces an extremely fine, even yarn. When the filament comes from the spinneret, it goes through a "funnel" in which it is stretched and twisted at the same time. The result is a highly twisted yarn that is much finer than viscose. Because of its fineness and evenness most of the cuprammonium produced in this country is woven into sheer fabrics, associated with the tradename of Bemberg. The yarn produced by the viscose method is more versatile; therefore, the greater part of the rayon today is produced by the viscose method.

Fabric from spun yarns. *U.S.D.A. Photograph*

Learn More About Rayon

Prepare a report on details in the discovery of rayon.

Make a chart illustrating the production of rayon.

Compare the basic process of making rayon with the natural process by which the silkworm creates silk filament.

Compare the two methods of making rayon. What are the differences in manufacture? How do the fibers of each method differ? Look through catalogs and identify brand names of each method.

Collect samples of rayon fabrics. Arrange an exhibit and discuss the differences in general appearance.

Learn the names of popular rayon fabrics.

Characteristics of rayon

Because of the continuous spinning process, the rayon filament is very long, even when compared to the length of the silk fiber.

Under the microscope, the two types of rayon fiber differ in appearance. Both have a luster like glass and are very uniform, but the viscose rayon fiber is marked by many long, spiral lines, whereas the cuprammonium fiber has no markings.

Since rayon is a cellulose fiber, it burns very much like cotton—ignites quickly and burns with a yellow blaze. The residue is a light, feathery ash and there is an odor of burning paper.

Since rayon is man-made, it is possible to control the manufacturing processes so as to produce yarns with a smooth, silklike texture or yarns

FMC Corporation, American Viscose Division
Cellulose is the raw material from which rayon is made. White sheets of cellulose that look very much like blotting paper are first treated with caustic soda.

The treated sheets of cellulose (alkali cellulose) are then crumbled in a mechanical shredder.

The crumbs are aged and then churned to permit the chemical reaction to continue. These crumbs are dissolved into the viscous solution from which the rayon yarn is spun.

The Fabric Story Today and Tomorrow

with a dull, fuzzy appearance. Rayon fibers can be made thick or thin and straight or crimped, as desired. They can be made into the smoothest of fabrics by use of continuous filament yarn or formed to make rough, nubby fabrics. The versatility of the rayon fiber makes it adaptable to many finishes and weaves. The rayon fabrics, however, are usually heavier than the same kind of silk fabric.

Rayon is stronger than wool, but weaker than the other natural fibers. Although it is only half as strong as silk, its strength is adequate for good fabric durability. All rayon yarns lose strength when wet; they cannot stand a great deal of strain.

Rayon does not possess the natural resilience of silk; therefore it wrinkles easily. It can be successfully treated, however, with a crease-resistant finish. Twisting the yarn tightly also makes it more elastic and the fabrics made from these highly twisted yarns—crepe, for instance—are more resistant to wrinkling.

Rayon absorbs moisture easily—even more than cotton and linen—and dries slowly. The high degree of absorbency, coupled with the fact that rayon is also a good heat conductor, makes rayon fabrics comfortable to wear in warm weather.

Rayon fibers also absorb dye readily and are colorfast to washing and sunlight. White rayon fabrics do not yellow with exposure to sunlight, as silk does.

Because rayon is such a smooth fiber, it sheds soil readily. Rayon fabrics may be washed or dry-cleaned successfully, but they should not be permitted to become too soiled. Rayon cannot take the treatment nec-

RAYON

Advantages	Disadvantages
Inexpensive	Weak when wet
Does not pill	Damaged by acid, mildew
Absorbent, comfortable	Shrinks unless treated
Static free	Requires care in laundering
No lint	
Sheds soil easily	Wrinkles easily
Moth resistant	Dries slowly
Not harmed by perspiration	

essary to remove heavy soil. It tends to stretch or sag because the rayon fiber is weaker when wet. Careful handling is necessary—avoid wringing and rough treatment.

Since rayon can withstand heat without damage, it can be laundered in hot water and ironed with a hot iron. Strong alkalies destroy rayon, so use a mild soap or detergent.

Like cotton, rayon is susceptible to mildew, damaged by acids, but not susceptible to moths or affected by perspiration. It shrinks the same as cotton, but shrinkage can be controlled with special finishes.

Hints for handling rayon

• LAUNDERING: Rayon requires careful handling. Wash only fabrics labeled washable. Use lukewarm water (100°). Hot water will not harm fiber but may cause fading. Use mild soap or detergent.

May be machine washed. Use a short wash time—not more than 5 minutes. Do not soak. Sheer or delicate fabrics should be hand washed.

Handle gently. Squeeze; do not rub or twist.

Rinse thoroughly. Roll in a terry towel to remove the excess moisture. Iron while damp.

- PRESSING: May use a hot iron, same as cotton. Press on the wrong side. Use a press cloth if necessary to press on the right side. May use a steam iron, but better results are obtained if ironed while still damp, rather than dry, and re-dampen.
- SEWING: Same as silk.

ACETATE

For many years the word rayon was used for all fibers made from cellulose. Acetate was considered one of the rayon fibers until, in 1952, Federal Trade Commission rules became effective, requiring acetate to be labeled a separate, distinct fiber. The definitions of each of the fibers read as follows:

"Rayon: Man-made textile fibers and filaments composed of regenerated cellulose and yarn, thread, or textile fabric made of such fibers and filaments."

"Acetate: Man-made textile fibers and filaments composed of cellulose acetate and yarn, thread, or textile fabric made of such fibers and filaments."

The reasons for classifying acetate as a distinct fiber and requiring it to be labeled "acetate" rather than "rayon" or "rayon acetate" are simple to understand. Rayon is made from pure cellulose; when the fibers or filaments emerge from the spinneret, they are still pure cellulose, though in a different physical form. Acetate is also made from cellulose obtained from wood pulp and cotton linters, but in this case acetic acid is added, making a new and chemically different substance, called cellulose acetate. Both chemical and physical characteristics differ from those of cellulose.

The rules say that it is unfair trade practice to make any claim or representation concerning either of these products so as to deceive purchaser or prospective purchasers. Fabric names such as "satin," "taffeta," or "crepe" may not be used alone. The approved terms are rayon satin, rayon taffeta, or rayon crepe, and acetate satin, acetate taffeta, or acetate crepe.

The modern process for making acetate was discovered in 1892, only a few years later than the discovery of the process for making rayon. It was first produced in commercial quantities in this country in 1925, considerably later than the first commercial production of rayon. When discovered it was used only for electrical insulation and photographic film. It was too expensive to use as a textile fiber. Mass production has made it one of the least costly and one of the most widely used man-made fibers today.

Learn More About Acetate

Review the basic process of making acetate. How does it differ from rayon?

Identify brand names of acetate fibers.

Examine samples of rayon and acetate fabrics. How are they similar? How are they different?

The Fabric Story Today and Tomorrow

Characteristics of acetate

Although rayon and acetate are two distinct fibers, they are still often confused. But since acetate is both vegetable and chemical, it differs from rayon in composition. Therefore you can expect it to have unique characteristics.

Under the microscope you can see that acetate fibers have fine line markings and a center groove. The fibers do not have the luster that rayon fibers have.

When acetate burns there is a blaze the same as rayon. However, acetate sputters and drips as it burns because the fabric melts. The residue is very hard and brittle and there is an odor of vinegar (acetic acid).

Acetate is considered one of the most pliable fibers, making it soft and pleasant to feel and excellent in draping quality. It is a rather weak fiber, however, and becomes even weaker when wet. Long exposure to light also weakens it, similarly to rayon.

Acetate absorbs only about half as much moisture as rayon. Therefore acetate fabrics dry quickly. Low moisture absorption also means that acetate does not absorb perspiration readily; it is likely to be uncomfortable for wear in warm weather. Acetate also builds up static electricity, making the fabric cling in cold weather.

Acetate does not wrinkle as easily as rayon. However, if the fabric does wrinkle with wear or in laundering, the creases are "set" and very difficult to remove.

Because acetate is a chemical fiber, it has a built-in resistance to moths, mildew, and mold, the same as rayon. It does not shrink but it is susceptible

ACETATE

Advantages	Disadvantages
Soft	Weak fiber, weaker when wet
Drapes well	
Dries quickly	
Does not shrink	Clings
Does not soil or stain easily	Uncomfortable in warm weather
	Builds up static electricity
Resistant to moths and mildew	Is subject to gas fading
	Creases are difficult to remove
	Requires special pressing care

to atmospheric conditions that cause the dyes to fade. This condition is called gas or fume fading.

Acetate dissolves in anything containing acetone, such as nail polish. This property is used as a means of identifying it. It is also easily damaged by anything containing alcohol, such as perfume, acetic acid, such as vinegar, and similar chemicals.

Acetate, like most of the synthetic fibers, is thermoplastic. This means that the fiber is softened or melted by heat—a property that has both advantages and disadvantages. A thermoplastic fiber can be damaged by application of too much heat. Ironing or pressing with a hot iron melts the fabric. Use only a warm, not hot iron.

Because of their thermoplastic quality, fabrics can be permanently pleated; permanently embossed designs or a moire finish are possible, and garments will hold their shape without shrinking or stretching. Once the fibers have been melted and then fused, the results are permanent. Even seams and hems that have been pressed in leave marks that are almost impossible to remove if one wishes to change them.

Hints for handling acetate

- GENERAL CARE: Store garments in a plastic bag to prevent fume fading.
- LAUNDERING: Acetates require careful handling and should usually be hand washed. Use warm water (100°) and mild soap or detergent. May be bleached, but avoid chlorine bleach. If machine washable, use short wash time—not more than 3 minutes—and short spin time. To prevent wrinkling, do not rub or wring.

Rinse thoroughly. Blot excess moisture with a towel. Then hang the garment to drip dry.

Press when damp dry, since sprinkling may cause water spotting.

- PRESSING: Set the iron to lowest heat setting. Press on the wrong side. Use a press cloth if it is necessary to press on the right side.
- SEWING: Same as silk.

Triacetate. Triacetate is a type of acetate produced by the Celanese Corporation of America under the trademarked name Arnel. In the production of acetate, acetone is used as the solvent in preparing the spinning solution. In the production of triacetate, another chemical—methylene dichloride—is used as the solvent. The result is a fiber similar to acetate in appearance but having many different properties.

Triacetate does not wrinkle as easily as acetate and the wrinkles that do occur fall out readily after hanging. The fiber is not weakened when wet and is not as sensitive to heat as acetate. Even boiling water will not damage it. Therefore it can be laundered by machine in hot water, like cotton. It can be dryer dried and ironed at a higher temperature—the wool or cotton setting. If the fabric has been properly heat-set, little or no ironing will be required because the garment retains its original shape after laundering.

Learn More About Cellulosic Fibers

Review the characteristics of rayon, acetate, and Arnel.

Review the care procedures for rayon, acetate, and Arnel.

Examine samples of Arnel fabrics. Compare them with samples of rayon and acetate fabrics. How are they similar? How are they different?

Outline tests for identifying silk, rayon, acetate, and Arnel fabrics. Using unidentified fabric samples, conduct the tests and identify the fabrics.

Synthetic Fibers

The man-made fibers rayon and acetate are made from the cellulose found in cotton linters and selected wood pulp. In the case of synthetic fibers, no natural substances such as cellulose is regenerated. Synthetic fibers are created from basic chemicals—carbon (C), hydrogen (H), oxygen (O), nitrogen (N), and sometimes sulphur (S), and chlorine (Cl). These chemicals are obtained from various raw materials—coal (carbon), petroleum and natural gas (carbon, hydrogen), air (nitrogen, oxygen), water (hydrogen, oxygen),

The Fabric Story Today and Tomorrow

and salt (chlorine). There are many long and complicated chemical and manufacturing processes before the starting materials are transformed into the thick liquid which is forced through the spinneret to form the finished fiber.

Are you familiar with these chemical terms

Element: The fundamental substance of matter; a chemical "building block." Oxygen is an element.

Compound: A combination of two or more elements. Water is a compound of hydrogen and oxygen.

Molecule: The smallest possible physical unit of an element or compound.

Molecular chain: Two or more molecules (units) of the same or different compounds hooked together like links in a chain.

Polymerization: The chemical reaction by which molecules (units) combine to form long chains. It may be a process of simple addition of units or a reaction in which units are split off and lost.

Polymer: A very complex compound consisting of many units (perhaps a thousand or more) joined in a chain.

The way in which chemicals are combined determines the characteristics of the resulting fiber. Each synthetic fiber has particular properties that make it especially adaptable for certain uses, but all fibers have several characteristics in common. These include:

- Very strong and lightweight.
- Resistant to abrasion and other types of wear.
- Extremely resilient and retain shape.
- Stabilized to resist shrinking and stretching, called dimensional stability.
- Low heat tolerance (thermoplastic).
- Retention of press.
- Resistant to moths, mildew.
- Resistant to damage from chemicals.
- Launder easily, dry quickly, and require little or no pressing.
- Low moisture absorbency.
- Accumulate static electricity.
- Absorb oil and grease, but are resistant to nonoily substances.

Because the synthetic fibers have similar properties, general care instructions apply to most of them. If the manufacturer does not provide specific instructions with his product, the following procedures are advisable.

Most are machine washable, preferably with a wash-and-wear cycle. Wash small loads at a time. Crowding causes wrinkles. Use warm water. Hot water will remove soil easily and will not harm the fiber, but it will cause wrinkling. The heat softens the fibers, making them more pliable and as a result susceptible to wrinkling. Use a short wash time—4 to 6 minutes for sturdy fabrics and 2 to 4 minutes for delicate fabrics. You may use soap or detergent.

Rinse thoroughly. NOTE: The use of a fabric softener in the last rinse will help reduce static electricity. Remove clothes from machine immediately. If permitted to remain damp in machine, wrinkling occurs.

The Man-Made Fibers

Immediately hang garments on a hanger (plastic or wooden to prevent rust). Smooth the collars, cuffs, and seams with fingers. May be dried in dryer on "air" setting—no heat. To avoid wrinkling, remove garments before they are completely dry and hang on hangers immediately.

Little or no pressing is necessary. If some touchup pressing is desired, use the lowest heat setting on the iron.

NYLON

Nylon is not the first man-made fiber, but it is the first true synthetic fiber to be produced. In 1928 the Du Pont Company was conducting research to discover why certain chemicals behaved the way they do. In the process they created a substance resembling taffy. This substance could be stretched into a long strand that was very strong and elastic. The strand looked very lustrous and silky and, although the research was not originally aimed at the discovery of a textile fiber, this development suggested the possibility. Intensive research got underway and nylon was born.

Nylon was first introduced to the public in 1938 in the form of bristles in toothbrushes. In 1940 the first nylon hosiery was put on the market, making nylon an instant success. In 1941 war with Japan cut off the silk supply and all the nylon produced was used for military purposes. At the end of the hostilities in 1945 nylon returned for civilian use, in the form of women's hosiery again. Since that time nylon has been used successfully in many different types of products—home furnishing and industrial items as well as apparel.

Nylon is sometimes described as being made from coal, air, and water. This is an over-simplification although basically it is derived from a hydro-carbon obtained from coal, nitrogen and oxygen from the air, and hydrogen from water. Nylon textile fibers are produced in the usual monofilament, multifilament, and staple forms of man-made fibers. In addition, it can be produced with a *crimp*. The result is a stretch yarn that can be stretched like a spring and will return to its original shape when released. Nylon can also be produced with *loops* on the fiber. The result is a yarn that has the texture of staple yet has all the characteristics of filament.

Learn More About Nylon

In the chemistry laboratory, watch a demonstration of making nylon fiber.

Burn a piece of nylon fabric. Note what happens. How would you describe the odor?

Examine a nylon filament under the microscope. Describe it.

Try untwisting a yarn from some nylon fabric. Can you tell how many filaments were twisted together?

Identify trade names used for nylon fibers.

Examine fabric samples made from each type of nylon yarn. How do they differ?

Examine samples of fabrics that are blends of nylon and other fibers. Make comparisons.

Prepare a display of apparel, home furnishing, and industrial nylon fabrics.

The Fabric Story Today and Tomorrow

The properties of nylon fabrics, of course, depend upon the type of yarn used.

Characteristics of nylon

The nylon fiber is stronger than any other commonly used textile fiber except glass. Weight for weight, it is stronger than steel wire and does not lose any strength when wet.

Nylon has strong resistance to abrasion, twisting, and pulling. It will stand an enormous amount of wear without breaking down. Because of its great strength and friction resistance, nylon is used for many industrial and commercial purposes.

Nylon is one of the most resilient fibers; therefore it retains its original shape very well. Nylon hosiery does not become baggy, fabrics crushed or creased by tying will usually hang out, and pile fabrics never look crushed.

Nylon is resistant to soil and it washes easily. Since nylon filaments are smooth, dirt does not stick to them readily. However, nylon *turns yellow* with age and picks up soil and color from other garments, causing it to *gray* readily. One pair of nylon hosiery is sufficient to discolor several white nylon articles when laundered together. Chlorine bleach also causes nylon to turn yellow and sunlight weakens the fiber.

Since nylon does not absorb moisture well, it dries very quickly after washing. The water runs off the fabric. It is also very *warm to wear* because it does not absorb perspiration. Lightweight, sheer, or open weave fabrics allow evaporation of moisture between the yarns and are more comfortable in warm weather.

NYLON

Advantages	Disadvantages
Very strong	Weakened by sunlight
Adds strength to blends	Warm to wear
Lightweight	Yellows with age
Resistant to soil	Grays readily
Can take great deal of strain	Colors not wash-fast
Retains shape well	Picks up dye and soil from other garments
Washes easily; dries quickly	
Requires little or no pressing	

Nylon, like other true synthetic fibers, is *sensitive to the application of heat*. When heat is properly applied, nylon can be permanently shaped or pleated. The sensitivity to heat also means that nylon should be washed in warm, not hot, water. Hot water may set permanent wrinkles. An iron that is too hot will melt the fabric, so nylon must be pressed with a cool or warm, but not hot, iron.

Nylon may be *blended with cotton* for increased strength and luster. Such a blend creates pressing problems, though, because cotton can stand a hot iron but nylon cannot.

Addition of nylon to wool adds strength and makes the fabric resistant to shrinkage.

Hints for handling nylon

- LAUNDERING: Follow the general laundering instructions for synthetic fibers. Wash often and pretreat badly soiled areas with liquid detergent.

Wash white nylon by itself. Use an oxygen bleach regularly to prevent graying. NOTE: Bleaches are not effective for restoring whiteness to already discolored fabric.

You may use hot water in the wash cycle, but use cold water for spin cycle to prevent deep wrinkles.

- PRESSING: Use a cool iron. You may use a steam iron, but may need to use a press cloth to prevent shine.
- SEWING: Difficult to sew smoothly or to ease curved edges together. Ravels readily, does not tear, slippery. Fabric shifts readily. Pin or hand baste before machine stitching.

Use sharp shears, chalk or thread markings (wax stains the fabric), and fine, sharp pins (silk, size 16) and needles (#11 or 14 machine needle). Place pins outside the stitching line to avoid marking the fabric. Use synthetic thread—nylon or dacron. All findings—interfacing, tape, lining, etc.—should preferably be of synthetic fiber also.

To avoid puckering when machine stitching, reduce the pressure on the presser foot and use a lower machine tension. Apply slight tension by holding fabric both in front of and in back of the needle, but do not pull. Stitch at a moderate, smooth pace. Use the throat plate with a small round hole. NOTE: Stitch sheer fabrics through tissue paper.

Press only when absolutely sure the stitching line, seam, or fold is final. Creases are difficult to remove once pressed in.

ACRYLIC FIBERS

(*Orlon, Acrilan, Creslan, Zefran*)

After nylon was launched, the Du Pont Company turned its attention to developing a continuous synthetic filament resembling silk and a staple resembling wool. The result of the research was Orlon, the first acrylic fiber and the second true synthetic fiber introduced in this country. The fiber was developed in the laboratory in 1940, but it was not until 1950 that actual commercial production was underway.

Acrylic fibers are produced from a chemical compound—acrylonitrile—formed as a result of combining natural gases, air, and water. The basic raw materials are coal, air, water, petroleum, limestone, and natural gases.

Acrylics are actually a form of plastic. An acrylic resin is used to make Lucite—a plastic used for combs, brush handles, and decorative objects because it resembles glass.

- ORLON is produced in both staple and filament form. Fabrics made from filament are silky and luxurious in texture. Those made from the staple have a bulky, warm feel and resemble fine wool. Orlon sweaters, for instance, are comparable to cashmere in softness and texture.
- ACRILAN is made only in the crimped staple form. It can be blended with other fibers to give the fabric a soft, rich, bulky feeling such as in jersey, materials for snow suits, ski suits, and regular suitings. Because of its light weight, heat retention, and resistance to moths, acrilan has achieved great importance in the home furnishing field in the form of blankets and carpeting.
- CRESLAN and ZEFRAN are very similar to the other acrylic fibers in most of their characteristics. Creslan is used for items in which bulkiness and

The Fabric Story Today and Tomorrow

warmth combined with light weight are desired. Zefran is generally used in blends with rayon, wool, or cotton.

Characteristics of the acrylic fiber

Basically the acrylics are thought of as substitutes for wool and are very often made into fleecy pile fabrics. The continuous filament is warm and feels wool-like. Acrylic staple is bulky, yet lightweight, and ounce for ounce has approximately 20% more insulating power than wool. Therefore acrylic fabrics that are as thick and as warm as wool are much lighter in weight.

Acrylics have a greater resistance to sun and weathering than any other fiber. This characteristic makes the fiber especially suitable for outdoor use.

Pilling (fiber ends form small balls on the surface of the fabric) is a problem with soft, bulky acrylic staple yarns. Static electricity is another problem, especially noticeable in dry cold weather.

Acrylics are somewhat more resistant to heat than other synthetic fibers, but are still thermoplastic. Too high a temperature or exposure to heat for a prolonged period causes yellowing.

Acrylics are being used alone in apparel fabrics, especially in sweaters and many kinds of knit goods, as well as being blended with other fibers. A blend with *nylon* results in softness and adds wrinkle resistance. When blended with *cotton* the resulting fabric is firm and crisp, resists wrinkles, does not soil easily, and can be ironed dry. When an acrylic is *added to wool or silk* it produces a washable, wrinkle-resistant fabric. When

ACRYLIC FIBERS

Advantages	*Disadvantages*
Resembles wool	Forms pills
Warm, yet lightweight	Yellows with oxygen bleaches
Does not mat	Yellows with heat
Bulks well	
Strong	Colors not fast to washing
Resilient	Collects static electricity

blended with *cashmere*, the fabric is stronger but still very soft and luxurious.

Modacrylics (*Dynel* and *Verel*) are very similar to acrylic fibers in characteristics. They were even thought of as acrylics until the Textile Fiber Products Identification Act required that they be grouped separately. Then they were classed as modacrylic or modified acrylic.

According to rules by the F.T.C., acrylics are any fiber composed of at least 85% of the chemical compound acrylonitrile whereas modacrylics are composed of less than 85% but more than 35% of the same compound. They are produced by converting salt, ammonia, and water into a gas and combining this gas with the compound acrylonitrile. The result is a powder which in turn is dissolved and put through the spinneret.

Modacrylic fabrics are also very warm, soft, and fluffy but they are heavier than acrylics. They are the most *flame resistant* of any of the synthetic fibers yet are extremely sensitive to high temperatures. They sometimes *melt under the iron* even at low temperatures, and steam pressing should be avoided. The application of too much heat causes them to become stiff and boardlike.

Dynel, because of its soft warm feel, is made into furlike pile fabrics. Blended with Orlon, it has attained popularity in the coat field as a fabric resembling expensive fur but at a moderate price.

Hints for handling acrylic fibers

- LAUNDERING: Follow the general laundering instructions for synthetic fibers. You may use chlorine bleach to remove bad stains. Wash sweaters inside out to prevent pilling. If pilling occurs, the garment may be shaved with a safety razor.

- SEWING: Not difficult to sew smoothly, even by machine. No special techniques are necessary. You may use either a synthetic or mercerized thread.

Learn More About Acrylic Fibers

Review the outstanding characteristics of each of the acrylic and modacrylic fibers.

Burn samples of each of the fibers. Note the results and make comparisons.

Examine the fibers under the microscope. Describe them.

Prepare a display of acrylic fibers, yarns, and fabrics.

Examine samples of acrylic fabrics as well as blends of the acrylics with other fibers. Make comparisons.

POLYESTER FIBERS
(Dacron, Fortrel, Kodel, Vycron)

The research that led to the discovery of nylon spurred British chemists to investigate the possibility of producing fibers from the test tube. In the early 1940's they were experimenting with polyesters (*poly* = many; *ester* = a chemical compound formed by replacing the hydrogen in an acid with a hydrocarbon). They succeeded in developing a fiber which they called *Terylene*. The Du Pont Company bought the right to produce this fiber in the United States and in 1951 introduced a polyester fiber which they named Dacron.

Learn More About Polyester Fibers

Burn a polyester fabric. Note the results. Compare with the other synthetics.

Examine a polyester filament under the microscope. Describe it. Compare it with the other synthetics.

Identify the tradenames used for polyester fibers. Examine fabric samples made from each type of yarn. How do they differ?

Prepare a display illustrating the use and advantages of fiberfill.

Examine samples of polyester fabrics and blends of polyester fibers with other fibers. Make comparisons.

Although the basic elements for polyester fibers are derived from petroleum, coal, air, and water—similarly to nylon—polyesters are chemically different from any other fiber. They are produced from two very plentiful and inexpensive chemical compounds—one a coal-tar derivative

The Fabric Story Today and Tomorrow

and the other an alcohol that is commonly used in antifreeze for automobiles.

Production methods are similar to those used for other synthetic fibers. The chemicals are "cooked" until the proper combination is obtained. The result is a hard, porcelainlike substance. This substance is chipped into flakes which are melted and forced through the spinneret—called melt spinning.

The continuous filament as it comes from the spinneret is used for apparel fabrics. A specially produced staple—"fiberfill"—can be used as a filling for pillows and quilts.

Characteristics of polyester fibers

The polyester fiber has excellent resilience and fabrics are extremely resistant to wrinkling, whether wet or dry. Usually they need no pressing after washing and they retain their pressed appearance even after many wearings.

The polyesters are also extremely strong. Only nylon and glass fibers are stronger. Because of their high strength and excellent resilience, polyesters provide great advantages when blended with other fibers.

Polyesters have a very low absorbency, even lower than other synthetic fibers. For this reason, polyesters dry quickly, as do other synthetics, and they do not stain easily. Most spots can easily be removed by wiping with a damp sponge, since the substance remains on the surface of the fabric. Low absorbency also makes a garment *uncomfortable to wear*.

The fiber may be blended with wool to produce a suiting fabric similar to a tropical worsted that is wrin-

POLYESTER FIBERS	
Advantages	*Disadvantages*
Extremely strong	Absorbs body oils and grease
Adds strength to blends	Uncomfortable when wet
Resists wrinkling, wet or dry	
Holds a crease	
Very durable	Picks up lint
Does not stretch or sag	Pills
Easily spot cleaned	Collects static electricity

kle resistant, holds a crease, and is stronger and longer wearing. A blend with nylon produces a lingerie fabric that is *not as transparent* as all-nylon. When *blended with cotton*, the result is a fabric that is lightweight, cool, quick drying, and requires little or no pressing. Blends of polyester fiber with cotton or rayon can be given a permanent press finish so that the finished garment will need absolutely no ironing.

Hints for handling polyesters

• LAUNDERING: Follow the general laundering instructions for synthetic fibers. Because the fiber readily absorbs oil and grease, pretreat collars, cuffs, and badly soiled or spotted areas with a soap or detergent paste. The use of a fabric softener in the final rinse will reduce the lint pick-up. The regular use of bleach keeps white fabrics bright.

• SEWING: Same as nylon.

Polyurethane fiber (Spandex)

This fiber is a comparatively recent development in the textile field. In the late 1940's scientists began to investigate the possibility of a synthetic yarn with all the desirable qualities of rubber. The first Spandex fiber—Fiber K, later given the name Lycra—was introduced commercially by the Du Pont Company in 1959. Like nylon, it was an immediate success and in a short time Spandex fibers almost replaced rubber as a textile fiber.

According to the F.T.C. rules, the fiber forming substance in Spandex must be at least 85% polyurethane. As with the other synthetic fibers, the raw material sources are common elements. One of them is castor oil. The chemical processes involved, however, are the most complicated of the synthetic fibers. In any polymer, molecules are linked together to form a long chain. To create Spandex, the molecules are linked together in a very special way. Soft sections are alternated with hard sections and the result is an "elastomer." The soft sections can be stretched and will return to original length when released, creating the elasticity. The hard sections hold the chain together, giving form to the structure.

Polyurethane can be created in two forms—fiber and foam. Spandex is the fiber form. The fiber can be used alone or it can be covered with another fiber—nylon, cotton, rayon, or acetate—to give these fibers stretch characteristics. Most popular uses are in stretch fabrics or for foundation garments, brassieres, support hose, and bathing suits.

To create foam, the polyurethane is combined with large quantities of air and poured into thin sheets. The foam is very soft, yet strong, and has excellent insulative characteristics. In the textile field it is bonded to other fabrics to form a warm yet lightweight interlining.

Characteristics of Spandex

Spandex fibers are lightweight and soft, yet very strong. Weight for weight they are much stronger and more durable than rubber.

Elasticity is the outstanding characteristic. Spandex can be stretched as much as 500% without breaking. It can be stretched over and over again and will always return instantly to its original length when released. The fiber also retains this elasticity through repeated machine washings and dryings.

Spandex, unlike rubber, does not deteriorate by oxidation. Although it may turn yellow from exposure to heat and light and from body oils and perspiration, the fiber is not weakened. Chlorine bleach will weaken the fiber.

Care suggestions

If Spandex is combined with other fibers, the garment should be cleaned or laundered according to the characteristics of the other fiber. To *launder* garments that are made of Spandex alone, follow these suggestions:

May be machine washed, but hand washing is recommended for delicate garments. Use warm water (not over 140°) and regular soap or detergent. Pretreat heavily soiled areas with a liquid detergent or a paste made from a soap or detergent.

Wash white garments by themselves, not with other colors. You may use an oxygen or perborate bleach, but *do not use a chlorine bleach.*

May be line dried or machine dried at a low heat setting (not over 180°). No ironing is necessary.

In review:

What are the three main steps in the production of all manmade fibers?

Define: filament, staple, monofilament, multifilament. How do they differ in appearance?

What is the basic substance from which rayon is made?

What qualities of rayon make it a poor choice for stockings?

How can rayon be made to look like silk? linen?

What are the advantages of rayon? the disadvantages?

Outline the general care procedures for rayon.

How does acetate differ from rayon in composition? in properties? in care procedures?

In what ways are acetate and triacetate similar? In what ways are they different?

What determines the characteristics of synthetic fibers?

What characteristics do all synthetic fibers have in common?

Outline the general care procedures for all synthetic fibers.

Compare leading synthetics as to strength, elasticity, composition, and appearance.

What kinds of nylon yarns can be produced?

What are the advantages of a nylon-cotton combination? the disadvantages? of a nylon and wool combination?

What are the basic characteristics of acrylic fibers?

Compare acrylic fibers with wool.

What is the difference between acrylic and modacrylic?

How do polyesters differ chemically from other synthetic fibers?

What are the advantages of a blend of polyester and wool? polyester and nylon? polyester and cotton? polyester and rayon?

In what two forms can polyurethane be produced? How is each form used?

HOW CLOTH IS MADE

There is a logical sequence in the manufacture of all cloth from fiber to finished product. Fibers are first converted into yarn, the yarns are then woven or otherwise made into the cloth, and finishing processes convert the newly constructed cloth into finished consumer goods.

Fiber to yarn

There are two main types of yarns—filament and spun. From your study of fibers you learned that a filament was a single continuous fiber. You also learned that there is only one natural filament fiber—silk—and that all the man-made fibers are produced in filament form. The yarns made from the continuous filament fibers are called *filament yarns*. The construction of filament yarns involves nothing more than twisting together several strands of the fiber.

Spun yarn is also produced by a twisting process in which many staple fibers are twisted together. Staple,

How Cloth is Made

you remember, is made from short lengths of fibers. The other three natural fibers—cotton, linen, and wool—are staple fibers, and man-made fibers may be produced in staple form by cutting the filament into short lengths. The short lengths must be both spun and twisted to produce yarns. Before spinning, the fibers go through several preparation processes. First they must be straightened and arranged in a parallel position—a process known as carding. If the fibers are to be made into fine yarns, there is an additional straightening process—combing. The fibers are then drawn out into thin weblike strips. The strip is given a slight twist, just enough to hold the fibers together, forming a "roving" strand. The roving is wound on spools ready to be spun and twisted into yarn.

Because of the differences in the construction of filament and spun yarns, there are differences in appearance between fabrics made from them. Since there are almost no fiber ends on fabrics made from filament yarns, the surface is smoother and more lustrous. Fabrics made of spun yarns generally have more or less fuzz unless it is removed or flattened by a special finishing process.

Novelty yarns used for decorative or textured effects can be produced

---

Learn More About Yarns

Unravel a sample of any woven fabric to obtain a yarn. Untwist the yarn. Note how it separates into individual strands.

Twist together a few strands of cotton batting into a yarn to illustrate very simply the spinning of a fiber into a yarn.

Using fibers, charts, and diagrams illustrate and discuss the processes of: picking, cleaning, carding, combing, drawing out, roving, spinning.

Compare samples of unbleached muslin and fine percale. Note the differences in texture. What are the reasons for the differences?

Unravel several different fabric samples and classify the yarns as spun or filament. Note the appearance of the fabric made from each type of yarn. List differences.

Discuss how the type of yarn affects the care and the durability of the fabric.

By twisting yarns differently, it is possible to change both appearance and physical properties. Take a raveling and twist it first loosely; then tightly. Note the differences in both the appearance and the strength of the resulting yarn. Fabric made from yarn with a strong twist is firm and perhaps even harsh, whereas fabric made from slightly twisted yarn is soft and pliable. Examine yarns from soft, rough fabrics and from firm, hard-finished fabrics. Compare them for the amount of twist. Experiment with pulling apart and breaking both loosely and tightly twisted yarns. A tightly twisted yarn is stronger than one that has only a slight twist. Compare spun and filament yarns for amount of twist. The difference can be explained by the fact that fine yarns require more twisting.

by variations in the spinning and twisting process. *Slub yarns* have soft, thick, untwisted areas at intervals throughout their length, creating a pleasing, textured effect. Fabrics with textures resembling linen or raw silk are made from these yarns. Shantung is an example of a fabric made from slub yarns.

Rough-surfaced yarns with irregular loops or "bumps" can be created by holding one yarn more taut than the other when twisting them together. The looser one will twist itself to form the loop. Some examples of this type of yarn are ratine and bouclé. *Ratine yarns* have small, tight loops on the surface. *Bouclé yarns* are softer than ratine because the yarn is not twisted as tightly and the loops are more pronounced. Both of these yarns are used a great deal for knitted fabrics.

The pebbly surface of *crepe fabrics* is produced by using very tightly twisted yarns, alternating the direction of the twist. These are referred to as S and Z yarns, indicating the direction of the twist.

A twist to the right is the same direction as the slant of the letter S, whereas a twist to the left is the same as the letter Z.

Unravel a yarn from a crepe fabric and hold the yarn in a vertical position. Can you determine the direction of the twist?

When the yarns are placed alternately—usually done in two's or four's—they kink in opposite directions. The result is a crinkly crepe effect. Crepe fabrics produced in this way are true crepe. Some examples are canton crepe, crepe de chine, and georgette. NOTE: Such fabrics as seersucker, crinkle crepe, or plissé have the crepe effect but it is produced in the weaving or by a finishing process. Therefore they are not considered true crepes.

A texturing process can be applied to the man-made fibers resulting in either a *stretch yarn* (one which has the ability to stretch when pulled and will return to its original size when released, like elastic) or a *bulk yarn* (a relatively soft, thick, fuzzy appearing yarn similar to wool). The process for both involves producing a permanent curl, loop, or crimp along the filament by twisting the yarn into the desired shape or position, heat-setting the yarn, then untwisting it.

The shape and depth of the crimp determines the resulting characteristics of the yarn. A zigzag shape gives bulk but not stretch. A deep, rounded crimp results in stretchability. Some variations are the loop which also gives bulk but not stretch and the coil, producing stretch. Some bulk yarns are Ban Lon (Joseph Bancroft and Sons Co.) and Taslan (Du Pont Co.). Helenca (Heverlein Patent Corp.) and Agilon

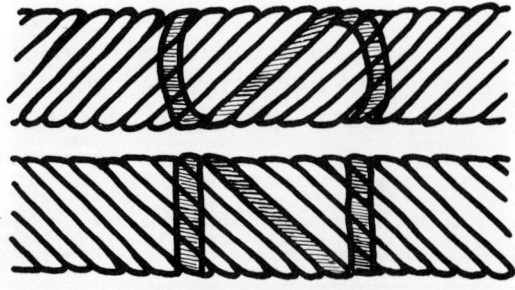

S and Z twist.

Zig-zag.

Crimp.

Loop.

Coil.

How Cloth is Made

(Deering Milliken Research Corp.) are examples of the stretch yarns produced by a texturing process.

Yarns may be classified according to their structure as single or multiple ply. *Ply* refers to the number of strands or yarns twisted together. Untwist a single ply yarn and it separates into individual fibers. Untwist a multiple ply yarn and it separates first into individual yarns which may in turn be untwisted into fibers. Such yarns are called two-ply, three-ply, and so on, according to the number of yarns used.

Most fabrics are made from single or one-ply yarns. Twisting two or more yarns together produces a stronger, heavier yarn. Therefore multiple-ply yarns are used when durability is the main concern (heavy men's shirts, work clothes, industrial fabrics) or when the fibers are extremely fine.

Yarns may be further classified as *simple yarns* or *blended yarns*. A simple yarn consists of only one fiber—all cotton, all wool, and so on. In a blended yarn, two or more fibers have been spun together.

Blending combines the desirable characteristics of both fibers. A blend of dacron polyester and cotton makes a very popular *blouse fabric*. This blend combines the softness and absorbency of cotton with the easy-care features of the polyester fiber. The blouse is comfortable to wear, dries quickly after laundering, and requires little or no pressing.

As noted before, blends can also be used to offset undesirable characteristics in one of the fibers. The addition of nylon to wool, for example, adds strength and makes the fabric resistant to shrinkage. The addition of cotton to nylon controls static electricity.

Blending always refers to the mixing of fibers before the spinning process and should not be confused with combination. In blending, different fibers are combined and spun into a single yarn.

A *combination yarn* is a multiple-ply yarn, each ply consisting of a different fiber. Combination may also refer to a fabric that is produced from different yarns. For example, the lengthwise yarns may be wool and the crosswise yarns a polyester fiber.

Learn More About Yarns

Collect labels and hang tags from clothing articles made from blends. Examine the information on the tag.

Examine samples of blend fabrics. Compare them with samples of fabrics of one fiber only. Determine the advantages and disadvantages of the particular blend.

Outline some tests that can be used to determine the presence of the fibers studied. Test unidentified fabric samples to determine their content.

Yarn to fabric

Fabric is made by one of four processes—felting, bonding, weaving, or knitting. In the **felting** process, there are no yarns. The fibers themselves are pressed together to form the fabric. Wool, hair fibers, and the fibers from fur-bearing animals (rabbit and beaver, for example) are the only fibers capable of being felted. The felting characteristic is associated with the scaly structure of the fibers

The Fabric Story Today and Tomorrow

which mat and interlock to form a dense fabric. Felting involves moisture, heat, and pressure. The fibers are moistened, exposed to steam, and passed between rollers. The pressure interlocks and mats them together.

Wool fibers alone do not make the best quality felt. Such felts have a dull appearance and feel harsh and rough. Felt made from fur fibers, especially beaver, is stronger and a finer quality.

Since felt has no yarns, it cannot ravel. Because the fibers have not been twisted, felt is a weak fabric with no elasticity. Therefore it is not very suitable for clothing, but it is widely used for hats, slippers, pennants, and padding or insulation.

Bonding is a process that makes use of an adhesive substance to hold together either random fibers, forming a fabric similar to felt, or separate layers of fabric, attaching them permanently to form a single fabric. Nonwoven fabrics which consist only of fibers are made by this process. The fibers are laid in a sheet and a bonding agent applied. Like felt, there are no yarns, so the fabric does not fray or ravel. Gift wrapping ribbons are an example of nonwoven fabric, and in clothing these fabrics are used for interfacing material.

Laminating, by which a thin layer of foam is permanently attached to the outer fabric, is an example of the bonded method. The foam adds warmth with little weight, eliminating the need for an interlining. Fabrics with a tricot lining bonded to the outer fabric have gained wide popularity in the clothing field because the need for a separate underlining has been eliminated.

Most fabrics are **woven,** a process of interlacing two or more yarns at an angle to each other. Perhaps you did some type of weaving when you were a child—a basket of paper strips or a loop pot holder on a small hand loom. That simple weaving process—passing the yarn over and under other yarns—is the same method by which the yarns are interlaced to make cloth on the giant looms that produce our modern fabrics.

All weaves consist of warp yarns that run the entire length of the fabric parallel to the selvage, and weft yarns (also called filling because they are the yarns that "fill in" to form the fabric) that run across the fabric from selvage to selvage.

Warp yarns are generally stronger and more firm than filling yarns because they are held under tension as they are woven. Give a piece of fabric a firm tug on both the lengthwise threads and crosswise threads. You will find that the fabric does not stretch in the lengthwise direction, whereas there is a slight give crosswise. Warp threads do not stretch as easily as filling. For this reason garments that are cut lengthwise—with the warp threads running up and down—hold their shape better and hemlines are less likely to sag.

In preparation for weaving, the loom is threaded with as many warp threads as are necessary for the width of the material. In the actual weaving process the warp yarns are raised, forming an opening through which a shuttle passes, carrying the filling yarns. After each passage of the shuttle, the filling yarn is pushed firmly against the fabric already formed. Then the harness holding the warp yarns changes position, forming a new opening for the next passage of the shuttle. This procedure is repeated till the required yardage is complete.

Quality

The way in which fabrics are woven is one factor in determining the quality of the fabric. Compact, closely woven fabrics are more firm and therefore more durable than loosely woven ones. Generally, household fabrics and clothing serve best if tightly woven. It is possible to check fabric for closeness of weave by holding it to the light, but a more accurate way is to do a thread count. Thread count refers to the number of warp and filling yarns in a square inch of fabric. A close weave has more. By using a pick glass—a magnifying glass mounted on a stand that has a square opening in the base—it is possible to count the number of yarns. Do a thread count on sample fabrics and then test the firmness of the same fabrics by pulling them in a rotating manner. Do the yarns hold firm or do they slip? Compact, firm, closely woven fabrics are more apt to hold their shape and less likely to shrink, making them more serviceable and longer wearing.

There are three basic weaving patterns—plain, twill, and satin—each with a characteristic appearance. Variations are used to produce different and complicated effects, but the structure of each is based upon one of these three.

The Plain Weave

Also known as homespun or taffeta weave, this is a simple process of "un-

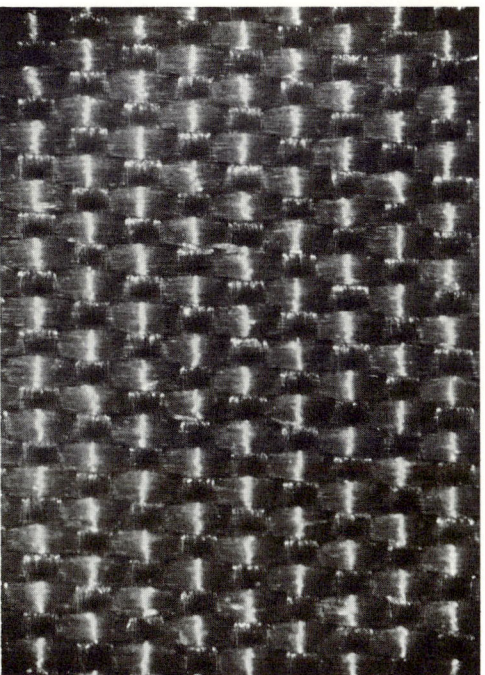

U.S.D.A. Photograph
Plain weave.

der-one-and-over-one." It is the most commonly used of the three weaves, the easiest and, consequently, the least expensive to produce. The plain weave is durable and gives excellent service when closely woven from strong yarns.

Some examples of fabrics made in the plain weave include: gingham, muslin, percale, organdy, lawn, madras, voile, dress linen, crepe, taffeta.

The *basket weave* is a variation of the plain weave. In the basket weave two or more filling yarns cross the same number of warp yarns in the same under-and-over manner. This weave is so named because baskets are woven in the same pattern. The resulting cloth stretches easily because it is loosely woven.

Some examples include: monk's cloth, oxford shirting.

All of these fabric swatches are samples of the plain weave and its variations. Different colored yarns are used to form the patterns. Can you identify the rib weave? the basket weave?

Turner Jones Co., Inc.

The *rib weave* is another variation of the plain weave. The ribbed effect is created by using heavier yarns in one direction than in the other. Usually the heavier yarns are in the filling, producing the crosswise ribs. NOTE: If the ribbed yarns are too coarse, the fabric will not wear well. The fine yarns will break under the strain of the heavier yarn and the fabric will split apart.

Some examples include: poplin, broadcloth, faille, ottoman, and bengaline.

Examples of warp-ribbed fabrics include: pique, dimity.

The *leno weave*, another variation of the plain weave, produces an open or lacelike fabric. This weave is also known as the gauze weave, but is not to be confused with the weave used to make gauze bandages and cheesecloth (a loose plain weave).

U.S.D.A. Photograph
Twill weave.

The Twill Weave

This has a distinct design characterized by diagonal lines or ridges running across the fabric either from right to left or left to right.

The ridges are formed by passing yarns over more than one yarn (but not more than four) before passing under a yarn. In each row, the filling yarn moves the design one step to the right or left to form the diagonal line. The most used twill is a 2–2, meaning the filling yarn passes over two yarns and under two. By changing the direction of the diagonal, variations can be produced—herringbone, for example, which is popular for suiting.

Twill fabrics are usually tightly woven from strong threads. Therefore they are especially strong and durable, giving excellent wear.

Some examples include: gabardine, serge, covert, flannel, surah, denim.

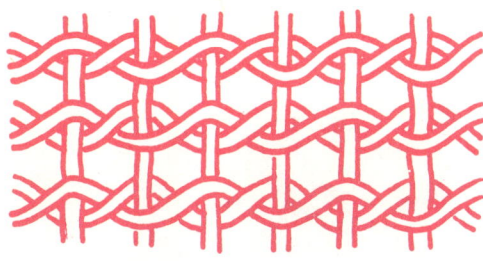

Leno weave.

The leno or gauze weave is produced by crossing or twisting two warp threads after each filling thread has been added. The result is a continuous figure eight as the warp threads cross the filling threads. Because of the twisted warp threads, the leno weave makes a firm, durable fabric, even though open.

An example: marquisette.

The Fabric Story Today and Tomorrow

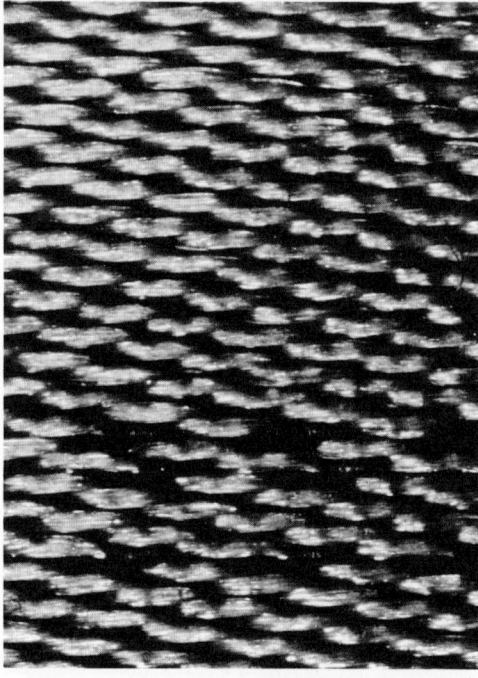

Satin weave. U.S.D.A. Photograph

The Satin Weave

This is very much like the twill weave except there are no visible diagonal lines. Long floats (yarns that pass over other yarns) arranged so as to avoid any distinct pattern create a lustrous sheen characteristic of the satin weave. In order to produce this shimmering quality, only yarns made from silk or other smooth, lustrous fibers are used. Then the yarns are given only a slight twist so as to preserve the greatest possible sheen.

Satin is usually woven with the floats in the warp yarns. The floats are arranged so that they pass under only one yarn at random; then they may float over as many as fifteen yarns. When the fabric is closely woven, only the floats are visible on the right side, creating a smooth, unbroken, glossy surface.

Closely woven satin is surprisingly firm and durable. Because of the long floats on the surface, however, the fabric is likely to snag easily.

Sateen refers to a fabric woven just the reverse of satin, with the floats in the filling yarns. Therefore the luster appears crosswise. It is also the name given to a cotton fabric woven in the satin weave. Naturally this cotton fabric does not have the same high gloss as satin.

Variations of the Basic Weaves

These create special effects. They include pile weaving, figure weaving, and double weaving. All three are more complicated and in most cases involve more than two sets of threads. Nevertheless, their construction still involves one of the three basic weaves.

Pile weaving adds a third dimension—depth—to the fabric. An extra

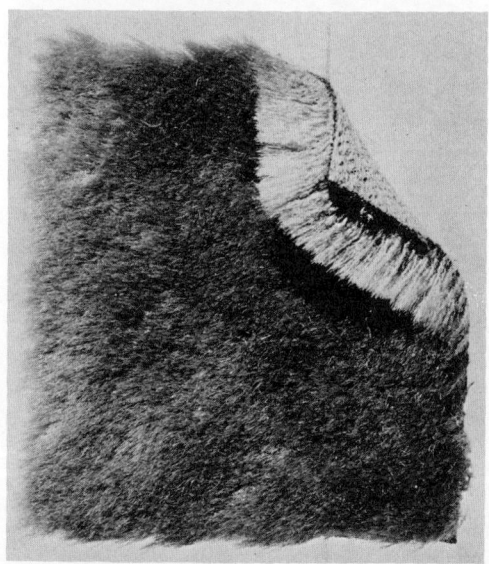

Pile weave. U.S.D.A. Photograph

How Cloth is Made

Figure weave.   U.S.D.A. Photograph

set of yarns, either warp or filling, is woven into the basic structure. These additional yarns extend above the surface of the fabric in the form of loops. The loops may be cut or left alone depending upon the effect desired.

An example of a looped-surfaced fabric: terry cloth.

Examples of cut pile fabrics include: velvet, velveteen, corduroy, velour, plush.

Figure weaving includes two kinds of construction. In one a third set of yarns is introduced to produce the design. In the other no extra yarns are introduced but a change in weave produces the design. *Swivel* and *lappet weaves* are examples of the first kind of construction. In both of these,

U.S.D.A. Photograph

Jacquard weave.

135

Jacquard weave is typical of the second type of figure weaving construction. An especially equipped loom, named for its inventor Joseph Marie Jacquard, is necessary. The design is created by combining different weaves—perhaps plain or twill for the design and plain or satin for the background. To identify this type of weave compare the two sides of the fabric. What is design on one side, either texture or color, is background fabric on the other side, and vice versa. For example, on one side the design may be plain weave and a satin weave background. On the other side just the opposite is true—the design is satin weave and the background plain weave.

Some examples include: damask, brocade, matelassé, tapestry.

Double weaving produces two separate pieces of fabric combined as one. Each is woven at the same time with separate sets of yarns. An additional set of yarns alternates between the two pieces, holding them together. This type of construction is used primarily for blankets, overcoatings, and upholstery fabrics. Cut pile fabrics can be produced inexpensively by this method. The extra yarns are inserted very densely and then the two pieces of fabric are cut apart.

Knitted fabrics are constructed by looping or interlocking yarns instead of interlacing as in weaving. Perhaps you have done some hand knitting or watched someone knit and are familiar with the process of using needles to form interlocking loops from a single yarn. Commercial knitting done by machine was developed from the same procedure.

J. P. Stevens and Co., Inc.
A punch card system automatically controls the weaving of intricate patterns on a modern Jacquard loom.

a small design is superimposed on top of the fabric. Swivel involves weaving the design with an extra filling thread, whereas in lappet the designs are stitched to the surface as the fabric is woven. The lappet weave, resembling embroidery, is the more desirable of the two methods. The threads are securely attached and the design cannot be pulled out easily. In fabrics made by the swivel method the thread ends are loose, making the design less durable.

An example: dotted Swiss.

How Cloth is Made

There are two basic kinds of knitting—*warp knit* and *weft* or *filling knit*. Weft knitting, which is similar to hand knitting and has the same general characteristics, is done with only one yarn and may be knit into either a straight or circular piece. On the right side of the fabric vertical rows of loops form vertical wales or ribs that can be clearly seen. On the wrong side there are horizontal ridges called courses. A disadvantage of this construction is the tendency to run if a thread is broken.

Jersey is a typical example of a weft knit fabric.

Warp knit fabrics are made with several yarns at one time and can be done only by the flat or straight knit method. The resulting fabric has lengthwise *wales* only. Warp knit fabrics are stronger and more firm than weft knits, but they do not stretch as readily. Neither do they snag as easily nor run when one of the loops is broken because the loops are interlaced so that every stitch is interlocked.

Tricot is an example of warp knitting. Run-resistant and non-run mesh used for hosiery are also produced by the warp knit method.

Double knitting, similar to double weaving, produces a fabric that can best be described as "twice-knit." A double set of needles knits two pieces of fabric and interlocks them in one operation. This is done only by the weft knit method, one side having fine ribs and the reverse side a diamond-like pattern. The double knits, which have gained tremendous popularity in the apparel field, are heavier and hold their shape better than single knits.

Knit garments fit well and are comfortable to wear because the fabric is elastic, soft, and porous. Due to the interlooping construction, the fabric can stretch in any direction with movements of the body and does not wrinkle, making it particularly suitable for underclothing. Yet, for this same reason, a knit garment tends to lose its shape with continued wear.

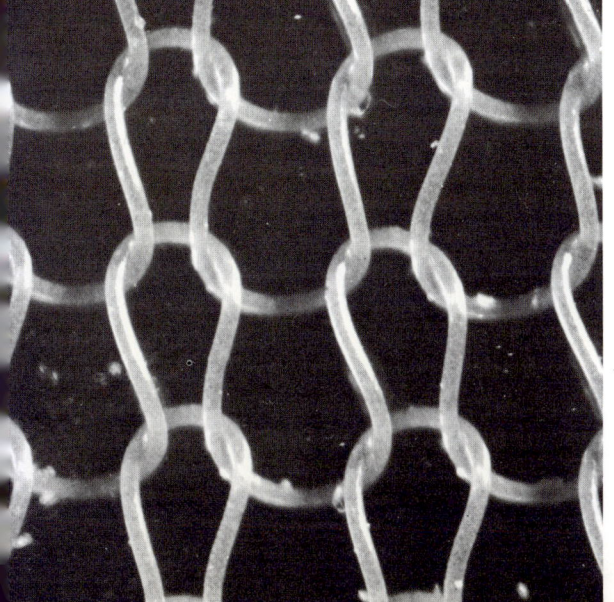

Filling knit.

U.S.D.A. Photograph

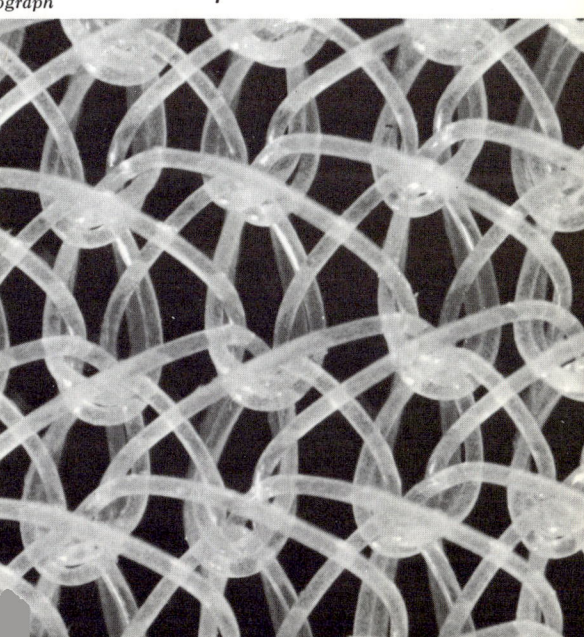

Warp knit.

The Fabric Story Today and Tomorrow

The open construction of knit-wear allows free passage of air through the fabric, thus aiding evaporation of perspiration. Nylon undergarments are much more comfortable to wear if made from a knit fabric rather than a tightly woven one.

Perhaps the biggest advantage knit fabrics have over woven fabrics is the natural quality of stretchability. A fabric that stretches with body movement and returns to its original shape makes a garment more comfortable.

Stretch Weaves

Manufacturers of fabrics have discovered how to add this desirable stretch property to woven fabrics. There are three methods used to produce stretch fabrics—yarn textured, core-spun, and mechanical. We have already discussed the *texturing process* (page 128) in which synthetic fibers are given a permanent crimp, resulting in a stretch yarn. In the *core-spun process,* rigid fibers are wrapped around Spandex yarn. Fabrics made by this process stretch the most and recover their original shape best. *Mechanical stretch* is the newest and least expensive method. First woven fabrics are treated chemically to crimp the yarns, causing artificial shrinking. Then, when the fabric is pulled, it can be stretched to what would have been its natural finished width.

Stretch fabrics may be classified according to the *direction of the stretch* as well as the *degree of stretch.* Fabrics may be woven with the stretch in either the lengthwise or crosswise direction or in both directions. Lengthwise stretch produces action fabrics particularly suitable for slacks, shorts, and other sportswear. Crosswise stretch provides freedom of movement, comfort, and smoothness of fit in all types of garments for everyday wear. Two-way or power stretch, which stretches in both directions and holds the body, is used primarily for swim suits and foundation garments.

Learn More About Fabric Construction

Examine several fabric swatches to identify the method of construction for each.

Prepare a report on the history of weaving.

Visit a textile mill to observe how cloth is produced; a knitting mill to observe commercial knitting.

Compare the different weaves and knits as to appearance, strength, and durability.

Examine samples of percale with different price ranges. Make comparisons as to firmness of weave, closeness of weave, and thread count.

Determine the advantages and disadvantages of knit fabrics compared to woven fabrics.

Compare samples of different types of knit fabrics. Label each as to type and use.

Display samples of bonded fabrics. Identify these and classify them according to use.

Test felt and other nonwoven fabrics for strength. Compare them with woven and knitted fabrics.

Study examples of each type of stretch construction. Compare the samples for amount of stretch and recovery.

How Cloth is Made

*Hints for handling
various fabric constructions*

Twill weave will require special consideration when selecting a pattern and placing the pattern on the fabric if the diagonal rib is prominent.

Select a style with set-in sleeves. Avoid bias seams, bias bands, and kimono sleeves. Avoid gored or flared skirts. The diagonal line will run in different directions because of the bias cut of the seam.

Place all pattern pieces on the fabric in the same direction. Preferably the diagonal line should run from left to right. Shading may occur if the direction is reversed.

Pile weave requires special care when cleaning, pressing, and sewing.

Corduroy is machine washable. Use warm water (not over 140°) and mild soap. Turn the garment wrong side out to avoid lint accumulation on the fabric. To avoid heavy creases do not twist or wring. Squeeze gently if washing by hand. In the machine, use a short washing cycle. A fabric softener in the last rinse water fluffs up the pile.

Corduroy may be dried in the automatic dryer. Use a medium heat setting and remove the item when only damp dry. Place on a hanger to finish drying, smoothing the garment with your hands. When dry, gently brush the fabric, brushing the nap downward.

Little if any ironing will be required. If necessary, use steam. *Do not place the iron directly on the fabric,* but hold it a little above.

Velvet and deep-pile hair fabrics should be dry cleaned. To freshen between wearings, brush with a soft brush to remove dust and lint. Steam a garment by hanging for about an hour in a steam-filled bathroom. Brush the pile at least once during the steaming process.

To freshen a spot that has been crushed, cover the fabric with a damp press cloth and pass it back and forth over an upright iron. The steam will penetrate the fabric and fluff up the pile.

- PRESSING: Avoid placing an iron directly on a pile fabric, even on the wrong side, whenever possible. Use a velvet pressing board or needle board. This is a piece of heavy canvas with upright bits of wire or needles. Place the pile side of the fabric down against the needles and press gently on the wrong side with a steam iron or a damp press cloth. If a needle board is not available, it is possible to substitute a thick padding of heavy terry towels or a strip of velvet fabric. Press with the pile, using as little pressure as possible. Brush lightly with the pile.
- SEWING: When cutting a garment, place all pattern pieces in the same direction to avoid shading. The pile running upward, from hemline toward neckline, gives a dark, rich color. To determine the direction of the pile, run your fingers over the surface. If the fabric feels smooth, the pile is going in the same direction as your fingers. If the fabric feels rough, the pile is going in the opposite direction.

Use lining fabric for facings to eliminate bulk.

Use silk thread to avoid leaving a mark on velvet. Pin holes will also mar the surface, so use fine, sharp pins and fine needles.

The Fabric Story Today and Tomorrow

Adjust the pressure on the presser foot, using as little as possible to avoid crushing and marking the fabric. Use a medium stitch (10 to 12 per inch) and stitch slowly, in the same direction as the pile. Avoid ripping, since machine stitches may leave permanent marks. Avoid top stitching that will crush the pile.

For *deep-pile fabrics,* such as imitation furs, use a loose tension, light pressure, long stitch, coarse needle, and heavy duty thread. Hand basting before stitching on the machine may prevent creeping and puckering. Smooth the pile away from the seam line toward the garment before stitching. Slash all darts and shear the pile in the seam allowances. Use finger pressing, since steam pressing mats the pile. To flatten seams and darts, catch the edges to the back of the fabric with invisible stitches.

Laminated fabrics

- CARE: The fabric may be laundered or dry-cleaned, depending upon the outer fabric. The permanence of the bonding is not affected by soaps, detergents or by dry-cleaning solvents. Dry-cleaning solvents may discolor the foam, but will not otherwise damage it.
- PRESSING: Little or no ironing after laundering is required, depending upon the outer fabric. Set the temperature of the iron according to the outer fabric. You may use either a steam iron or damp press cloth. Do not place the iron directly on the foam. Place brown paper over the foam so the iron will glide easily. NOTE: It is difficult to press a laminated fabric flat because of the springy nature of the foam.
- SEWING: Select a pattern with simple lines, preferably an unfitted style. Avoid complicated details and set-in sleeves, especially if the outer fabric is woven. Any detail that requires easing in fullness will be difficult. Neither interfacing nor interlining is necessary. Use a plain fabric for facings to eliminate bulk.

Fold the fabric with the foam side out to pin the pattern on so that the foam sides will not stick together. Use sharp shears and fine needles.

When stitching, place tissue paper on both sides of the foam so the fabric will feed through the machine evenly. To start the fabric through the machine smoothly, turn the balance wheel by hand for the first few stitches. Use medium tension, minimum pressure, and a medium to long stitch. Stitch at a moderate speed. Remove pins rather than stitch over them.

Grade the seams to eliminate bulk. Top stitching helps to flatten seams and edges. NOTE: Hemming stitches must catch the outer fabric since the foam will not hold the stitches.

Pre-lined (bonded) fabrics

- CARE: May be laundered or dry-cleaned according to instructions for the outer fabric.
- PRESSING: Can use a steam setting on most bonded fabrics. If outer fabric requires a higher temperature than the lining fabric (for example, cotton outer fabric—hot iron; and acetate lining fabric—warm iron) press the fabric on the side requiring the higher temperature.
- SEWING: Bonded fabrics are frequently easier to work with than the outer fabric alone because they are

more firm. Pattern selection need not be limited except to those styles suitable for the outer fabric. In most cases, there is no special sewing problem.

Cut the pattern on the right side so you can see the grain line of the outer fabric. If the fabric is off-grain, it cannot be straightened but must be used "as is." The yarns are locked in position by the bonding agent.

Grade the seams to eliminate bulk. If the fabric is especially bulky, separate the backing from the face fabric in the seam allowance and trim the backing close to the stitching.

Knit fabrics

- CARE: Dry-clean wool knits as well as blends of synthetics and wool. Cotton and synthetic knits may be hand washed.

Knits that may stretch should be stored flat. Others may be hung on padded or shaped hangers to avoid creases along the shoulder line.

- PRESSING: Most knits require little if any pressing. If steaming is desired, hold a steam iron just above the fabric or place a damp press cloth on it and hold the iron just above the cloth. *Do not iron knits.* Use a pressing motion—lower and lift. The back and forth ironing motion will stretch the fabric.

- SEWING: Choose a simple style with as few seams as possible. Avoid patterns that are cut on the bias. Tubular knits should be cut open, cutting along a single lengthwise rib. This rib is the grain line, not the fold line. Baste along one rib near the center to mark the straight grain. Remove the fold line by steam pressing. If the line is difficult to remove, it may be necessary to rearrange the pattern pieces to avoid placing them on this line.

Double knits do not require linings. Single knits are more satisfactory if lined.

Use thread markings, fine needles, synthetic or mercerized thread, and an average-length or small zig-zag stitch. Use a medium tension for single knits, a looser tension for double knits. Stitch slowly and smoothly, stretching lengthwise seams slightly as you go.

Sew the seam binding into shoulder and waistline seams to avoid stretching. *For the hem,* pink the edge and stay-stitch; then invisibly catch the raw edge to the garment.

Stretch fabrics

- CARE: Rest a stretch garment between wearings to give the fabric a chance to return to its original size.

Stretch fabrics may usually be machine washed, but check the label. Wash frequently. Use cold or warm water, any soap or detergent, but *avoid chlorine bleach,* which may weaken the fabric. Set the washer for a short washtime. Fabrics containing wool should be dry-cleaned.

May be dried in the automatic dryer at low heat or on the wash-and-wear setting. Remove from the dryer when still slightly damp. Overdrying may cause excessive wrinkling and shrinking.

- PRESSING: You may steam press. Avoid stretching the fabric when pressing. Use moderate temperature and press in the direction opposite to the stretch.

- SEWING: There needs to be no restriction on the style that can be used, but simple lines are easiest. Use the

The Fabric Story Today and Tomorrow

same size pattern you would for any other fabric. The garment should have the neat but not tight fit of any non-stretch garment.

If the fabric was stretched when it was rolled on the bolt, it needs a chance to relax. Do not use the fabric for at least 24 hours after it was unrolled. When placing pattern pieces on the fabric, be sure the stretch is going in the proper direction for the garment.

Use sharp scissors and sharp pins, placing them at right angles to the stretch. Use medium to fine needles, light pressure, loose tension, short machine stitch, or small zig-zag stitch.

Synthetic threads have more stretch than mercerized. Avoid stretching the fabric as you sew, but it will be necessary to hold the fabric taut when stitching with mercerized thread or a straight stitch. Test the stitch by pulling the seams. If the thread breaks, shorten the stitch or loosen the tension until the seam can take the pull without breaking.

FABRIC FINISHES

After the yarns have been woven or knitted into fabric, the job is still not complete. Most fabrics require several finishing processes to convert into finished consumer goods. The fabric that comes from the loom or knitting machine is called *greige* or *gray goods*. Some preparatory finishing processes are necessary merely to make gray goods usable. Other finishes may be applied to change the appearance or texture of the fabric and make it more attractive. Still other finishes are used to produce certain characteristics or add desirable qualities of service and durability, thus improving the performance of the fabric.

It is not as important to know how the finishing processes are carried out as it is to know how they affect the fabrics. Following is a list of some of the more important finishing processes and their purpose or effect on the fabric.

Preparatory finishes

- CLEANING: Removes all foreign substances that may still be clinging to the fibers. The fabric may be washed, scoured, or dry-cleaned.
- BLEACHING: Necessary to remove all the natural coloring matter in the fibers so as to obtain clear whites. Even though a fabric is to be dyed, it is essential first to remove the impurities that could interfere with clear, even coloring. Most bleaching is done chemically, using different chemicals for different fibers. Cotton may be bleached by merely washing the fabric and exposing it to the sun. Some linens are "grass bleached" by long exposure to sunlight, air, and moisture.
- SHRINKAGE CONTROL: Processes can be applied to both woven and knit fabrics as a most important finishing treatment. The actual shrinking may be accomplished mechanically, with chemicals, with water, or with steam.

In review:

What is the usual sequence in the manufacture of all cloth?

What are the two types of yarn? Describe each.

How does the length of the fiber affect the appearance of the fabric?

Define: carding, combing, roving.

How does twisting affect the appearance and physical properties of the yarn?

Describe: slub, ratine, bouclé.

How is crepe produced? stretch yarn? bulk yarn?

Define ply.

What is the difference between simple yarn and blended yarn? between blending and combining?

What are the four processes by which fabric is made? Describe each.

Define: warp, weft, filling, selvage.

What is thread count? How does it affect the appearance and quality of the fabric?

Describe and cite examples of each of the following: plain weave, basket weave, rib weave, leno weave.

In what way are the twill weave and satin weave similar? different?

Describe pile weaving, figure weaving, and double weaving. Examples.

How does knitting differ from weaving?

Describe the difference between warp knit and weft knit. Cite examples of items in which each is used.

What is double knit?

What are advantages of knit fabrics over woven? disadvantages?

Describe the three methods of producing stretch fabrics. What are advantages and disadvantages of each?

- **LABELING**: F.T.C. rulings concerning the labeling of shrinkage approve the use of the terms *shrunk* or *preshrunk*, but the label must also state the amount of residual shrinkage or how much more the fabric can be expected to shrink. Sanforizing, for instance is a patented mechanical shrinkage control process used on cotton and linen that guarantees an item will not shrink more than 1%.
- **SINGEING**: Removes any unwanted substance—lint, threads, fuzz, or fiber ends—from fabric, leaving a smooth surface. This is accomplished by passing fabric rapidly through a flame.
- **CALENDERING**: Smooths and presses the fabric by passing it through heated rollers. This is actually an ironing process. The result is a flat, smooth surface. It may also impart a luster to the fabric.
- **TENTERING**: Restores irregular cloth to the proper, even dimensions by using steam to stretch it and shrink it where necessary. Pins or clips attached to the selvage edges hold the fabric in the correct position as it passes through the tentering machine. Perhaps you have noticed tiny holes in the selvage of some fabrics. These are marks the pins make. When properly done this process also sets the lengthwise and crosswise yarns at right angles to each other. If the fabric starts through the machine with the yarns not at right angles, the finished fabric will be off-grain.
- **CRABBING**: A process similar to tentering, used on wool fabric to set the

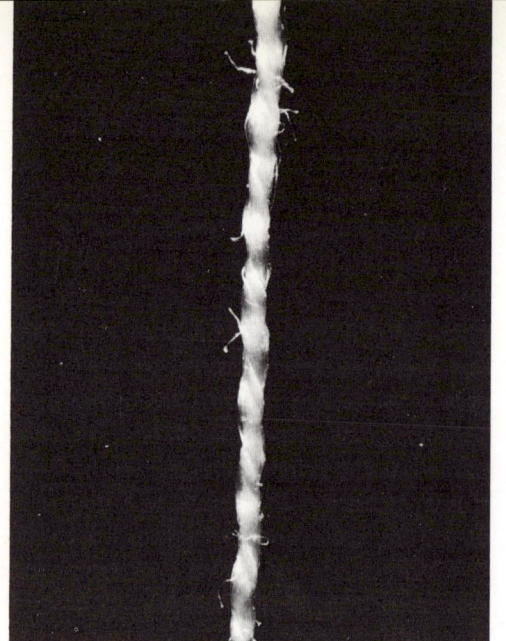

Mercerized yarn. U.S.D.A. Photograph *Non-mercerized yarn.*

width and position of the yarns. The fabric passes over the rollers—first through steam and then into cold water; then it is pressed.

Finishes that Affect Appearance

- MERCERIZING: As previously noted, is a chemical process used to produce

---

Learn More About Fabric Finishes

Compare samples of bleached and unbleached muslin. Note the differences.

Identify the trade names of shrinkage control processes.

Interpret residual shrinkage figures into the number of inches a certain size fabric or garment may shrink.

Test sample fabrics for shrinkage by laundering them in hot, soapy water. Compare the measurements of the washed sample with those of unwashed samples.

---

luster in cotton and linen. It also strengthens the fibers and makes them more absorbent. This process may take place in either the yarn or fabric stage. The yarn or fabric is treated under tension in a caustic soda solution, rinsed, exposed to a warm acid bath, rinsed again, and dried.

- SIZING: A substance added to a fabric to give additional firmness, weight, and stiffness. This may be a temporary soluble starch that washes out, or with a permanent chemical sizing that lasts for the life of the garment. NOTE: Soluble sizing is frequently used to disguise poor-quality, loosely woven fabric. The starch fills in the openings, giving the fabric the appearance of being compact and closely woven.

- NAPPING: Creates the opposite effect from singeing. It produces a fluffy, soft-textured fabric by brushing up the fiber ends that extend out from the surface of the cloth. The nap is raised by passing the cloth over a revolving cylinder covered with fine metal teeth. Cotton and wool flannels and wool broadcloths are examples of fabrics finished with the napping process. NOTE: Do not confuse the napped fabrics with fabrics of pile-weave construction. *Nap* is merely surface fuzziness created by brushing. *Pile* is depth or thickness produced by extra yarns.

- SHEARING: A process that cuts the thread ends of both napped and pile fabrics to an even length so that the surface is smooth and regular. The fabric passes through a shearing machine that operates much like a lawn mower.
- SUEDING: A variation of brushing and napping in which the fiber ends are sheared very close to the surface of the fabric.
- CREPE EFFECTS: Usually not permanent—can be created by certain chemical finishing processes. For instance, to create plissé, cotton fabric is printed with caustic soda. When the fabric dries the part covered with soda shrinks, causing the other areas to pucker. The result is a fabric resembling seersucker.
- EMBOSSING: Produces textured effects on the surface of the fabric. The cloth is run through heated, engraved rollers and the design is transferred from the roller to the cloth. This process can be used on any fabric except wool. It is permanent on fabrics made from thermoplastic fibers and can be made permanent on other fabrics by setting the design with a resin finish.
- DYEING AND PRINTING: Processes by which color is added to fabric. Dyeing may be done at any of the three stages of fabric construction—to the fibers (stock-dyed), to the yarns (yarn-dyed) or, after weaving, to the fabric (piece-dyed). In the *dyeing process* the substance is immersed in a solution so that the dye completely saturates it. Some of the man-made fibers are dyed in the solution stage before it is forced through the spinneret to form filaments. A solution-dyed fabric such as this is said to have a sealed-in color because the dye is part of the filament itself.

Several different types of dyes are used for fabric. They may be classified according to their origin as *natural* (those obtained from plant, animal, and mineral sources), *artificial* (coal tar derivatives), and *synthetic* (chemicals). Some dyes have an affinity for certain fibers but do not react well with others. Some are susceptible to fading in sunlight or laundering; others are damaged by dry-cleaning agents, gas fumes, perspiration, and other hazards. Beauty of color is an important consideration, but color fastness is of greater importance. No color is absolutely fadeproof, but a dye should be colorfast to the ordinary conditions of daily use. Vat dyes—referring to dye that is insoluble in water, not to the use of a vat or tank in the dyeing process—are the most resistant to sunlight and washing. The dye is rendered soluble by a chemical process, the fabric is soaked in the dye solution, and exposure to air and steam converts the dye back to its insoluble state, locking the color into the fiber.

- PRINTING: The process by which patterns or color designs are applied to fabric. Printed surfaces can be distinguished from those that have been dyed by examining both sides of the

J. P. Stevens and Co., Inc.

The artist's drawing board is the "beginning of a fabric." Here the design or pattern is created.

fabric. When a fabric is printed there is a definite right and wrong side because the color seldom penetrates completely. As a result the design is not as distinct on one side, whereas dye colors are the same on both sides of the fabric.

When a pattern is *woven in*, using threads of different colors, the design is always straight with the threads of the fabric. A fabric printed with stripes or geometric patterns may not have the pleasing effect of the woven pattern if the design is not printed straight.

Color prints are made by direct printing or by the discharge or extract method. In direct printing, the color is applied by passing the cloth through engraved rollers, one roller for each color in the design.

Screen printing is another direct printing method done by hand. A frame containing a fine mesh is used. The mesh is covered with lacquer and the design etched in the lacquer. The frame is placed on top of the fabric and the dye poured on and forced through the openings in the lacquer, thus printing the design on the fabric. This method can be used to print knit fabrics which would stretch from the pressure of rollers.

In the *discharge* method, the fabric is first piece-dyed, and then the design is made by bleaching or removing the color from the spots that form the pattern.

Learn More About Appearance Finishes

Compare mercerized and non-mercerized threads for appearance and strength.

Examine cotton fabrics of different price ranges to determine the presence of sizing. Wash fabrics that contain sizing and compare with unwashed samples of the same fabric.

Test sample fabrics for colorfastness to washing according to the following methods:

- *Launder a sample of colored fabric and compare it with the original fabric that has not been laundered.*
- *Sew a sample of colored fabric to a piece of white cloth, wash it, and check for bleeding onto the white cloth.*
- *Immerse a sample of colored fabric into water containing bleach or strong compounds similar to those used in a commercial laundry. Compare with the original fabric that has not been laundered.*

Test sample fabrics for colorfastness to dry-cleaning by using a launderometer and dry-cleaning solvents.

Test sample fabrics for colorfastness to light by one of the following methods:

- *Cover half a piece of fabric with opaque paper. Expose the other half to outdoor light for two weeks. Compare both halves.*
- *Expose sample fabrics in a fadeometer for definite periods of time, depending upon the amount of exposure the fabric would receive in normal usage.*

Test sample fabrics for colorfastness to crocking by rubbing the dry fabric against a white cloth. Repeat the test with a wet piece of the fabric. Notice whether the color rubs off on the white cloth.

Test sample fabrics for fastness to perspiration by soaking each sample in a weak acetic acid solution for 10 minutes. Roll it in a piece of undyed cloth and permit it to dry gradually. Check for dye on the undyed cloth.

Finishes That Improve Performance

- WRINKLE RESISTANCE: Processes have been developed that make cottons, linens, and spun rayons resistant to creasing or wrinkling. The same treatment—which consists of the application of synthetic resin to the fabric—imparts other special properties, including resistance to perspiration, odor, and mildew as well as improved wash-and-wear qualities. Any fabrics treated with a crease or wrinkle resistant finish maintain a fresh look for long periods of time and require little or no ironing after laundering.

There are some minus factors in that the fabric will not be as absorbent, static electricity may accumulate, and grease and oil stains will be difficult to remove.

Some examples include: "Regulated," "Disciplined," "Wrinklshed."

- WATER-REPELLENT: Finishes do not make fabrics absolutely waterproof, but they do keep the fabric from absorbing water. Such substances as resins, waxes, or oils are used to coat the fabric. Water repellent fabrics are still porous, so are comfortable to wear. To make fabric waterproof, it must be coated with a rubber or plastic which closes the pores, making the fabric uncomfortable to wear.

Some examples include: Zelan, Cravenette.

- MOTHPROOFING: Chemicals can be applied to wools or wool blends to protect the fabric from damage by moths. This gives a permanent finish that lasts for the usable life of the fabric. It withstands washing and dry-cleaning.

Some examples include: "Mitin," "Eulan."

- INSULATION: Finishes that add warmth to a fabric without weight. Metallic particles, usually aluminum, are sprayed on the fabric. This coating keeps body heat in by reflecting it back and prevents both heat and cold from entering. The *milium treatment*, as it is called, is used for lining fabrics both for wearing apparel and for window draperies.

- STAIN-RESISTANT: Finishes are of two kinds. Silicone resins protect the fabric from water-borne stains as well as impart water repellency. Another type of chemical finish has been developed that protects the fabric from both water-borne and oil-borne stains.

Some examples include: Unisec, Sylmer, Zepel, and Scotchgard.

The Fabric Story Today and Tomorrow

- WASH-AND-WEAR: The quality that means quick drying and little or no ironing, may exist because of the fiber content of the fabric or because of a chemical finish applied to a fabric. 100% synthetic fibers and blends that contain over 50% of a synthetic fiber produce fabrics with wash-and-wear qualities. Cotton, when treated with chemical resins, gains wash-and-wear characteristics.

  Some examples include: Ban-Care, Belfast

- DURABLE PRESS: An absolutely no-iron, permanently pressed finish that can be applied to blends of cotton, rayon, or acetate with polyester or nylon. A chemical finish is first applied to the fabric. Then the fabric itself may be cured—or after a garment is made the fabric may be cured—by baking it in a 350° oven. The heat creates a reaction between the chemical finish and the fabric, causing the finish to be absorbed. The whole process may be likened to the familiar "brown-and-serve" baked goods, which are partially cooked in the bakery and then finished in a second baking process.

  Once a garment is cured it keeps its newly pressed appearance permanently and ironing is never necessary. Styling details such as pleats and creases remain after laundering and the fabric is still smooth and wrinkle free.

  Some examples include: Koratron, Everprest, Super-Crease, Dan-Press, Cone-Prest.

Learn More About Fabric Finishes

Using your knowledge of the physical characteristics of the fibers, determine why animal fibers are naturally resistant to wrinkling, whereas vegetable fibers are not.

Using samples of treated and untreated cloth, test wrinkle resistance by folding the samples several times and fastening them with a clothes pin. Leave overnight. Unfasten and note whether or not wrinkles disappear or hang out.

Experiment by laundering fabrics that have a crease-resistant finish. Determine water temperature, washing procedures, ironing, and special precautions before beginning.

Compare the results of drip-drying, spin-drying, and dryer-drying with a wash-and-wear blouse.

Examine labels from water-repellent finishes for information concerning care and durability of the finish.

Test fabric samples having a spot-resistant finish by subjecting them to both oil and water stains. Determine the effectiveness of the finish.

Determine the permanence of the finish by washing or cleaning the fabrics and again subjecting them to spots and stains. Clean once more.

HINTS FOR HANDLING FABRICS WITH SPECIAL FINISHES

Wash-and-wear

- CARE: May be laundered in the automatic washer with a wash-and-wear cycle or, if the machine can be regulated, for a short wash cycle and a cool rinse. NOTE: Spinning may cause wrinkling.

  Drip-dry, smoothing the seams, collars, cuffs, and edges with the fingers. May also be dried in the automatic dryer if there is a wash-and-wear cycle that ends the drying period with cool air to prevent wrinkling. Remove from the dryer as soon as it stops and place the garment on a hanger. Some touch-up pressing may be necessary.

- SEWING: The finish locks the fibers in place. If the fabric is off-grain, it cannot be straightened. It is also difficult to ease in, so avoid styles with set-in sleeves, curved seams, etc.

Either mercerized or synthetic thread may be used. Use fine needles and fine, sharp pins. Use medium to long machine stitch, and light pressure. A slightly loose tension prevents puckers. Stitch with a steady, smooth speed.

You may use a steam iron, but do not press seams or folds until you are certain they are final. Pressed-in creases are very difficult to remove.

Durable Press

- CARE: Launder in lukewarm water according to the method for the synthetic fiber in the blend. May be washed in the automatic machine, but wash the garment wrong side out to prevent wear at the creases. Pretreat stains with a liquid detergent.

Dry in the automatic dryer to eliminate wrinkles. Remove from the dryer as soon as it stops and place on a hanger. If the garment is hung to drip-dry, some touch-up ironing may be necessary.

- SEWING: Select a simple style with few details. Fabric cannot be eased in, so avoid set-in sleeves, curved seams, etc.

Use mercerized thread, medium to long machine stitch, light pressure, fine machine needle, and as loose a tension as possible.

Ready-to-wear garments are cured after the garment is made, but a fabric for home sewing has to be cured before it reaches the store. Garments made from this fabric cannot be completely "no-iron." The smooth areas of the garment will be wrinkle-free, but seams, folded edges, and creases will not be flat because there is no way to set them.

Alterations are difficult if not impossible because creases in the garment at seam lines and hemlines cannot be removed.

Our scientists are constantly at work—experimenting, conducting research, developing new products, and improving existing products. Many of the fibers on the market today did not even exist ten years ago. What does tomorrow hold?

There may be disposable clothes made from paper or very inexpensive fabric. Throw them away after using them for a dirty work job. If you get caught in a rainstorm, buy a raincoat from a vending machine. It will keep you dry and can be thrown away when the rain stops. Perhaps it will be an unexpected trip out of town for an important meeting. Pick up a "one-wear" paper suit in a machine at the airport on the way to the plane.

Glass fiber clothes will be spotproof and will never wear out. Fabrics that you can wipe clean with a damp cloth will never need washing or ironing. There may be no need for dry-cleaning either, because even wool clothes will go in the automatic washer—and

The Fabric Story Today and Tomorrow

won't have to be pressed. Clothes may be glued together rather than stitched. All this and more may become realities.

The story of fabrics has no ending. With the rapid and constant changes, it is difficult to keep up to date and well informed. Trade associations and many manufacturers issue educational materials that are helpful. Scan newspapers and magazines for textile information articles. Investigate books, pamphlets, and trade journals for available information. Analyze labels for textile information. Keep abreast of the times.

You will find it rewarding because the more you learn the more use you can make of the fabric treasures that are being created for us.

In review:

What is meant by gray goods?

Describe the purpose and effect on the fabric of each of the following finishing processes: cleaning, bleaching, singeing, calendering, tentering, crabbing.

How can shrinkage be controlled?

Why is sizing added to fabric?

What is the difference between nap and pile?

What is sueding?

What is the difference between printing and dyeing?

At what stages of production can dye be applied?

What is vat dye?

What are the two methods of applying pattern to finished fabric?

What are the advantages of woven-in pattern as compared to applied pattern?

What are the disadvantages to wrinkle-resistant fabrics?

In what ways do water-repellent and waterproof fabrics differ?

What are the differences between wash-and-wear and durable press?

Outline general care procedures for durable press.

Chapter 5

Merchandising Clothing—A Fascinating Business

DISTRIBUTION OR "MARKETING"

Moving a product from the producer to the consumer—a process known as distribution—follows certain patterns and may involve many people. The producer or manufacturer makes the product. The manufacturer's agent sells to wholesalers or large retail stores. The wholesaler buys large quantities of the product and resells in smaller quantities to the retailer. (A *distributor* is a wholesaler who has exclusive rights to handle the products of a certain manufacturer in a given territory.) The retailer sells the product in smaller quantities, perhaps only one at a time. Finally, there is the consumer who buys and uses the product.

This process of distribution, also called "marketing" because it involves buying and selling, may involve only one step. In its simplest form the consumer may buy directly from the producer, as in the case of the homemaker who buys vegetables directly from the farmer. Some companies also sell their products directly to consumers through door-to-door salesmen. For instance the Fuller brush man is an American institution, as is the Avon lady. However, most products we obtain indirectly. The product may have been bought and sold many times before it reaches the ultimate consumer. All those who buy and sell the merchandise on its way from producer to consumer—the middlemen—add their mark-up to the cost, but it allows for such large scale production that we pay less than if purchased from a custom manufacturer.

We are primarily interested in the retailing aspect of the distribution process—especially the retail store rather than catalog selling. The retail store is the last link between the producer and the consumer. It is a principal outlet for the manufacturer and the leading source of supply for the consumer. It is important that those preparing for employment in the retailing business understand its scope and are aware of currect trends. To

151

perform any of the retailing operations demands specialized skills and knowledge.

One very important retailing operation—merchandising—deals directly with the selling of products to the consumer; it involves the planning and promotion of the sale as well as the actual selling. Regardless of the size or type of retail store, the merchandising process is the same: the product must be bought, advertised, displayed, sold, and accounted for. The process can be divided into three main parts: (1) control of stock—including buying, planning, and recording; (2) planning of sales promotional events—including advertising and display; and (3) the actual exchange of the product for money.

Over 2½ million people are employed as salespersons in retail businesses. The stores in which they work may vary in size from the small specialty shop that employs only one or two to the department store that employs hundreds. The success of any retail business, regardless of size, depends to a great extent upon its sales personnel. They represent the company to the buying public; they make the sales that are necessary for the store's success. Courteous, efficient service results in satisfied customers and in turn builds a good reputation for the store.

Work of Salesperson

A salesperson may have different duties and responsibilities depending upon the type of merchandise sold and the type of store. Most salespersons make out sales or charge slips, receive payment, make change, and give receipts. They may also be responsible for wrapping or merely sacking purchases. In self-service stores where customers make their own selections, these routine duties—plus perhaps telling customers where to find items and suggesting additional merchandise for sale—may be the extent of their responsibilities. They merely "wait on" customers.

In selling many types of wearing apparel, however, the salesperson's main responsibility is to assist the customer as much as possible. A great deal of time may be spent showing different styles and colors, trying clothes on, suggesting ways of wearing them, pointing out desirable features, and answering questions about construction and care. The successful salesperson creates a desire to buy and helps the customer make a final selection. This requires skill in dealing with customers as well as knowledge of the merchandise.

In addition to these selling responsibilities, salespersons are usually expected to keep the merchandise in order and their working areas neat and clean. In *small stores* they may also be called upon to perform some duties in the other two aspects of merchandising, such as: check in merchandise and put it in stock, mark price tags, take stock counts and inventories, prepare displays and sales promotions, and perhaps even suggest merchandise to be ordered.

The customer consultant

A successful salesperson acts as a customer consultant. He or she performs a service function—to provide the customers with information and guidance in helping them solve their buying problems. He knows his

Distribution or "Marketing"

store—its policies, practices, and services. He knows his customers—their wants, needs, and buying motives. He knows sound selling techniques and how to appeal to the customers so that they will respond by buying. He knows the mechanics of selling and how to perform the routine jobs quickly and efficiently. He also knows his merchandise thoroughly—its qualities and usefulness to customers. In clothing, this knowledge of merchandise includes (1) a good background in *design, color,* and *fabrics;* (2) a knowledge of *fashion, good taste,* and *appropriateness* in dress; and (3) an understanding of *construction* and *quality* of workmanship. All of this background knowledge helps the salesperson perform his primary function—to satisfy the customers.

THE STORE

The American manner of living is constantly changing, so the modern retail stores must reflect these changes. We have come a long way from trading posts, the Yankee peddler, and the general stores of the eighteenth and nineteenth centuries. Retailing today includes stores of all sizes and kinds, each offering different products and services.

The **independent store** is individually owned and operated. It is often

The "dry goods" store of horse-and-buggy days was the forerunner of today's modern department store. Here milady found all her fashion needs—dress goods to fashion her own, the latest ready-made styles, maybe even an import or two, and trimmings galore. The Golden Rule stores represented a true belief in doing one's best for the customer. Today's department store allows return privileges and other conveniences that excel the past.

J. C. Penney Co.

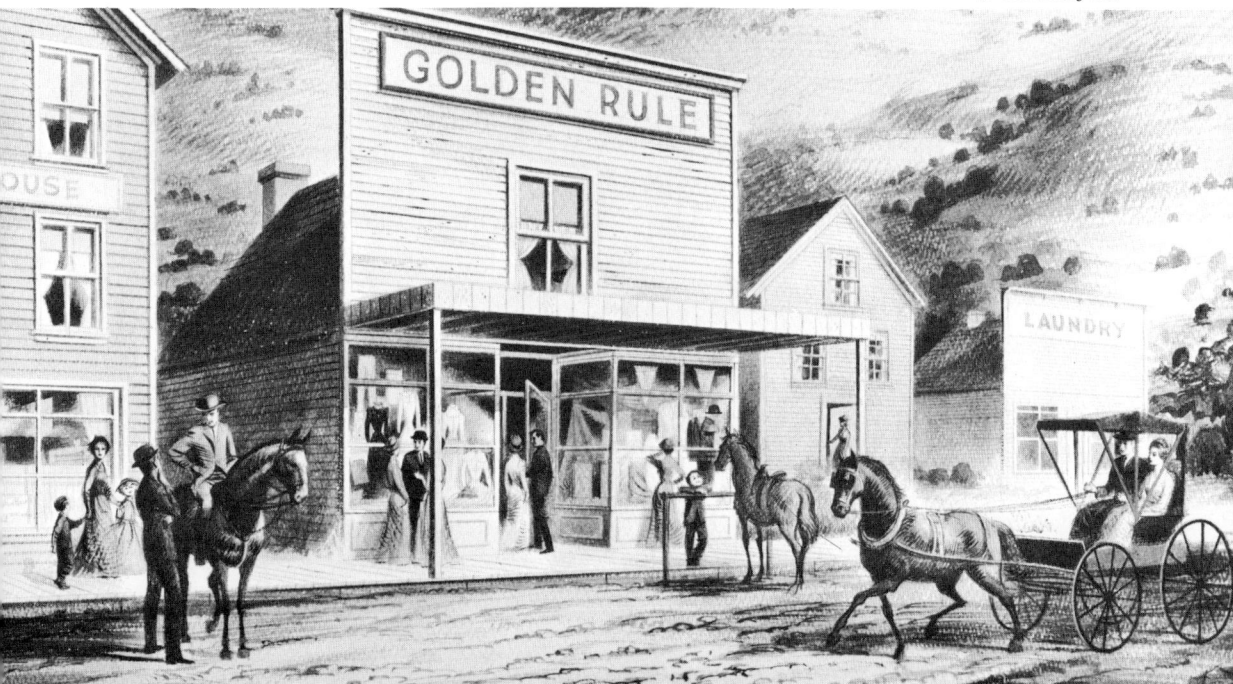

J. C. Penney Co.

Today's modern store is a far cry from the general store of old. One thing remains the same, however—modern woman can still find all her fashion needs, plus much more, under one roof, plus "Golden Rule" service.

small in size, perhaps employing only one or two people. It may even be a one-man operation in which the owner himself performs all the managerial functions. At most, he and his wife operate the business, with no additional employees.

Merchandise is often priced higher in such a store because the volume of busines is low. Merchandise is bought from the wholesaler in small quantities, making the cost higher; in turn, the retail price must be higher in order to realize a profit.

Frequently the customers are well known to the independent store owner. They may even be friends and neighbors, in the case of the neighborhood store. There is a personal contact—personal preferences are catered to and special services are often available. Merchandise may be ordered with a particular customer in mind or especially ordered on the customer's request.

Employment in the somewhat larger independent store offers an excellent opportunity to gain valuable experience because, although small, it still must perform the retailing functions that are common to all stores. Although there is little chance for promotion, one can learn the business and perhaps establish a store of one's own.

In contrast to the small-scale, independently owned stores are **chain stores** that are centrally owned and operated. As few as four stores may constitute a chain, but many large-scale chains have stores numbering in the hundreds.

This type of organization has many advantages. All stores in the chain handle similar merchandise, so buying is simplified. Merchandise is

The Store

Specialty shops, such as this men's clothing store, deal with one line of merchandise. Customers can perhaps find all their clothing needs, from underclothing to accessories, in the one store.

Department Store Journal

bought in large quantities, often directly from the manufacturer instead of through a wholesaler; or produced by the chain using its own brand. Therefore the cost is lower and as a result the consumer price is also lower.

Specialty shops handle only one type of merchandise; for example, children's clothing, men's furnishings, women's clothing, or perhaps they specialize in only one specific line, such as ski apparel at a winter resort. They may deal in only a certain price or size range, offering a complete selection in that line. These shops are often small and independently owned. They usually stress customer service. Like the independent store, this type of retailing offers excellent experience. Although the merchandise is limited, the retailing functions of the store are the same.

Variety stores, unlike one-line specialty shops, handle a wide assortment of merchandise, usually in the lower price range. The "five-and-ten" got its name because it handled primarily items that sold from five and ten cents up to a dollar. This is no longer true, although the name still holds.

The trend today is toward an even wider assortment of merchandise, including fashions, food, and furniture. Although dealers have increased the upper price limit, the merchandise may still be classified in the lower price range for any particular type.

Very often in a small community a variety store may be independently owned, but generally it is a part of a large chain, regional or national. The business is mainly cash and carry; the store offers very few customer services. It is usually a self-service operation in which the customers make their own selections without the help of a salesperson. Employees in this type of store usually have no actual selling responsibilities. Rather, they work with stock and act as cashiers and wrappers or sackers.

A **department store,** as already noted, is a combination of many specialty areas in one building, or a group of buildings, operating under a central management. The main store may occupy an entire city block and be several stories high. Along with today's population shift to the suburbs, the downtown stores have established suburban branches which are often smaller versions of the main store.

The forerunner of today's department store was the dry-goods store specializing in textile fabrics and related items. Gradually other kinds of merchandise were added until now almost any item—food, pet supplies,

Department Store Journal
A bridal salon, specializing in clothes for the bride and the wedding party, is an example of the many "specialty shops" that make up the large department store.

auto accessories, or garden supplies, as well as the usual fashions and home furnishings—may be purchased in the large department store. A person can do almost all of his shopping there.

A department store may be independently owned, but often it is connected with an association or a chain to take advantage of the buying and operating practices of that type of organization.

Because of its size the department store can organize each of the retailing activities—buying, advertising, display, selling, operating, and control—in a separate department under the leadership of specialists in each particular field.

However, the need for increased personnel, added supervision, and extended bookkeeping and record keeping that goes with a business of this size increases operating expenses. The large volume of sales in a store of this kind make it possible to obtain merchandise at a good price; however, the increased cost of operating a large business often means that the retail prices are also increased. The department stores have felt competition keenly, and to offset the "higher price" claim, they point up their unique features and strong points:

- A large selection of quality merchandise is available from all over the world.
- Many long-established stores have built a reputation of integrity in the community, so they "stand behind" their merchandise. Some even operate their own testing laboratories for establishing high quality standards.
- They stress customer satisfaction. Customers may shop in a relaxed manner in attractive surroundings.

They receive personal service and assistance with their shopping. There are many extra services available, such as charge accounts and other liberal payment plans, mail and phone ordering, delivery and return privileges, and personal shopping and home selection service. In addition many stores include such departments as appliance and clothing repair, home decorating and remodeling, travel and ticket agencies, rental services, gift wrapping, and restaurants—all with an eye for attracting customers.

In spite of all the services available, there are some who feel that the large department store lacks the personal relationship possible in a smaller store.

Employment opportunities in a large department store are excellent because there are many beginning jobs available—both in selling and non-selling departments—and there are opportunities for advancement. A salesperson may advance to such a position as head of stock, supervisor of a department, department manager, assistant buyer, or buyer. Promotion is usually slow, however, unless the person has the background and training that prepare him for a better job or has been specifically hired with executive training in mind.

Discount stores have given the department store perhaps its keenest competition. They too offer a wide variety of merchandise, but no specialty service. Often they are located in a low-rent area, in a simply constructed building resembling a warehouse inside and out, and usually have large parking facilities. Merchandise is arranged for availability, not attractiveness—crowded on racks or shelves and often merely stacked

Self-service is the rule at discount stores. All the merchandise available is displayed on racks and counters. Customers make their own selections and pay for them at the cashier's lane.

on the floor. Because of low overhead, the discount store may undersell those stores with expensive services and surroundings. They stress self-service, cash and carry, and low prices. They depend upon a large turnover of stock, at a low mark-up price, to produce profit.

NOTE: Credit may be used to stimulate business in discount stores. They may have "charge-it" days with special low-price items ("leaders"). Cash is not accepted, so as to establish a large number of steady, credit customers.

Mail-order houses offer "at-home" shopping for those who prefer. Originally designed for the rural customer who could not get to the city store, mail-order houses are now being used by anyone who prefers to shop at home. The customer selects merchandise from a catalog, orders by mail, usually sending payment with the order, and receives the merchandise by mail or express. Not only can credit and installment terms be arranged, but most reputable mail-order houses include a money-back guarantee, or substitute of superior products, if the merchandise is not satisfactory or is out of stock.

Regardless of the type or size of the store, you see that they all have certain activities in common. **Remember,** the way in which the store is organized to perform these activities, however, does vary. In the small store, they may all be performed by one person, but the complex store is organized into specialized departments according to the type of activity. Also, the process of running the store is divided into three kinds of work: buying, selling, and operating or controlling.

In a one-man business, *buying* may be done in an informal, sometimes even haphazard manner. The store owner checks items that are low in stock or that he is out of, perhaps just by glancing at the shelves. He may make a mental note of the items customers request that he doesn't have. Then perhaps he fills in an order sheet and sends it to the wholesaler or orders directly from a salesman who stops at the store. Often there is little formal thought or pre-planning, because the proprietor knows his stock so well.

In a large retailing operation, *buying* must be very carefully planned and executed. First the customers the store serves are studied—their interests, their likes and dislikes, even their education and financial standing. A knowledge of customers' wants and buying habits as well as past sales records help to determine what type of merchandise and how much of it to buy. Then a carefully prepared budget determines the amount of money to be spent for each type of merchandise. Through past experience, this is broken down further into the amount to be spent or number of items to be purchased for each price range, size, color, etc. Possessing a great deal of knowledge and experience, a buyer, who is a specialist in a particular field, is then ready to purchase merchandise according to the plans. If he did not, the risk would be enormous, since so much has to be purchased. He may buy from salesmen or go directly to the market source—perhaps even abroad if nec-

Department Store Economist

This window display, designed to promote the sale of fabrics, is both eye-catching and informative. The way the fabrics are grouped suggests ways of coordinating them and the models show them made up in appropriate pattern styles. A special fabric finish is featured, emphasizing the special qualities of the featured fabrics.

essary—where he can make the best buys in the type of merchandise suitable for his customers and at the price he wishes to pay.

Remember, the main reason for a store's existence is to sell merchandise; all other functions—including buying—are important only as they relate to *selling. Personal selling* therefore directly involves the salesperson and, as we have noted, the responsibilities of the salesperson vary depending upon the type and size of the store. In addition, advertising and display both play a part in selling merchandise. They are classified as *non-personal selling* activities.

Besides mail campaigns, TV, radio, and printed advertising, a window or counter display may catch the customer's eye and "sell" that particular item. Special events such as fashion shows are also non-personal display techniques.

There are many store activities that have no direct relationship to the selling of merchandise but are necessary to the *operation* or *control* of any business. Store *maintenance*—general cleaning, repairs, and upkeep of the building—and security fall in this category. *Supplies* and equipment have to be purchased, personnel have to be hired and trained, merchandise

Department Store Economist

A fashion show is a natural attention-getter for women, so what better way to promote the sale of patterns and fabrics than with a "sewing" fashion show! Very possibly each woman in the audience will be an immediate customer as she sees herself in one of the styles. Holding the show right in the fabric department makes it extra convenient for purchasing.

must be received, marked, and stored, and often the delivery of merchandise is a complicated matter. *Records* of accounts must be kept, so that the state of business is always up to date. The *extra customer services* that may be provided such as lounges, check rooms, restaurants, information desks, etc., though not absolutely necessary for business, add to the shopper's convenience so in turn help business. All of these things are in turn grouped together as operating activities.

Customers learn to associate stores with certain policies—"It's a pleasure doing business there," or, "You can always find what you want at _____," or, "They are difficult to deal with when something isn't satisfactory." Every store builds an image in the minds of customers; it is this image that attracts some and causes others to avoid shopping there. The services offered, the atmosphere and physical appearance, the quality and type of merchandise handled are all responsible. Not all people place the same value on things. To some the physical characteristics are important—spaciousness, tasteful decor, air conditioning, etc. To others, this means little, but buying at discount prices is appealing. Therefore the type of customer that *generally* accepts a store is also a part of a store's image.

The Store

To get back to selling, the type of personnel employed in a store is a strong contributing factor to its image. The salesperson represents the store to the public. Increasing importance is being placed on professional attitude and manner. The hiring and training of personnel are geared toward achieving "professional" employees who possess not only the knowledge and skill for selling, but also pride in a job well done and a loyalty toward their work. Your attitude toward people and your work, your manner of behavior and personality, even your appearance and manner of dress are all a part of your professional manner.

All personnel, including those who work out the displays, contribute to the image.

Some stores outline definite dress codes which they expect their employees to follow. A business-like appearance creates a favorable appearance. Salespersons, especially those working with clothing, should dress "quietly" so that they emphasize rather than detract from the merchandise. Impress the customer with

The atmosphere of this department—a feeling of spaciousness, an uncluttered look, and the elegant decor—creates an impression of luxury and prestige. Appearances in this case suggest higher-priced merchandise.

Department Store Journal

Merchandising Clothing—A Fascinating Business

your courtesy and ability, rather than call attention to your wearing apparel. Follow these guides to help you achieve a professional look:

Wear:

    Tailored dresses, suits, or separates—well fitting, clean, pressed, and in good repair.

    Pleasant, subtle colors—dark in preference to pastel, subdued in preference to bright.

    Comfortable street shoes—polished and in good repair.

    Stockings.

    Simple hair style and make-up—clean and well-groomed.

Don't wear:

    Extreme styles.
    Low necklines.
    Tight sweaters.
    Cocktail-type dresses.
    Transparent fabrics.
    Bright prints and plaids.
    Casual play shoes.

Some other points to remember that will help you achieve a professional manner include:

    Use simple, correct English.
    Learn the right terms for your department.
    Avoid slang expressions.
    Speak distinctly.
    Keep the tone of your voice pleasant—soft, well-modulated.
    Don't chew gum.
    Avoid "standing around" with the other salespersons.
    Be pleasant and cooperative with your co-workers.
    Don't complain or criticize—especially in front of customers.

In review:

What are the steps a product follows from producer to consumer?

What is meant by merchandising? Explain the three phases of the merchandising process.

Explain the difference between "waiting on" customers and selling.

What are main differences between independent stores and chain stores?

How do the retailing operations differ in a small store from those in a department store?

List important services provided by retail stores.

What main factors are instrumental in building a store's image?

For further discussion:

Economic and social factors involved in distribution.

Advantages of competition and the free enterprise system.

Contemporary trends in retailing.

The organization of retail stores.

Factors that determine store policy.

Customer services.

SOUND SELLING TECHNIQUES

Real salesmanship is more than handing merchandise across the counter. Nor is it high-pressure selling. It involves giving customers personal service by finding merchandise that best suits their needs and desires. It means *opening doors* for customers, but not *forcing them through*.

A successful salesperson acquires skill in dealing with customers, which in turn results in sales. From the moment a person enters a store or a particular department, the relationship between that person and the salesperson can make the difference between a satisfied or a dissatisfied customer—between a sale and "no-sale."

Compare yourself with a hostess, performing much the same service in the store as you do for a guest in your home. As a hostess you greet your guests pleasantly when they arrive, you endeavor to make their visit worthwhile by pursuing subjects or engaging in activities in which they are interested, you make them feel you sincerely enjoyed spending time with them, and you invite them to return soon. Good salesmanship uses the same techniques: approach the customer, determine her needs and present merchandise that will satisfy those needs, complete the sale. Just as a guest in your home enjoys her visit and is eager to return, your customers should be pleased with their purchases and your service. More than that, good salesmanship not only increases your sales but results in satisfied customers who come back again and again to your store and you.

Everyday you will come in contact with all kinds of people—most of them very pleasant, but some will naturally try your patience. Practice courtesy at all times, even with the difficult customers. No matter how exasperating the situation, nothing is gained by being rude or disrespectful. Put yourself in the customer's place. Use the Golden Rule. Think of yourself in the customer's place. You will find it much less annoying, regardless of the person's manner or appearance. In all of your relationships, strive to convey the feeling of wanting to help. *It makes your work mean something to you.*

Your attitude reveals your feelings sometimes even more clearly than

Don't you feel that her neat, well-groomed appearance and friendly, warm manner are bound to appeal to customers?
Department Store Economist

Merchandising Clothing—A Fascinating Business

what you say. The customer can sense a semblance of disrespect or a feeling of superiority, no matter how successfully you may feel you are concealing it. It has a way of showing through. Perhaps it is the tone of your voice (sarcastic), your facial expression (a raised eyebrow), an unconscious, bad comment (It's too expensive for you?), or a revealing gesture (a shrug of the shoulder).

Why be a salesperson if you don't sell anything? It is fun to sell! It is an empty life if you just stand there, wishing you were someplace else.

Not every customer contact ends in an immediate sale, but each contact is an opportunity to establish good will for both you and the store and perhaps results in future sales. A sale made merely for the "sale's sake" may mean the merchandise will be returned and the customer is dissatisfied. Dissatisfied customers do not return. To build a following of steady customers, remember these points in all of your customer contacts:

People like to be made to feel important.

People are mainly interested in themselves. Talk to them about themselves—"you" and "yours," not "I" and "mine."

Get them to talk. Listen attentively and glance at them often as you work.

Agree with them. (If that is not possible, don't disagree!)

Be tactful and considerate of their feelings.

Display genuine enthusiasm, but do not sound like a fake.

Do not force a sale against someone's will.

Give customers your undivided attention, one at a time.

Always be alert to their comfort and convenience.

Be as courteous, patient, sincere, and interested as you can.

Here are suggestions to help you carry out the above, which may seem difficult on the surface:

• **Remember,** a sale may be made or lost in the customer approach even before any merchandise is shown. Think of the customer as a friend. Welcome the person with a smile and a warm, friendly greeting, and by name, if you know it. Add some pertinent remark. "Good morning, Mrs. Brown. Did you enjoy your trip?" She's flattered to think you remembered. People react positively when they are made to feel important. *To repeat*, learn to recognize them and call them by name. What you say isn't as important as the way you say it. Show that you are happy to see them and are genuinely interested, but avoid being overly familiar or solicitous. They will sense your attitude immediately. A pleasant, sincere manner starts the sale on the way to success.

• Customers appreciate prompt attention, but avoid what may appear to be "pouncing on them" as soon as they enter. Time the approach to advantage, perhaps as they near a display or start to examine some merchandise. If they pause to look at a garment, there is a glimmer of interest. Use this as an opening and include a reference to it in your ap-

Sound Selling Techniques

proach. "Good afternoon. That's one of the new spring pastels. It is quite popular."

• Avoid such overused phrases as "May I help you?" or "Is there something I can do for you?" They are cold and impersonal remarks with little meaning. How much more sensible to talk to the customer about the merchandise rather than distracting her with a question that might drive her away. Such a question as "May I help you?" has a slightly superior tone to it, implying, "I know more than you do; therefore I am more important." Such a question also gives an opportunity to reply negatively—"No thank you, just looking"—and disregard you completely. Always phrase a question so that the other person must judge an item as favorably as possible.

• Encourage the customer to look —her interest may be aroused by something she sees. Perhaps the most common complaints about salespersons are at opposite extremes: Either, "You can never find a salesperson when you want one," or, "Salespeople never leave you alone." If the customer indicates an interest just in looking, assure him or her that you are happy about it. Then leave the person alone—don't hover around. You may have a better chance of making a sale if the customer can examine merchandise freely at leisure. Be on the alert, however, for any indication that the person is ready for assistance and approach again at this time. In that way you will not annoy by either pestering or ignoring a person.

• Take time to acknowledge the presence of someone else who is waiting, even if you are already busy with a customer.

If you are busy with something other than another customer, leave it as promptly as possible to give your attention to the customer. Never be guilty of ignoring a waiting customer while you engage in a personal conversation, arrange merchandise, or busy yourself with such similar activities. Never tell the customer curtly "I'm busy." Stop what you are doing and give the customer prompt attention. A neglected customer, or one spoken to impolitely, builds up antagonism. The person may become angry and leave.

• Knowing what merchandise to show is an important selling technique. Find out what the customer wants. When you greet him or her, the person will probably tell you. If not, ask. Then try to find out why the customer wants to buy. If a lady, where is she going to wear it? Is there a special occasion? Try to determine how much she wants to spend. Does she have a particular color preference? Draw out the information by asking a few pertinent questions, if necessary, but avoid a rapid-fire cross-examination. Let her tell you what *she* wants. Note that the same is true for men, especially if they are buying shirts. They may depend on you a lot for ties or jewelry. If buying women's things, they generally need much help!

Start with what the customer asks for. If he or she knows exactly what is wanted and you have it, a sale is made with little effort on your part. Note, however, that if you don't have the specific item, you may still be able to "sell" the customer. Don't stop at,

Merchandising Clothing—A Fascinating Business

"Sorry, we don't have any." Suggest a substitute, being sure the article you suggest is, as good as, if not better than the requested item and will serve the same purpose. In no way should you imply that the requested item is inferior.

• If a customer is in doubt about what is wanted, you must make suggestions. If you know the customer, you may have learned through experience the desired color, style, etc. and what may suit best. You know the type and price range of merchandise bought in the past. You can call upon past experience to select a good buy, a particular fondness, or a certain manufacturer. If you don't know the person, follow the leads that are given you and try to "figure out" likes and dislikes so that you can show merchandise that will be interesting.

• A "just-looking" customer may be persuaded to buy something that fills a need or satisfies a desire. Encourage the person to look, but first you can do some selling. Mention the advertised merchandise, call attention to an unusual value, point out the "new arrivals," etc. A timely suggestion may be all that is needed to persuade.

• **Remember,** learn to know your customers—their wants and needs, their likes and dislikes. This selling suggestion pays in two ways. You will increase your sales because you will be able to satisfy the customer. You will also build a following of regular customers. You have made them feel important because you remember them, and they in turn will remember you. You learn to know the customers by looking and listening.

• Observe the customer. The clothes a woman or girl is wearing are a clue to her taste—tailored or feminine, conservative or gay, etc. **Caution:** You can get an idea of her preferences in clothing, but avoid the pitfall of making snap judgments on appearance alone. The way a person is dressed may have nothing to do with her ability to buy. You may be tempted to feel a person can't afford something because she isn't well-dressed, but you have no definite way of knowing and must be careful not to imply such a feeling.

• Encourage the customer to look, and then be alert to the person's reactions to everything. What colors attract? What styles are rejected? Does the customer check labels, indicating an interest in care or durability? How about the price tag? Note facial expressions, a nod of approval, a pause or flipping something aside. Watch the eyes and take note of what makes them interested. The way a lady handles a garment, or holds it up for a look in the mirror or keeps going back to it, all indicate an interest.

• Encourage the customer to talk and then listen attentively to what is said. This will tell you wants, needs, desires, likes, and dislikes. Listen between the lines too, because what people say and what they mean are often quite different. "I don't like anything *too* unusual," may mean "I really do, but I'm a little afraid to wear it." The customer may be looking for encouragement and really wants to be convinced that he or she is doing the right thing. A good listener can usually find clues for knowing people better.

| Philippe Bodinat for Laurence Gross | Ole Borden for Rembrandt | Wilson Folmar | Martin Friedricks for Henry Friedricks | Victor Joris for Cuddlecoat |

15 Americans line up for Miss Bergdorf. What makes the best young talents in America run for their designing pads? None other than that fabulous all-American creature who runs on not-so-standard time, our own Miss B. And what have these 15 gifted Americans done just for her? Nothing less than a super, streamlined collection that belongs to no other girl in the whole fashion world. All you see here and more, more. On Floor Five. Now. **BERGDORF GOODMAN**
ON THE PLAZA • NEW YORK   5TH AVENUE AT 58TH STREET

| Kasper for Joan Leslie | David Kidd for Barberini | John Mullen for Arkay | Alan Philips for Gino Charles | Shannon Rodgers for Jerry Silverman |
| Gunther Ruecker for Ginala | Pat Sandler for Highlight | Elinor Simmons for Malcolm Starr | Don Simonelli for Modelia | Philippe Tournaye for Modelia |

Vogue

This advertisement promoting designer fashions appeared in a nationally circulated magazine as part of one store's special promotion. Make use of special aides such as this spread—refer to them, mention the magazine by name, and suggest the featured merchandise—to increase your sales.

Merchandising Clothing—A Fascinating Business

• What price merchandise to show may present a problem. Price can be a sore subject—a source of embarrassment to customers. Few people like to admit, "I can't pay that much," because it tends to make them feel inferior. Actually, those who do admit it are usually the ones who can afford to pay the price. Most people will pretend they have some other reason for wanting to see something else. Listen carefully to what the customer says and how it is said. With practice you can develop the ability to "hear" between words for the true meaning.

—Start with merchandise in the medium price range. Then you can move up or down without embarrassment to anyone. Watch the customer's reaction. If the person checks the price tag, drops the item, and asks "What else do you have?" look for lower priced merchandise. Show this with the same amount of enthusiasm and interest, and tactfully remove the higher priced item from consideration as quickly as possible.

—A lady customer may indicate that the price is higher than she wants to pay, but still seems hesitant to put the item down. Perhaps she continues to examine it, handling it fondly. Maybe she admires herself in it, removing it slowly and reluctantly. She may look at other merchandise, but keeps coming back to it. Even though it is more than she wants or intended to pay, she probably can afford it. She is trying to justify paying more. She wants a reason to ease her conscience and to convince herself she isn't being extravagant. You may be able to provide the reason with some comment about its advantages—"You'll be able to wear it for many seasons" or "The color goes so well with so many things." Undoubtedly true!

—If the price of an item doesn't meet with any objections, don't hesitate to show some higher-priced items also. The customer might pay a higher price if convinced of its advantages. Call attention to the better quality fabric, higher fashion, better construction and workmanship, style details, greater durability, etc. This goes for men as well as women. Concentrate on the price range you feel the customer can afford. However, remember that most customers aren't interested in the least expensive merchandise but in the best value for the money.

• How much merchandise to show can also influence the sale. Show all that is necessary to satisfy the customer—all that is available, if necessary—but only a few articles at a time. Two or three are sufficient to give the customer a selection; too much at once may only confuse or discourage the sale. If no interest is expressed in an item, take it away and replace it with another. When something pleases, there is no need to show any more. Let the customer feel, however, that you are happy to show all you can until you find something satisfactory. By quickly determining the customer's wants, you should be able to select wisely and not have to show everything. Perhaps the customer will purchase the first item shown, but will be better satisfied with an opportunity to compare other merchandise.

• The mechanics of displaying and handling the merchandise can increase the possibility of a sale. Your reaction and enthusiasm toward mer-

Sound Selling Techniques

Know These Points

Appearance: *color, texture, design.*

Appropriateness: *occasion, time and place, season, customer's wants and needs.*

Becomingness: *for customer's figure, coloring, personality, taste.*

Comfort

Convenience: *easy-care, wear often.*

Durability: *practical, strong.*

Quality: *fabric, workmanship, special, general.*

Style: *simplicity, classic, fashion-right.*

---

chandise as you display it influences the customer. Always handle it with pride and care, and show it effectively. Show each item separately, holding it up or apart from other merchandise, and take time to emphasize any unique selling point. Use your hands—point to features, drape the fabric, demonstrate a style detail.

• **Know what you are saying.** The more effectively you make your points as you display and describe the merchandise, the more you create a desire to buy. A customer doesn't like to be pressured, but she does want honest information and intelligent guidance. • Talk enough to show that you are interested, but not so much that you appear to be pushing the sale. Let the customer help. Follow her lead and emphasize fit, style, color, comfort, or care depending upon her indicated interest. Ask her opinion. She may have some ideas you haven't thought of. Answer her questions intelligently and honestly. Tell her what the merchandise will do for her: "This coat will cut down your cleaning bills because it can be wiped clean with a damp cloth." Point out the advantages of the merchandise: "This shirt will never need ironing." If there are any disadvantages, point them out: "We cannot guarantee that this coat will clean successfully." The honesty of such an admission will be appreciated.

• Be prepared to meet the customer's objections. Sometimes it is possible to anticipate them and actually answer them before they arise. When they do arise, however, they deserve careful consideration, skillful handling, and an honest, direct answer. Often they can be turned into selling points by saying something that makes a reason for buying: "Thin, soft winter wools are really in this year," or give the question another meaning: "Yes, the fabric is soft, but a firmer fabric would not drape so becomingly."

Check Your Selling IQ

What do you do if your customer requests a color that is not becoming to her? (Show her another? Agree, but still suggest something else? Pretend the color isn't in this season?)

What do you say to a customer who likes knits, but says they are not flattering to her figure? (Suppose she is correct? Wrong?)

What do you do if a customer likes a style, but it is not becoming to her? (Criticize the style? Say it isn't right for her or him?)

What do you do if a garment does not fit well, needs too many alterations?

What do you do if there is a flaw or defect in a garment?

Merchandising Clothing—A Fascinating Business

Most customers, either consciously or unconsciously, are looking for reasons why they should buy. Even when they know exactly what they want, your reasons are needed to make them feel they are doing the right thing. Support the customer's reasons for buying—mention the item's appeal and benefits so that the person feels good about taking it.

- **Good timing** is essential to closing the sale successfully. The best psychological moment to take definite action is when the customer is "ready." Watch a lady customer for some indication—she brightens, she expresses enthusiastic *satisfaction*, she raises no more objections, she isn't interested in seeing any other merchandise—note some such action, remark, or expression. The alert salesperson senses the customer's readiness or satisfaction and practices techniques, designed to help in the final step, so that she says, "I'll take it." You don't push the customer into the sale, but your comments can be instrumental in helping her make a positive decision—*if you really think it is best for her.*

Sometimes a customer has difficulty reaching a decision. You may lose a sale unless you learn to help. Often only reassurance is needed. Sum up the reasons why not to purchase and weigh these against the reasons for purchasing. This process can help the person think through the purchase, helps relieve doubts, and may bring a definite decision. **Remember,** you want to narrow down the choices, not show things for hours.

- The method used to bring the sale to a close varies with the customer and the type of merchandise. All through the sales transaction you have concentrated on producing affirmative feelings. If you have paved the way well, the closing will be natural—just another in a *series* of affirmative decisions. Don't try too hard or be too obvious. The customer will sense any hint of anxiety; an overanxious attitude may kill the sale. Here are some suggestions for bringing the sale to a successful close:

Closing Suggestions

Rather than let the sale depend upon one item, provide a choice between "this" and "that." Then instead of deciding simply yes or no, the problem becomes "which one."

- **Then ask primary questions** that require "Yes" answers: "You feel the green one looks best on you, don't you?" "Doesn't it go well with your coloring? It brings out the color of your eyes."
- Next, assume that the customer is going to buy; ask such pertinent questions as, "Which color can you use?" "They come three in a box; is one box sufficient?" "Do you want two or three?" "May I charge it or do you wish to pay cash?" Her answers to these *secondary* questions lead up to the completion of the sale.
- Finally, make suggestions that, if accepted, will also mean the completion of the sale. "The fitter can mark the hem for you." "If you want to wear it, I'll be happy to wrap the one you are wearing and send it for you."
- After the customer makes up her mind, you have an opportunity to suggest an additional purchase. Such suggestive selling can help you increase your sales and the customer

Sound Selling Techniques

will usually welcome suggestions if they are suitable and made in the proper manner. Your *attitude* is very important. The customer must sense that you are showing a genuine interest—not high-pressuring. **Remember,** with a dress, suit or even lesser purchases, other things naturally are needed—accessories of many kinds.

Fitting Room Pointers

When the lady customer is ready to go to the fitting room, ask her to follow you. Don't just point the way and leave her on her own; you lead the way.

Push back the curtain and let the customer enter first.

Hang the clothes on a hook. It's a good idea to take no more than three items into the fitting room at a time. Remove those the customer isn't interested in or is finished with and bring in others as necessary.

Point out lip tissues, if available, and suggest their use to prevent damage to the merchandise.

Offer your assistance—for opening and closing back zippers, for instance—but generally leave the customer alone to change.

Don't leave the customer unattended for a long period of time, however. Return frequently to offer your assistance and show an interest.

Keep the conversation related to the merchandise and try to limit it to what will promote the sale. Be friendly—but don't waste valuable time "entertaining" customers.

After the customer leaves, remove all clothes from the fitting room.

—Make a definite suggestion; don't merely ask, "Is there anything else?" Put yourself in the customer's place. If you had just made the purchase, what else would you like or need to go with it?—a blouse to go with the suit? jewelry to go with the basic dress? gloves, scarf, or hat to go with the coat? Then be direct. "Let me show you the new smoke ring scarves. They are so attractive on this basic dress."

—Men, too, accept suggestions for a tie, handkerchief, sox.

—Include reasons with the suggestions. The customer may need to be convinced of the advantage of the extra purchase. If your suggestions strike home, the person may immediately think of other reasons for buying accessories.

—Suggest related items by showing them rather than just talking about them, if this is possible. Don't ask, "Would you like a blouse to go with this suit?" Instead, casually show a blouse and make some pertinent comment about how well the two look together. Display a tie with a minimum of talk and let it sell itself. The sight or feel of the merchandise may be enough temptation to persuade.

• *Also,* suggest the advantages of buying an additional quantity, where applicable. In the case of hosiery for example, a simple reference to one stocking "running" before the other suggests the advantage of buying more than one pair.

• **For today and the future,** call customers' attention to advertised merchandise or sale items, letting them know how long prices will last. They may appreciate the opportunity to take advantage of buying at a "good

(Continued on page 173)

Department Store Economist
By showing this half slip, color-coordinated to go with the bra and girdle the customer has just purchased, the salesperson has planted the "desire." The result will probably be a larger sale.

Go-Together Selling Pointers

Companion items—they go together like salt and pepper; sell one, show the other, you may sell both. For example: sell a lady's suit, show a blouse. Sell a fine man's golfing sweater—show a sport shirt.

Complementary merchandise—it will add prestige to the first purchase. For example: appropriate women's accessories, or personalizing tie clasp or cuff links with name or monogram.

Special price—other merchandise at an extra good buy, a special promotion, a clearance. Most people love a bargain.

Convenience items—they will cause great inconvenience when you don't have them—like hosiery, needles, thread, etc. You perform a real service by reminding customers to keep them on hand.

Advertised merchandise—if it is a very desirable item featured in an ad, call it to the attention of each of your customers.

Seasonal items—the many items made-to-order for weather, special events, and holidays (rain and snow, back-to-school, sports, birthdays, etc.). If they buy one, show another. For example: sell a swim suit, show a beach bag or beach coat.

Gift merchandise—customers could keep them on hand for future gifts. Most people are usually pleased to find solutions to their coming gift problems. For example: sell an apron, suggest one to put away for a gift.

Special interest merchandise—those items you show because the customer has talked about a hobby, a trip, etc. The person will usually like to think you have shown an interest. For example: show resort clothing or handy travel kits. **Caution:** Do not seem to force expensive things on the customer, unless asked.

Related merchandise from other departments—items that complement or accessorize the merchandise from your department. For example: sell shoes, suggest hose; sell a suit, suggest jewelry.

Products to use in caring for the merchandise—cleaners, polishes, protecting storage cases, etc. For example; sell gloves, show the special soap for washing them.

Sound Selling Techniques

price." You might even mention merchandise in another department that is being sold at a special price.

• Take advantage of the fact that people are naturally interested in what is new—the fashionable "go-togethers"—and your customers will be particularly interested. You might say "By the way, have you seen the new ____? This goes very well with your purchase."

• After the sale is finished, saying good-bye to the customer should be just as friendly as the approach was. Let the person know you were happy to be of service, say thank you, and express the desire for future meetings. The final remark should be pleasant and sincere. "It was a pleasure to help you; come again." "Thank you. I know you'll enjoy your coat." "Have a pleasant vacation. Stop in when you return." If the customer leaves with a friendly feeling and a good impression, you have further established good will.

• Even if the result is "no-sale," be just as courteous as if there had been a sale. Don't let the customer sense any disappointment or impatience on your part. Assure the person that you are truly sorry you have not been able to satisfy needs at this time. Your continued pleasant manner will impress the customer favorably. It is good for you as a person, as well as for the store, if you leave a good impression. **Remember,** you do not have to gush all over anyone—just be pleasant and courteous.

In review:

Define salesmanship.

How can you best handle a difficult customer?

What do you do if a customer is waiting and you are busy?

How can you determine what merchandise to show a customer?

How can you help persuade a "just looking" customer to buy?

What is a good way to approach the matter of price?

What is the danger in showing too many pieces of merchandise?

List some pointers in showing merchandise to advantage.

How can you handle customer objections?

What is suggestive selling?

For further discussion:

Appropriate dress and behavior for a salesperson.

Customer relationships.

Factors that establish good will; build a following.

Store training programs.

Personal qualifications for successful salesmanship.

Buyer resistance.

"The customer is always right."

To gain experience:

Practice customer approaches; initiating a possible sale; closing the sale; selling a specific item.

Role-play a complete sales transaction; a difficult customer; a "no-sale."

Observe salespeople; make notes of good and poor selling techniques and customer relations. (Do not interfere with the person's work or let others know that you are criticizing or studying sales methods.)

MECHANICS OF SELLING

To complete any transaction, (1) the sale must be recorded, (2) payment must be received or arranged for, (3) the merchandise has to be wrapped or sacked, and (4) perhaps arrangements have to be made to deliver it to the customer. Salespersons may be responsible for some or all of these routine jobs and should be able to execute them accurately and smoothly. Each store has its own system that includes special instructions to its personnel, but a basic understanding of the procedures involved is very helpful.

Types of Sales Transactions

- CASH TAKE: The customer pays for the merchandise and takes it away.
- CASH SEND: The customer pays for the merchandise and the store delivers it.
- CHARGE TAKE: The customer has the merchandise charged to his or her account and takes it away.
- CHARGE SEND: The customer has the merchandise charged to his or her account and the store delivers it.
- C.O.D.: The store delivers the merchandise. Then the customer pays the deliveryman for it—*Cash On Delivery*. It can also be mailed C.O.D. There may be an additional charge for this service.
- WILL CALL: The customer pays cash—or charges the merchandise—and the store holds it until the customer calls for it.
- LAYAWAY: The customer puts a deposit on the merchandise and the store holds it until the customer completes payment, at which time she receives the merchandise. There is usually no additional charge made for this service.
- TIME PAYMENT: The customer agrees to pay so much per month for merchandise and takes it with her. There is an additional interest charge made for this service. Some stores

Prospective employees attend training classes where they are informed of store policies and procedures and they receive instruction in the use of various store forms.
Department Store Journal

honor a 90 day cash time payment with no additional charge.

Recording the Sale

The store has to have information about each sale—what is sold, when, in what department, by whom, what kind of sale (cash, charge, etc.), the amount of the sale, any other charges (tax, for example), and to whom the sale was made in the case of credit or delivery. Such information is essential for the numerous records that are kept in the retailing business—inventory controls, sales analyses, financial reports, credit accounts, even personnel sales records. The salesperson is often responsible for executing such recordings rapidly, accurately, and with ease.

Each store has its own system—cash register slip, sales check, or a combination. In the case of clothing, stores often make use of the *price tag* also in recording the sale. The tag is generally perforated, perhaps in three sections, each section containing the identical information. In addition to the price and size, code numbers may designate the (1) department, (2) the type of merchandise, (3) the manufacturer, (4) the color, style, even the date the merchandise was put in stock. *At the time of purchase, one section is removed* and kept for the store's stock control record. *The other sections remain attached* to the garment and become the customer's record in case of adjustment or return.

For ordinary *cash-take* sales, the cash register record is usually all that is necessary. Modern cash registers can record all the necessary information listed above except the custom-

Department Store Journal

Coded numbers on the price tag, indicating the department and kind of merchandise, enable you to transfer the information from the tag to the tape via the keys of the cash register—along with the price. Always check carefully with the tag to be sure no mistake is made.

er's name and address. The information from the price tag is recorded with the appropriate keys on the register—department keys and price keys. There may even be keys to designate detailed types of merchandise; for example: (1) fur-trimmed coats, (2) plain coats, (3) raincoats, etc. There are keys to designate the type of sale—cash or charge. If tax is involved, there are keys that indicate tax charges. Each salesperson has a separate key with his symbol on the register. By depressing all appropriate keys, the complete information is printed on a "detail tape," providing a record for the store. A printed receipt, containing the same information, plus the date, store name, and register number is provided for the customer.

Many cash registers also make it possible to insert a separate sales check and print the information on it also. What information is on the keyboards of supermarkets in your locality? Notice while you are waiting. It will help you understand the system.

Department Store Journal

The detail strip provides a printed record of every transaction that is entered by the cash register. The information on the tape provides the store with a record of total sales for each department and for each salesperson.

The cash register provides a printed receipt for the customer, showing the department number, price, type of sale, salesperson number, and date of sale. Be sure the information is accurate; then wrap the receipt with the merchandise. It is the customer's proof of purchase.

For certain transactions—a charge sale, or a "send" transaction—a sales check is still necessary. There are many different types of forms used; some entirely handwritten, some printed on the cash register. Although the form may differ, all sales checks provide basically the same information:

• *Customer's name and address,* for charge and delivery purposes. NOTE: There may be two name and address sections—charge to and send to—to provide for the transaction that is charged to one person and sent to another. If it is a charge-take, or charge and send to the same person, fill in the charge section and mark the other one TAKE or SAME, whichever is appropriate. If *handwritten,* be sure the name and address are correct and legible. Carelessness may result in nondelivery or a mistake in the account.

• *Customer's signature and identification,* for a charge transaction. If the store has a charge-card system, no other identification is necessary. Compare the signature on the plate with the customer's. Without a card, *proper identification* is usually required. The identification should contain the customer's signature—a good example is a driver's license.

• *Authorization of the customer's charge.* If the customer does not have a charge card, or if the sale is a charge-take over a certain amount, most stores require the salesperson to "check the account" before releasing the merchandise. A call to the credit department is the general procedure.

• *Merchandise information,* including a description of the merchandise, the number of items, price per item,

(Continued on page 180)

Mechanics of Selling

The cash register receipt is all that is needed for recording a "cash-take" transaction.

**Joseph Horne Co.
Pittsburgh**

1 0 0 1 3 4 . 2 8 # 1

7 2 4 - 0 5 . 0 0 S/L 3

- 0 0 - 0 5 . 0 0 C/A

REGISTER No. 463

7 2 7 2 7 APR 72

**Joseph Horne Co.
Pittsburgh**

- 0 0 - 0 5 . 0 0 C/A

REGISTER No. 463

7 2 7 2 7 APR 72

1605

JOSEPH HORNE CO.

AUTHORIZATION

CHARGE TO

ACCOUNT NO.

NAME

ADDRESS

REG. NO.	DATE	TRANS. NO.	DEPT.	AMOUNT	
	JUL 27	9299	636-35.75		2
	JUL 27	9299	00-35.75		A
	JUL 27	9299	00-35.75		A

THIS MACHINE PRINTED SALESCHECK HAS BEEN DESIGNED TO SAVE YOU TIME IN SHOPPING.

13720   PURCHASED BY

Joseph Horne Co., Pittsburgh
A sales slip is necessary for any charge transaction. This particular slip is for a "charge-take." The name and address can be printed from the charge plate or handwritten if there is no plate. All other information has been printed by the cash register. This type of slip may be made in duplicate—one copy for the customer and one for the credit department. Some stores, however, print only one copy—for the credit department—and use the cash register receipt for the customer.

Merchandising Clothing—A Fascinating Business

Joseph Horne Co., Pittsburgh

Additional information is required for all "send" transactions—the name and address of the person to whom the purchase is to be sent. This type of sales slip is made in triplicate. One copy is given to the customer at the time of purchase. One copy goes to the credit department, in case there is a charge transaction. The third copy goes with the merchandise to the delivery department. This third copy is perforated—one part is the address label, the other a receipt that is put in with the merchandise.

Mechanics of Selling

| JOSEPH HORNE CO. | DEPT. 467 | AUTHORIZATION |

SEND TO
NAME _____ APT. NO. ____
ADDRESS *Same*
INSTRUCTIONS

SALESPERSON 8998   DEPT. 467

PURCHASED BY
ACCOUNT NO. 32 4?? 352 2
NAME CLORIANNA HOLTMAN
ADDRESS 356 COLLINS DR
PGH PA   15231

CASH | ~~CHARGE~~ | T.P.A. | C.O.D. | DUE
MO. 2 / DAY 9 / YR. 72 | SALESPERSON 8998 | 364855

QTY	DESCRIPTION	DEPT. · AMOUNT · CLASS
1	dress	19.00

PURCHASER - ORDER NO. - INSP. - IDENT. | PKGS. ENCL.

Joseph Horne Co., Pittsburgh

The sales slip may be printed on the cash register or filled in by hand. If printed on the cash register, it is not necessary to fill in the date, salesperson number, department, etc.—the register prints all this information. When writing the slip by hand, however, be sure to fill in all the information accurately and legibly.

Merchandising Clothing—A Fascinating Business

total price, tax or other charges. If the sales check is printed on the cash register, the total price is computed for you. On *handwritten sales checks,* you have to figure the total price. You must be accurate. A simple arithmetic mistake costs money.

• *General information*—same as recorded on a cash register, including *date, department number, salesperson's number* or *letter,* and *type of sale* (cash, charge, etc.).

• *Receipt* or *voucher* to give to the customer as proof of purchase. There may be a tear-off strip or the entire check may be made in duplicate. One part goes with the merchandise, the other to the credit department. When the salescheck is printed on the cash register, the register receipt is issued to the customer.

Recording Your Sales

Each salesperson usually must keep a record of his or her own sales. Perhaps he lists each sale on a card or a page of his sales book. Then at the end of the day he totals the *transactions* (number of sales) and *production* (amount sold).

This recording can also be done on the cash register. Each time any person makes a sale, the record is printed on the detail tape in the register. At the end of the day, you can set the register to take a sales reading, insert a card just as you would a charge slip, and press your key. The register automatically totals the amount you have sold and prints it on the production card. The register also counts the number of sales made on each person's key—pressing the key changes the number. This number, visible through a window on the register, can be transferred to the card, completing the daily record. *At the end of the week,* add the number of sales and the amount sold, giving the weekly production report.

Commissions and Production

Some salespersons work on commission; for them, a great part of their pay depends upon their sales. To others, raises depend upon their production; again, the more sales, the better the pay. A great deal of emphasis is put on production. Stores have even determined how much each salesperson "costs" them in terms of the amount sold. Perhaps the person is even told how much he is expected to sell by the hour. Sales become very important. To some salespeople, they become even more important than customer service. Avoid becoming overly aggressive either in pressuring customers to buy or in "grabbing" them. For pleasant relationships with your co-workers, practice fair consideration. Others could herd sales away from you, if you made enemies.

Handling Money

There are certain approved procedures for handling money that should be learned and then practiced until they become habit.

• Always ring up the sale before wrapping or sacking the merchandise to prevent mistakes.

• Unless the customer gives you the correct amount of money, state the price and the amount given you. For example: "That is $3.15 out of $5.00." —Keep the bill in plain sight until the customer receives the change. Place it on the change plate above the cash drawer of the register while you re-

cord the sale and make change. Then there will be no question as to how much money the customer gave you.
- Record the sale on the cash register, checking the figures you ring up. *If you make a mistake,* mark the slip "Void" and proceed with a new one. NOTE: You may have to have a void okayed by someone in authority.
- Count the change, using as few coins as possible—a dime in preference to two nickels; a fifty cent piece (if available) in preference to two quarters, etc.

—In figuring the amount of change, count up from the price to the amount given you. For example: $3.15 (10¢), $3.25 (25¢), $3.50 (50¢), $4.00 ($1.00), $5.00. In this way you will be sure of the correct change. NOTE: Some cash registers figure the change for you.

—Hand the change to the customer one coin or bill at a time, "counting up" just as you did when figuring the change. NOTE: Always finish with "Thank you."
- Place the money the customer gives you in the cash drawer. Place all bills face up, in one direction, and the coins in the proper compartments. *Be sure to close the cash drawer.*
- The importance of accuracy with money cannot be overemphasized.

Work of the Cash Register

At "opening" a certain amount of change is in the cash drawer. • All transactions are recorded on the register tape. • If any cash is removed from the drawer, a receipt is issued. • At "closing" the money is counted and recorded on some form of tally sheet. Intake and outgo must balance.

Different stores have different recording and checking procedures. Perhaps the tally sheet, the register tape, any cash removal receipts, and the cash drawer are all turned in to the auditing department, where a check is made. **Remember,** everything must balance. Some stores hold employees responsible for a "short" register, deducting the amount from the person's pay.

Wrapping or Sacking

Some form of covering protects the merchandise from exposure and serves as a form of "proof of purchase," protecting the customer from suspicion of shoplifting. The process may be as simple as inserting the merchandise in a paper bag or may involve deluxe gift wrapping or wrapping for mailing. In many stores, the salesperson is responsible for ordinary wrapping of merchandise that is sold.

- *A box* is more suitable for clothing than a bag because there is less danger of wrinkling and crushing the garment. Some stores now use "box-bags" which are less expensive than boxes. Because they are made of paper, like a bag, they are lightweight. Customers find them more convenient and easier to handle than a box because they are soft and flexible. They protect the garment better than a bag, however, because they have the contour of a box and are waterproof. When closed, an air cushion prevents crushing and wrinkling.

NOTE: The wrapping supplies are costly. Don't be wasteful. Try to use the correct size bag or box.

—There is a definite technique to packaging clothing so that there will be a minimum of wrinkling. (1) Use

Merchandising Clothing—A Fascinating Business

the proper size box. If the box is too small, no amount of care will prevent wrinkling from overcrowding. (2) Fold the garment as few times as possible, cushioning each fold with tissue paper.

SKIRTS: Fold in thirds lengthwise to fit the box; then crosswise, where necessary (near the hipline).

JACKETS: Button the jacket. Place upside down on a counter, with sleeves lying lengthwise against the jacket. (They tend to fall into place naturally.) Fold the jacket crosswise to fit the box.

COATS: Button the coat. Place it upside down on a counter. Fold in thirds lengthwise from the shoulder, turning in just enough so the coat fits the box. (The sleeves tend to fold themselves naturally. Be sure they are smooth and flat.) Then fold the coat crosswise to fit the box.

DRESSES: Close all fasteners. Fold the same as a coat.

If there is a belt, be sure to enclose it in the box.

—Be sure the customer's receipt is in the package with the merchandise. NOTE: If the customer is going to stop back for the package, give him or her a voucher and tape or staple the receipt to the outside of the package. Then it can be quickly identified by comparing the customer's voucher with the receipt.

—Close the package securely so that it will not come open. In most cases, either tape or self-locking boxes are used. If it is necessary to tie the package, however, be sure it is tied securely. Practice over and over on a box until you can do it easily and neatly. For convenience in carrying, a handle of some sort may be attached. *For deliveries,* attach the address label securely to the outside of the package.

• *Gift wrapping* and *wrapping for mailing* are usually handled in separate departments in large stores. If the salesperson has to perform this duty, learn the proper technique for wrapping packages neatly and then practice until you can do it easily and well.

Handling (Preventing) Returns and Customer Complaints

How you handle these two areas is an important factor in promoting good will or creating customer ill-will. The best method is a *preventive.*

Some articles of clothing are not returnable—hats, bathing suits, etc. Emphasize this fact to the customer *during the sale* so that she will make her selection very carefully. **Remember,** don't pressure the customer to buy: she may do so just to please you or to get away, but such a purchase is almost always returned. Avoid "on-approval" sales whenever possible. When a customer is in doubt, avoid the negative approach: "Why not take it with you? If you aren't satisfied you can always return it." Such a suggestion displays an interest in your sales total, not in customer service and satisfaction. Such purchases are most likely to be returned.

Of course, returned merchandise adds to the store's expenses. Additional handling is involved to re-mark it and put it back in stock. Additional bookkeeping is involved in both stock records and customer accounts. It may even mean a delivery man picking up the merchandise.

In spite of the additional expense, most stores permit returns because of good will. They have been known to accept merchandise that has been worn, is damaged, or was even purchased at another store rather than incur the customer's anger and ill-will. As a matter of good public relations, most stores subscribe to the policy that the customer is always right, even when they are aware this is not the truth.

Who handles the return depends upon the store's policy—a salesperson with an "OK" by someone in authority, a supervisor, a section manager, or a clerical employee at the service desk. The actual procedure to follow is also a matter of the individual store's policy. In the case of a *charge sale*, returned merchandise is credited to the customer's account. When the sale is *cash*, however, some stores refund the money, or the store may issue a merchandise certificate. The forms used vary with the store; special instructions are part of personnel training.

Customer *complaints* follow much the same pattern as returns. Some sort of adjustment is usually involved, and merchandise may be returned. Most stores welcome legitimate complaints. They are concerned about the quality of merchandise they handle and strive to maintain high standards. They would rather the customer return to a store for an adjustment than be dissatisfied, do nothing, blame the store, complain to friends, and stop doing business with the firm.

Mechanics of Selling

Prevention

The alert salesperson can often do a great deal to prevent customer complaints. For example, if a fabric or garment requires special care, emphasize this fact to the customer *during the sale*. Point out the care instructions, to prevent improper handling that may result in damage to the article. Be honest about any *disadvantages* concerning the merchandise. *Be alert for flaws* or defects and don't sell merchandise that you know is damaged. Something minor may be repaired or adjusted, but call it to the customer's attention. Don't try to "put something over" on the person.

Handling the complaint and the making of a satisfactory adjustment is usually the responsibility of someone in authority—a supervisor, the section manager, or the adjustment department. If you become involved with a customer and a complaint, remember, never argue with the customer. Be courteous at all times.

As one of their customer services some stores operate *testing laboratories* in which they investigate the customer complaints and test the merchandise. Experts in these laboratories may also inspect random samplings from a shipment, checking it for quality and conformity to their standards. The stores consider it their responsibility—and good business—to alert manufacturers about inferior or faulty merchandise. If there is a defect or flaw, rather than handle inferior goods, they may return it to the manufacturer.

Using the Telephone

The telephone plays a large part in retailing. For the customer, it is an

Department Store Journal
When taking a telephone order, carefully write down the information the customer gives you.

easy way to shop without leaving home. For the stores, it pays to have telephone order departments with special operators who handle the orders. For the salesperson, it is a helpful device to boost sales—call customers when new merchandise is received, or a "sale" is in progress, or there is going to be a mark-down on an item in which the customer is interested, or special merchandise is available, or similar news.

• There are certain fundamental *telephone techniques* that are essential to successful telephone selling: Practice the use of basic, courteous telephone manners. • Answer the telephone cheerfully, identifying yourself and the store or department, as, "Ready-to-wear, Miss Smith. May I help you?" • The tone of your voice is especially important. It should be soft, yet clear and pleasant.

—If a call comes in for a specific person, acknowledge the request—don't just drop the phone. "Just a moment, I'll call her," or, "She is out to lunch. May I have her call you when she returns?" or, "She is off the floor right now. May I give her a message?" Then be sure the person gets the message. If it is necessary to call a person, don't shout the name near the mouthpiece. Put the phone down or cover the mouthpiece with your hand.

—The phone is very often at a wrapping desk or near the cash register. Be conscious of the open line. Your remarks to others can be clearly heard by the person on the other end of the line. Griping, arguing, discussing customers, etc. are in poor taste in front of customers and embarrassing for the person on the phone who cannot help but overhear.

—When talking, give the person on the phone your undivided attention. Avoid (1) talking to anyone else while you are on the phone or (2) picking up the telephone and not answering it until you finish another conversation. *Listen attentively* so you don't have to ask the customer to repeat, but be sure you fully understand the person's request.

—Excuse yourself if you must leave the phone to get information the phone customer wants. Then try not to keep the person waiting more than a few moments. Know your merchandise—what is available, the sizes, colors, and prices—so the information is at your fingertips.

—Suggestive selling can be accomplished beautifully over the telephone if you know your merchandise and can effectively describe it. Your ability to paint word pictures helps the customer visualize the merchandise and your enthusiasm, reflected in your voice, helps create a desire to buy. Note: Be alert to the inflection of the customer's voice—it reveals her interest.

—Be sure to obtain the *necessary facts* for the completion of the phone sale and record them accurately: an exact description of the merchandise wanted—style, size, color, quantity, etc.; the name and address of the person to whom the merchandise is to be charged and sent. To be sure they are correct, repeat them as the customer gives them to you.

—Thank the customer for calling.

NOTE: The telephone is a business tool and all calls should be limited to store business. Except for emergencies, avoid personal calls—both incoming and outgoing.

Preparing Merchandise for Sale

In a typical department store, handling the merchandise from the time it arrives at the store until it reaches the selling floor is the responsibility of the receiving department, where it is opened, checked, marked, and distributed.

• When a shipment arrives, a receiving clerk counts the unopened packages and compares the actual number with that on the delivery receipt. He also examines the packages for any visible shipping damages and notes the condition of the shipment on the receipt. A complete, accurate *record* is kept of all shipments, including the date of arrival, the manufacturer or wholesaler, the number of packages, the method of transportation, the charges, the condition of the shipment, and other pertinent information. This record, as a check on whether a shipment is received, is valuable in case of loss or damage.

• Next the cartons are opened and the merchandise sorted. In the case of standard pre-packaged items—such as boxed shirts, packaged panties, or hosiery—it is not necessary to open each packing carton and count the number of individual boxes or packages. The description and number are usually clearly marked on the outside of the carton, so all that is necessary is to count the number of cartons. However, in the case of items that vary in size, color, and style, it is necessary to count the individual ones. They are *stacked* according to size, *counted*, and the quantity received *checked against the manufacturer's or wholesaler's invoice*. Any irregularities—shortage or excess—are noted at this time and reported immediately for adjustment.

—At this stage, also, many stores have the merchandise inspected for quality —material, workmanship, conformity to the manufacturer's sample or description—to be sure that it meets their standards and that no substitution has been made. This check is usually made by the *buyer* or the assistant buyer, who knows what was ordered.

Merchandising Clothing—A Fascinating Business

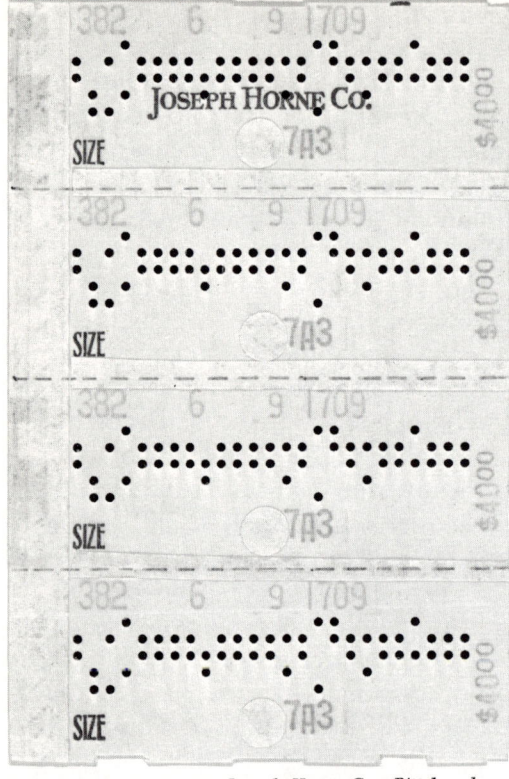

Joseph Horne Co., Pittsburgh

Some typical price tags.

• The buyer also lets the receiving department know the retail selling price for each item (it may be included on either the invoice or the purchase order) so that the *markers* can make the price tags and attach them to the merchandise. There are various types of *price tickets* used—hang tags for articles of clothing, gummed stickers for merchandise in boxes, sewn-on, pinned, or stapled tickets for such articles as gloves, sweaters, and lingerie. Most price tickets will include the following information:

Store name and location.
Department number.
Type of merchandise (coat, suit, etc.).
Manufacturer.
Style number.
Color.
Size.
Price.
Date put in stock.

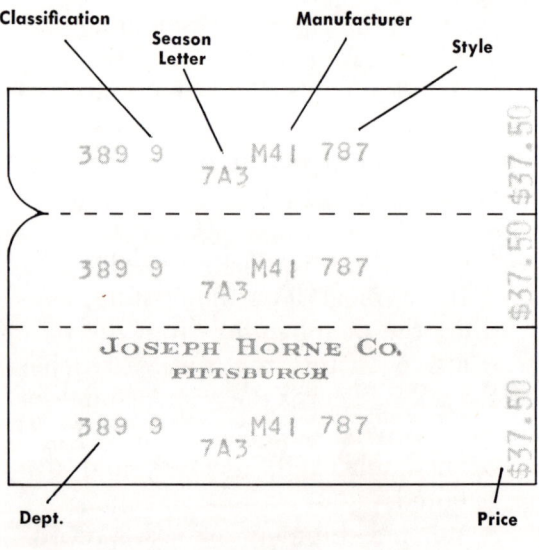

All the numbers on the price tag stand for something.

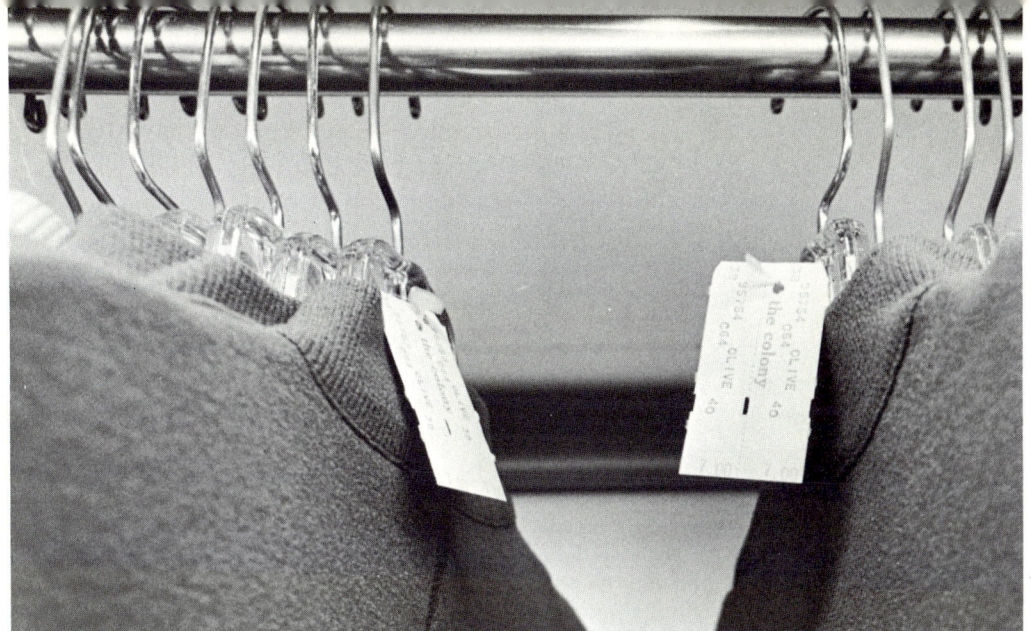
This merchandise is tagged and ready for transfer to the selling floor.

—Much of the information, as you see on the sample tag, is coded. The *date* the merchandise is put in stock, for example, is shown with numbers and letters. One system may be to give each *3 month season* a letter (A for January through March, B for April through June, etc.) and each month in the season a number. For the year, only the last numeral may be used. Therefore a date 8A3 means the merchandise was put in stock in March, 1968. (Always start with the year.)

In most cases, the price tags are printed by machine, counted, can be recorded as they are printed, and—except for gummed labels—are even attached to the merchandise by machine. All but the gummed labels can be perforated, also, so that one portion can be detached at the time of purchase, for the sales record (see page 175).

For *mark-downs*, the same price tag is usually used—cross out the original selling price and write in by hand the marked-down price. For a *special sale* or promotion, very often new price tags are attached.

Sales stock handling:

From the receiving department, the merchandise is transferred to the various selling departments. Here it is placed either on open display or in easily accessible storage spaces at the selling area. What there isn't room for on the floor is placed in reserve stock in a stockroom or storage area near the selling area.

• Usually everyone in the selling department is expected to do some stock work. "Entering stock" (making a record of the receipt of merchandise for stock control) and arranging it for sale may be part of the salesperson's responsibilities.

—The *arrangement* of merchandise is an important aspect of retailing because properly arranged stock can facilitate the sale of goods. First, it looks more attractive. A neat, orderly department is more likely to appeal to

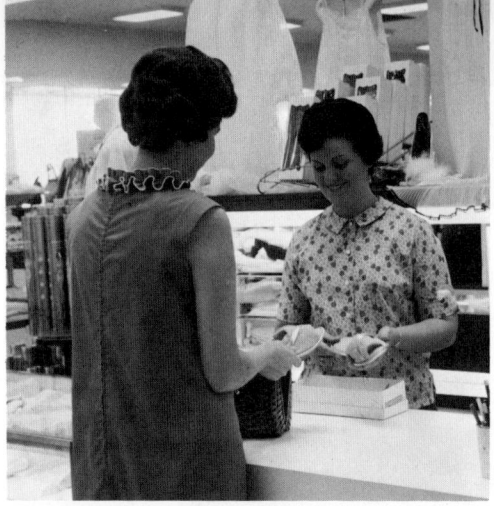

Department Store Journal

Suggest a pair of slippers to the customer who has just bought a robe and nightie set. You can often make a sale. Having articles that are worn together stocked in the same department makes suggestive selling easy.

the customer than one in a state of confusion and disarray. A logically planned arrangement also helps the salesperson learn where merchandise is located so it can be found more easily and quickly. Properly arranged merchandise can be counted easily and restocked when the supply gets low. Customers, too, can locate merchandise.

There are some specific principles involved in the stock arrangements. There should be a logical, easily understood system. In a dress department, for example, all women's sizes may be in one section, all half sizes together in another, etc. Or perhaps the knits are all together, the "after-fives" together, etc.

In "fashion goods" a fast turn-over is essential because of the time factor. As fashions change, stock must be cleared to keep ahead of trends. Therefore the arrangement should provide for selling older stock first. Rotate the merchandise by placing new stock in back of or under merchandise already on the shelf.

Slow movers may be "pushed"—moved to a front rack or displayed prominently—to encourage sales. Suggestive selling is easier if the customer sees all items that go together—ties near shirts, robes near sleepwear, etc. The customer can be tempted to fill needs in other ways also. Fast selling items placed close to slow movers call attention to them. Attractive, profitable, "mood" items should be displayed up front, along main aisles or traffic lanes, or in some such conspicuous place. Items that are standard—that customers buy regularly, that they come to the store for specifically—can be placed farther back in the department. Customers will seek them out.

There are two theories on displaying *sale* or *strongly advertised* merchandise—up front where it attracts the most attention or in the back so the customer sees other merchandise while heading for the sale items. In any case the arrangement should be varied occasionally so the department keeps an exciting, new, different look.

Care of stock:

Soiled and damaged merchandise is a real loser, so keep the merchandise clean and in good order at all times. Especially in ready-to-wear you must guard against soiling and careless handling when trying on clothes. • Encourage customers to hold tissue between their lips so that they don't get lipstick on the clothes. • Encourage them to put straight skirts on and off over the head instead of stepping into or out of them so as not to break the zipper. • Keep your own hands clean. • Rough nails, too, can snag fabrics.

After you finish with each cus-

Mechanics of Selling

tomer, return the merchandise you have shown to its proper place. • Hang garments neatly with the zipper and buttons closed, belts fastened, etc. • On the rack, garments are hung with *smaller sizes to the left*—larger to the right. The *front* of the garment *faces the left* so the customer can examine it conveniently. The *end garment at the right* of the rack is an exception. Turn it *toward the right* so that as a customer approaches the rack she sees the front of a garment, not the back. • Merchandise that is *folded* for storage should be folded carefully and neatly stacked on the shelves. • *Plastic covers* can be used to protect merchandise from soiling. **Remember,** always keep the stock and the department in order.

Merchandise records:

Accurate information about the merchandise—what is selling, what isn't; what stock is plentiful, what is running low—helps the store decide what to reorder, when to reorder, what to mark down, what to promote specially, etc.

For ready-to-wear, many stores maintain a "unit-control system" by which they keep a very complete record of each item of merchandise. For example, when a shipment of dresses is received, a *stock card* is made out for each style. On this card is recorded: the date of the purchase order, the number ordered, the date received, the number of each size and color received, the manufacturer, the cost, and the selling price. Entries are made on the card for every transaction that occurs—a sale, a customer return, a transfer to a branch store, a return to the manufacturer—showing the balance on hand at all times. The information for these entries is obtained from sales slips or from the

This robe department is located next to the sleepwear for customer convenience. Such an arrangement helps suggestive selling also. Notice how neat and orderly the department is.

Department Store Journal

stubs torn off the price tag when an item is sold. If the stock doesn't "move" quickly, it may be marked down and the mark-down recorded on the card also. With such a continuing inventory system, it is possible always to know the stock "picture" at a glance.

Stock counts may be taken periodically—perhaps as often as weekly—to check the "on hand" figure on the unit control card with the actual merchandise in stock. In case of a shortage—for instance, the card says there should be seven items in stock, but only six are found—a recheck is made to try to locate an error either in recording or counting. If no error is found, the item is listed as a shortage and may even be assumed to have been stolen. If unaccounted shortages occur frequently, extra security pre-

Department Store Journal
When the stock control record shows that an article is not moving well, some action is indicated. Here the buyer and section manager are contemplating a markdown.

A typical stock card.
Joseph Horne Co., Pittsburgh

DATE		DATE		DATE		DATE		DATE		DATE		DATE		DATE				
COST		COST		COST		COST		RETAIL		RETAIL		RETAIL		RETAIL				
DATE	TRANSACTION	PRICE VAR.	MAIN BAL.	MUSIC BAL.	2 BAL.	3 BAL.	4 BAL.	5 BAL.	6 BAL.	7 BAL.	8 BAL.	DATE	ORDER NO.	ON ORDER
MFR.			MODEL		FINISH	DATE		DATE		DATE		80-10-112		
						COMM. RATE		COMM. RATE		COMM. RATE				

Mechanics of Selling

4068		INVENTORY SHEET			DATE		
COUNTED AND CALLED BY	ENTERED BY	DEPT. MGR'S. APPROVAL	LOCATION			DEPT.	CLASS
RECOUNTED AND CALLED BY	ENTRIES CHECKED BY	DEPT. AUDITOR'S APPROVAL	FIXTURE	SHELF		389	9

	DESCRIPTION	SEASON LETTER	QUANTITY	PRICE PER UNIT DOLLARS	CENTS	EXTENSION
	Raincoat	7A	6	37	50	
	Raincoat	7C	4	35	00	
	Raincoat	7A	5	19	00	

OVER 18 MONTHS	PRIOR SEASON (6 MO.)	PREVIOUS QUARTER (3 MO.)	PRE-MARK "P"	TOTAL
	PREVIOUS SEASON (6 MO.)	CURRENT QUARTER (3 MO.)	NON-MARK "V"	
AGE ANALYSIS BY		EXTENSION BY		

N⁰ 77919

Joseph Horne Co., Pittsburgh

A typical inventory sheet.

Merchandising Clothing—A Fascinating Business

cautions are indicated to protect the stock and prevent shoplifting.

Full *inventories* are a complete count of all the merchandise in stock. Many stores take inventory twice a year—say, in January and July. Such a complete count not only shows what is in stock and how long it has been held (for buying or sale purposes), but it also lets the retailer know the dollar value of the merchandise on hand. This information, showing the amount of money invested in stock and the amount of profit made during a given period, is used in preparing the store's financial report or balance sheet.

Stores usually try to reduce stock as much as possible before taking inventory by holding *pre-inventory sales*. What is left after the sale is sorted and arranged in order, in preparation for actual counting. The forms used differ with different stores, but all the merchandise is listed in some way —(1) a description to identify it, (2) how long it has been in stock, (3) how many of each item are in stock, and (4) the price per item. To prevent errors, usually *two people work together* to do the actual recording. One counts the merchandise and calls it to the other, who repeats what is called and records it on inventory sheets. A correct inventory depends upon *accuracy* in counting and entering, and on *clearly written letters* and *figures*.

In review:

What are the logical steps in completing a sale?

Explain the main types of sales transactions.

What general information is it necessary to record for each sale? For what reason is each item recorded?

What purposes does the cash register receipt serve? For what transaction is it the only record necessary?

What additional information is necessary for a charge sale? a send?

What is considered suitable customer identification for accepting a check?

What purposes does a salesperson's production report serve?

Outline the approved procedures for handling a cash sale.

How can you help prevent returns? customer complaints?

What is meant by legitimate complaints? Why do stores usually welcome them?

What are the logical steps in preparing merchandise for sale?

What is the salesperson's responsibility toward the merchandise?

For further discussion:

Merchandise display.
Arrangement of stock.
Care of merchandise.
Inventory control.
Sales analysis.

To gain experience:

Practice filling in sales slips; using a cash register; making change.

Practice folding and packaging articles of clothing; wrapping packages.

Practice telephone procedures.

Prepare a counter display; show case display; window display.

KNOWING YOUR MERCHANDISE

To sell successfully and to feel happy while working, it is essential that you really know what you are selling. Customers want information about the merchandise they buy and if you know its style features, its principal characteristics—what it is made of, how it is made, how to care for it, when and where it is worn or otherwise used—you can talk about it intelligently. You can learn to turn merchandise information into selling points that will help customers reach buying decisions. The more you know, the more help you are to your customers. Knowledge gives you confidence and in turn customers gain confidence in you also. In such a way you build a following and make a place for yourself.

Remember, it is easy to learn details if you try a little every day.

- *Fabric* is the common ingredient for most clothing merchandise, so *fabric knowledge* is especially important. An entire chapter has been devoted to textile information to help you become well-informed. New fibers, new finishes, new textures, however, appear with each new season. Therefore your study of textiles is a continuing one. Keep informed on the latest information available by reading the labels and descriptive material on the merchandise, articles in magazines, trade journals, and newspapers, and accounts of developments from manufacturers.
- *Style factors* are perhaps the prime consideration for most customers

The fashion coordinator informs the ready-to-wear sales personnel about the season's fashions, colors, and fabrics.

Seventeen-at-School

when they purchase clothing. **Remember,** the salesperson should first clearly understand the difference between style and fashion. As we know, style in clothing indicates a specific shape or design; fashion is a style that is popularly accepted at the particular time. For example: the A-line skirt is a specific shape and the empire waistline is a specific design; both of these may be in style, but the skirt length or the trim of the waist may not be in fashion at a particular time. A simple pump with the wrong heel can be in style but out of fashion; high-button shoes may be a fad (fashion) of the younger set, but the entire style is out with adults.

—*Fashion* is often unpredictable and always changing, even for shirtwaist styles. A salesperson must keep up to date with the fashion picture—the look, the fabrics, the colors. Buyers and the fashion department of large department stores usually hold periodic fashion clinics for the sales personnel to acquaint them with current fashions. Fashion magazines, trade newspapers, and material from manufacturers also keep you informed.

• Next, know *suitability*. Customers are interested in being fashion right, but they also want to wear clothes that are becoming to them. A basic knowledge of color, line, and design can help you advise customers on selection of clothing that is best suited to them. Many customers also look to the salesperson for advice on what clothing is appropriate for various occasions—what to wear when and with what. The customer hopes that you are an expert on fashion. Become one! Be informed. Read all the fashion and fabric information you can.

Carroll Reed Ski Sh

The classically tailored shirt dress, the jacketed sheath dress ensemble, and the separates shown in this display are all color coordinated to create a versatile wardrobe. By showing well-matched companion items such as these blouses that are especially good with the skirt or slacks you can often increase your sale.

The Expert's Guide

This next section is intended to help you become well informed. It contains information about specific items of clothing and accessories—about *fabrics, construction, workmanship,* and *fit* as applied to each type of garment. It suggests a *professional vocabulary,* to help you present the merchandise to the customer. It should further help you translate your fashion *knowledge* into *sales.*

READY-TO-WEAR

Dresses

Styling

- **Sheath:** a straight, slim dress; shaped at the waistline; may or may not have a waistline seam.
- **Shift:** loose fitting dress that hangs straight from the shoulder; straight, tubular shape.
- **Skimmer:** A-line shift, flaring out slightly in the skirt.
- **Princess:** cut in single pieces from shoulder to hem; shaped to form a close-fitting bodice and flared skirt.
- **Blouson:** a loose fitting bodice, gathered at the waist in some manner (drawstring, belt, seam, etc.) causing it to blouse.
- **Tent:** hangs from the shoulder, flaring out to a very wide skirt.
- **Empire:** high waistline (just under the bustline), straight skirt.
- **Babydoll:** high waistline (just under the bustline), slight gathering where lower portion of dress joins bodice.
- **Smock:** lower portion of dress gathered to a shoulder yoke.
- **Coat dress:** tailored dress with a coat-like appearance and coat-like front closing.
- **Shirtwaist:** one-piece, tailored dress with a bodice similar to a man's tailored shirt.
- **Basic:** plain, simple dress with no decoration or trimming; can be changed in appearance with the use of different trim and accessories.
- **Morning:** house dress.
- **Daytime:** not as elaborate as afternoon; not as tailored as business; appropriate for luncheons and general day wear.

Shift. *McCall's Patterns*

Skimmer.

Merchandising Clothing—A Fascinating Business

Princess line skimmer.

Baby doll.

Blouson.

Coat dress.

McCall's Patterns

- **Afternoon:** appropriate for daytime social functions; somewhat dressier than for regular wear; more luxurious fabric.
- **Cocktail:** informal, but very dressy; luxurious fabric; suitable for late afternoon and evening; also called "after-five" dress.
- **Dinner:** often long, not as formal as evening dress; shoulders covered and has sleeves.
- **Formal:** full-length, décolleté (low-cut—often strapless) front and back; no sleeves.

Formal.

McCall's Patterns

After-five dresses.

Merchandising Clothing—A Fascinating Business

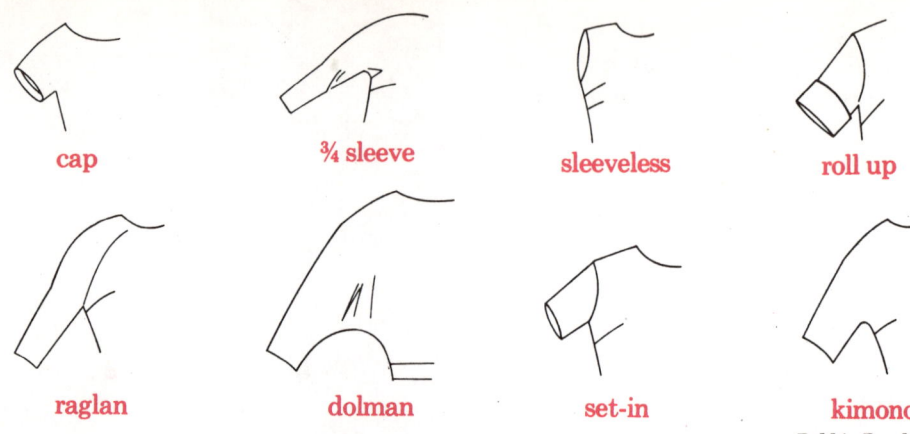

Sleeve styles.

Workmanship

Here are some general points to check in all garments:

- Is the garment *cut on grain?* If not, it will not hang properly; it will twist around the body and is likely to stretch out of shape. The lengthwise grain should be perpendicular to the floor (straight up and down) and the crosswise grain should *cross* it squarely at right angles.
- Is the stitching *small, straight,* and *secure?* Long machine stitches are for basting and won't hold as well as regular length stitches. The stitch should be a lock stitch, just like the stitch made by the home sewing machine. This stitch will not pull out. NOTE: Some inexpensive garments are sewn with a chain stitch—pull the under thread, and all the stitches will pull out.
- Are the seams *wide enough* and free from puckers? Wide seams lie flatter and will take more strain than narrow ones. It will be possible to enlarge a garment, if necessary, when the seams are wide.
- Have the seams been pressed properly? If the material ravels, have the

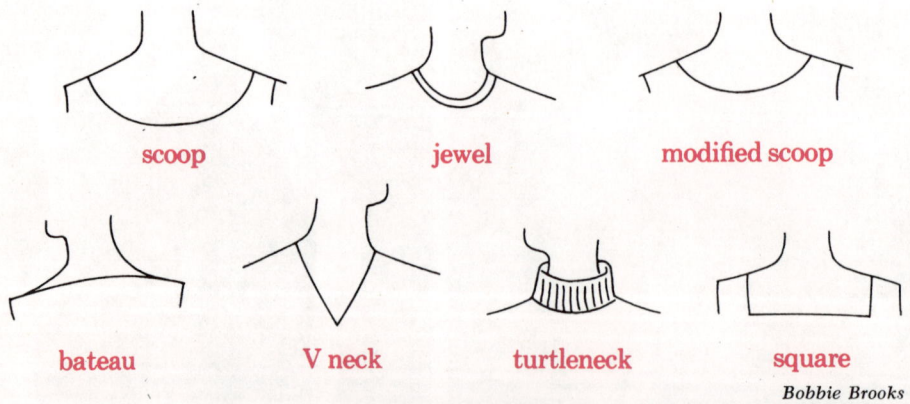

Neckline styles.

edges of the seams been finished to keep them from fraying? Very often these finishings are ignored in inexpensive garments.

• If the garment has plaids or stripes, are they carefully *matched*? Check the side and center seams. Do they match in both directions? Other matching points are sleeves, armholes, collars, and pockets. A large print also looks better if it has been matched and if some thought is given to the placement of the print on the garment. Careful matching is a sign of good quality, besides adding to the appearance of the garment.

• Are *slide fasteners* neatly stitched and inconspicuous? They should be completely covered and lie flat. The fastener should be lightweight yet durable and should not slip open.

• Are buttons, hooks and eyes, or snaps *sewn securely* in place? Better quality clothes often have extra buttons attached for use in case one is lost.

• Are *buttonholes* straight, of proper length, and neatly, securely stitched? They should fit easily over the buttons—not so short that it is necessary to force the buttons through, but not so long that the buttons slip out. Better quality garments use self-bound buttonholes, if the type of garment and the weight and weave of the fabric permit. Look for them on a wool coat or suit, for instance, but not on a cotton shirt. *Machine-worked* buttonholes should be evenly and firmly stitched. The stitches should be close together and extend into the fabric far enough so that they won't pull out.

• Are the *hems* flat and invisible? Stitches should be invisible on the outside; there should not be a ridge showing at the hemline. A straight or slightly flared skirt should have an ample but not deep hem. A very full flared skirt will seem less bulky and look better with a small hem. Deep hems are attractive in sheer and lightweight gathered or pleated skirts. All hems, whether sleeve, blouse, or skirt, should be finished after the seams are sewn together. NOTE: For inexpensive garments, the hems are often completed before the seams. This is speedy construction, but not good quality.

Size

• PRE-TEEN or SUB-TEEN: for the short, immature, young figure; sizes range from 6S to 14S.

• TEEN: for the young, developing, still growing figure; sizes range from 10T to 16T.

• JUNIOR: for the well-proportioned, short waisted, fully developed figure with small, high bustline. Sizes range from 5 to 17.

• MISSES: for the well-developed, nicely proportioned figure—taller and longer waisted than the junior. Sizes range from 6 or 8 to 18 or 20. Also available in petite for the short women with Misses proportions and in Tall for the person 5'8" and over.

• WOMEN'S: designed for full figure of average height—heavier than Misses. Sizes range from 20 to 48 or 50.

• HALF SIZE: designed for the mature, short waisted figure—not as tall as Misses or Women's. Sizes range from 8½ or 10½ to 26½.

Ready-to-wear sizes are not standardized. Since different manufacturers may cut garments differently, you

Merchandising Clothing—A Fascinating Business

cannot rely on stated size. A person able to wear a size seven in some makes, requires size nine in others.

Fitting

Check the following points:
- Does the *neckline* fit smoothly? Any wrinkles? Does it gape? Does it choke?
- If the *sleeves* are set-in, is the armhole seam at the tip of the shoulder? Do the sleeves hang straight without wrinkling or twisting? Can the person move the arms forward and reach up without straining?
- Does the *bodice* fit without straining or wrinkling? If it is a shell, does it fit snugly without gaping at the armholes? Does the bustline dart point to the fullest part of the bust?
- If there is a *waistline seam*, is it at the natural waistline? Check both front and back to be sure the seam does not show above or below the belt.
- If the *skirt* is slim, does it hang straight without "cupping" under at the hipline. Is there any strain at the seams? Note whether or not the hem needs to be straightened.
- Have the customer sit, stand, walk, move her arms, reach, and bend. Make certain the garment is *comfortable*. Also fit means a great deal to appearance.
- Avoid selling clothes that require much *alteration*. The length of a sleeve or a skirt can usually be changed easily. Major alterations,

Department stores often devote separate floors or sections of a floor to each size range. In this section, for example, only junior-size clothing is available. A "junior" customer can see all the clothing available in her size in this one area.

Department Store Journal

however, may spoil the lines of the garment.

Coats

Fabric

Almost every fiber is found in coats. Wool and other hair fibers are most common. Other fabrics that may be used include:
- SYNTHETICS: Orlon, dynel (to imitate fur).
- LEATHER: genuine or vinyl.
- SUEDE: a finish applied to leather to give it a nap.
- CORDUROY: popular for sportswear and all-weather fashions.
- BLENDS: dacron and cotton broadcloth for rainwear.

Whatever the fiber, the fabric should have a firm weave to withstand wear. *Lining fabrics* should be closely woven, non-bulky, smooth, so that the garment will slip on and off easily; colorfast, and resistant to the effects of perspiration. A slightly stiff lining fabric adds extra body to the garment and helps to prevent wrinkling.

Carroll Reed Ski Shops

The coat—a basic piece around which to build a wardrobe. This one has the shawl collar and single-breasted styling, pairs with a Glen plaid skirt and soft wool knit pullovers, for that "country casual" look. The cowhide tote and deerskin gloves are excellent companions for wool and country tweeds. A well-planned display of this type promotes sales.

This double-breasted plaid top coat has a special water-repellent finish, making it a very practical all-weather coat.

SYL-MER®

Styling
- Box: plain, loose coat; often short; hangs straight from shoulders, resembling a square box.
- CHESTERFIELD: a single-breasted, straight coat; fly-front or straight button closing; notched lapel and collar, often velvet.
- COACHMAN: double-breasted, fitted coat; notched lapel and wide collar.
- ALL-WEATHER COAT: water-repellent, usually of top-coat weight; may have a removable lining for extra warmth.

Merchandising Clothing—A Fascinating Business

- REEFER: single or double-breasted, fitted.
- SWAGGER: loose-fitting, flared coat.
- TRENCH COAT: loose-fitting, double-breasted, belted coat with flaps or pockets; resembling military coat.
- TUXEDO: straight coat with a flat collar that extends around the neck and down the entire length of the garment.
- TOPCOAT: lightweight coat to be worn in cool weather.
- OVERCOAT: warm, heavy coat to be worn in cold weather.
- RAINCOAT: waterproof, lightweight coat.

Workmanship
Lining
- SEAMS—generous, in line with the garment seams, tacked to garment seams.
- STITCHES—neat, close together, secure.
- PLEAT—the full length of the back to allow for freedom of movement; keeps the lining from straining.

Outer garment
- *Seams*—flat, well-pressed.
- *Hem*—invisible on the outside.
- *Buttons*—attractive, good quality, securely attached with a "stem" of thread.
- *Buttonholes*—correct size, preferably bound, machine suitable for casual wear.
- *Lapels, collar, front edges*—well pressed; sharp, flat edges.

Size
Same as dress, but start with one size smaller than the regular dress size. Manufacturers cut coats slightly larger than dresses so that they will fit over other clothes comfortably.
NOTE: A coat should always be tried on over the type of clothing with which a person plans to wear it. If they want to wear a coat over a suit, for example, they should try it on over a suit to make sure it will be comfortable.

Fitting
- COLLAR: close at neckline; lies flat at back of the neck.
- SHOULDER: seams straight; no wrinkles under the arm or across the back.
- SLEEVES: hang straight; cover the wrist bone when the arm is bent (if full length).
- GENERAL FIT: should not strain across the back when arms are folded or raised; should fall in straight line from shoulders; should button without strain or pull.
- FITTED COAT: more comfortable if waistline is slightly below normal waist.
- LENGTH: full-length coat should be slightly longer than the clothes worn under it.

SUITS

Fabric
Almost any fiber may be used. The fabric should be a suitable weight for the style. In general, the fabric is heavier than dress weight, not as heavy as coat weight.

Styling
- DRESSMAKER: a soft, semi-tailored or dressy suit; may be unlined; often made of a lighter weight fabric than the usual "suit-weight."
- TAILORED: simple, trim, fitted lines;

Tailored.

Dressmaker.

Cardigan.

Pants suit.

Ensemble—dress and jacket.
McCall's Patterns

Merchandising Clothing—A Fascinating Business

precisely tailored (interfacing, seaming, and pressing; perfection in construction details), resembling a man's suit; made of suit-weight fabrics similar to those used in men's suits.
- **Costume**: a dress and coat or jacket designed to be worn together.
- **Ensemble**: another term for costume.
- **Slack suit**: also called *pants suit*; slacks and jacket of the same fabric.
- **Cardigan jacket**: straight cut, collarless, may or may not button.
- **Chanel type**: straight cut, open down front, no collar, no buttons.
- **Bolero**: short jacket.
- **Blazer**: semi-fitted, single-breasted, notched collar, patch pockets.
- **Pea jacket**: straight, loose, short, double-breasted jacket similar to type worn in the navy.

Workmanship
See skirt and coat.

Size
Same as dress.

Fitting
See skirt and coat.

SEPARATES

Skirts

Fabric
The fabric should be a suitable weight for the style. A gathered skirt, for example, will look better in a medium or light weight fabric than in a heavy or bulky one. Almost any fiber may be used.

Styling
- **A-line**: close-fitting to the hipline, very slight flare below the hipline to hem, resembling the letter A.
- **Bell**: curved out from waistline, resembling the shape of a bell; usually lined with a stiff fabric to hold the shape.
- **Circle**: a complete circle of fabric, hanging in folds from waistline to hem.
- **Dirndl**: full, gathered skirt.
- **Divided**: culotte; looks like a flared skirt, but actually has leg sections.
- **Flared**: wider at hemline.
- **Gored**: made from shaped pieces, each piece narrow at top and wider at hemline; may have as many as 24 pieces; called 2 gore, 4 gore, etc.
- **Pleated**: folds of fabric.
  - *Soft pleats*—stitched across the top only; also called unpressed.
  - *Stitched pleats*—edge of pleat stitched down from waistline to hipline.
  - *Knife*—narrow pleats all turned in the same direction.
  - *Box*—folded edges turn in opposite directions, away from each other.
  - *Inverted*—folded edges turn toward each other, just the reverse of the box pleat.
  - *Accordion*—permanently pressed in, resembles an accordion.
- **Sheath**: slim, straight skirt.
- **Wrap-around**: skirt opens out flat; one side folds or laps over the other; either buttons or ties in place.

Workmanship
Better quality straight skirts are lined to prevent stretching and

wrinkling. Skirts with flare may be underlined to give added body.
- SEAMS: wide, lie flat, well-pressed.
- SLIDE FASTENER: lies flat, completely covered, inserted neatly.
- WAISTBAND: reinforced to keep it from stretching or losing its shape; hooks and eyes attached securely or neat buttonhole and buttons sewn securely.
- HEM: even width, raw edge appropriately finished, invisible stitches, well-pressed, no ridge visible on the right side.

Size

By the waist measurement: 23, 24, 26, etc.

By dress size: Junior—9, 11, etc. Misses—10, 12, 14, etc.

Proportioned to height: Petite, Average, Tall.

Fitting

- WAISTBAND: snug enough to hold the skirt in place.
- SLIM SKIRT: hangs straight. No "cupping" in the back. Smooth at the hipline. Enough fullness for comfort. No straining or wrinkling.
- PLEATED SKIRT: pleats should hang straight; if they "break" open the skirt is too tight.
- FULL SKIRT: fullness evenly distributed and hangs evenly.
- HEMLINE: even distance from floor; attractive length in keeping with prevailing fashion.

BLOUSES

Fabric

Labels tell the fiber content. The following are some popular fabrics used for shirts and blouses:

Separates: *Skirts, jacket, blouses, pullovers, shells—designed to be mixed and matched.*

Sportswear: *Slacks, skirts, pants toppers, pullovers, and skimmers for a well-coordinated, basic casual summer wardrobe—even adds a gay, poppy-rimmed sunshader.*
Carroll Reed Ski Shops

Merchandising Clothing—A Fascinating Business

- **Cotton:** oxford (modified basket weave), broadcloth (plain weave with slight rib), easy-care (special finishing process).
- **Blends:** such as 65% dacron and 35% cotton, permanent-press.
- **Synthetics:** such as dacron, acetate.
- **Silk:** shantung, crepe, surah.

Fabrics for washable blouses should be color-fast, absorbent, fully shrunk or "sanforized," and easy to care for. Permanent-press finish is especially desirable.

Workmanship

- **Stitching:** smooth, flat, secure, straight, even, no puckering.
- **Seams:** raw edges finished, no loose threads.
- **Hems, sleeves, cuffs:** neatly finished, no raw edges.
- **Collar:** edges held in place with edge stitching or understitching. undercollar doesn't show; collar points are even; lies flat, with no puckering.
- **Interfacing:** should be used in collars, cuffs, and facings; may be omitted for special soft effects; lies flat, smooth, no puckering.
- **Buttons:** washable if blouse is washable; firmly sewn to two thicknesses of fabric; spaced evenly in relation to buttonholes.
- **Buttonholes:** evenly worked; no fraying; no loose threads; reinforced at both ends; proper size for buttons.

Size

Shirts and blouses are sized by the bust measurement. Both dress size and bust measurement may appear on the label; for example, size 12—bust 34. This practice is known as double "ticketing."

Fitting

- A *blouse* should have enough looseness for comfort, yet not be so loose that it hangs. There should be no wrinkling, pulling, or straining. If a tuck-in style, it should be long enough to stay in the skirt, even when the arms are raised.
- *Collars* should fit close to the neck; they should neither gape nor choke.

The *armhole* seam should be at the edge of the shoulder. It should fall straight down, not at an angle, from the tip of the shoulder in both the front and the back. The armholes should be comfortable, neither too large nor binding.

- *Sleeve* length should be in style and comfortable. If the blouse has long sleeves, the sleeve should reach the bottom of the wrist bone when the arm is bent. The width of the sleeve is also important. There should be enough ease to be comfortable; the sleeve should not bind or strain when the arm is bent.
- If the blouse is intended to be worn under a suit, set-in sleeves will be most comfortable. Other styles have a bulkier armhole.

Care of Blouse

Check the label for care instructions. Some blouses can be laundered in the machine; for some, hand washing is recommended; for some, dry cleaning. Some require ironing; for some, touch-up pressing is sufficient; for others, no ironing is needed.

The care usually depends upon the fiber content, the fabric finishing process, and the styling in some cases.

Some terms you should know:

- **Drip-dry:** Hang on a hanger to dry.

Separates

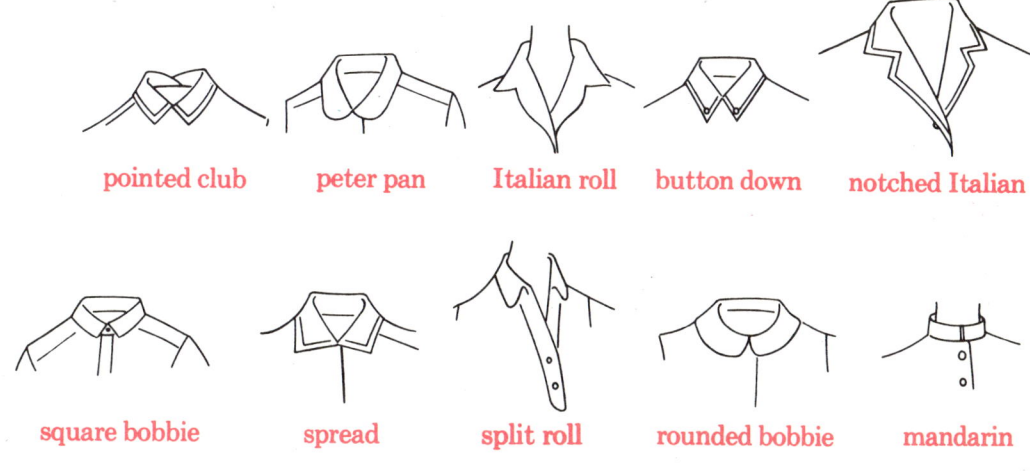

Collar styles.
Bobbie Brooks

Finger-press the seams and edges so they will dry smoothly.

• WASH-AND-WEAR (*an older term*): May be washed in the washer on a gentle cycle, but should not be spun dry. Best if hung on a hanger to dry, unless the dryer has a wash-and-wear cycle. Usually requires some touch-up pressing.

• AUTOMATIC WASH-AND-WEAR: May go through the spin cycle of the washing machine and may also be tumble dried.

• PERMANENT PRESS: If washed and dried correctly, will require no pressing. Special cycle required on both washer and dryer for best results, because fibers should be cooled before entering the spin cycle.

SWEATERS

Fibers

• WOOL (lamb or sheep): warm, durable.

• CASHMERE (hair of Kashmir goat): luxurious, soft, not so durable, very expensive.

• MOHAIR (hair of Angora kid): fine, lustrous, strong, often blended with wool for softness.

• ANGORA (hair of Angora goat): soft, fluffy, often blended with wool or nylon for strength.

• BLEND (fur fiber, wool, nylon): luxurious feel, better wear, lower price.

• SYNTHETIC (nylon, orlon, banlon): mothproof, won't shrink, easily laundered, quick drying, looks like wool but less expensive.

Construction

• *Yarns:* high bulk—soft, light, stretchy worsted-spun (long fibers)—strong, firm; woolen-spun (short fibers)—hairy, fuzzy

• *Method: full-fashioned*—knit to shape; fashioning marks at armhole and neck; more expensive; better fit; better shape retention.

—*cut and sewn*—seams are visible; may sag and twist; hand sewn stitches may be used to imitate fashion markings.

Merchandising Clothing—A Fascinating Business

Style
- CARDIGAN: open down the front.
- PULLOVER: open just at the neck.

Workmanship
- *Knit* should be firm and close. Gauge, or number of strands per inch, determines the firmness of the knit.

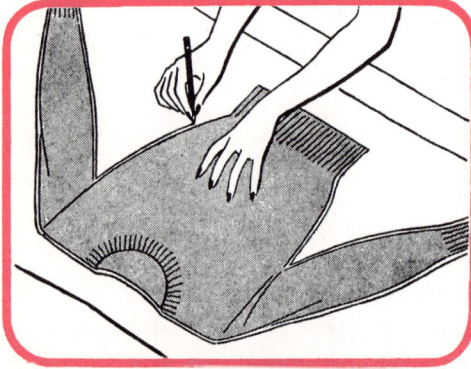

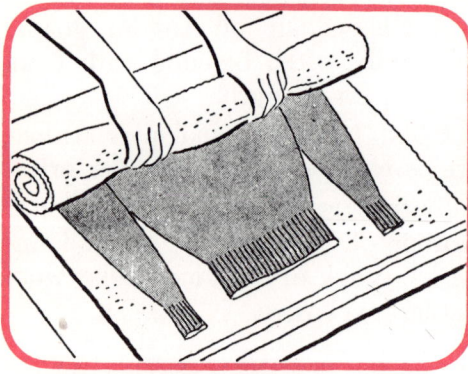

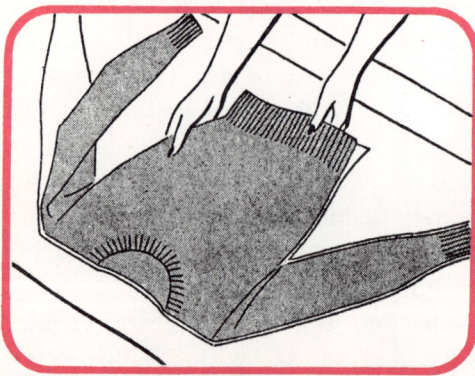

Ivory Flakes
How to wash sweaters.

- The *ribbing* at the neck, sleeves, and bottom of the sweater should be firm. Stretch it gently. If it springs back quickly, it is firm.

—The ribbing should be knitted in, not sewn on. "Knitted-in" is smooth and firm, wears longer, and won't stretch out of shape readily.

- *Openings* should not ripple. They may be faced with ribbon or be a knit band. If ribbon is used, it should be washable.
- *Buttons* should be washable and secure.
- *Buttonholes* should be straight and firmly sewn.

Size

Sweaters are sized by bust measurement. However, actual sizes are usually smaller than other ready-made garments because of the stretch of the fabric. It is better to buy sweaters a *size larger* than you ordinarily need.

Sizes can also vary several inches with style and manufacturer. If possible, a person should try on a sweater to be sure it is neither too snug nor too loose.

NOTE: Better sweaters are knit oversize, then shrunk to exact measurement. Lower price sweaters are often stretched to size and will be smaller after washing.

Care

Call attention to the care instructions on the label. Some sweaters may be washed; others should be dry cleaned.

We recommend the following procedure for washing:

- Turn the sweater *wrong side out*. Button any buttons. Wash by hand, squeezing the sweater in lukewarm water with mild suds—or use special cold water soaps. Squeeze gently; never wring. Rinse thoroughly. Roll in a thick turkish towel to absorb excess moisture.

- *Synthetic* fibers can be dried on a towel.
- *Wool* sweaters should be blocked in one of the following ways:
  1. Use an adjustable wooden or metal sweater frame.
  2. When the sweater is new, draw its outline on heavy cardboard. Cut out three pieces—body and two sleeves. Insert these pieces in the wet sweater.
  3. Before washing, draw an outline of the sweater on wrapping paper. Manipulate and pull the damp sweater to fit the outline. Check during the drying to see that it keeps its shape.

- Lightly steam-press a sweater when it is dry, to give it a "just-like-new" appearance.

We recommend that sweaters be stored flat in a drawer or box. Hung on a hanger, they may stretch out of shape.

SPORTSWEAR

Shorts and Slacks

Fabric

Should be sturdy, firm, closely woven, opaque. Some suitable fabrics include: cotton gabardine, denim, twill, sailcloth, chino, wool flannel, corduroy, and wool gabardine. Stretch fabrics are popular for sportswear because they permit freedom of movement.

Style

- SHORT SHORTS: very short.
- BOY SHORTS: short, often with a cuff.
- JAMAICA: mid-thigh.
- BERMUDA: just above the knee.
- CLAM DIGGERS: just below the knee.
- PEDAL PUSHERS: mid-calf, ¾ length.
- CAPRI PANTS: above the ankle.
- SLACKS: ankle length; tapered,

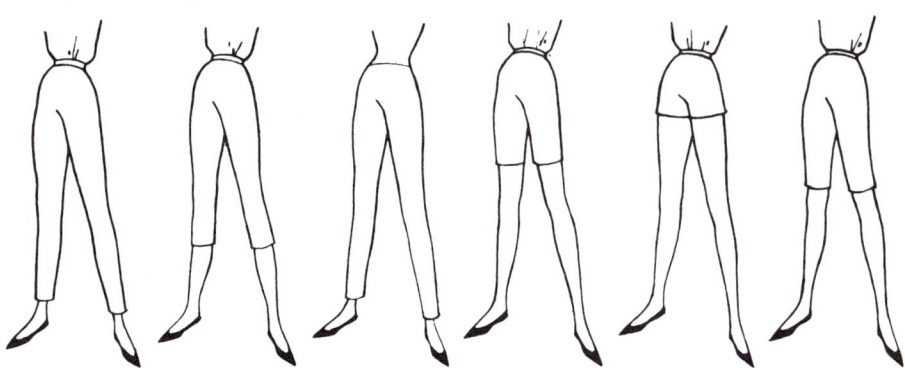

capris   pedal pushers   hip huggers   Jamaicas   short shorts   Bermudas

Bobbie Brooks

Pants styles.

Peter Pan Swimwear
One piece, classic sheath styling.

straight (stove pipe) or bell-bottom; cuffed or plain. Hip huggers rest on the hip.

Workmanship

Sturdy, generous, reinforced seams. Small stitches, no loose threads. Double-stitched crotch seam. Lapped under the zipper closing. Waistband reinforced to keep it from stretching. Hooks and eyes attached securely. Neat buttonholes and buttons sewn securely.

Size

Same as skirt.
Slacks are available in proportioned lengths—short, average, and tall.

Fitting

Waistband snug enough to hold in place.

Sufficiently loose to allow for freedom of movement.
Garments of stretch fabric should fit no tighter than garments of conventional fabrics.
Sufficient length in crotch for comfort.

SWIM WEAR

Fabric

Stretch nylon, cotton knit, wool knit, elasticized rayon or cotton.

Style

- ONE PIECE; TWO PIECE; BIKINI (abbreviated two piece).
- STRAPLESS: built-up straps; detachable straps; halter style.
- SHEATH: one piece, skirt panel in front only, elasticized legs.
- MAILLOT: brief, panty legs; no skirt panel.
- TAPERED-LEG SHORTS: the lower portion like a pair of shorts, often cuffed, with short elasticized tights underneath.
- ALL-OVER SHIRRED: "lastex," stretch to fit.
- DRESSMAKER: very short, full skirt; may be princess line or attached skirt.

Workmanship

Seams smooth and strong.
Adjustable bra with uplift lining.
Adjustable straps, securely anchored.
Extra heavy zippers.
An elasticized panel in front for "tummy" control.
Extra length in back to prevent "hiking-up."

Size

Same as dress sizes.

Fitting

- Proper procedure for putting on a swimsuit:

    Fold suit in half and hold open.

    Hold firmly at sides and step into it.

    Ease it up gently.

    When the suit has been drawn up over the hips, turn it gradually to the right side, easing it up over the top of the body.

    Lean forward, as you do in putting on a bra, to fill in the bra cups.

    Adjust straps, close zipper, etc.

    Have customer stand, sit, bend, stretch, raise arms, etc. and check the following points for fit:

- GENERAL FIT: snug enough to feel secure, allowing freedom of movement; sufficient length for comfort without riding-up.
- BUSTLINE (strapless): should fill

The classic shirt of sheer fabric in coordinated styling makes an attractive "cover-up" coat, for the one-piece and two-piece "hipster." Note the long torso styling on the one-piece created by contrasting braid trim.
Peter Pan Swimwear

De Weese Designs
The two-piece bikini and the swim-tunic with separate panty.

out cups, have adequate support; bra should stay in place as person moves and bends.

- SHOULDER STRAPS: correct length, don't cut shoulders, don't fall off shoulders.
- HIPLINE: should not ride-up at the thighs; no straining or bulging.
- CROTCH: wide enough for complete coverage.
- LEG OPENINGS: should neither bind nor gap.

Care

Wash by hand in warm water with mild soap after every wearing to remove salt and sand or chlorides. Rinse thoroughly and dry out of direct heat or sunlight.

A swimsuit will wear better if allowed to rest between wearings. *Two suits* permit the customer to wear one and rest one.

211

FOUNDATION GARMENTS

GIRDLES

Fabric

- **ALL ELASTIC**: gives the greatest stretch.
    - *Lastex*—rubber; used alone, but most often wrapped with cotton, rayon, or nylon.
    - *Spandex*—a synthetic stretch fiber; soft, lightweight; strong, comfortable; resists body oils, perspiration; easy care, machine washable.
- **NON-ELASTIC OR RIGID**: gives firm control.
    - *Cotton*—absorbent, easily laundered.
    - *Rayon*—durable, lightweight, easily laundered.
    - *Nylon*—strong, lightweight, gives easy care.
- **COMBINATION OF ELASTIC AND RIGID**: gives stretch in certain areas, control in others.
    - *Plush*—a thick pile fabric—usually cotton—used along edges to prevent irritation.
    - *Boning*—originally was real whalebone; now coated steel or plastic; used for extra control and support, to help flatten and to prevent wrinkling or "rolling."

Styling

- **GARTER BELT**: not a girdle substitute because it gives no support; its function is to hold up stockings only.
- **TWO-WAY STRETCH**: all elastic, no seams. Very comfortable to wear because it permits complete freedom of action—it stretches both in length and width as body movement requires. Best suited for the slim or average figure. Smooths the figure, but gives little support. A pull-on type, either panty or straight.
- **PANTY GIRDLE**: has leg sections, in contrast to a conventional straight girdle. May have a detachable crotch, for easy laundering. Often has detachable garters, so it can be worn without stockings. There are various lengths:
    - *Briefs*—like panties, only elastic; good for use under a bathing suit, shorts, or full skirts.
    - *Regular length*—the same length as a regular straight girdle.
    - *Long-leg*—covers the heaviest part of the thigh; trims the hipline, slims the thighs, and gives a smooth line; has hidden garters on the inside of the leg; good under slim skirts and slacks.
- **PANEL AND SEAMS**: combination elastic and rigid. Gives extra control. For a large stomach—a firm front panel; a firm rear panel for a prominent derriere; firm side panels for large hips. May be either pull-on type or step-in (have a zipper closing). May have light boning also for extra support. Available in both panty and straight, waistline and waistband styling.
- **WAISTLINE GIRDLE**: comes just to the waistline; a *waistband* girdle has a wide waistband that nips in the waist. The center of the waistband should fit at the waistline.
- **ALL-IN-ONE**: a corselet, combination of bra and girdle in one garment. Gives smooth, unbroken line. May be pull-on or step-in styling. Available with low back or strapless for evening

Foundation Garments

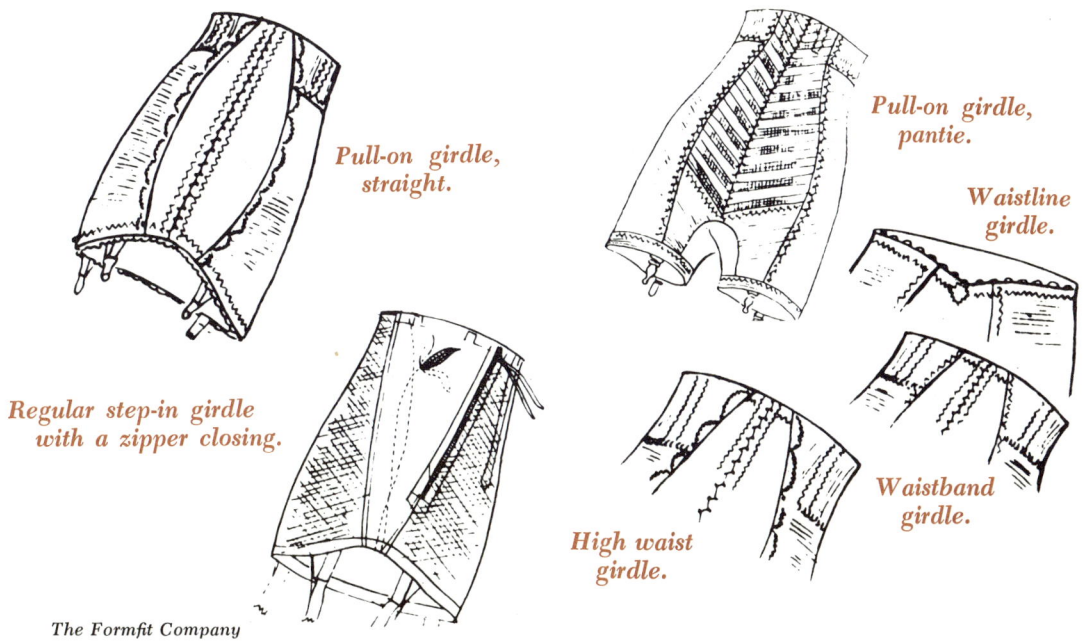

Pull-on girdle, straight.

Pull-on girdle, pantie.

Waistline girdle.

Regular step-in girdle with a zipper closing.

High waist girdle.

Waistband girdle.

The Formfit Company

dress also. A short version is available—the "merry widow"—that is not much more than a waist-cinching garter belt.

- CORSET: heavily boned, often laced, and made from heavier fabrics. Used for large, difficult figures or when extra, rigid support is desirable. Specially designed garments for figure irregularities, maternity, correctional and post-operative supports fall in this class, but these must be *professionally fitted*.

Workmanship

Top and bottom should be lined in a soft fabric for comfort.

There should be no raw edges visible and no loose threads.

Supporters should be securely attached and covered with ribbon for a smooth line.

Seams should be flat and smooth; stitches should be small.

Size

Pull-on girdles are sized according to waist measurement as follows:

- PETITE: 22″–23″
- SMALL: 24″–25″
- MEDIUM: 26″–28″
- LARGE: 29″–30″
- EXTRA LARGE: 31″–32″
- STEP-IN GARMENTS: sized by the *waist* measurement (size 26, 27, 28, 29, etc.) and the *hip* development (straight, average, and full). To obtain the correct figure type, subtract the waist measurement from the hip measurement. For straight, there is 8 or less inches difference; average, 9 to 11 inches; and full, more than 11 inches.

Regular girdles also come in different lengths, from 12 to 18 inches. To obtain the correct length, measure from the natural waistline to the base of the buttocks and add 2 inches for sitting.

Merchandising Clothing—A Fascinating Business

Fitting

Have the customer follow this procedure when putting on a girdle:

- Fold the garment in half with the top folded down toward the outside.
- Step into the garment and pull it into position on the body. NOTE: the garters will be in place. Crossing the legs permits the garment to slip up easier. **Caution:** Hold the fabric with the fingers, not the fingernails—the nails might break or cause a hole.
- When the bottom half is in position, roll the top half up to the waistline. It will roll easily without any tugging and pulling.
- To remove a girdle, reverse this procedure.
- For a *step-in* girdle, it is not necessary to fold down the top half of the girdle before stepping into it. Otherwise, the procedure is the same. When the girdle is in position, fasten the hooks under the zipper and close the zipper.

Check the following fitting points:

- If there is a waistband, its center should be at the waistline. If the girdle rolls at the top, it is either too long or too high at the waist.
- The girdle should fit smoothly and be snug. If it binds, it is too tight. If the flesh bulges, either at the waist or the hip, the girdle is either too tight, too short, or both.
- Have the customer bend, stretch, and sit. The girdle should give support, yet be comfortable. If it rides up, it is too short.
- For a panty girdle, check the length from the waist to the crotch to be sure it does not bind.
- For sanitary reasons, a girdle should always be *tried on* over panties. In *actual use*, however, a trimmer look is achieved if the garment is worn next to the skin.

Care

Advise the customers to alternate wearing girdles so that they will last longer. Encourage them to have at least three: wear one, wash one, and rest one.

Care in putting them on also prolongs life.

Girdles should be washed frequently, because perspiration and body oils may discolor and weaken the fibers.

Recommend this procedure for *washing* girdles:

- Launder them in the washing machine only if the manufacturer's label says they are machine-washable.
- Use lukewarm water and mild suds or a product specifically made for laundering elastic garments. Avoid very hot water and strong detergents. They weaken elastic.
- Squeeze gently, but never twist or wring. If there is soil around the waistline or lower edge, rub gently with a soft brush.
- Rinse thoroughly as many times as necessary until the water is clear.
- Roll garment in a towel to absorb excess moisture.
- Allow to dry at room temperature, away from heat or direct sunlight.
- Do not hang the garment.

BRAS

Fabric

Most bras are made from cotton or nylon in solid fabric, lace, or net. Spandex and blends are also used.

Lingerie

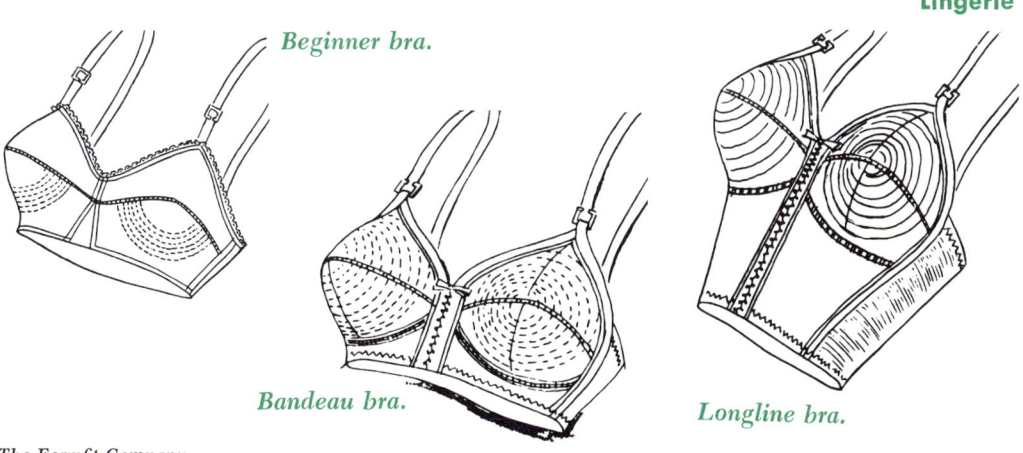

Beginner bra.
Bandeau bra.
Longline bra.

The Formfit Company

- ELASTIC: lastex or spandex.
- LINING: jersey-type rayon, acetate, or blend.
- PADDING: rubber foam, polyester foam, or "fiber-fill."
- BONING
- WIRES

Styling

- TEEN BRA: a beginner bra, designed primarily for coverage. Shallow cups, wide separation between, no support band between.
- CONTOUR: pre-shaped cups lightly lined with foam. Gives shape and firmness; doesn't necessarily increase size.
- BANDEAU: a short bra with a support band under the cups. Molds, uplifts, supports. Special features—elastic sections, circular stitched cups (accentuate size), bias section cups (uplift), set-in pockets (added support), detachable straps.
- LONGLINE: a bandeau bra with a long midriff section extending 3 to 6 inches below the cups (to the waistline or slightly below). Often has hooks to attach to the girdle. Gives support, a smooth unbroken line, and controls "midriff bulge."
- STRAPLESS: either no straps or detachable. Designed to wear under off-the-shoulder and strapless clothes. Molded, wired, or boned. May be either short or longline.
- PADDED: added thickness in cups; foam rubber, polyfoam, or fiber-fill

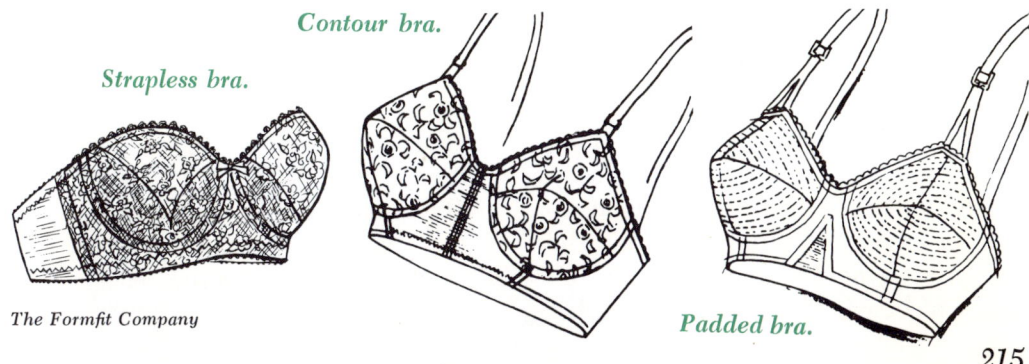

Strapless bra.
Contour bra.
Padded bra.

The Formfit Company

padding stitched in. Increases size. Designed to give the effect of a better proportioned figure. Some are available with pockets for inserting separately purchased "falsies."

Workmanship

- SHOULDER STRAPS: should have either buckles or elastic inserts, or be made of all stretch fabric for adjusting the length.
- BACK CLOSING: should have elastic at both sides and at least two sets of hooks and eyes; should be adjustable.
- DIAPHRAGM BAND: should be securely attached to bra and have an elastic insert for "give" and freedom of movement.
- STITCHES: should be secure; there should be no loose threads.
- SEAMS: these should be finished smoothly.

Size

Bras are sized in even numbers (32, 34, 36, etc.) and according to the following cup sizes:

AA—very small, breasts not fully developed.
A —small; needs little support.
B —average; needs shaping and lifting.
C —larger; needs firm support.
D —very large; needs extra firm support.
E —pendulous; needs a great deal of support and special fitting.

To determine bra size, take a snug measurement around the rib cage directly under the bust. Add 5 inches to this measurement. For example, if the rib measurement is 27 inches, the bra size will be 32. If the measurement is not an even number—for example; rib measurement is 28 inches, plus 5 inches, equals 33 inches—fit the customer in a larger size (in this case, size 34) rather than the smaller size. NOTE: The adjustable back closing allows for an inch size adjustment.

To determine cup size, take a loose measurement around the fullest part of the bust. Compare this measurement with the bra size. If the figure is less, the customer needs an AA cup; if it is the same, an A cup; 1 inch more, a B cup; 2 inches more, a C cup, etc.

Fitting

Instruct the customer to lean forward from the waist when putting on a bra. Then the bust will lie naturally in the cups. Hook the bra in the inside hook if there are two; in the middle hook if there are three.

Check the following points in fitting:

- A bra should support the bust in a natural position, usually midway between the shoulder and the elbow.
- The bust should fill the cups. If it doesn't, the cup is too large.
- There should be no bulges at the top of the bra. If there are, the cup is too small.
- There should be no wrinkles under the arm. If there are, the cup or the bra is too small.
- The bra band should be well down across the back. If it isn't, the straps are too tight.
- The straps should give support without cutting into the shoulders.
- The bra should remain in position even when a person reaches or stretches. If it doesn't, it is too large.

Care

Wash after every wearing.

Unless wired, most bras can be washed in the machine. Many are also machine dryable.

Avoid very hot water and strong detergents. They weaken elastic.

LINGERIE

SLIPS

Fabric

- COTTON: cool, absorbs moisture, doesn't cling, launders easily, may require ironing.
- RAYON: inexpensive, but requires more care.
- SILK: expensive, delicate.
- SYNTHETIC (nylon most popular): strong, durable, may cling, may pill, may become grayed or yellowed.
- BLENDS: dacron and cotton; give easy care, are comfortable.

Fabrics may be either *woven* (crepe, satin, or taffeta) or *knit*. Tricot is a popular knit fabric used for lingerie. Conventional or circular knits have no ribs, whereas tricot has vertical ribs on the right side and horizontal ribs on the wrong side (see page 137).

Qualities desired: soft, lightweight, non-transparent, nonstatic (it won't cling), easy care, color fast (if not white), shrinkage controlled.

Style

- FULL: with sheer garments, with no belt or no waistline seam.
- HALF: with separates, suits, or when garment has a belt.
- PETTICOATS: with full skirts.
- TAILORED: usually plain with no lace or decoration.
- TRIMMED: lace inserts, edgings, etc.
- STRAIGHT CUT: will not ride up.
- PANELED: two seams in front and back, providing width below the hipline.
- BIAS CUT: smooth fit, fabric conforms to figure.
- SHADOW PANEL: double fabric either front only, front and back panel, or all-around.

Workmanship

- SEAMS: double or edge stitched in woven fabrics; overcast in tricot fabrics.
- HEMS: narrow, with two or more rows of stitching in woven fabrics; close zig-zag stitching used in knit fabrics.
- SHOULDER STRAPS: firm fabric; attached securely to the body of the slip not just to the trim; adjustable.
- TRIMMING: firmly attached, washable.

Size

Full slips are sized according to the bust measurement (32 to 44) or the dress size. They come in teen, junior, misses, and half sizes.

A half slip is sized according to the waist measurement—usually small, medium, and large—similar to girdle sizes.

Slips may also be proportioned according to height—short, average, and tall.

Fitting

A slip should be slightly shorter than the skirt worn with it. It should fit smoothly, allowing for freedom of movement, with no strain yet no excess fullness.

Merchandising Clothing—A Fascinating Business

PANTIES

Fabric

Most panties are made from cotton, rayon, or nylon.

The fabric should be run-resistant, easy to launder; require no ironing.

Styling

- **BRIEFS:** short, snug fitting.
- **STEP-INS:** various lengths, loose fitting legs.
- **PETTI-PANTS:** fitted leg; mid-thigh length.

Workmanship

- **Elastic at waist:** have plenty of give, enclosed in waistline, securely attached with a zigzag stitch to permit stretching without breaking.
- **Seams:** smooth, flat, raw edges finished.
- **Crotch:** double thickness of fabric.

Size

Panties are sized by the hip measurement as follows:
- SIZE 3: 30″–31″
-       4: 32″–33″
-       5: 34″–35″
-       6: 36″–37″
-       7: 38″–39″

Fitting

Panties should fit fairly snugly, be smooth, yet have comfortable stretch; they should not bind.

SLEEPWEAR

Fabric

- NYLON TRICOT.
- COTTON: batiste, plissé, flannelette, challis, broadcloth.
- BLENDS.
- SILK CHIFFON.

Styling

- **GOWNS:** full length, waltz length, shorty length; tailored or lace trimmed; straight or bias cut; straps, built-up shoulders, gathered onto a neck band, or short puffed sleeves; flared or straight; hang straight from shoulder, yoke or bra type styling, or mid-section inserts.
- **GRANNY GOWN:** high, yoke neck; full length; long sleeves shirred in at the bottom with a ruffle.
- **PAJAMAS:** *full length*—generally tailored like a man's, shirt-like top; *baby doll*—two-piece, loose fitting top and short full panties gathered in with elastic; *bermuda*—short length trousers, above the knee; *ski pajama*—challis or flannelette, trouser legs shirred in at the bottom.

Sizing

By the bust measurement—32, 34, 36, etc.

LOUNGE WEAR

Fabrics

Same as those used for gowns or pajamas, plus chenille, quilted, terry, corduroy, velvet, wool flannel, etc.

Styling

- **TAILORED ROBES:** usually long, straight, resembling a coat with notched collar and long sleeves; often belted.
- **DUSTERS:** short, loose fitting coat-type coverall garment.
- **HOUSECOAT:** Usually long, open down the front, either fitted or loose.
- **HOSTESS GOWN:** the same styling as

a housecoat, but usually of a luxurious fabric.
- **Negligee or peignoir**: sheer, full, flowing garment with long sleeves, usually with gown of same fabric, long or short.
- **Bed jacket**: short jacket, usually loose fitting, with high neck and long sleeves; for use when sitting up in bed.

Size
Same as dress.

Hosiery

Fabric
Most hosiery is made from nylon. Silk, rayon, and cotton are also used. Cantrece is a kind of nylon yarn with a built-in crimp, giving hosiery extraordinary resilience, resulting in a stocking that clings to the leg and doesn't wrinkle.
- **Plain knit**: sheer, elastic, smooth texture; a break causes a run.
- **Mesh knit**: run-proof or run-resistant, less flexible, may break at points of strain. A break causes a hole, not a run; or it will run up from the hole, but not down.
- **Stretch**: made from yarns specially constructed for greater stretchability (see page 128). Fits snugly, prevents wrinkles on slim legs, prevents binding on heavy legs.
- **Denier**: size of thread, used to determine sheerness.

  Lower denier—fine, fragile thread; 10, 12, 15 denier are very sheer dress or evening sheers.

  Higher denier—heavier thread, less likely to break; 20, 30 denier are not so sheer—walking or business weight.

- **Gauge**: number of stitches in each 1½ inches across full-fashioned stockings. The higher the gauge, the closer knit, more elastic the stocking. Denier and gauge are usually in proportion to each other—the lower the denier, the higher the gauge.
- **Needle count**: measurement of the stitches across seamless stockings.

Styling
- **Socks**: end at various points below the knee (knee socks, anklets, etc.). Socks are usually circular knit with no seams, using from medium to heavy yarn. The most popular fibers are:

  Cotton—durable, comfortable, machine washable.

  Wool—warm, shrinks if laundered improperly.

  Orlon—resembles wool, warm, easy care.

  Nylon—strongest, not absorbent.

- **Stockings**: lightweight fabrics; knee length to full length; also available in ankle length for wear under slacks and in panty-stockings (one-piece).
- **Full-fashioned**: (seamed) knit flat, then seamed from head to toe. Knit to the shape of the leg; permanent shape. *Fashion markings* are the small marks on either side of the back seam where stitches have been decreased to give shape to the stocking. NOTE: Stockings with seams make the leg look slimmer.
- **Seamless** (circular knit): knit in a tube from top to toe. Shaped either by heat or by tightening the yarn during the knitting. With seamless stockings there is no worry about keeping the seams straight, but they do not slim the leg.

Workmanship

Close knit—better fit, better appearance, better wear.

Clear texture, no streaks.

Dull finish rather than shiny.

Even stitches, straight seams.

Reinforced heel and toe.

Deep welt at top of stocking.

- IRREGULAR: slight flaws in fabric, color, or size—will not affect wear.
- SECONDS: slight mistakes in construction—may or may not affect wear.

Size

Stockings are sized from 8 to 11 according to the measurement from heel to toe. For example, a size 10 stocking measures 10 inches from heel to toe.

For comfort, suggest a stocking slightly longer than the foot. For a very wide foot, suggest a half-size larger.

Stockings are also proportioned (short—28", average—29"–30", and tall—up to 34") according to the measurement from the base of the heel to the top of the stocking. To find the correct length, measure from the base of the heel to the garter on the girdle. For a heavy leg, suggest a longer stocking.

Fitting

A stocking should fit snugly, with no wrinkling or bagging, yet not so snug as to bind. There should be no strain when sitting or bending the knee.

Supporters should be fastened to the top part of the welt (upper reinforced section) without folding or stretching the stocking.

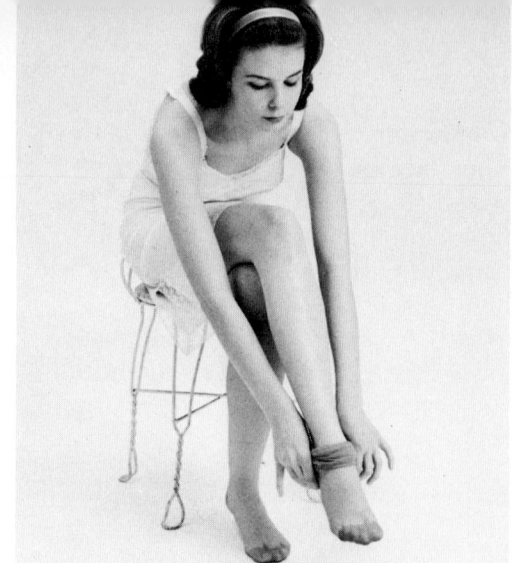

How to put on stockings.

Isis Nylons

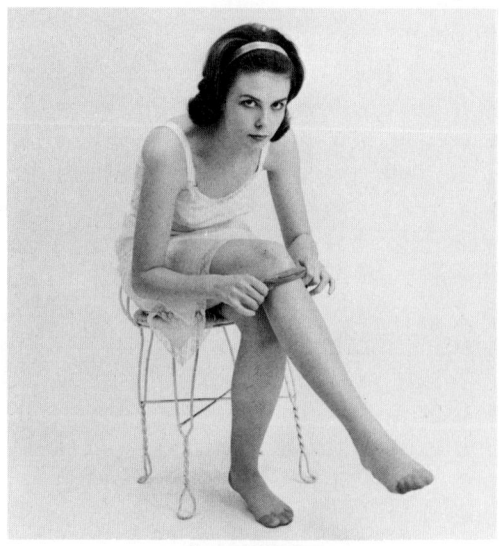

Pull stockings up.

Fasten back supporters first; then sit to fasten the front supporters.

Care

Sell at least two pairs of the same style and color. In case of a runner, the mate can be used as a "spare."

- To put on stockings:

  Roll down to the toe. Place foot in carefully. *Be sure toe nails are smooth.*

  Note: Rough hands and nails can cause snags. Suggest a pair of "cosmetic gloves" for use when handling stockings. It is best to *remove finger and wrist jewelry.*

  Pull stocking up on leg carefully.

  Check to see that the seams are straight. With stretch stockings, be sure that the heel is in the proper position and stretch the stocking open while pulling it up on the leg.

  Fasten the back supporters first. Sit down to fasten the front supporters. This allows for room to bend the knee.

- Washing stockings:

  Wash after every wearing.

  Use lukewarm water and mild suds.

  Squeeze suds through stockings. Do not soak or wring.

  Rinse thoroughly.

  Squeeze out excess water with a towel.

  Dry on a smooth rod. Do not hang with wooden clothespins.

ACCESSORIES

Shoes

Fabric

All shoes must be labeled, indicating whether materials used are natural or man-made.

- Leather: (cowhide) tough, strong, most widely used.
- Kid: from goats—fine, resilient, porous.
- Calf: pliable, fine, smooth, not easily scuffed.
- Suede: either buffed calf or kid.
- Reptile: alligator or lizard; expensive, very durable, not easily scuffed, doesn't crack, shrink, or stretch.
- Patent: either calf or kid that has been varnished or enameled; airtight, watertight, no give, cracks easily.
- Woven fabrics: either linen, canvas, or satin; lose their shape easily and do not give proper support.
- Simulated leather: (plastic) long wearing, but it doesn't "breathe;" usually makes the feet very warm and may cause blisters.
- Straw: popular for summer, but doesn't wear well.
- Synthetics: "Corfam" and others —resemble leather, scuff-resistant, water-repellent, easy-care (wipe with a damp cloth), shape retentive, breathes; made in smooth, textured, or napped finish.

Styling

- Flat: very low heel or no heel.
- Loafer: trade name for moccasin type shoe.
- Open-toed: front of shoe cut so toes are exposed.
- Open-heeled: back of shoe cut so heels are exposed.
- Oxford: ends just below ankle, held on with laces across the instep.
- Saddle oxford: flat-heeled and has a section across the instep of a contrasting colored leather.
- Play: any kind of shoe for casual wear.

- **Pump**: low cut, no straps or ties; step-in.
- **Opera pump**: classic, plain.
- **D'Orsay pump**: cut very low at sides.
- **Sling pump**: heelless, strap around heel.
- **Sandal**: heelless, low cut, held on with straps.
- **Scuff**: no heel, just a strip across the instep.
- **Slipper**: soft sole.
- **Sneaker**: sports shoe; canvas top, rubber sole; ties.
- **Thong**: a strap fits between the large toe and the toe next to it.
- **Walking**: low or medium heel; often ties.

Heel styles

- **Cuban**: medium height, straight heel.
- **Flat**: low, broad.
- **French**: high, curved.
- **Military**: straight like Cuban, but lower and broader.
- **Spike**: very high, narrow.
- **Stacked**: separate pieces or layers, attached together, uncovered.
- **Wedge**: continuation of the sole; a flat platform. Entire bottom of the shoe, from the toe to the back of the heel, rests on the ground.

Workmanship

There are three kinds of construction, usually combined: sewn, cemented, and nailed. The type used depends upon the material and style of the shoe, as well as its use.

Most of the construction is hidden, so quality is hard to judge. The *lining* can be used as a guide: should be smooth, wrinkle-free, even stitching, no loose threads.

Parts of a shoe

- **Vamp**: front of shoe from toe to instep.
- **Throat**: top of vamp.
- **Tip**: toe section.
- **Quarter**: back of shoe from instep to center of heel.
- **Tongue**: portion under laces, protects the foot.
- **Counter**: reinforcement around heel under the quarter, helps maintain shape and snug fit.
- **Lining**: cover the inside.
- **Sole**: outside, bottom of the shoe.
- **Insole**: inside, under the foot.
- **Shank**: curved portion between the heel and the ball of the foot.
- **Heel**: the support under the heel part of the foot.
- **Lift**: a protector attached to the bottom of the heel; can be replaced when worn out.

Rainwear styles

- **Overshoe**: designed to be worn over regular shoes; made of rubber, plastic, or waterproof fabric (nylon). Also called *galosh* (generally in the plural).
- **Toe rubber**: covers the toe of the shoe only; held on by a heel strap.
- **Boot**: some worn over regular shoes, some designed to be worn without shoes (shoe boot); extends above the ankle—midcalf, knee high; often have a zipper closing if close fitting.
- **Stadium boot**: ankle-high, fur-lined; fastened with zipper or ties; worn over shoes.

Size

- **Foot length**: from heel to toe. 7, 7½, 8, etc. The difference between each half size is only ⅙ inch; each full size, only ⅓ inch.

- FOOT WIDTH: at the widest part of the foot; 5A (very narrow) to E (very wide). The circumference of the last (the last is the mold over which a shoe is made—gives a shoe shape) increases ¼ inch with each different width.
- ARCH LENGTH: from heel to the ball of the foot. No specific designation; will differ in shoes of the same size, depending upon the last.

Fitting

It is best to fit shoes in the afternoon when the foot has expanded.

Measure both feet; one may be larger than the other. If so, fit the larger foot; the other shoe can be padded to fit. Measure the length in both a sitting and a standing position.

Try on both shoes. Have the customer stand up and walk around to check the fit. Check the following points:

- The shoe should support the foot at the three weight-bearing points: (1) base of the heel, (2) base of the large toe, (3) base of the small toe.
- There should be space enough to allow the toes to move freely.
- There should be about ½ inch between the end of the longest toe and the tip of the shoe.
- The broadest part of the foot should be at the widest part of the shoe. (The shoe and the foot both bend at this point; they should bend together.)
- The shoe should not slip at the heel. Some shoes are made in two widths—one for the main part of the shoe and the other for the heel. This is known as *combination last*. If the shoe seems to fit well but the heel slips, the customer may need a narrower heel width.
- Shoes should not pinch, cut across the instep, or gape at the sides. The toes should not turn up; neither should the foot bulge over the side of the shoe. In the case of *toeless* or *heelless* shoes, neither the toe nor the heel should extend beyond the end of the shoe.

Care

If a shoe fits well, it will wear longer and look better.

Shoes should be permitted to air between wearings. It is better if they are not worn two days in a row.

Keep heels straightened.

Clean and shine shoes frequently.

If shoes get wet, wipe them clean and dry them slowly away from direct heat. Stuff them with paper to preserve their shape while drying.

To preserve their shape when not on the foot, insert shoe trees.

GLOVES

Fabric

- FOR DRESS: kidskin, satin, lace, or net.
- FOR DAYTIME: cotton, nylon, wool, or leather.
- FOR CASUAL WEAR: pigskin, knit, or fur.

White, black, and beige gloves are basic. They may be worn with almost any color. Colored gloves may be chosen either to harmonize with or accent clothing. Select them to go with dress, coat, and shoes.

Styling

Glove lengths are measured from the base of the thumb to the top edge

Merchandising Clothing—A Fascinating Business

Accessories are the finishing touches. Handbag and gloves complete the picture.
a. Envelope bag—closes like an envelope.
b. Pouch—attached to a rigid frame.

c. Satchel—resembles a piece of hand luggage.
d. Shoulder bag—long strap worn over the shoulder.

Jaclyn Handbags

of the glove. This length is expressed in "buttons" (slightly larger than an inch) rather than inches.

- **Wrist-length** gloves may be worn with sleeveless daytime dresses, evening dresses, or with ¾ length sleeves.
- "**Two-button**" (approximately 2 inches from the base of the thumb to the end of the glove) are appropriate with long-sleeved coats and suits.
- "**Eight-button**" look well with either ¾ length or very short sleeves.
- "**Twelve-button**" may be worn with elbow-length or short sleeves.
- "**Twenty-button**" gloves are very formal, should be worn only with strapless gowns.

Workmanship

All stitches should be small and evenly spaced.

There are four methods of sewing gloves together:

- 1. **Inseam**: seams are stitched on the inside, and the glove is turned right side out. No stitches visible; no raw edges showing; easiest to make; least expensive; fairly durable.
- 2. **Outseam**: regular seam, but with raw edges on the outside. Often sewn by hand with a running stitch; bulky; used for sports gloves.
- 3. **Overseam**: raw edges on the outside. Seams are overcast by hand or machine; fine stitches; attractive; not very durable.
- 4. **Piqué (p.k.) seam**: one edge lapped over the other; one raw edge showing. Most difficult to make; most expensive; most durable.

Size

Gloves are sized according to the measurement, in inches, around the knuckles. Sizes range from 5½ to 8.

Stretchable gloves and mittens are usually sized small (5½ to 6), medium (6½ to 7), and large (7½ to 8).

Fitting

Always try on gloves. To put them on, insert the fingers first, then the thumb. Don't pull them on; work them on.

The glove fingers should be as long as the fingers. Gloves should fit without straining, binding, or wrinkling.

YARD GOODS

A thorough knowledge of textiles will be a great help to you in selling yard goods. You should know *fibers* and their outstanding characteristics, fabric construction, and fabric finishes. You should know the *names of fabrics* and be able to identify them. You should be able to picture how a fabric will look when used for a certain style so that you can advise customers about the suitability of a fabric for a pattern. Customers may also look to you for advice concerning suitability of fabric or *style* to the individual (color, line, design, etc.). You should be familiar with the special *sewing techniques* necessary for various fabrics, as well as proper care procedures.

You should know which fabrics are *suitable for beginners* and which require expert sewing ability. Your study of textiles (Chapter 4) and Color, Line, and Design (Chapter 3) will prove valuable to you every day on the selling floor. The more knowledge you have, the better able you will be to advise customers in their fabric selection so that they will achieve successful results.

There is a certain amount of basic sewing information that will also be valuable because customers quite often look to the salesperson for help in the following areas:

What size pattern?

It may be necessary to take the customer's measurements and help her select the correct size and type of pattern. For this information, refer to page 273.

How much fabric?

Learn to read the chart on the back of the pattern envelope that tells you how much fabric to buy. The view the person is going to make will determine which set of figures to look at on the chart. If she is making View 2, you can eliminate all of the chart except that section devoted to View 2.

You must know the *width* of the material. Generally cotton and linen fabrics are 35–36 inches wide; silks, 39–42 inches; rayons and synthetics, 44–45 inches; and wool or wool blends, 54–60 inches. These widths do not always hold true, but they serve as a guide. If in doubt, check the label at the end of the bolt or measure the fabric.

On a yardage chart, you will find different sets of figures for fabrics "with nap" and "without nap." The word nap on the yardage chart is used for any material that must be cut all in one direction (nap, pile, one-way design). As you learned in your study of fabrics, nap actually means the short fuzzy fibers formed by brushing the surface of some fabrics (see page 145). With such a fabric, all pattern pieces must be cut in the same directions so that the nap will go one way. To do this requires more material.

To read the chart easily, find the proper fabric width and type. Run your finger across this line until you reach the column for the person's size (at the top of chart). This is the amount of material needed. Sometimes people feel that they should buy a little extra "just in case." Not only is this not necessary; it is actually a waste. The only time more is needed is in the case of a plaid, stripe or large print that must be matched. The extra amount varies from ¼ to ½ yard, depending upon the size of the plaid or print and the number of pattern pieces.

Be sure to check for *contrasting fabric*—yokes, collars, cuffs, bands, etc.

Yardage is *measured* either with a yardstick, along a solid metal rule, or in an automatic fabric measuring machine, but never with a tape measure (it stretches and isn't accurate). The most accurate method is with the *automatic measurer:* As the fabric is drawn through, the length is continuously recorded on a dial. When the desired amount is reached, mark with a slash by depressing a lever. After removing the fabric, press a button returning the dial to "0" and the machine is ready for another use. (These machines have a table that figures the *price* of the amount measured.)

Yard Goods

NOTE: Fabric should be *torn* from the bolt whenever possible. It is difficult to cut fabric straight (on one thread) unless there is a woven pattern. If you tear it, however, it tears along one thread and will be straight.

Interfacing

This is extra material inserted between the garment and the facing to prevent stretching. It adds firmness and body to collars, cuffs, and lapels. It strengthens and reinforces an area that may receive strain, such as under buttons and buttonholes. Some patterns only recommend interfacing or say that it is optional. In such cases, inform your customers that they will achieve a smarter, more professional effect if they use it. Interfacing can make the difference between a "homemade" and a professional looking garment.

There are fabrics made especially for interfacing. These are of two types, *woven* and *non-woven*. Woven interfacings have grain, whereas the non-woven fabrics resemble lightweight felt; they have no threads and may be cut in any direction. Both types come in various widths and weights. In general the non-woven interfacings are stiffer than the woven, but there is a "bias" non-woven type (it stretches in all directions) that is more flexible than the regular. *Iron-on* interfacings, both woven and non-woven, are also available, but these are most successful when used in small areas.

Some woven interfacing fabrics include:
- HYMO: generic name for hair canvas; trade-names—Armo, Sta-Shape. Light to heavy in weight; used for tailoring suits and coats, must be dry cleaned.
- FORMITE: medium weight for dress fabrics.
- SIBONNE: lightweight, comes in soft and crisp finish.
- STAFLEX: medium weight, irons on.
- SUPER SIRI: both soft and firm.
- VERIFORM: lightweight.

Some non-woven interfacing fabrics include:
- KEYBACK: light to heavy; also available in iron-on.
- PELLON: regular in light to heavy; also all bias.
- PELOMITE: iron-on, is of medium weight.
- STAFLEX: iron-on.

Some regular dress fabrics, such as lawn, taffeta, organdy, percale, or muslin may also be used for interfacing.

Since there are so many different interfacings and many of them can be used with the same fabrics, helping your customer select the right one may present a problem. The type of fabric chosen for the interfacing depends first upon the garment fabric—its color, its weight, and whether or not it is washable. There are no definite rules to follow except that the interfacing fabric should not be heavier than the outer fabric. A heavy fabric requires a firm interfacing, whereas a lighter fabric requires a lighter interfacing. If the garment is washable, the interfacing should also be washable. Salespersons should recommend *shrinking* all woven interfacings before using them.

The choice of interfacing also depends upon the *purpose* it is to serve. If used to stiffen, a stiff fabric must be used. If the interfacing is to be used for reinforcement, a soft fabric should be selected. Drape the garment fabric over the interfacing and ask: Does it feel right? Will it accomplish its purpose?

Underlining

This is fabric used as backing for the outer fabric. In construction, the underlining is *basted to the outer fabric* first; then the two pieces of fabric are handled as one to make the garment. Underlining gives more body to a garment and keeps it from stretching out of shape. Firmly woven fabrics such as taffeta or sheath lining can be used as well as fabrics made especially for this purpose—SiBonne, Siri, Undercurrent, and Veriform are examples. In *tailoring*, coats and jackets of loosely woven or lightweight fabric may be completely underlined with the regular interfacing fabrics also.

If there is no separate yardage chart, sell the same amount of underlining fabric as needed for the outer garment in fabric of the same width. Be sure to recommend a washable underlining fabric if the outer fabric is washable.

Lining

This gives a finished appearance to a garment by covering all the raw edges. It also contributes to a "smooth feel." In contrast to an underlining, a lining is *construced separately* from the outer garment and sewn into it. A lining fabric should be *smooth* so that the garment will slip on and off easily. It should be *color fast* and resistant to the effects of perspiration. It should be *closely woven* to withstand wear; also if it is firm or slightly stiff it will add extra body to the garment and help prevent wrinkling. NOTE: Generally the color should be close to the outer fabric or blend with it. If a contrasting color or print is desired, check to see that the lining doesn't show through the outer fabric.

Some fabrics used for linings include:
- EARL GLO: a trade-name for a fine twill lining fabric; acetate, perspiration proof, fade proof.
- CREPE: rayon or silk; firmly woven, soft.
- TISSUE TAFFETA: rayon, lightweight, firm.
- SATIN: rayon or silk; lightweight, slippery.
- QUILTED: two layers of cloth with wadding between, stitched together like a quilt; warm, bulky.
- MILIUM: insulated lining; right side is either twill, satin, or taffeta; reverse side is coated with metallic insulator; warm, lightweight.
- LAMINATED: foam permanently bonded to fabric; lightweight, less bulky, warm.
- SUNBAK: a trade-name for a satin lining fabric with a napped wool backing.

Interlining

This is extra fabric inserted between the lining and the outer fabric for warmth. It may be a separate fabric specifically designed for this purpose (wool interlining), or it may be in combination with the lining (quilted, laminated, Sunbak).

Yard Goods

What notions?

Check the notion list on the back of the pattern envelope and remind the customer of the sewing supplies she needs for the garment she is making. Most people plan to buy all their supplies when they buy the pattern and fabric. In this way, they will be able to match colors easily and will have them when they need them.

Threads

Select thread one shade darker than the fabric—it "sews-in" lighter than it appears on the spool. Your knowledge of fabric will help you advise the customer on the best type of thread to use—*mercerized cotton* for most general sewing; *heavy duty* for heavy fabrics; *silk* for silk and wool; *synthetic* for man-made fibers and blends.

Zipper

Available in metal and nylon. Nylon zippers require special care when ironing (avoid hot iron or they melt). Be sure to check the type needed—dress, skirt, neckline, separating, etc.—and the length.

Seam binding

- WOVEN EDGE—a ribbon-like band with no raw edges, straight grain, does not stretch.
- BIAS—raw edges folded under; cut on bias, stretches, useful for binding seams and finishing curved edges. Available in rayon (bias seam binding) and cotton (bias tape—both single fold and double fold).
- *Iron-on seam* binding—woven edge seam binding with an adhesive that can be attached by pressing with a warm, dry iron. It can be removed (press and peel off while warm) and re-used.

Fasteners

Buttons (check the number needed; size is usually suggested also), snaps, hooks and eyes, frogs, buckles, and special clasps.

Trimmings

Braid, rick-rack, fringe, etc. if needed. The amount, width, etc. are listed either on the notion or yardage list.

In review:

Explain the difference between style and fashion.

What construction points can be stressed in selling ready-to-wear?

Describe the figure type for each of the following size ranges: junior, misses, women's, half-size.

How are each of the following sized: dresses, blouses, coats, skirts, sweaters, slips, girdles?

What fabric characteristics are desirable for a washable blouse? a winter coat? lining fabric? slips?

What purpose does elastic serve in a girdle? the rigid fabric? boning? plush?

What are the advantages and disadvantages of the following slip fabrics: cotton, nylon, a blend of dacron and cotton?

What fitting points do you check in dresses? coats?

What are the advantages of bias cut slips?

Define denier and gauge. Which stocking is more sheer—30 denier, 51 gauge or 15 denier, 10 gauge?

What is the difference between irregular and seconds?

Outline the proper procedure for putting on a swimsuit; a girdle; a bra; hosiery.

How would you advise a customer to care for a wool sweater? a permanent-press blouse? a nylon swimsuit? a spandex girdle? a cotton bra? nylon stockings? orlon socks?

What is the difference between interfacing, underlining, lining, and interlining?

For further discussion

What to wear when.

What to wear with what.

Appropriate clothing for specific occasions.

The fashion picture—the look, the fabrics, the colors of the current season.

To gain experience

Using the merchandise information available, prepare a list of selling points for the following:
- nylon tricot slip
- three-piece wool knit suit
- spandex long-leg pantie girdle
- dacron-cotton blend tailored shirt
- silk blouse
- irregular seamless mesh stockings
- velvet cocktail dress
- tailored linen sheath
- orlon slip-on sweater
- elasticized cotton one-piece swimsuit

Prepare a merchandise manual for one of the clothing categories. Include style features, fabrics used, construction features, care instructions, any special characteristics, when and how worn, etc.

Prepare a display of fabrics popularly used for each category of clothing. Identify by name and outline any pertinent information about the fabric such as fiber content, special finishes, and care instructions.

Chapter 6

Industrial Sewing

The stitching industry is among the largest manufacturing industries in the United States today. Take a minute to list as many stitched articles as you can. Clothing naturally heads the list; then think of household linens and accessories, home furnishings, sporting goods, toys, travel accessories, closet accessories, utility garments and uniforms, automobile accessories—even space suits. Just a partial list will reveal the wide expanse of the sewing industry and the large number of employment possibilities.

At present, the apparel industry employs well over a million people. New York City is the center of the industry, but there are garment plants located throughout the United States. The employment outlook indicates that many thousands of new workers will be needed each year in the future. Since 80% of the employees in this industry are women, every year many new workers are needed just to replace those who leave to marry or raise families. Then, too, the population is expected to continue increasing. As population increases, the need for clothing and other fabric items will increase further. The trend toward more women working outside the home and increased numbers of people in "white-collar" occupations will also increase the demand for clothing. Whatever the reason, increased demand means a rise in employment in the industry.

Most of the employment opportunities in the sewing industry will be for sewing machine operators, using fast power-driven sewing machines. These machines are heavier than the home sewing machine and are capable of sewing at a much greater rate of speed. The home sewing machine stitches at the rate of approximately 900 stitches per minute, whereas the power-driven industrial machine is capable of 4,000 stitches per minute. Industrial sewing depends upon the speed of the machine. Wherever commercial sewing is done—in manufacturing plants, alteration workrooms, tailoring or dressmaking shops, slip cover and drapery workrooms, clothing maintenance establishments—industrial machines are used.

Thorough training in the use of the power-driven machine is essential for anyone seeking employment in the

Industrial Sewing

stitching industry. The apprentice system is no longer wide-spread and employers find it expensive and impractical to hire novices without any training in power-machine sewing. While learning, the beginner may spoil material, damage the machine, or even injure herself. However, *thoroughly trained* beginners can find employment even though they have had no job experience. Specific duties vary with each branch of the industry, but a person who can skillfully operate the lockstitch industrial machine and has sewing knowledge and ability can easily learn to perform the construction techniques required by a particular manufacturer.

The basic techniques of power control mastered on the lockstitch industrial machine can also be applied to more highly specialized machines. These are now designed to duplicate any stitching that formerly had to be done by hand and they perform the task with much greater speed and efficiency. The possibilities are almost unlimited. There are machines for stitching cylindrical articles, such as sleeves or trouser legs—and odd shaped articles, such as shoes and purses. There are multiple-needle machines—as many as 36 needles—for making as many rows of stitching in one operation. There are machines for blind stitching, embroidery, design work, and fancy stitching. There are buttonhole machines that automatically space the buttonholes, cut them, work the edges, bar and tack the ends, and cut the threads. Another machine sews on buttons and snaps.

Industrial sewing is a rewarding, productive vocation fully equal to

A large garment factory employs hundreds of sewing machine operators.
Jerry Soalt for ILGWU "Justice"

The Singer Co.
A high speed buttonholer that stitches evenly around the buttonhole, automatically trims the thread, and cuts the buttonhole after stitching.

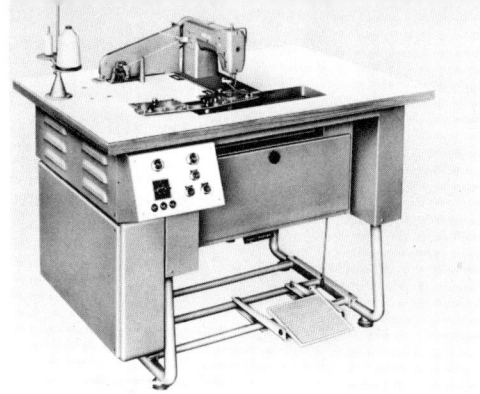

Garment Finishing Equipment Corp.
An automatic sewing unit designed for attaching shirt collars and cuffs accurately and in one high-speed operation.

any clerical occupation in respectability and financial return. There is also a great deal of personal satisfaction to be derived from the work because it is productively creative and the end results are immediately apparent. It is classified as a semi-skilled vocation. Many of the same abilities usually associated with more highly skilled vocations are evident. These include finger dexterity, a keen sense of touch, coordination—in mind, eye, hands, and feet—skill, speed, precision, as well as the ability to exercise good judgment and an understanding of sewing construction processes. The best machine available is only as good as the operator.

Most operators must be able to do routine work rapidly, but a beginner often works under supervision at relatively simple tasks such as sewing straight seams. She may do nothing but stitch shoulder seams. Then she may progress to other simple types of construction work such as assembling garment pieces. She usually repeats the same sewing operation on identical pieces. A high degree of speed is essential to all volume production and thorough training in the use of the power-driven machine enables the operator to develop the skill necessary to work at the steady, fast pace required for commercial sewing. Later, as an experienced operator with superior skill and ability, she may advance to more complicated or specialized construction work—perhaps even producing sample garments according to the designer's specifications.

A multiple needle machine and a smocking attachment are used to produce decorative stitching patterns at high speed.
S. & W. Sewing Machine

Industrial Sewing

Safety

The importance of *safety* on the job cannot be overemphasized. Accident prevention is the responsibility of every machine operator. Efficient, safe workers take no chances. They know that to do so is foolhardy and may result in personal injury, lost time, and in decreased earnings, whereas following safe working procedures results in personal security, increased production, and higher earnings. Employers prefer safe, efficient workers who protect themselves and others from injury, and the property and equipment they use from damage. *Learn the safety rules and regulations involved; then always comply with these rules.* Develop good work habits and be safety conscious at all times.

Dress for the Job

Dressing *properly* for work is the first general rule to follow. Wear comfortable, neat, suitable clothing. Fussy clothing is not only out of place but also can be dangerous. Avoid wearing anything that can get caught in the machinery. Loose or bulky sweaters, ties or streamers, ruffles or frills, loose fitting smocks, large buttons, and long flowing hair are all dangerous to your safety around moving machinery. Jewelry is also out of place in the workroom. It might result in injury to you and damage to the material on which you are working. Simple, tailored clothing is both appropriate and safe.

Posture at the Machine

Practice good posture until it becomes a habit. Poor posture contributes to ill health, fatigue, reduced efficiency, and in turn to the increased possibility of accidents. It is especially important to sit properly at the machine. Sit deep on the seat of the chair with *your* back against the back of the chair. Sit erect, with your back straight and head up. Don't stoop or tilt the chair. If it is necessary to bend forward to get closer to the work, lean from the hips or bend the neck slightly. Don't allow the back to curve, the shoulders to slump, or the head to hang above the machine. For proper balance, sit close to the machine directly facing it, having the machine needle in line with the center of your body.

Remaining in one position over a prolonged period of time is tiring. *Occasionally change your position.* Get up and move around. Breathe deeply several times. Rotate your head and shoulders. Such breaks are relaxing and help to relieve tension. You will return to work with renewed energy and work more efficiently.

Self Care and Order

Cleanliness, neatness, and orderliness are essential for safety and to produce an acceptable, salable finished product. A worker should be neat if she expects favorable treatment and she must have clean hands that are free from excess perspiration so that she will not soil or damage the fabric. The work area should be clean and orderly at all times, the work surface of the machine clear, the aisles clear, and the floor area free from oil, water, or anything that may cause a person to slip and fall. Each worker is responsible for the condition of her work area. She must correct any haz-

Power-Driven Machines

ards or conditions that might result in an accident or damage to the finished product.

Some additional **general safety rules** to follow:

- Do not put pins or needles in your mouth.
- Do not put open scissors or other sharp objects on the machine.
- Always concentrate on your own work; don't let your mind wander while operating the machine.
- Report any accident and treat any injury immediately, no matter how minor.
- Keep equipment in proper working condition. Immediately report any broken equipment. Do not attempt to make any adjustments or repairs about which you are not absolutely sure.
- Replace burned out light bulbs promptly.
- Turn off the motor when machine is not in use.
- Learn the location of switches, plug-ins, and fuses. In case of an emergency, learn how to turn off the main switch.
- Hold the *plug*, not the cord, when disconnecting electric cords.
- Use extreme care. Carelessness causes accidents. Be sure before you proceed; if in doubt, don't. Caution is still the best safety device known.
- Above all, obey all the rules that govern your safety.

Learn to Control a Power-Driven Machine

To understand the working principles of the machine, an operator should be familiar with the parts involved and the purpose each plays in the efficient operation of the machine. Learn the location and purpose of each of the following parts:

- MOTOR: The power unit that drives the machine.
- SWITCH: A key or button that turns on the electricity for one individual motor.
- TREADLE: The platform on which the feet are placed. Controls the motion of the machine.
- PRESSER FOOT: The metal foot attached to the bottom of the presser bar. Holds the cloth in place against the feed dog as the machine stitches. Can be raised or lowered as desired.
- PRESSER BAR LIFTER: A hand lever at the back of the presser bar. Lifts and lowers the presser foot.
- KNEE PRESS: A lever mounted under the table; raises and lowers the presser foot as the knee is pressed against it and released.
- FEED DOG: Metal plate with teeth, located directly under the presser foot. The teeth come up through the openings in the throat plate and move the cloth along with each stitch.
- BALANCE WHEEL: The wheel to the right of the head of the machine. A belt drives the wheel, which revolves once with each stitch.

To learn how sensitive the machine is, practice starting and stopping. Sit well back in the chair, directly in front of the machine. Be sure you are close enough to be comfortable. Keep your back straight and, for this first practice lesson, keep both hands in your lap. Lift the presser foot with the presser bar lifter and leave the presser foot up when operating the machine without fabric. (If there is nothing between the presser foot and the feed dog, the constant rubbing of metal against metal will wear down

Industrial Sewing

the teeth.) Turn on the switch, place both feet on the treadle, and you are ready to start the machine.

The movement of your feet on the treadle controls the motion of the machine. Press forward on the treadle with the ball of the foot; the machine starts. The more you press, the faster the machine goes. To stop the machine, release the foot pressure. Press back on the heels; the brakes are applied and the machine stops immediately. NOTE: It is not necessary, or even safe practice, to turn the balance wheel to start or stop the machine. Keep your hands in your lap. Practice the foot movement several times, starting and stopping until you have the feel of the machine.

- **SAFETY TIPS**

  Practice good posture.

  Keep hands in your lap.

  Do not start or stop the machine by turning the balance wheel with your hand.

  Lower the presser foot and needle and turn off the motor when the machine is not in use.

Next, practice running the machine as slowly as possible. It is true that it is capable of sewing at a very high rate of speed, and speed is essential in industry. The speed can be controlled at will, however, and the ability to control the machine is very important. Learn to control the machine first; speed will come automatically. An efficient operator learns to stop the machine at a desired point, with the needle in the desired position, without any hand adjustment. To accomplish this saves time, which in turn increases efficiency, but the operator must be skillful. Considerable practice is necessary to gain this control.

Stitching charts are helpful in learning to control the machine skillfully. The perforations the needle makes in the paper will show how well you followed the lines.

Practice Straight Stitching

Use a chart with ruled straight lines. Raise the needle by turning the balance wheel. Press the knee against the knee press lever to raise the presser foot just far enough to slip the paper into place. The needle should be directly over the beginning of a line. The use of the knee press to raise and lower the presser foot is a great time saver and adds to the operator's efficiency by freeing the hands to adjust the position of the item to be sewn. Practice using it until it be-

Practice exercise for stitching on paper— straight line stitching.

Practice Turning Corners

comes automatic. Remember, it is necessary to raise the presser foot only far enough to move the paper easily. It is not necessary to raise it very much.

When the paper is in position, lower the presser foot by releasing the knee press, and begin to stitch. Remember that the object is to stitch straight, not necessarily fast. Practice control and do not race the machine. Use both hands to guide the paper. Hold the paper lightly with the left hand. Guide the paper into the machine with the right hand. Be careful to keep both hands away from the needle. It is not necessary to push, or pull, the paper through the machine. Let the machine carry it; you merely guide.

It is important to learn to stop the machine at a definite point. As you near the end of the paper, slow the machine so that you can stop at the end and not run off. Stop completely, with the needle up; raise the presser foot with the knee press and remove the paper. NOTE: Always remove work by drawing it back behind the presser foot. Move the chart into position with the needle over the start of the next line. Lower the presser foot and stitch on the line. Repeat until all the lines on the chart are stitched.

Next, practice stitching straight on paper without any drawn lines, using the presser foot as a guide. Place the side of the presser foot on the edge of the paper and stitch its entire length, keeping the presser foot on the edge. For the next row, keep the side of the presser foot on the row of stitching. Continue stitching in this manner until the paper is completed.

- **SAFETY TIPS**

    Keep hands away from the needle.

    Do not pull the material through the machine.

    Control the speed of the machine; stitch slowly.

    Relax!

Practice Turning Corners

Use charts with square corners and sharp angle turns. This practice exercise requires straight stitching and the ability to stop the machine at a definite point. Stitch along the line, slowing up as you reach the turning point. Stop stitching exactly at the corner. As you become more skillful, you will learn to stop the machine with the needle down in the material. If the needle is up when you stop, it

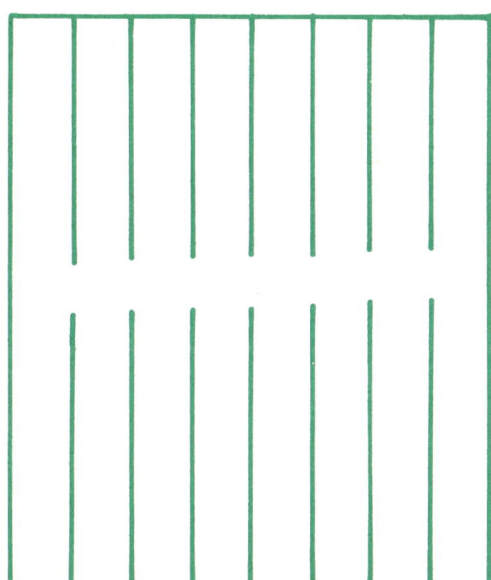

Practice exercise for stitching on paper—broken lines. Learn to control the machine so that you can stop at a definite point.

237

Industrial Sewing

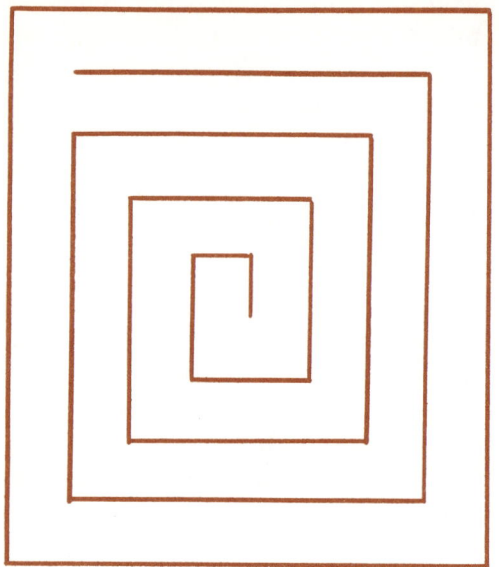

Square corners.

Sharp angle turns.

Wavy lines.

Circle.

will be necessary to lower it by turning the balance wheel by hand. The needle serves as a pivot and must be down to hold the material in place at the corner.

Raise the presser foot with the knee press and turn the paper to the desired angle. Lower the presser foot by releasing the knee press and continue stitching on the line. Stitch the entire chart, turning all corners the same way. Considerable practice will be necessary to develop perfect control.
Remember: Concentrate on stopping the machine at an exact spot, with the needle down.

Practice Stitching Curves

- **SAFETY TIPS**

  Do not use the hand as a brake to stop the machine.

  If it is necessary to turn the balance wheel by hand, do so only after the machine has stopped completely.

Practice Stitching Curves

Use both a circle chart and one with wavy lines. The secret of learning to stitch curves successfully is to stitch slowly at first and keep an even, steady pace. Hold the paper very lightly with the left hand, having the fingers spread apart. Turn the paper in a circular motion the whole time, making the hand movement the same as the speed of the machine. Avoid the need to make a sudden drastic turn; turn the paper slightly with every stitch. It should not be necessary to raise the presser foot at any time.

Learn to Thread the Machine

The specific method for threading differs with machine models, but all machines have similar parts with which you should be familiar.

- **SPOOL PIN**: Spindle which holds the spool of thread.
- **THREAD GUIDES**: Hold the thread in position as it passes from the spool to the needle.
- **UPPER TENSION**: Controls the delivery of the upper thread. Keeps the thread from becoming too loose or too tight, thus helping to make a perfect stitch.
- **LOWER TENSION**: A spring on the bobbin case controls the delivery of the bobbin thread. The upper and

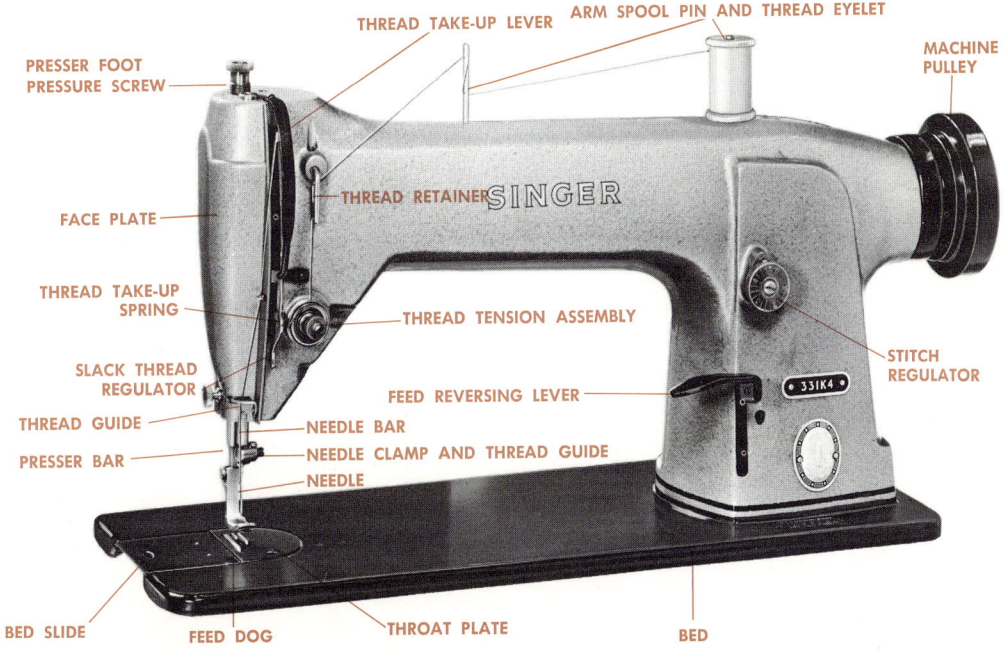

The Singer Co.

Principal parts on head of a power-driven lockstitch machine.

Industrial Sewing

lower tension must be in perfect balance to make a perfect stitch.
- THREAD TAKE-UP SPRING: A wire in back of the upper tension.
- SLACK THREAD REGULATOR: A metal hook at the upper tension.
- THREAD TAKE-UP LEVER: Moves up and down with each stitch, pulling up the slack in the thread. As the needle goes down, the upper thread passes around the bobbin case. As the needle comes up, the take-up lever pulls up the slack in the thread, pulling the upper thread around the bobbin thread to make the locked stitch.
- NEEDLE: Carries the upper thread down through the fabric to make the stitch.
- NEEDLE BAR: Holds the needle and moves it up and down with each stitch.
- THROAT PLATE: A plate directly under the presser foot. The needle passes through a hole in the throat plate. The feed dog moves upward through the throat plate.
- BED PLATE: A flat plate which opens to give access to the bobbin.
- BOBBIN: Spool which holds the supply of lower thread.
- BOBBIN CASE: A container which holds the bobbin. The upper thread passes around the bobbin case, catching the lower thread to form the locked stitch.
- BOBBIN LATCH: A hinge on the bobbin case. Hold it to insert and remove the bobbin case.
- BOBBIN WINDER: A mechanism for filling bobbins automatically.
  - The bobbin winder spindle holds the bobbin.
  - A thread guide near the bobbin winder tension holds the thread in position.
  - The tension discs control the delivery of the thread as the bobbin is being filled.
- THUMB SCREW: One that can be adjusted with the thumb and forefinger.
- STITCH REGULATOR: Controls the length of the stitch by lengthening or shortening the stroke of the feed dog.

Directions for Upper Threading

Watch a demonstration of threading the machine and follow the steps in the instructions manual of the machine you are using. The threading for each individual machine may vary somewhat, but the following steps will generally be similar:
- Raise the thread take-up lever to the highest point.
- Place thread on spool holder.
- Put thread through holes in thread retainer.
- Bring thread down between the tension plates and over the wire spring.
- Take the thread under the slack thread regulator and back of the thread guide.
- Put the thread through the eye of the thread take-up lever.
- Take the thread through the thread guides.
- Put the thread through the eye of the needle. The direction depends upon the particular machine. For the machine pictured, the thread goes through the eye of the needle from left to right. (The thread is on the left side of the needle after passing through the last thread guide; therefore, the needle is threaded from left to right.)
- Draw the thread through the needle until you have about 3 inches of thread with which to start sewing.

Directions for Upper Threading

Upper threading.

The Singer Co.

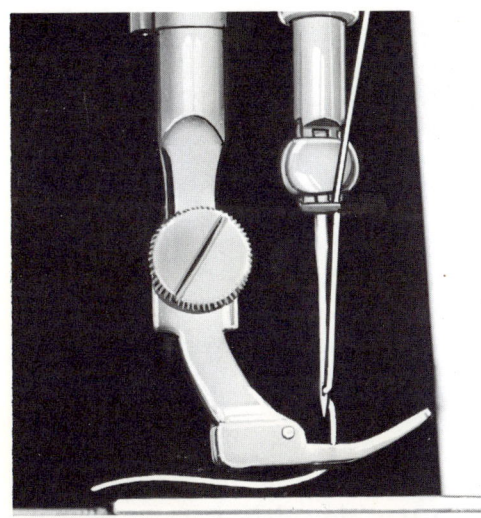

The Singer Co.
Needle threads from left to right.

- **SAFETY TIP**

  Keep your feet off the treadle when threading the machine.

To save time, it is possible to change the upper thread without re-threading the machine. Break the thread near the spool and tie the end of the thread from the machine to the new thread with a square knot.

Make a square knot.

Industrial Sewing

Raise the presser foot to release the tension and pull the end of the thread gently until the knot goes through the eye of the needle. The new thread will be pulled through the upper threading.

Directions for Winding the Bobbin

Unless the thread is wound evenly on the bobbin it will not move smoothly when stitching and the result is stitching troubles. Follow these steps for winding the bobbin correctly. NOTE: There may be variations depending upon the machine you are using.

Winding the bobbin.

The Singer Co.

- Place the thread on the bobbin winder spool pin.
- Draw the thread between the tension discs and guides.
- Wrap the thread around the bobbin a few turns.
- Place the bobbin on the spindle of the bobbin winder. Be sure it is pushed on as far as it will go.
- Press the bobbin winder against the pulley and run the machine.
- Let the tension discs control the flow of thread. It is not necessary to hold or guide the thread. The bobbin winder stops automatically when the bobbin is full.
- To save time, bobbins can be wound while stitching. If you wind one bobbin while sewing with another, there will always be a full bobbin ready when needed.

- **HELPFUL HINTS**

  Never keep the presser foot down when operating the machine without fabric.

  Be sure to raise the presser foot if you fill the bobbin when you are not stitching.

  Remove all thread ends from the bobbin before refilling.

Directions for Under Threading

The method for threading the lower part of the machine may vary in different models. Watch a demonstration and follow the directions from the instruction manual for the particular machine.

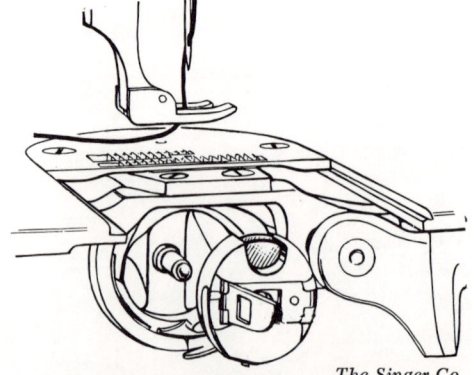

The Singer Co.
Removing bobbin case.

To remove the bobbin case, have the thread take-up lever at the highest point. Tip the machine back or open the hinged bed plate, depending upon the machine model, so that

Directions for Under Threading

you can reach the bobbin case. Open the latch on the bobbin case and pull it out. As long as the latch is open, the bobbin stays in the case. Close the latch, turn the case upside down, and the bobbin falls out.

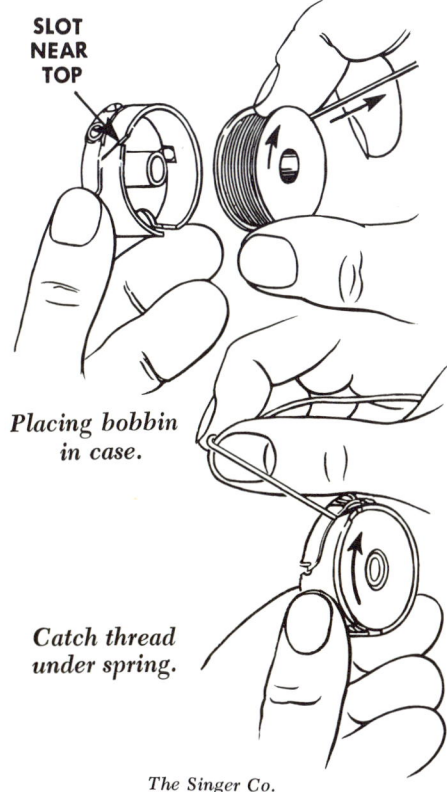

Placing bobbin in case.

Catch thread under spring.

The Singer Co.

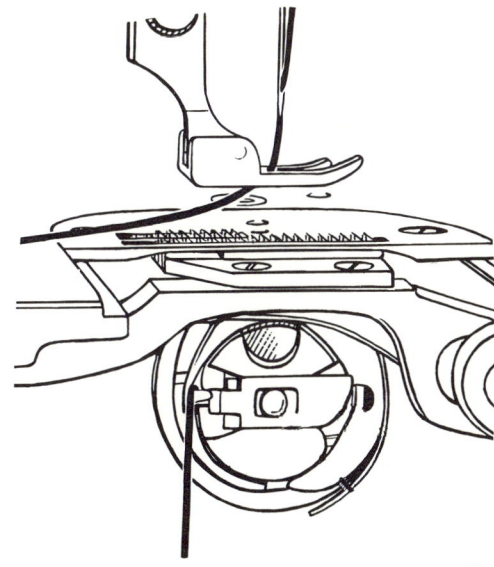

Replace bobbin case.
The Singer Co.

To replace the filled bobbin in the case, hold the bobbin so that the thread unwinds in the proper direction for your machine. If the thread is not going in the proper direction, a loose stitch will result. Put the bobbin in the case. Place the thread through the slot in the case and under the tension spring. Allow at least 3 inches of thread to hang free.

To replace the case, hold the latch and put the case on the center pin of the bobbin case holder. Release the latch and push the case back until you hear the latch click into position. Be sure that the bobbin case is all the way in and that the thread is not caught in the latch. If the case is not correctly placed, it may cause the machine to lock or break the needle.

- **SAFETY TIPS**

    Use both hands to raise the head of the machine.

    Keep both feet off the treadle.

    Do not place the bobbin case in the machine when the needle is down.

    Close the bed plate before operating machine.

To bring the lower thread to the top, hold the needle thread lightly. Turn the balance wheel toward you for one complete turn. The needle will bring the lower thread up through the hole in the throat plate. Place both threads under the presser

Industrial Sewing

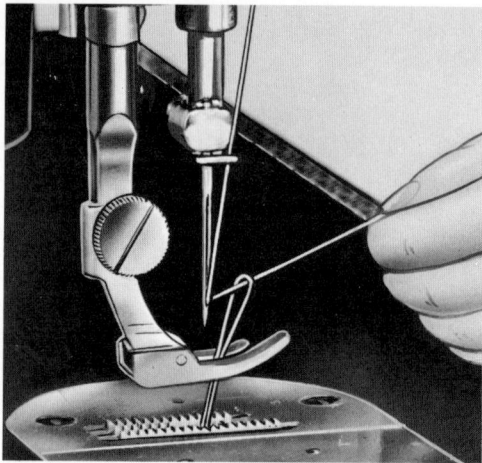

Bring up lower thread. — The Singer Co.

foot and straight back. Now you are ready to sew.

Check the Length of the Stitch

Long stitches are better suited to heavy, thick materials and short stitches to thin delicate fabrics. Change the stitch regulator to obtain a satisfactory length. In some cases, the stitch regulator is a thumb screw. Turn it to the right to shorten the stitch or to the left to lengthen it. On some machines, move the stitch regulator lever up to shorten the stitch and down to lengthen it.

Test the Thread Tensions

Good stitching is impossible when either upper or lower tension is not correct. You can tell whether the tension is correct by examining samples of stitching.

If the tensions are in perfect adjustment, the stitching will appear the same on both sides, as in the diagram below. Upper and lower threads are locked in position in the center of the thickness of the material.

If the tension on the upper thread is too tight—or the lower tension is too loose—the upper thread will be in a straight line on the surface of the material. *There will be looped stitches on top of the material.*

If the tension on the upper thread is too loose—or the lower tension is too tight—the lower thread will lie in a straight line on the bottom of the material. *There will be looped stitches on the underneath side.*

Adjust the upper tension by turning the thumb nut in front of the tension discs. In most cases, turn to the right or to a higher number to tighten the tension and turn to the left or to a lower number to loosen the tension. *Always lower the presser foot when adjusting the upper tension.*

Good stitch.

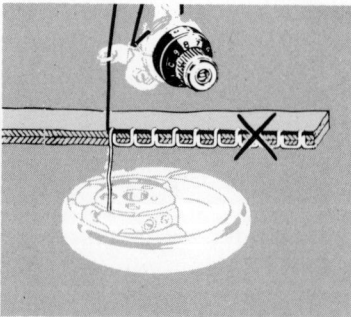

Tight upper tension.

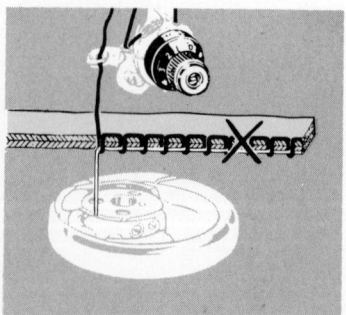

Loose upper tension.

Machine Adjustments

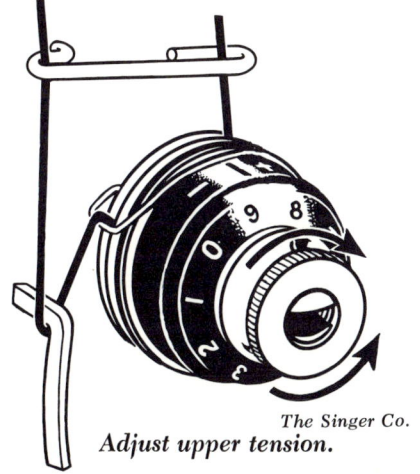

Adjust upper tension. — The Singer Co.

Once the lower thread tension has been adjusted correctly, it is usually possible to obtain a correct stitch by adjusting the upper tension only. To adjust the lower tension, turn the screw on the tension spring of the bobbin case. Remember that turning to the right tightens the tension and to the left loosens.

Adjust lower tension.

Practice the same stitching exercises on cloth that you did with paper. Include: following a straight line, turning square corners, making smooth starts and accurate stops at a definite point, stitching curved lines.

HELPFUL HINTS

- *Always check the machine stitch on a double thickness of scrap material. Is the stitch an appropriate length? Is the tension properly regulated? Is the thread the correct size and color?*
- *Tighten the upper tension slightly more than usual when using a long stitch.*
- *Use a looser upper tension with silk and nylon thread than with cotton.*
- *Place both threads under the presser foot and behind it before starting to stitch. Do not start the machine until the presser foot is down and fingers are away from the needle.*
- **Do not** *pull the material through the machine. Let the machine feed the material; you merely guide it.*
- **Do not** *remove the work from the machine until the machine has stopped completely.*
- *To remove the work easily, press the knee press to the extreme right. This releases the upper tension and the thread pulls more easily. Then draw the fabric gently toward the back of the machine away from you.*
- *Follow all safety rules.*

Learn To Make Simple Machine Adjustments

A sewing machine operator is not hired as a mechanic. If the machine is in need of repair, notify the proper person or call a service man. Do not attempt to repair a machine yourself or make any adjustments you have not been trained to do.

However, an efficient operator is able to detect any trouble with stitching or operation and is able to make minor adjustments. You have already learned how to adjust the length of the stitch and to regulate the tension. There are other simple adjustments you should know how to make.

- *Regulate the pressure on the material.* The presser foot holds the material in place against the feed dog. If

Industrial Sewing

the pressure of the foot against the material is too heavy, the machine will run hard and there may be an imprint of the presser foot on the material. A delicate fabric such as lace may even be cut by too much pressure. Yet if there is not enough pressure, the material will not move smoothly through the machine and may cause skipped stitches. The thumb screw on top of the presser bar adjusts the pressure. **Remember:** Turn the screw to the right to increase and to the left to decrease it.

- *Replace a needle.* Raise the needle bar to the highest point by turning the balance wheel. Loosen the screw near the bottom of the needle bar. Place the needle up into the bar as far as it will go and tighten the screw.

It is important that the needle be placed in the proper position. Its flat side should be against the needle bar and the long groove should be on the side the thread enters. For example, if the thread goes through the needle from left to right, the long groove will be on the left. If the needle is in backwards, the thread will break as you stitch.

Be sure to use the correct type and size of needle. If the needle is not the right length, it will not complete the stitch. If it is too fine for the material, it will break. A needle that is too coarse may damage the material, and a dull needle will catch the threads and pucker the material.

Avoid bending or breaking needles by following these suggestions:

- *Be sure* the presser foot or any attachment is tightly fastened.
- *Be sure* the needle goes through the middle of the hole in the throat plate.
- *Do not pull* material through the machine while stitching.
- *Slow down* when stitching across heavy thicknesses of material.
- *Pull* material to the back when removing it from the machine.
- *Be sure* the presser foot is up and the needle is out of the material before removing the work from the machine.

- SAFETY TIP

  Keep your feet off the treadle when replacing the needle.

To Correct Common Stitching Difficulties

Incorrect stitching means wasted time and effort because the stitches will have to be removed. In the process, the material may be damaged and a piece of work spoiled. Be sure the machine is stitching correctly before you start to work. Check the stitch on scrap material first. If there is some stitching difficulty, you should understand what causes it and how to correct it.

- *Looped stitches* indicate incorrect tension. **Remember,** if the loops are underneath, tighten the upper tension. If the loops are on top of the material, either loosen the upper tension or tighten the lower tension. Check the threading, also. Perhaps the upper thread is not between the tension discs or the lower thread is not correctly placed in the bobbin case.
- *Incorrect feeding* of the material through the machine may have a number of causes. The pressure of the presser foot on the material may be too light. The teeth of the feed dog

may be worn down or the feed dog may have worked loose. Perhaps the needle is bent or the stitch regulator may be in "neutral"—turned so far that the material does not move.

• If the *needle thread breaks,* check for the following: Is the machine threaded correctly? Is the upper tension too tight? Is the needle bent, dull, or set backward? Is the needle too fine for the thread or the material? Is there a rough edge on the needle hole in the throat plate or on the edge of the presser foot?

• If the *lower thread breaks,* check for the following: Is the bobbin threaded correctly? Is the lower tension too tight? Is the thread wound evenly on the bobbin? Is the bobbin too full? Are there any sharp or rough edges on the bobbin case, on the rotary hook, or on the under side of the throat plate?

• *Skipped stitches* mean that something is probably wrong with either the needle or the machine timing. Is the needle dull, bent, or set improperly? Is it too fine for the thread? Is it intended for use in some other machine? If the needle is correct in every way, obtain the services of the repairman to check the *timing.*

To Adjust the Bobbin Winder

An incorrectly wound bobbin can cause stitching difficulties. If the bobbin winder is not in proper adjustment, the thread cannot be wound smoothly and evenly.

• If the *thread is too loose* on the bobbin, the bobbin winder tension is not tight enough. Tighten the screw on the tension discs until the thread winds smoothly. *If the tension is too tight,* the thread will break as the bobbin is being filled.

• If the *thread is wound on one side* of the bobbin, the tension bracket is out of line and the thread is not centered on the bobbin. Loosen the screw that holds the tension in position and slide the bracket until it is centered. If the bobbin is wound high on the right side, move the bracket to the left and vice versa.

• The latch that holds the bobbin in position on the bobbin winder also determines the amount of thread wound on the bobbin. If the *bobbin winds too full,* loosen the screw that holds the latch in position. Tighten the screw *if the bobbin is not full enough.*

• If there is insufficient pressure to hold the bobbin winder against the pulley, the bobbin cannot be wound. Loosen the adjustment screw, press the bobbin winder against the pulley, and tighten the adjustment screw.

• SAFETY TIPS

   Make only those adjustments you have been trained to do.

   If in doubt, don't experiment.

   Report trouble to the proper person, and if the machine is in need of repair call a qualified service man.

To Adjust the Knee Press Lever

Using the knee press to raise and lower the presser foot leaves both hands free to manipulate the material. For comfort and efficiency, however, the lever must be in a comfortable position for the operator. The flat side of the lever should rest

Industrial Sewing

against the right leg just above the knee. If the knee press is not in the proper position, a sore leg as well as decreased speed and efficiency could result.
- Sit down directly in front of the machine, well back in the chair.
- Place both feet on the treadle.
- Loosen the setscrew on the knee press.
- Adjust the lever to fit against the leg comfortably. It is possible to raise or lower the lever as well as move it farther in or out.
- When the lever is in a comfortable position, tighten the setscrew.

To Adjust the Foot Treadle

For comfort and freedom of movement the foot treadle must be at a comfortable angle for the operator. If it is too high, the feet and ankles will feel cramped. If it is too low, the leg and ankle muscles will be strained. Either way, the feet and legs will ache as a result of being held in an uncomfortable position for an extended period of time.
- Sit down directly in front of the machine, well back in the chair.
- Place both feet on the treadle. Is the position comfortable? Can you move your feet freely, without any strain or pull?
- Loosen the setscrew on the treadle.
- Raise or lower the treadle until the position is comfortable.
- Tighten the setscrew.

Learn to Care for the Sewing Machine

Efficient, long-lasting service from a sewing machine—with the least amount of trouble and expense—depends upon the care a machine receives and the way in which it is used. An efficient machine is clean, well-oiled, in proper adjustment, and in good repair. It is the operator's responsibility to see that the machine is kept in good condition.

To Clean the Machine

A machine in constant use should be cleaned at least once a week. When sewing on fabrics that are soft and have a great deal of lint, more frequent cleaning is necessary—perhaps even daily. If dust and lint are permitted to accumulate they cause wear and reduce a machine's efficiency.
- Remove the thread and bobbin case.
- Open the bed slide and remove the throat plate.
- With a lint brush, remove all accumulated dust, oily lint, and loose threads from the mechanism.

- **SAFETY TIP**
  Turn off the motor when cleaning the machine.

To Oil the Machine

Frequent, proper oiling is also essential to keep the machine in good working condition. If a machine needs oil, there is strain on the motor, excessive wear on the mechanism, and the machine runs slowly. Too much oil, on the other hand, is just as harmful. It may also result in spotting the fabric. It is *not the amount of oil* but *the frequency of oiling* that keeps the machine in good running condition and prevents unnecessary wear. Note: Some machines are self-oiling. They have a reservoir that drips automatically, oiling all moving parts during operation. Otherwise, if the machine is not so equipped, it is necessary to oil it manually.

- Clean the machine first and wipe all dust from the exposed parts and the table.
- Follow the oiling diagrams in the instruction manual for the particular machine.
- Place one or two drops of oil in all places indicated.
- Place one or two drops of oil wherever movable parts are in contact.
- Run the machine after oiling.
- Avoid oil spots on fabric. Wipe excess oil.
- Stitch on a scrap of material to absorb excess oil.
- Be sure that both the machine and thread are free of oil before starting to stitch.
- SAFETY TIPS

Never oil the machine manually while it is in operation.

Use both hands to raise and lower the head of the machine.

Be careful not to spill oil on the floor.

If some does spill, clean it immediately.

Do not oil or grease the motor. That is a job for the serviceman.

Learn Time-Saving Stitching Techniques

Although we should strive first for accuracy in sewing and let speed develop naturally with proficiency, we realize that speed is essential to production sewing. In order to increase the production, most manufacturing plants use the "section work" method of sewing. In this method, the work is broken down into simple operations. Each operator is responsible for just one of these. For instance, one person

Each girl is responsible for one step.

Garment Union

Industrial Sewing

may do nothing but stitch shoulder seams, another collars, another the sleeves, and still another zippers. As a person repeats one construction process over and over, the same skills are practiced. Her speed increases, the quality of her work improves, and she becomes a more efficient operator.

There are some specific skills and techniques that are employed in production work because they are *time savers*. To increase your speed and efficiency, practice them until you can do them easily and automatically.

Time Savers

Backstitching or *staying* is a quick, efficient way to secure threads at the beginning and the end of stitching. Because the stitches are retraced, they are reinforced and will not rip out easily.

To backstitch, follow this procedure
- Raise the presser foot just far enough to place the fabric into position. Of course, the stitching starts at the edge of the material.
- Start stitching without lowering the presser foot. Move the material back and forth quickly by hand. The stay should be no more than ¼ inch long and the stitches should be straight, one row directly on top of the other.
- Lower the presser foot and continue to stitch the entire seam.
- At the end of the seam, raise the presser foot slightly and stay the end of the seam in the same manner.

It is important to raise the presser foot just far enough to move the material freely without causing any strain that might break the thread or needle. If the presser foot is raised too high, the upper tension will be released and the thread will feed too fast, resulting in looped stitches.

Practice backstitching until you can do it quickly, easily, and neatly.

Stitching without pinning or basting

Skill in handling fabric is essential for learning this time-saving technique. The seam must be stitched evenly, without stretching or puckering. As the fabric moves through the machine, the presser foot tends to push the top layer forward while the feed dog pulls the underneath layer in the opposite direction. To feed the fabric properly, it is necessary to hold it correctly.

Practice stitching seams without pinning or basting them.

Practice stitching on the bias. Bias material stretches and can be pulled out of shape very easily. Careful handling is necessary to prevent stretching the material when guiding it.

Helpful Hints
- *Place the larger part of the material to the left of the presser foot. There is more room for the fabric on the machine table and it is easier to manipulate and guide the work under the machine arm.*
- *Guide the work gently. Do not pull it through the machine.*
- *Be sure of seam allowance before stitching. Incorrect width seams result in inaccurately sized garments.*
- *Remove the work from the machine by pulling it gently toward the back.*

- Hold the underneath layer firmly with the right hand as you guide the material.
- Ease in the top layer of material with the left hand.

Skillful, correct hand movement will prevent one layer from becoming either loosely full or tighter than the other. With practice, sensitive fingers learn to apply pressure or tension at the right instant, to ease in or even to stretch the fabric slightly where necessary. Concentrate on *correct hand position and movement*. Poorly handled fabric results in seams that sag, bulge, or pucker.

Keep Work Connected

Instead of cutting threads at the end of a seam and removing the work completely from the machine, feed in the next piece. Keep stitching from one seam to another. The threads can be cut and the parts separated after they are stitched. Not only does this technique save time, but it saves thread as well and the work is much neater looking.

Save time by picking up the next piece of work, if possible, with one hand while guiding the stitching with the other hand. Then a piece of work is ready to feed into the machine immediately.

Keep pushing the work ahead as you sew from one piece to the next. The pieces will eventually fall off the table into the bin. Picking up the material and tossing it into the bin is wasted motion as well as time.

Rip Properly

Hopefully we say, ripping should be unnecessary! Work carefully and concentrate on what you are doing so that it will be done correctly. If rip you must, however, learn to do it correctly so that you do not tear or damage the material. Pull out the threads with your fingers—first from one side until the thread breaks, then from the other side. A seam ripper may also be used, with caution, but avoid tearing the stitches apart or using scissors to cut the stitches.

- **SAFETY TIPS**

    Keep the work area clear at all times.

    Keep scissors closed when not in use.

    Always keep fingers a safe distance from the needle.

    Keep your eyes on your hands as you work.

    Do not talk with your neighbor while sewing.

    Concentrate! Give your work undivided attention.

    Avoid waste and accidents that result in injury and loss of material or supplies.

    Stay alert! Think!

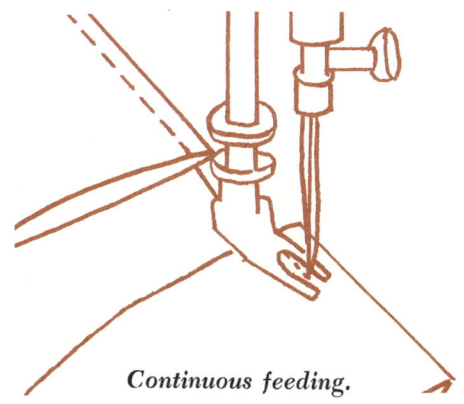

Continuous feeding.

Markers.

Jerry Soalt for ILGWU "Justice"

Steps in Garment Production

Although a sewing machine operator is mainly concerned with the actual stitching, she should understand the cutting process well enough to notice mistakes. Only sample garments or very high quality custom garments are cut individually. In production work a *machine spreader* automatically spreads the material evenly in neat layers on a table. Each layer is the exact length needed for the particular garment to be made. Several garments are cut at once—there may be well over a hundred layers. A slight error in the stack can cause a piece to be miscut.

Markers trace the pieces to be cut on the top layer of material or onto large sheets of paper the exact size of the layer of fabric. They must arrange the pattern pieces so as to use the fabric to best advantage and get the most cuttings possible from a given quantity of material. If there is a design that must be matched, the cutting must be planned so that sewn garment pieces will be matched.

Cutter.

Cutters go around the pattern pieces with an electric machine that cuts through all layers at once. Small slashes in the edge of the material indicate matching points for assembling the pieces.

Assemblers prepare the fabric pieces for the sewing room. They mark the location of any construction details. They sort the pieces according to color, size, and design of fabric. Then they gather together and bundle all the fabric pieces and notions required for each garment. This bundle is ticketed and sent to the sewing department.

In the *sewing department,* as you know, each operator performs her

Jerry Soalt for ILGWU "Justice"
Hand finishers.

Production chart.

		BOX	FOLD	PRESS	EXAM	TRIM	SEW BUTTONS	BUTTON HOLES	HEM	SET CUFF	TRN. CUFF
STYLE ___ LOT ___ SIZE ___ QTY. ___ OFFICE CONTROL 1 2 3 4 5	STYLE ___ LOT ___ SIZE ___ QTY. ___										
		ST. CUFF	SIDE SEAM	SET SLEEVE	SET COLLAR	JOIN SHOULDER	TP. ST. BAND	BAND COLLAR	TRN. COLLAR	SET COLLAR	TRIM COLLAR
FACTORY CONTROL PITTSBURGH 1 2 3 4 5	STYLE ___ LOT ___ SIZE ___ QTY. ___ ST. CUFF 1 2 3 4 5										

Industrial Sewing

OPERATOR'S DAILY QUALITY CHECK

EMPLOYEE NO. _____ NAME _____ OPERATION _____ MONTH _____

S. L.	LARGE STITCH
S. B.	BAD STITCH
P.	PUCKER
PL.	PLEAT
T. M.	POOR THREAD MATCH
N. I.	NOTCHES IGNORED
I. T.	INCORRECT TECHNIQUES
N. S.	SEAMS TOO NARROW
W. S.	SEAMS TOO WIDE
C. S.	SEAMS CROOKED
P. S.	SEAMS POORLY FINISHED
M. L.	MEASURES TOO LARGE
M. S.	MEASURES TOO SMALL
V.	MEASURES VARY
M. T.	MACHINE TROUBLE
O. S.	OIL STAINS
✓	WORK GOOD
X	ABSENT

WEEK OF _____ (MON., TUES., WED., THURS., FRI. — AM / PM)
WEEK OF _____ (AM / PM)
WEEK OF _____ (AM / PM)
WEEK OF _____ (AM / PM)
WEEK OF _____ (AM / PM)

Inspection chart.

specific job on the pieces. She cuts a section called a "ticket" for her job from the production ticket card and attaches it to her daily production card. Her pay is based upon her production, and the tickets show her daily output. Then the bundle is passed on to the next operator. In this way the bundles pass through a large number of sewing operations and the garment takes shape as it passes through the department.

As we have already noted, most of the work is done by machine. There may be a minimum of handwork done on top quality clothing as the garment nears completion. To repeat, although each operator specializes in only one operation, the successful sewer knows how to make every part of the garment. She checks her own work, is alert for errors, and keeps the work moving.

Inspectors or *checkers* examine the workmanship at random during construction. They may caution an operator about a procedure—perhaps the "staying" is too long—or they may mark pieces that have to be corrected or discarded before sending the bundle on to the next operation. The finished garment is also examined for

Jobs in Sewing Industry

defects in workmanship. Inspectors may sometimes make minor repairs themselves, such as skipped stitches or poor seams. If a defect cannot be corrected, however, the garment may be marked a "second" or discarded depending upon the nature of the mistake.

Trimmers and *cleaners* cut off all loose threads, remove any basting stitches, and brush lint and threads from the finished garments.

Pressers give the garments a final press after the sewing is completed. In the case of lightweight fabrics, standard quality and low-priced garments, the final press after the garment is completed is the only pressing done.

Better quality garments are pressed and shaped at regular steps during the sewing operations in order to produce a neater look and better fit.

Manufacturers cater to particular markets and produce merchandise to sell at specific price levels. The methods and techniques used and the standards of workmanship required by any manufacturer depend to a large extent upon the quality and style of the garment being produced. In general, higher priced, better quality clothing naturally requires more handwork and higher standards of workmanship than low cost clothing. It is true that in mass production, speed is the utmost concern. Quality of work is sacrificed somewhat for quantity and low-priced lines are even sewn together with a long basting stitch. It is *fast*, even though not appropriate.

An employee should know how the manufacturer wants his work done, what methods and techniques he

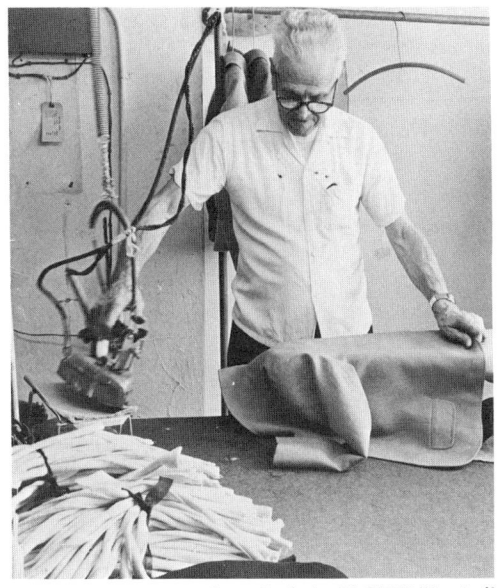

Jerry Soalt for ILGWU "Justice"
Presser.

Bobbie Brooks
After the final pressing.

255

The finished garment, folded and boxed, is sent to the distribution center where orders are filled.

Bobbie Brooks

In the packing area, boxed garments and hanging garments are packed for shipment to the customer.

Jobs in Sewing Industry

uses, and what standards he requires. Then he should proceed accordingly. Incidentally, while learning it is advisable always to maintain the highest standards. Careless habits are difficult to break. Take pride in your work and do your very best at all times. A careless, slipshod worker commands very little status, even in low price manufacture. *You have to be an expert,* no matter what the product is.

In review:

What is the difference between a home sewing machine and an industrial sewing machine?

What special abilities are necessary for industrial sewing?

In what ways can clothing be related to safety?

What is considered correct posture at the sewing machine?

What controls the motion of the machine?

What are the advantages of speed? the disadvantages?

Discuss the importance of accuracy versus speed.

What is the advantage of being able to have pin-point control of machine stops?

What are the advantages of the knee-press?

What is the secret of stitching curves successfully?

How can the upper thread be changed without rethreading?

Describe a perfect stitch.

What do you do if there are loops on the upper side of the fabric? on the underneath side?

What can cause a broken thread? skipped stitches? incorrect feeding of the fabric?

Outline general care procedures for the sewing machine.

Chapter 7

Basic Skills for Clothing Construction

Learning to sew well enough to be employed in any aspect of clothing construction requires mastering certain basic sewing skills. Once you have learned to control the power-driven sewing machine you have made a good start. Speed is important, especially in mass production, but you must also understand the various construction techniques and acquire proficiency in performing them. Your sewing ability determines the quality of construction of the wearing apparel you produce.

For mass production work you will be primarily interested in perfecting stitching techniques. In large volume sewing of wearing apparel, the individual purchaser is not known to the manufacturer. There is no fitting of garments—they are merely cut in assorted sizes and assembled. In order to save production time, during construction there is no basting and very little, if any, pinning. Most likely your job will consist of section work in which you will repeat a stitching process over and over again. Although mainly concerned with only one stitching operation, an understanding of all construction techniques helps you perform your job accurately and with pride, enables you to detect irregularities or mistakes in workmanship, and is essential for those interested in advancement. With superior skill and ability you may advance to a more complicated operation, to specialized construction work—perhaps making entire garments as samples, or to supervisory work.

In custom work, you may be creating garments for specific individuals. All aspects of construction are involved—measuring, cutting, assembling, fitting, finishing, and pressing—not merely stitching alone. It is assumed that you are already familiar with some of these processes and, having had some "home sewing" experience or training, it will be necessary merely to review them. More time will be devoted to establishing and perfecting the construction techniques with emphasis on commercial methods. Fitting techniques will be discussed in a later chapter.

THE MATERIALS YOU WORK WITH

Any worker must be familiar with the tools of the trade—the fabric she works on, the supplies she uses, the tools and equipment that help her perform her job. What are they? What are they used for? How are they used? How should they be cared for properly? A conscientious person realizes that she is responsible for the equipment she uses and only when it is of good quality and in proper order and working condition can she perform her job with the greatest efficiency. Therefore she learns how to use tools and equipment properly and exercises great care in their use so as to avoid accidents or damage to the equipment.

In the same manner, a conscientious worker exercises care in the use of all supplies. Careful handling, neatness, and the proper economical use of supplies is essential. Waste is costly. Carelessness means waste and can cause accidents that result in loss or damage to fabric and supplies. Be conscious at all times of maintaining good work habits.

Are you familiar with the tools of your trade?

Fabric

In Chapter 4, there were hints for handling and sewing fabrics with various fiber contents, of different constructions, and having special finishing processes. To help you achieve successful results, refer to these before stitching on a different fabric for the first time.

Are you familiar with these fabric terms?

- SELVAGE: The smooth finished edges of fabric, extending the entire length of the fabric.
- GRAIN: The threads that form the fabric.
- LENGTHWISE GRAIN: The lengthwise threads of the fabric. These are the warp threads that are placed on the loom first for weaving. Because the warp threads are held taut during the weaving process, there is no give or stretch to the lengthwise grain.
- CROSSWISE GRAIN: The crosswise threads of the fabric. These are the filling threads that are woven back and forth across the warp threads. Because they are not as firm as the warp threads, there is a slight stretch to the crosswise grain.
- TRUE GRAIN: The threads of the fabric cross each other at right angles. Other terms that refer to the same thing are straight grain or on grain.

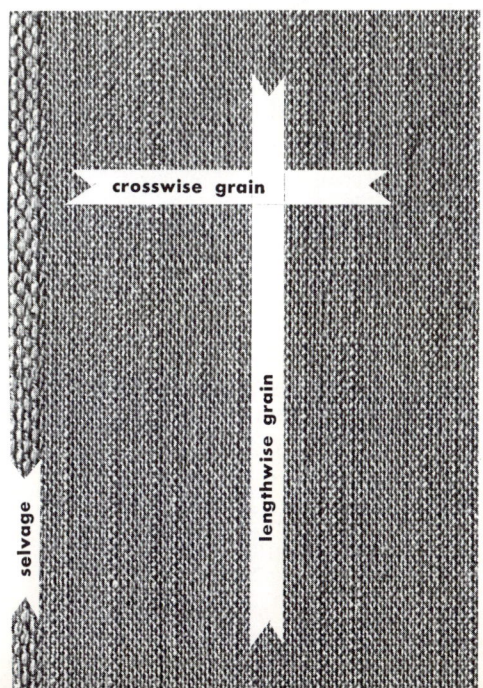

Fabric grain.
Educational Bureau, Coats & Clark Inc.

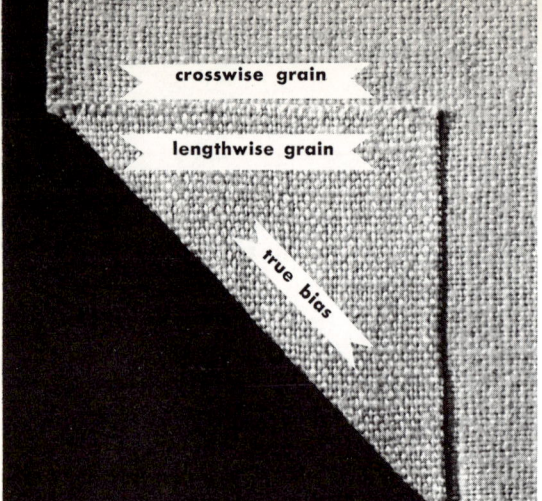

Educational Bureau, Coats & Clark Inc.
Bias.

- OFF GRAIN: The threads are not at right angles, but on a slant.
- BIAS: The diagonal of the fabric. True bias is the exact diagonal across the two grain lines. Any other angle is not true bias, but merely off grain. True bias has a great deal of stretch.
- WITH NAP: As you learned in your study of fabric construction, nap actually means the short fuzzy fiber ends formed by brushing the surface of some fabrics. With such a fabric, all garment pieces must be cut in the same direction. For convenience, the term "with nap" is often used to designate any fabric that must be cut in one direction whether a true napped fabric, a pile fabric such as velveteen or corduroy, or a "one-way" fabric that has a design such as a print, a plaid, or a stripe that repeats the pattern in only one direction.

THREAD

For commercial sewing, thread is available in either cones or tubes that hold a much greater quantity than the spools used for home sewing. For convenience ready wound paper bobbins are also available.

The selection of the correct thread is important to the appearance and the quality of a garment. It may not always be possible to have an exact color match, but the thread should blend with the color of the fabric so that it is inconspicuous. Since thread "works-in" a shade lighter than on the spool, choose a shade slightly darker than the fabric. The thread must be strong so that the stitches will not break, should be the correct size for the fabric, and be similar to the fabric in physical properties.

When both the thread and the fabric have the same physical properties they will react the same to washing, heat, chemicals, dry-cleaning, stretch, strain, and so forth. Whenever possible it is best to use thread of the same fiber origin—animal, vegetable, or synthetic—as the fabric itself. Cotton thread can be used successfully with most fibers. Silk thread is stronger than cotton and, being an animal fiber, it reacts the same as fabrics of animal fiber content. Therefore it is

Coats & Clark's Sales Corp.
Thread cones, holding large quantities of thread.

preferable for stitching wool and silk fabrics. For the same reason, synthetic threads (nylon or Dacron) are the best choice for stitching synthetic fibers. With blends, select the thread that is most similar to the predominant fiber.

There are still other important factors to consider in selecting thread for commercial sewing. Since the thread passes through the needle and the fabric very rapidly in a power driven machine, it may fray and break unless it is smooth and uniform. It must stand up under the friction and heat build-up that occurs with a machine that stitches at such a fast rate of speed. Cotton thread for industrial sewing is either treated with a lubricating agent (oiled thread), or polished or waxed to make it smooth, lint-free, and resistant to abrasion. These finishes also make the thread stronger.

Synthetic thread is the strongest of the three kinds of thread, but it can cause stitching difficulties. Synthetics are sensitive to heat, and the heat build-up may damage the thread. The high speed may also cause skipping or puckering, and the thread may split or shred from the combination of friction and high speed. Synthetic threads may be twisted—the usual method used for producing threads—or they may be bonded. In bonded thread the filaments are fused together with an adhesive agent into a single non-twisted thread. Bonded thread, having more resistance to abrasion than twisted thread, does not fray as easily. Synthetic threads may also be bulked (see page 128). Bulking eliminates the slippery quality characteristic of synthetics. This "slipperiness" can be the cause of skipped stitches and other stitching difficulties.

The proper weight of thread depends upon the fabric with which it is being used and the kind of article being stitched. Thread may be classified according to the number of cords or plies—the greater the number, the smoother and better the thread.

Cotton thread size is designated by a number representing a measure of the length of thread derived from a pound of cotton fiber. The standard measure is based on 840 yards of thread from one pound of cotton (size 1). Size 10 cotton thread means 10 × 840, or 8400 yards of thread from one pound. The numbers range all the way from 1 to 100—the higher the number the finer the thread. Some of the most commonly used thread sizes are:

- SIZE 8 (button or carpet thread): for sewing very heavy fabric (upholstery or awning). Also good for sewing on buttons.
- SIZE 40 (heavy duty): for sewing on heavy fabrics or on articles that receive hard wear or strain.
- SIZE 50 OR 60: for general use on medium weight fabrics.
- SIZE 70: for fine sewing on sheer fabrics.

There are two sizes of silk thread—A or D. "A" is suitable for general use and "D," also known as Buttonhole Twist, is used for buttons, buttonholes, loops, thread carriers, and other decorative or finishing details.

TOOLS AND EQUIPMENT

There are many tools to make sewing easier. It is important to use the proper equipment for the job and to

Basic Skills for Clothing Construction

Scissors.

Dressmaker's shears.

Scalloping shears.

Pinking shears.

J. Wiss and Sons Co.

use it correctly. Good equipment will give good service and last for years if cared for properly.

For Cutting

- **Scissors:** used for snipping threads, trimming, and clipping. They are small (6" or less) with narrow pointed blades and ring handles both the same size.
- **Shears:** used for cutting fabric when cutting individual garments. They have long cutting blades and either bent or straight handles of different sizes—a round handle for the thumb and a long handle for the fingers. Available for both right and left-handed.
- **Pinking shears:** used for finishing seams. They have blades that notch the fabric as they cut. There are also scalloping shears which cut scallops

Tools and Equipment

instead of notches. Available for both right and left-handed.

- BUTTONHOLE SCISSORS: used for cutting buttonholes by hand. They have blades that are notched, permitting you to start cutting away from the edge of the fabric. A setscrew permits setting the blades to cut a certain distance.

NOTE: *Keep scissors and shears sharp by using them only for cutting thread and fabric. For safety, keep the blades closed when not in use.*

- ELECTRIC SCISSORS: used for cutting out individual garments. They are convenient for cutting fabric quickly and accurately, and can be operated with ease by either right or left-handed.
- CUTTING MACHINE: an electrically driven cutting knife used for mass production cutting. The knife can cut through layers of fabric as high as nine inches, cutting perhaps more than a hundred garments at once.

For Measuring

- TAPE MEASURE: 60 inches long, useful for taking body measurements and

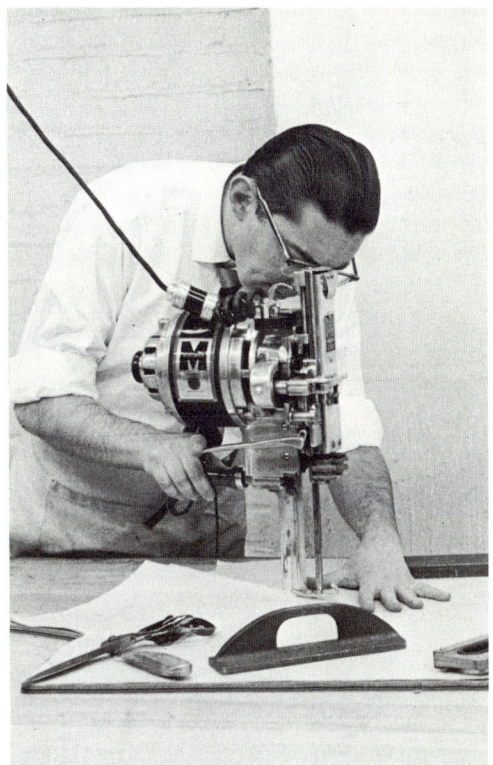

Electric cutting machine.   "Justice," ILGWU

other measuring jobs. It should be made of plastic or a firm fabric, treated to prevent stretching. Paper is not satisfactory. Metal ends prevent fraying. There are numbers on each side, starting at opposite ends for convenience in reading.

Electric scissors.   John Dritz and Sons, Inc.

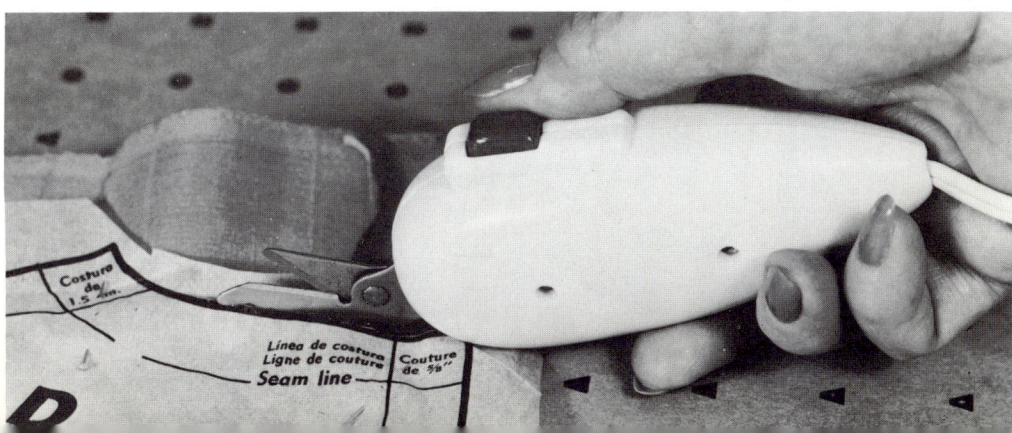

A measuring gauge.

A convenient tool for every measuring job.
Educational Bureau, Coats & Clark Inc.

• RULER: 12 or 15 inch plastic or wooden, used for measuring and marking straight lines. A small metal ruler (4 to 6 inch long) with a movable indicator to locate the marking spot is especially convenient for detail measuring.

• YARDSTICK: 36 inch, sturdy wood or flexible metal used for measuring on a flat surface or marking straight lines.

• GAUGE: plastic or metal with one curved side for turning and measuring hem widths. Heavy cardboard can be used to make a gauge of any size if there is a need. Merely cut a notch at the desired width, as shown in the above drawing.

• SKIRT MARKER: for measuring and marking an accurate, straight hemline. Both pin and chalk markers are available.

For Marking

• TAILOR'S CHALK: flat squares of chalk used for marking on fabric. There are two kinds—chalk and wax. The wax type will leave an oily mark on all fabrics except wool.

• TRACING WHEEL: used with dressmaker's carbon paper to transfer pattern markings to the fabric. There are three types—with sharp needle points, with dull saw-toothed edges, and the smooth wheel. The needle points work best on wool, but the other two are safer to use because there is no danger of making holes in the fabric.

• DRESSMAKER'S CARBON PAPER: used

with the tracing wheel to transfer pattern markings. It is available in several colors as well as white, but it is advisable to use the lightest color that will show on the fabric.

Educational Bureau, Coats & Clark Inc.
Tracing wheel and tailor's chalk.

For Sewing

● NEEDLES: *For machine sewing*—On one side of the needle there is a long groove that holds the thread as the needle goes through the cloth. In placing the needle in the machine, the long groove should be on the side the needle is threaded from. Needles vary in length and shape, and it is important to use the one intended for the particular make of machine you are using. There are various shaped points—round, wedge, or pointed—each designed for stitching a specific material. The round point is for stitching fabric. A type number indicates such variations in machine needles. Check the machine manual for the type to be used. The size of needle used depends upon the size of thread and the weight of fabric—size 9–11 for fine; 14–16, medium; and 17–18, heavy.

NOTE: *Be sure the needle is sharp. A dull needle may damage the fabric.*

● *For hand sewing*—There are two kinds of needles—Sharps (round eye) and Crewel (long eye). Sizes are numbered from 1 (very heavy) to 12 (very fine) and both kinds are available in the same sizes. Although Sharps are intended for general sewing and Crewel for embroidery, many prefer to use Crewel because the longer eye is easier to thread.

Needles.

● PINS: should be very fine and have sharp points that will not leave marks in the fabric. "Silk" pins are the finest. "Dressmaker" pins are also satisfactory, though not as thin.

● PIN CUSHION: Keep needles and pins handy while working. A wrist pin cushion is especially convenient for fitting.

● EMERY BAG: This is a strawberry shaped bag attached to many pin

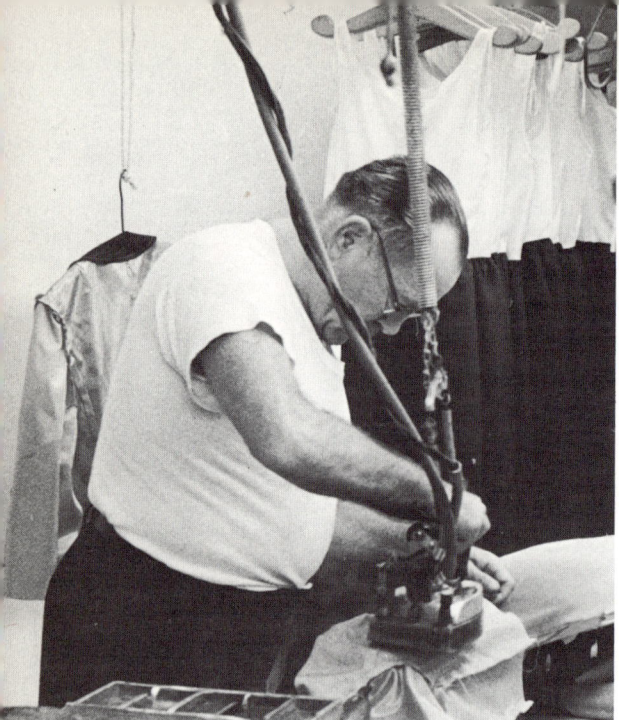

"Justice," ILGWU
A steam iron and pressing table are used for detail pressing during construction.

The steam press is operated with foot pedals, leaving the hands free to smooth the garment into position. If extra moisture is needed, it is available from the hose attachment directly above the press.
American Cleaners Equipment Sales

cushions. Clean rusty or sticky needles by pushing them through the bag a few times. Do not leave pin or needles in the emery bag, however, or they will rust.

• THIMBLE: used to push the needle through the fabric and makes hand sewing faster and easier. The thimble should fit snugly on the middle finger of the hand that holds the needle.

For Pressing

• HAND IRON: A regular household steam iron—with accurate temperature control—or an industrial iron, similar to the one in the above picture, with the steam and water controls mounted on the iron.

• IRONING BOARD: A sturdy, well-padded, regulation ironing board, preferably having a cloth covered frame or tray under the board to keep the garment from touching the floor. May also be smaller than the regulation board and be permanently mounted to a table, similar to those in the above picture.

• STEAM PRESS: A pressing machine having a stationary pressing surface (buck) and a movable top pressing surface (head) that can be raised and lowered to meet the pressing surface.

• PUFF IRON: A small round-shaped pressing device mounted on a stand, used for parts that are difficult to press by hand or machine.

• FORM FINISHER: A steam air finisher resembling a dress form. The garment is placed on the form and steam and air press it "from the inside out," shaping the garment and giving it a "finished appearance."

• PRESS CLOTH: a cloth placed over the fabric to prevent a shine from forming when pressing on the right

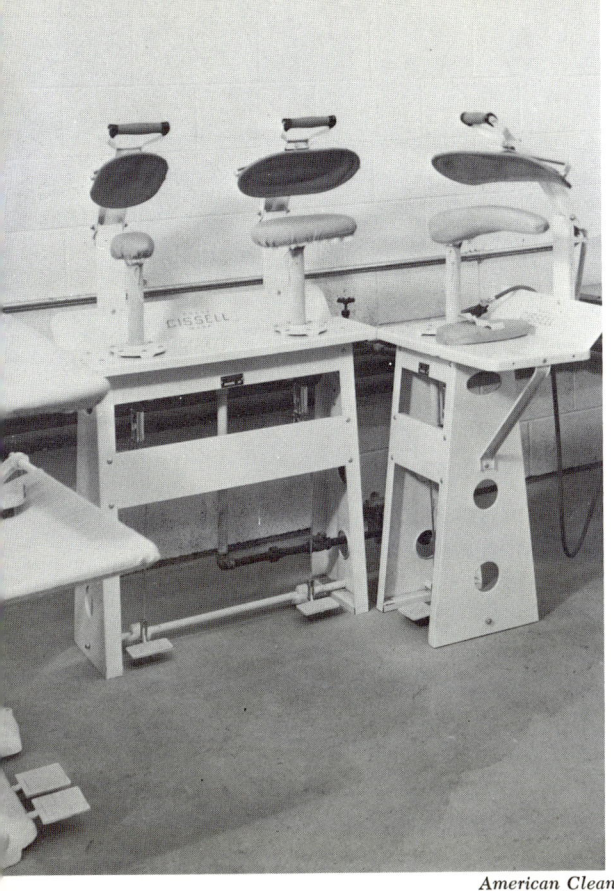
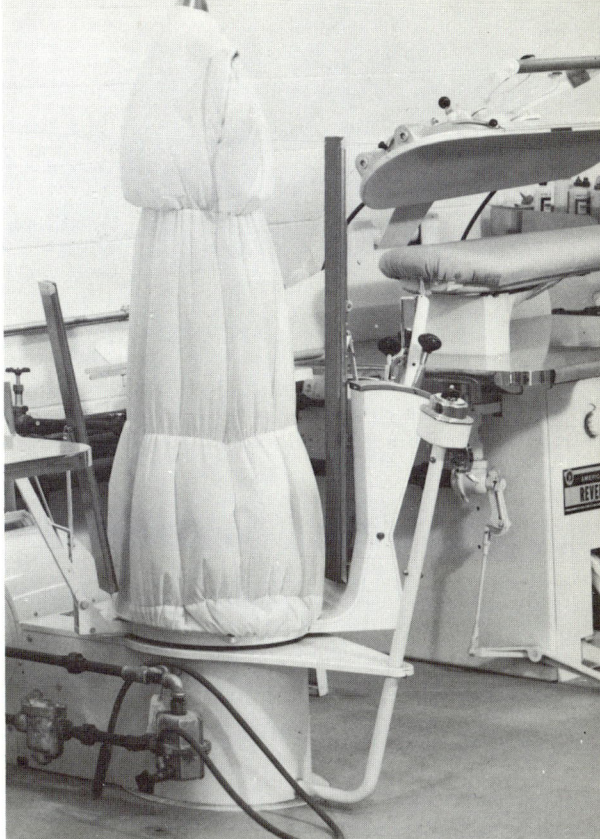

American Cleaners Equipment Sales

Various shaped pressing devices are available to make the pressing of hard-to-reach areas easier.

Place a garment on this form, inflate it, and the garment receives a fast, all-over, final press.

side. May be a chemically treated cloth or cheese cloth. If a regular household steam iron is used, a dampened press cloth supplies the extra moisture often needed for a "good press." A piece of lightweight wool cloth may be used when pressing wool. Velveteen makes a good press cloth for pressing pile fabrics without crushing the pile.

- SPONGE: To moisten the press cloth. A small artist's paint brush is also handy for applying moisture to the seam line.
- CLOTHES BRUSH: For brushing the nap after pressing to keep it from being flattened.
- NEEDLE BOARD: A piece of heavy canvas with upright pieces of wire (needles) used for pressing pile fabrics without crushing the pile. Place the pile side of the fabric face down against the needles.
- SLEEVE BOARD: A well-padded, small board useful for pressing sleeves as well as other small seams.
- POINT PRESSER: A narrow board with a pointed end, mounted on a stand. Useful for pressing corners and pointed edges, such as collars and lapels. Pull the corner over the point and press the seam open before turning right side out.
- SEAM ROLL: A tightly padded roll

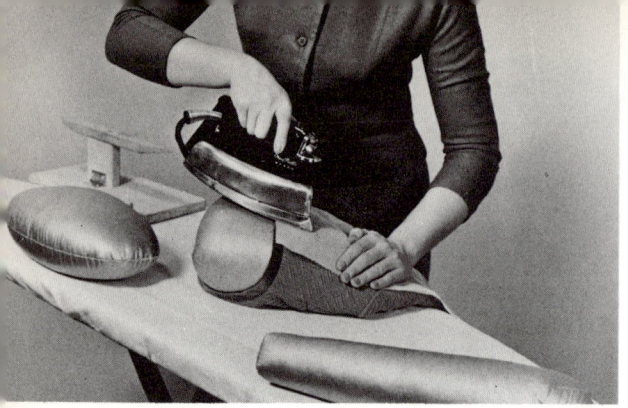

Contoured pressing cushions are helpful aids for pressing curved or hard-to-reach areas of a garment without wrinkles or fuss. —David Traum Co.

A pounding block can be used to flatten seams, hemlines, or pleats. —John Dritz & Sons, Inc.

useful for pressing seams without leaving an imprint of the seam edge on the right side of the fabric. Use the point of the iron only.

- PRESS MITT: A cushion that can be slipped over the hand or over the end of the sleeve board. Useful for pressing curved seams, darts, or other shaped areas. Can also be used to flatten seams in napped fabric.
- TAILOR'S HAM: A firmly packed cushion resembling a ham in shape with one end rounded and the other pointed. Used for tailor pressing and shaping lapels, collars, and other curved areas.
- POUNDING BLOCK: A piece of hard wood approximately 12 inches long and 2 inches thick used to flatten seams, hemlines, pleats and also to sharpen edges. Apply steam; then clap or pound the fabric sharply (on the right side) to force out the steam.

THE LANGUAGE OF SEWING

Are you familiar with these stitching terms?

- BASTING: a temporary stitch done by hand or machine (long stitch) to hold two pieces of fabric together for stitching. May also be used to locate construction markings (pocket or for buttonhole placement, for example) on the right side of the garment.
- PIN-BASTING: hold two pieces of fabric together for stitching by placing pins on the seam line. Place the head of the pin toward you for easy removal while stitching.
- ALTERATION BASTING: a slip-stitch (the thread slips through the fold of the fabric and catches a thread or two of the underneath fabric) used to baste a "pinned-down" alteration (see page 310). When the pins are removed the garment can be turned to the wrong side and spread flat for stitching. The new stitching line is clearly marked by the thread.
- STITCHING: permanent sewing done on the machine. The length of the stitch depends upon the weight of the fabric. Ten to twelve stitches per inch are suitable for most medium weight fabrics. This length stitch may be referred to as regular stitch as opposed to baste stitch.

The Language of Sewing (Continued)

- LOCK STITCH: a sewing machine stitch in which top thread and bobbin thread are interlocked at each stitch. Stitches do not rip out easily.
- CHAIN STITCH: the stitches are loops that are joined together much like the links of a chain. Stitches will rip out easily.
- GATHERING STITCH: a long machine stitch (six stitches to an inch). The underneath or bobbin thread is pulled to draw in the fabric to the desired length.
- EASE STITCHING: a long machine stitch (8 to 10 stitches to an inch) placed on the seam line. By pulling the under thread it is possible to draw in extra length or extra room on a longer edge of fabric and fit it to a shorter one without any visible gathering or puckering.
- DIRECTIONAL STITCHING: stitching with the grain of the fabric. "With the grain" is usually from the wide edge toward the narrow. To be sure, rub your finger along the edge of the fabric. If the threads lie flat, you are rubbing with the grain. Directional stitching is important for controlling the grain and to prevent stretching.
- STAY STITCHING: regular stitching on single thickness of fabric, just inside the seam allowance around bias or curved edges, to control the grain and keep fabric from stretching.
- BACK STITCHING: retracing stitches for approximately ¼ inch at the beginning and end of a line of stitching to secure the threads. Also called staying.
- TOP STITCHING: stitching on the right side of a garment. It may be stitched either close to a seam or fold, or ¼ inch or more away depending upon the appearance preferred. As well as being decorative, it may also serve to keep an edge in place, as around a collar, cuff, or pocket edge.

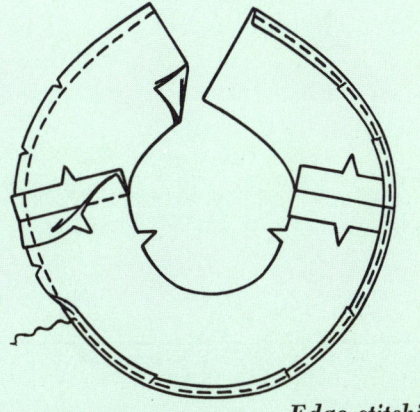

Edge stitching.

- EDGE STITCHING: stitching close to a turned edge (never more than ⅛ inch away from the fold). Keep the inner edge of the presser foot along the edge of the fabric to guide stitching.

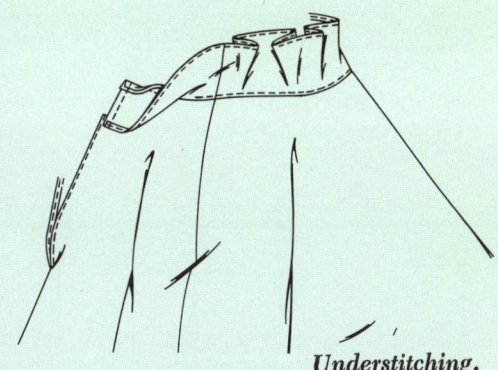

Understitching.

- UNDERSTITCHING: the stitching that holds the facing in position by sewing it to the seam. It is done on the right side of the facing, close to the seam line, and is not seen on the outside of the garment. The result is a neat, flat edge because the facing cannot roll to the outside of the garment.

The Language of Sewing (Continued)

- BLIND STITCHING: An invisible stitch used for hemming, catching only a thread of the outer fabric so that it is not noticeable on the right side of the garment. Can be done by hand or on the blind stitching machine.
- TACK: hold a part of a garment in position by attaching it to another invisibly with a few small stitches; for example, tack a facing to a seam.

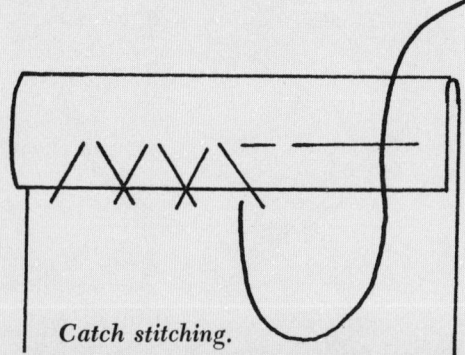
Catch stitching.

- CATCH STITCHING: diagonal stitches used to hold a raw edge in position; for example, attaching interfacing to a garment. The top stitch catches the raw edge; the bottom stitch, the garment with the threads crossing each other at every stitch. No stitches are visible on the right side.

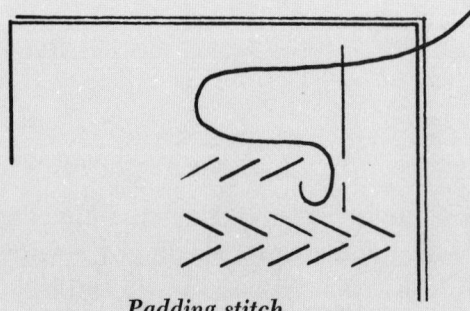
Padding stitch.

- PADDING STITCH: rows of diagonal stitches used in tailoring to hold two layers of fabric together; for example, interfacing to collar. The vertical stitches on the outside are small and barely seen because they catch only a thread or two of the fabric.

Are you familiar with these construction terms?

- REINFORCE: strengthen a point of strain in one of the following ways:
—*Small stitching:* place a row of small machine stitching on the seam line; for example, around a corner before clipping into the corner.

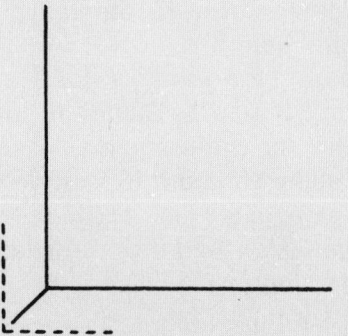
Reinforce a corner to be clipped.

—*Double stitching:* place a second row of machine stitching on top of or right beside the first row; for example, around the point of a slashed opening or around a curved seam.
—*Tape:* stitch tape to the seam as around the waistline or to the underarm seam of a kimono sleeve.
—*Extra fabric:* stitch a square of fabric to the point of a slash, as in a gusset.

- TRIM: cut away part of the fabric. A seam allowance may be "trimmed" to eliminate bulk. Cut to within ¼ inch of the stitching unless directions indicate "trim close to the stitching," in which case cut to within ⅛ inch. A power-driven machine may have a trimmer attached that trims the seam

The Language of Sewing (Continued)

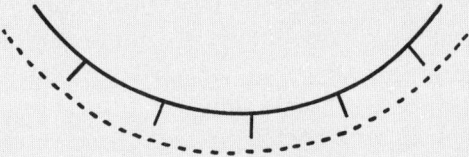
Clip a concave curve.

as it is being stitched. A corner may also be trimmed before it is turned by cutting across diagonally close to the stitching.

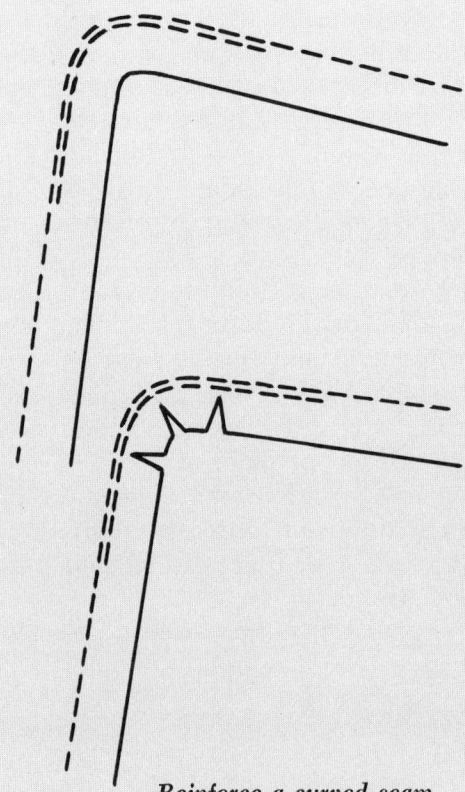
Reinforce a curved seam.

stitching, being careful not to cut the stitching.

- NOTCH: a triangular-shaped cut. Along the seam allowance notches are an aid for assembling the garment. Match the notches to join pieces together correctly.

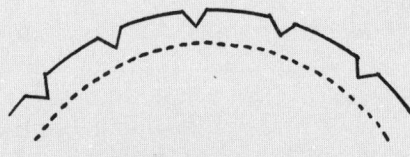
Notch a convex curve.

Notching a seam refers to cutting small V's out of the seam allowance. A convex curve (collars, scallops, etc.) should be notched to eliminate the excess fabric so that there will be no bulges visible on the right side when the seam is turned.

- SLASH: Cut open or apart with one straight cut of the shears.
- EASE: Sew together fabric pieces of unequal length without any puckering. The longer edge is "worked in" gradually so that the extra fullness is evenly distributed and hardly noticeable.
- PUCKER: an unwanted tuck or fold stitched into the seam. Also an undesirable pulling, wrinkling, drawing, or gathering along the seam.
- CLEAN FINISH: Finish the edge of a seam or the bottom edge of a facing by turning under the raw edge and "edge stitching" it separately.

- LAYER: also called grading. Trim the seam allowance to different widths to eliminate bulk—one edge ¼ inch, the other slightly lower. If there is also interfacing in the seam, trim it close to the stitching. Because of the different widths, there is no ridge visible on the outside of the garment.
- CLIP: Cut into the seam allowance from the edge of the fabric toward the stitching, as around a curved seam or into a corner. Clipping enables the seam to spread so that it will lie flat. Cut straight in toward the

The Language of Sewing (Continued)

- **Facing:** a piece of fabric sewn to the right side of a garment section and turned to the inside to finish a raw edge; for example, neck edge, collar, cuff, etc. There are three types of facings; fitted—cut the same shape as the section to be finished; self—cut in one piece with the garment and merely turned under; bias—a strip of fabric cut on the bias and eased around the edge to be finished.
- **Band:** a finish for a raw edge that is also decorative. Unlike a facing, it is visible on the right side of the garment because it is stitched to the wrong side and turned to the right side—just the opposite of a facing.
- **Binding:** a finish for a raw edge that encases the edge and has the same amount of fabric visible on both the right and wrong sides.
- **Interfacing:** an extra piece of fabric inserted between the facing and the garment. It adds firmness and body to such sections as collars, cuffs, and lapels. It strengthens and reinforces an area that may receive strain, such as under buttons and buttonholes. It prevents stretching or sagging of the fabric; for example, around neck edges.
- **Lining:** fabric used to cover the inside of a garment. The lining and the garment are constructed separately; then the lining is attached to the garment. A lining gives a finished appearance to a garment by covering all the raw edges. It also contributes to a "smooth feel."
- **Underlining:** fabric used as a backing for the outer fabric. The underlining is cut over the same pattern as the garment. The two pieces of fabric are sewn together and then handled as one piece of fabric during construction. The underlining serves much the same purpose as interfacing; to add body, reinforce, and prevent stretching.
- **Interlining:** extra fabric inserted between the lining and the outer fabric for warmth.

Taking Measurements

In all aspects of sewing except mass production, you will be concerned with body measurements. In custom sewing for a specific individual and in fitting and alteration work, measurements are very important. If you are selling in the fabric and pattern department, you will have to know how to take body measurements and determine sizes. Be accurate.

The four measurements on top of the next page are used to determine size. Dress patterns (coat and suit, also) are sold by bust measurement; skirts, slacks, and shorts by waist measurements.

Patterns are sold according to type—Junior, Petite, Misses, Women's, etc. These types have nothing to do with age. Instead, they describe a type of figure (see the charts). It is as important to use the correct type of pattern as the correct size. If a person with an immature, short figure selects a pattern for a fully developed, tall figure, the finished garment will not fit properly. To insure good fit the pattern should be designed for the figure. See pages 274 and 275 for the figure types.

There are additional measurements needed to check size and fit (see bottom of the next page):

McCall's Patterns

- **Bust:** Measure around the fullest part of the bust. Take it snug, but not too tight. Don't let the tape slip down across the back.
- **Waist:** Remove a belt. Measure around the natural waistline. Make it comfortable, but not too snug.
- **Hips:** Around the fullest part, approximately 7 inches below the waist. Not accurate if taken over a bulky or very full skirt.
- **Back Waist Length:** From the prominent bone at the base of the neck to the waistline. To locate the bone easily, bend the head forward.

1. **Front Waist Length:** From the base of neck at the shoulder to the point of the bust.
  —From the base of the neck at the shoulder, over the fullest part of the bust, to the waistline.
2. **Front Width:** From armhole to armhole, above the bust.
  —**Back Width:** From armhole to armhole, 4 inches and 6 inches below the base of the neck. (*Not shown.*)
3. **Shoulder Length:** From base of neck to top of arm.
4. **Sleeve Width:** Around fullest part of arm halfway between shoulder and elbow.
  —Around fullest part of arm halfway between elbow and wrist.
  —Around wrist.
5. **Sleeve Length:** Shoulder to elbow.
6. Shoulder to wristbone, with the arm bent at the elbow.
7. **Skirt Length:** From waistline to hem. Check both center and sides.

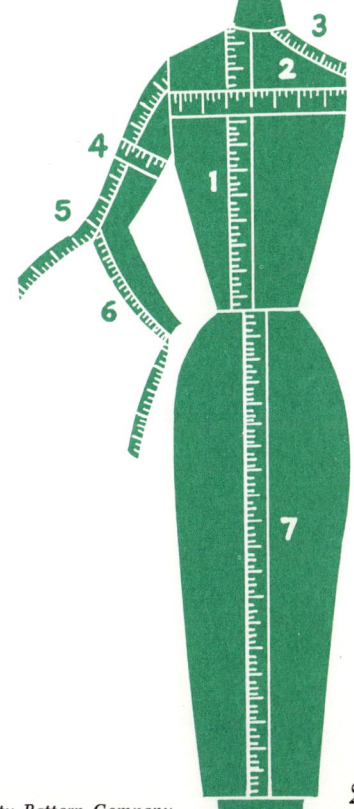

Educational Division, Simplicity Pattern Company

PATTERN SIZE MEASUREMENT CHART

(Buy patterns by your bust measurement, regardless of the size number shown on the envelope.)

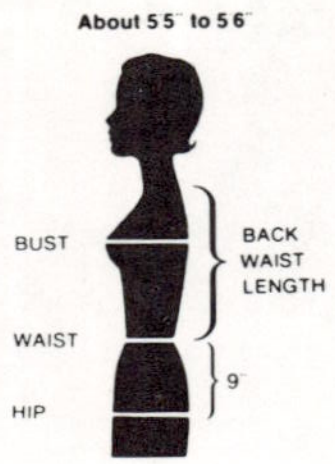

MISSES'

Misses' patterns are designed for a well proportioned, and developed figure; about 5'5" to 5'6" without shoes.

Size	6	8	10	12	14	16	18
Bust	30½	31½	32½	34	36	38	40
Waist	22	23	24	25½	27	29	31
Hip	32½	33½	34½	36	38	40	42
Back Waist Length	15½	15¾	16	16¼	16½	16¾	17

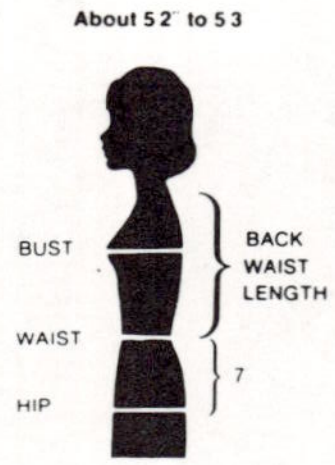

MISS PETITE

This new size range is designed for the shorter Miss figure; about 5'2" to 5'3" without shoes.

Size	6mp	8mp	10mp	12mp	14mp	16mp
Bust	30½	31½	32½	34	36	38
Waist	22½	23½	24½	26	27½	29½
Hip	32½	33½	34½	36	38	40
Back Waist Length	14½	14¾	15	15¼	15½	15¾

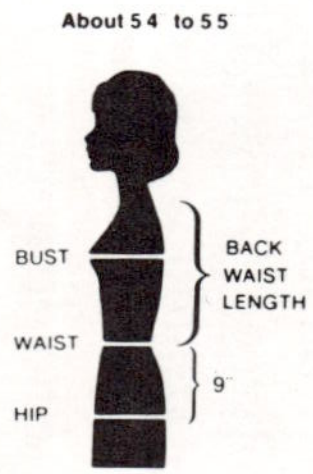

JUNIOR

Junior patterns are designed for a well proportioned, shorter waisted figure; about 5'4" to 5'5" without shoes.

Size	5	7	9	11	13	15
Bust	30	31	32	33½	35	37
Waist	21½	22½	23½	24½	26	28
Hip	32	33	34	35½	37	39
Back Waist Length	15	15¼	15½	15¾	16	16¼

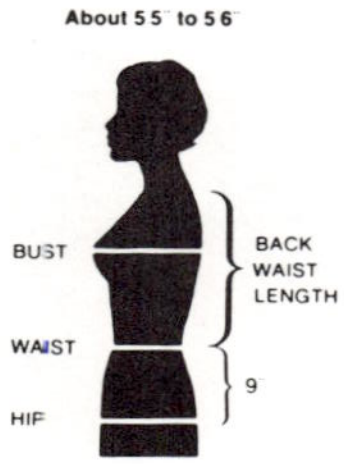

WOMEN'S

Women's patterns are designed for the larger, more fully mature figure; about 5'5" to 5'6" without shoes.

Size	38	40	42	44	46	48	50
Bust	42	44	46	48	50	52	54
Waist	34	36	38	40½	43	45½	48
Hip	44	46	48	50	52	54	56
Back Waist Length	17¼	17⅜	17½	17⅝	17¾	17⅞	18

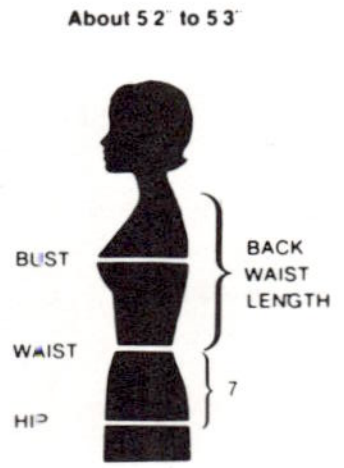

HALF-SIZE

Half-size patterns are for a fully developed figure with a short backwaist length. Waist and hip are larger in proportion to bust than other figure types; about 5'2" to 5'3" without shoes.

Size	10½	12½	14½	16½	18½	20½	22½	24½
Bust	33	35	37	39	41	43	45	47
Waist	26	28	30	32	34	36½	39	41½
Hip	35	37	39	41	43	45½	48	50½
Back Waist Length	15	15¼	15½	15¾	15⅞	16	16⅛	16¼

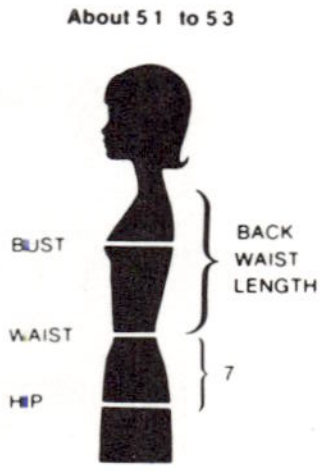

YOUNG JUNIOR/TEEN

This new size range is designed for the developing pre-teen and teen figures; about 5'1" to 5'3" without shoes.

Size	5/6	7/8	9/10	11/12	13/14	15/16
Bust	28	29	30½	32	33½	35
Waist	22	23	24	25	26	27
Hip	31	32	33½	35	36½	38
Back Waist Length	13½	14	14½	15	15⅜	15¾

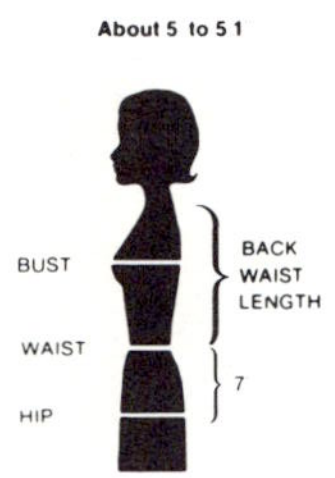

JUNIOR PETITE

Junior Petite patterns are designed for a well proportioned, petite figure; about 5′ to 5′1″ without shoes.

Size	3jp	5jp	7jp	9jp	11jp	13jp
Bust	30½	31	32	33	34	35
Waist	22	22½	23½	24½	25½	26½
Hip	31½	32	33	34	35	36
Back Waist Length	14	14¼	14½	14¾	15	15¼

SKIRTS, SLACKS & SHORTS:

Select by waist measurement or if hips are much larger in proportion to waist, select size by hip measurement.

Misses'

Waist	22	23	24	25½	27	29	31
Hip	32½	33½	34½	36	38	40	42

Miss Petite

Waist	22½	23½	24½	26	27½	29½
Hip	32½	33½	34½	36	38	40

Junior

Waist	21½	22½	23½	24½	26	28
Hip	32	33	34	35½	37	39

Junior Petite

Waist	22	22½	23½	24½	25½	26½
Hip	31½	32	33	34	35	36

Women's

Waist	34	36	38	40½	43	45½	48
Hip	44	46	48	50	52	54	56

Young Junior/Teen

Waist	22	23	24	25	26	27
Hip	31	32	33½	35	36½	38

BUY *ALL* PATTERNS IN THE FOLLOWING SIZE RANGES IN THE *SAME* SIZE YOU ARE ACCUSTOMED TO BUYING.

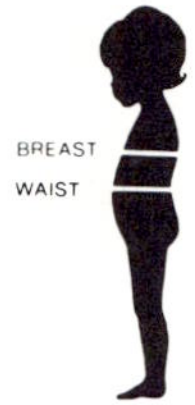

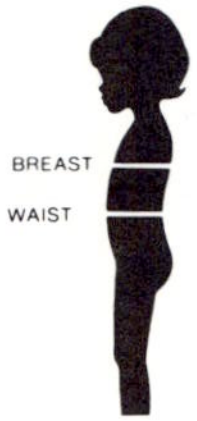

CHILDREN'S MEASUREMENTS

Measure around the breast, but not to snugly.
Toddler patterns are designed for a figure between that of a baby and child.

Dress Lengths from Back Neck Base to Lower Edge

Size	½	1	2	3	4	5	6	6X
Toddler	14″	15″	16″	17″	18″			
Child		17″	18″	19″	20″	22″	24″	25″

TODDLERS'

Size	½	1	2	3	4
Breast	19	20	21	22	23
Waist	19	19½	20	20½	21

CHILDREN'S

Size	1	2	3	4	5	6	6X
Breast	20	21	22	23	24	25	25½
Waist	19½	20	20½	21	21½	22	22½
Hip				24	25	26	26½

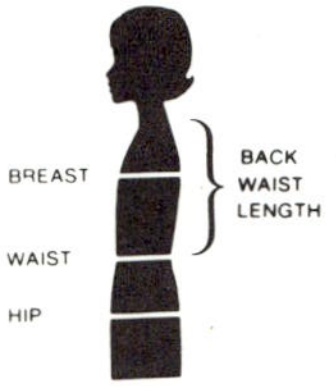

GIRLS'

Girls' patterns are designed for the girl who has not yet begun to mature. See below chart for approximate heights without shoes.

Size	7	8	10	12	14
Breast	26	27	28½	30	32
Waist	23	23½	24½	25½	26½
Hip	27	28	30	32	34
Back Waist Length	11½	12	12¾	13½	14¼
Approx. Heights	50″	52″	56″	58½″	61″

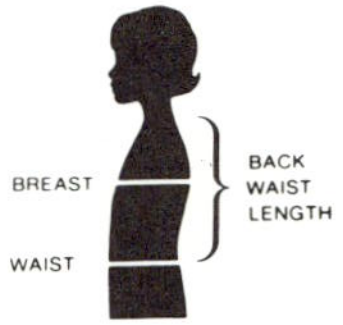

CHUBBIE

Chubbie patterns are designed for the growing girl who is over the average weight for her age and height. See below for approximate heights, without shoes.

Size	8½c	10½c	12½c	14½c
Breast	30	31½	33	34½
Waist	28	29	30	31
Hip	33	34½	36	37½

Basic Skills for Clothing Construction

Using a Commercial Pattern

Commercial patterns have a language all their own. Study a pattern to become acquainted with the terms and symbols used. See page 277.

- CUTTING LINE: All the pattern pieces are printed on one large piece of tissue paper for accuracy, and then cut apart by machines, leaving a margin around each piece. On some patterns the cutting line is indicated by a heavy solid line; on others, there is a double line. For accurate cutting on heavyweight or bulky fabrics, it is best to cut the margin off the pattern before pinning it to the fabric. Then cut around the edge of the paper, instead of through paper, to cut the garment out of the fabric.

- FOLD LINE: Some pattern pieces are marked to be placed on a fold of the fabric for cutting. You do not cut along the fold lines. The fabric piece will be twice the size of the tissue paper when cut. The fold line may be indicated by a heavy broken line or a very light solid line marked "place on fold."

  A fold line on a pattern piece may also indicate where a section is to be folded during construction; for example, through the center of a cuff or waistband, or a self-facing.

- GRAIN LINE: If a pattern piece is not to be placed on a fold of the fabric, there will be a straight line or arrow marked "place on straight grain of fabric." This line must be placed on one thread, preferably on the lengthwise grain, parallel to the selvage. The garment will hang correctly only if it is cut accurately on-grain and this line assists in placing the pattern on the fabric correctly.

- SEAM ALLOWANCE: All commercial patterns now have a standard ⅝ inch seam allowance. On most patterns this allowance is marked with a light broken line inside the cutting line. Some indicate with arrows the direction in which you should stitch.

- CENTER LINES: The center front and center back on the pattern may be a fold line, a seam line, or merely a line—as is the case of a garment that buttons down the front or back. Most patterns indicate these by printing "center front" or "center back" on the line.

- NOTCHES: Notches are the triangular markings along the cutting lines of the pattern. They help to put the garment together correctly by indicating where the pattern pieces are to be joined. On some patterns the notches are numbered to indicate the sequence of matching.

- MATCHING POINTS: Different size circles help in fitting pieces together. For example: a circle at the top of a sleeve is placed at the shoulder seam, a circle on a collar is placed at the shoulder seam, the end of the collar is placed at the circle on the bodice, etc. Some patterns use squares and triangles as well as circles to mark matching points.

- LOCATION LINES: The placement of buttonholes, pockets, and other construction details are indicated by solid lines. The fold line for a hem may also be indicated with a solid line.

- ALTERATION LINES: Lines drawn across a pattern piece and marked "lengthen or shorten here," indicate where the pattern can be altered, if necessary. Some patterns even print a

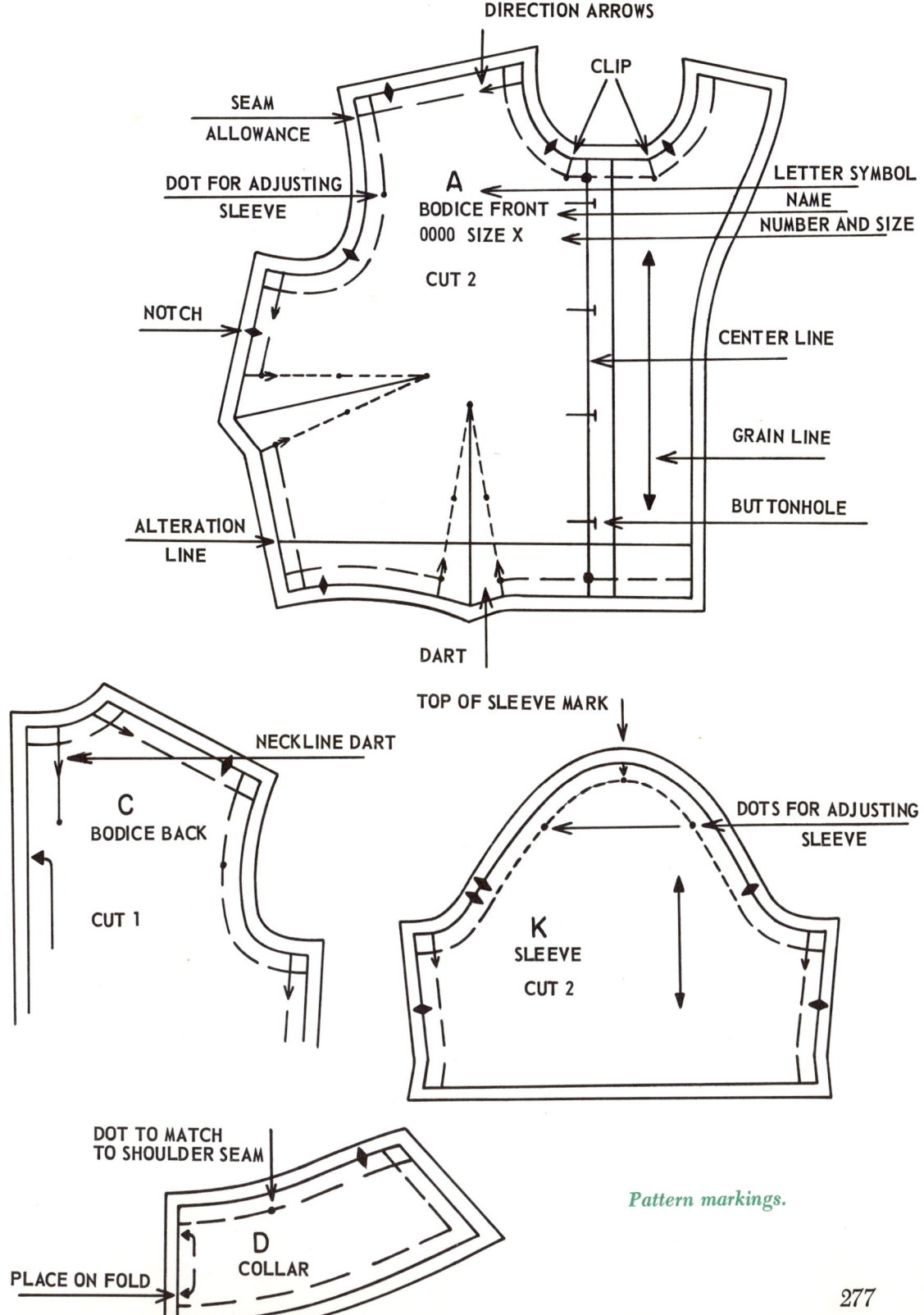

Pattern markings.

Basic Skills for Clothing Construction

ruler on the tissue paper at the alteration point to simplify the measuring. If a pattern piece can be lengthened or shortened at the bottom, as in the case of a full skirt, there are no alteration lines drawn on the pattern, but the words "lengthen or shorten here" are printed near the cutting line.

To lengthen at the bottom of the pattern piece, pin or tape a piece of tissue paper to the bottom. Measure the amount needed and draw a new

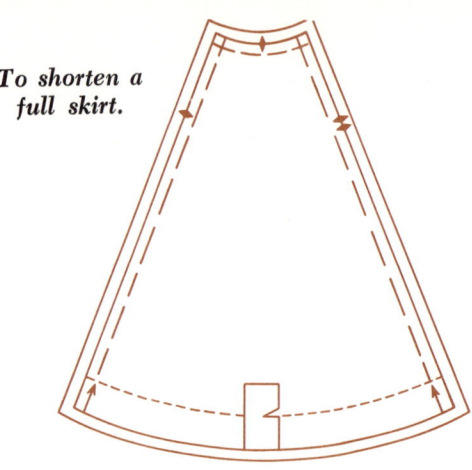

To shorten a full skirt.

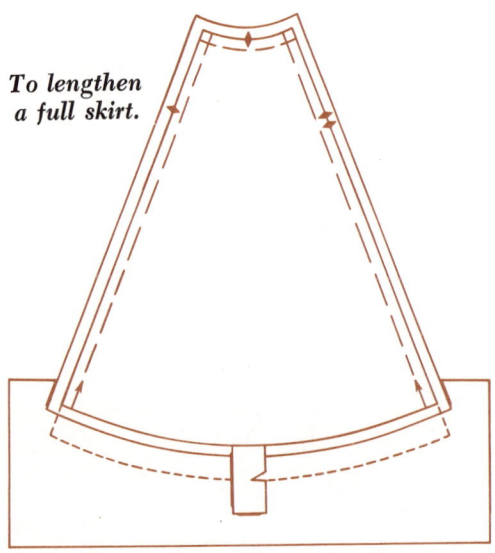

To lengthen a full skirt.

To lengthen at an alteration line, cut the pattern apart on the line. Pin or tape one part of the pattern piece to tissue paper. Measure the amount needed and draw a line across the tissue paper at this point. Pin the other part of the pattern piece to this line, keeping the grain line markings straight.

To shorten, measure from the alteration line the amount that needs to be shortened and draw a second line across the pattern. Fold the pattern on one line and bring the folded edge to the second line. Pin or tape in place. Keep the grain line markings

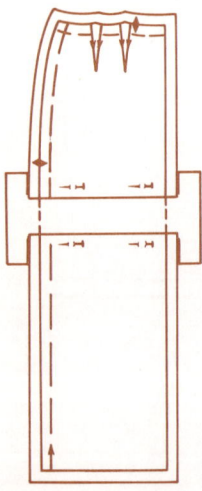

cutting line. It is also possible to add the desired length after the pattern is pinned to the fabric. Measure the extra and mark it with chalk directly on the fabric. To shorten, cut off the required amount from the lower edge of the pattern.

To lengthen a straight skirt.

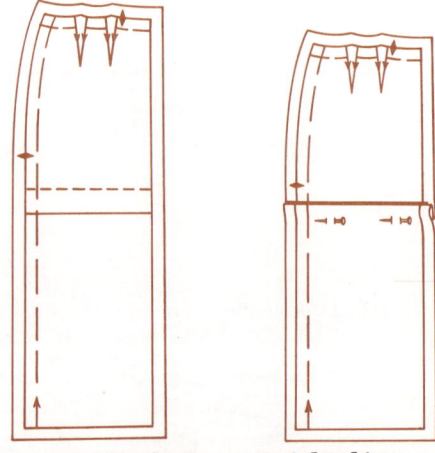

To shorten a straight skirt.

straight and straighten the cutting line.

Some patterns have two different sizes printed on the same pattern piece. For example, there may be two cutting lines—one for size 14 and one for size 16. A pattern of this type makes it possible to "cut to fit" for the figure that needs one size in the bodice and perhaps another size for the skirt.

Proportioned patterns come in different lengths—short, medium, and tall. There may be a separate pattern piece in the envelope for each or the pattern may be for the tall length with an alteration line marked for each of the others.

• CONSTRUCTION MARKINGS: Dart outlines, pleat lines, slash marks, and other construction details are indicated on the pattern with printed lines. Often sewing instructions are included; for example, beside the dart outline may be printed "Fold on solid line, stitch on broken line." There may be marks indicating how far to stitch a seam or where to place gathers, etc. Examine a pattern carefully to identify all the markings.

THE CUTTING PROCESS

In mass-production sewing, the cutting process is quite different from that used by the home sewer or in custom sewing where only one garment is cut at a time. In all probability you would not even be concerned with cutting. However, you should understand the process and the techniques involved and if you plan to do any custom sewing or tailoring you need to know how to cut out a garment accurately and with as little waste as possible.

• PREPARATION OF FABRIC: All fabric is woven grain perfect with the lengthwise threads and the crosswise threads at perfect right angles. If it is tentered properly (see page 143), it is probably still grain perfect when ready for use. In the finishing processes, however, it may be stretched out of shape so that it is no longer on grain. In mass production work, where speed is the prime consideration, fabric is used "as-is" whether grain perfect or not. In custom work, and better quality dressmaking, however, more consideration is given to details. Before using fabric, check the grain. First straighten the raw edges (straight means on one thread) by tearing across the fabric, pulling one thread across, or marking along a thread. Then fold the fabric in half lengthwise with the selvages together and smooth it on a flat surface. If the raw edges are even, the fabric is grain perfect; if not, the fabric should be straightened before using.

To straighten: Stretch the entire length of the fabric on the true bias, pulling it gently but firmly. Recheck for straightness and repeat the process, if necessary, until the fabric is grain perfect.

Wool will not respond to stretching alone. In your study of fabrics you learned that wool is resilient; it springs back to position. However, when it is damp, it will be possible to manipulate the fabric into shape. Place the fabric on a sheet that is thoroughly damp but not wet. Fold the sheet over the fabric; then loosely fold end over end for the length of the fabric. Cover with a bath towel or place in a plastic bag. Leave the wool in the sheet for several hours or over-

FOLDS

There are four possible kinds of folds:

A *lengthwise fold* in which the fold is parallel to the selvage.

A *crosswise fold* in which the fold goes across the fabric from selvage to selvage.

A *partial fold* in which the fabric is folded only part way. Part of the fabric is single thickness. To be sure this fold is straight, measure it in several places from the fold to the selvage or straight end. A partial fold may be either lengthwise or crosswise.

A *double fold* in which both ends of the fabric are folded so that the selvages, or ends, meet in the middle. A double fold may be either lengthwise or crosswise.

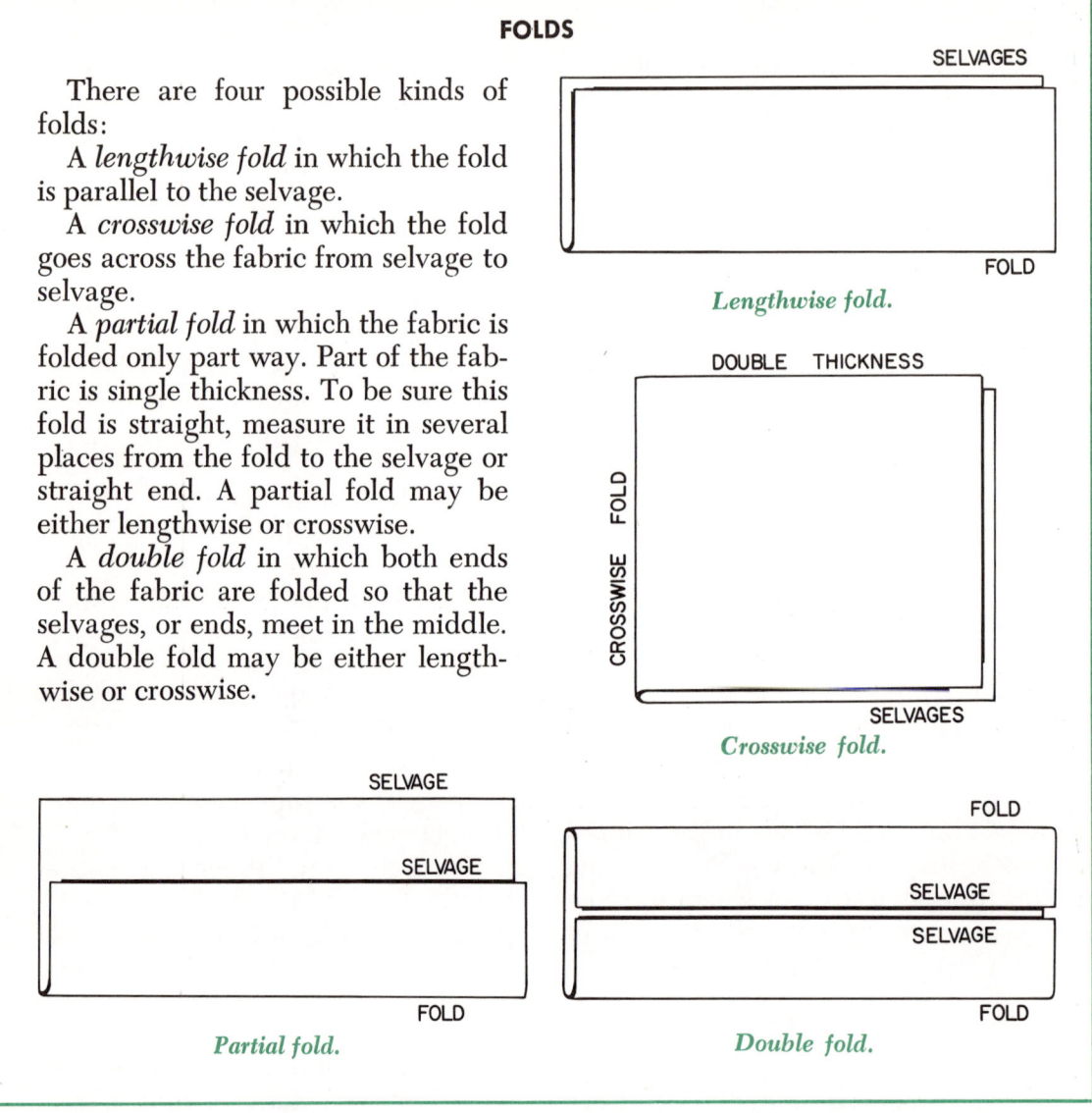

Lengthwise fold.

Crosswise fold.

Partial fold.

Double fold.

night. Unwrap and let dry in a flat position, manipulating into shape to straighten the grain. Press lightly with a steam iron, being careful not to stretch it.

Some fabrics cannot be straightened. If a resin finish has been applied to the fabric (for example; wash and wear, or wrinkle resistant) the finish has set the threads into position. In bonded fabrics, also, the threads are set in position. If these fabrics are not grain perfect, there is nothing that can be done to straighten them, because the threads cannot be moved. They have to be used "as-is."

In mass production, a machine spreader automatically spreads the fabric evenly in neat layers, each

The Cutting Process

layer the exact length needed for the particular garment to be made. Although more than one hundred garments may be cut out at once, all pattern pieces for each individual garment are cut singly. If two of a kind are required for the same garment—for instance, sleeves—the pattern is cut twice. In cutting individual garments, the fabric can be folded and one cutting will produce both pieces. Preferably fold the fabric wrong side out. It will be easier to transfer pattern markings to the fabric, the fabric will not become soiled, and the pieces will be in position to sew them together without additional handling.

When working with a "one-way" fabric, only a lengthwise fold may be used—never a crosswise fold. Mark the direction of a "one-way" with arrows; then fold the fabric crosswise to see what happens. Notice that the arrows on the two layers go in different directions. If a garment were cut on this type of fold, the design or nap would be going in different directions. If the width of the pattern pieces requires the wider area of a crosswise fold, fold the fabric crosswise as far as needed. Then cut the fold. Turn the under layer so that the bottom edge becomes the top. Then check the arrows and you will find that they are going in the same direction.

• PATTERN PLACEMENT: In mass production the pattern pieces may be traced on the top layer of fabric or the entire layout may be printed on a large sheet of paper the exact size of the layer of fabric. This paper is then placed on top of the fabric as a guide for cutting. In either case, the pattern placement has been planned very carefully so as to use the fabric to best advantage and with the least amount of waste. At the same time all pieces are placed accurately and on grain. If there is a design to be matched, in better clothing the placement is planned so that garment pieces will be matched when sewn together.

In the same manner, when cutting individual garments, the pattern must be placed on the fabric very carefully and accurately to insure success. First be sure that both pattern and fabric are wrinkle-free. Press them if necessary, using a cool, dry iron on paper patterns. Then merely place all the pattern pieces on the fabric, fitting them as close together as possible. When you are sure the pattern is arranged in a way that makes best use of the fabric, you are ready to pin each piece in place permanently.

Use enough pins to hold the pattern securely, but not so many that the fabric bulges. Place the pins about three or four inches apart, with the points toward the edge of the pattern. Be careful that they do not extend past the cutting line. Make sure that all corners are pinned securely by placing the pins diagonally into each corner. Keep the fabric flat on the table while pinning, smoothing the paper as you go.

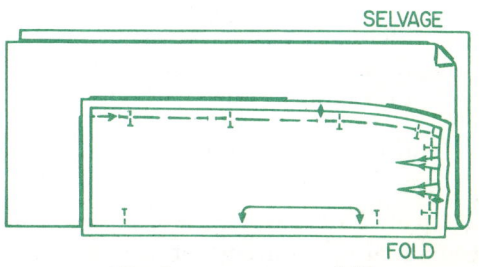

Pinning pattern on fold.

Basic Skills for Clothing Construction

If the pattern piece is to be placed on the fold of the fabric, pin along the fold line first, making sure that the line is exactly on the fold of the fabric for its entire length. Then, pin around the other edges.

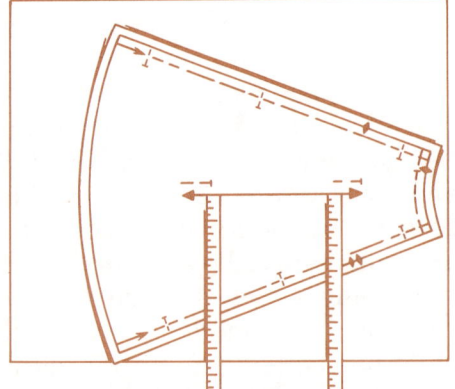

Pinning pattern on straight grain.

If there is a grain line on the pattern, this must be pinned in position first to insure having the garment piece on grain. Here are the steps to follow to get the grain line on the straight grain of the fabric:

—Place the pattern so that the grain line looks straight.

—Pin one end of the line to the fabric.

—Measure from the pinned end of the line to the selvage.

—Check the other end of the line. It must measure the same distance from the selvage. If it doesn't, move it until it does and then pin it in place.

Grain is very important to the appearance of the finished garment. The grain line must be on the straight of the fabric (a thread of the fabric). When the grain line is pinned in position, continue pinning the edges of the pattern to the fabric.

Here are some additional items concerning commercial pattern cutting layouts that may need explanation.

Place the pattern pieces on the fabric exactly as shown on the layout. When cutting on double fabric, it does not matter whether the pattern piece is right side up or upside down. Often pieces can be fit closer together by turning them over. Perhaps the pattern pieces that are to be turned upside down will be shaded on the layout.

When cutting on single thickness, place the pattern right side up on the right side of the fabric. If the piece is to be cut again, turn the pattern wrong side up for the second cutting to insure having opposites; for example, a right sleeve and a left sleeve rather than two right sleeves.

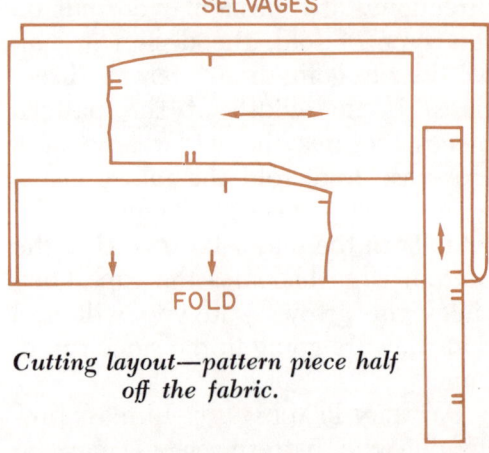

Cutting layout—pattern piece half off the fabric.

If a pattern piece extends beyond the fold of the fabric, as in the above diagram, unfold the fabric after cutting all other pieces and pin it to a single thickness.

The Cutting Process

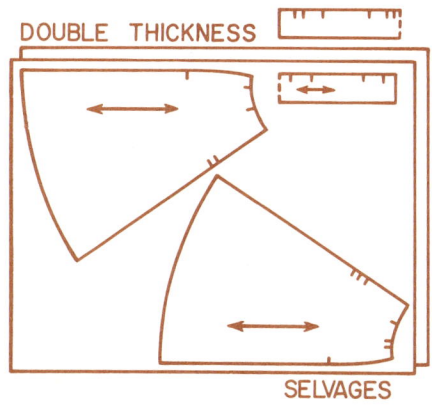

Cutting layout—not enough room for a pattern piece.

In the above diagram, there was not room to place the entire waistband on the fabric. The pattern has been cut in half; half is on the fabric and the other half is shown above the fabric. In this case, cut out all other pieces. Separate the remaining fabric and pin each part of the pattern piece to single fabric. When cutting, add seam allowance where the pattern was separated so the two pieces may be sewn together.

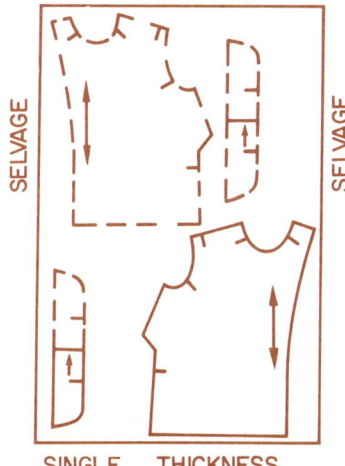

Cutting layout—pattern piece drawn twice.

If a pattern piece is drawn twice on the layout, it must be cut a second time. The first cutting is usually drawn with a solid line—the second, with a dotted line. When pinning the pattern to the fabric, save enough space for the second piece or trace the pattern onto tissue paper so that you can pin all pattern pieces at one time. Remember to place the patterns so that you will have one for the right side and one for the left—first cutting, right side up; second cutting, upside down.

Notice the two collar pieces in the diagram, lower left. The arrow indicates that they should be cut "on the fold"; however, they are placed on single fabric. To do this, place the fold line on straight grain and pin the duplicate piece beside the first piece with fold lines matching. The entire piece is then cut as one.

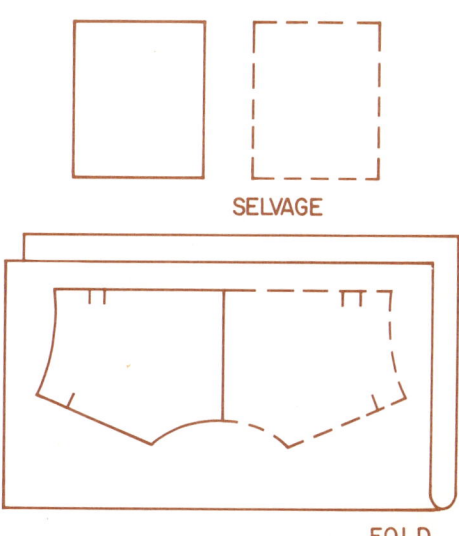

Cutting layout—pattern piece completely off the fabric.

In the above diagram, two pattern pieces are drawn completely off the

283

Basic Skills for Clothing Construction

fabric. If you examine such layouts carefully, you will notice that the pattern piece off the fabric is always placed beside a piece on the layout that is either similar in shape or requires the same amount of fabric. The piece of pattern already on the fabric is to be cut of single fabric from the top layer only. The piece beside the layout is to be cut of single fabric from the bottom layer directly underneath.

• CUTTING AND MARKING: Either dressmaker shears or electric scissors may be used to cut individual garments. Cut accurately. A mistake here could be very costly. Here are some suggestions:

—Use sharp shears. Pinking shears are intended for finishing, not cutting out. They do not give an accurate cutting line.

—Keep the fabric flat on the table. Move around the table rather than move the fabric as you work. Hold the fabric flat with one hand as you cut with the other.

—Cut with long strokes of the shears.

—Follow the cutting line carefully. Do not cut fold lines.

In mass production, notches are indicated by small slashes in the edge of the fabric. When cutting individual garments, it is safer to cut notches outward, into the scrap fabric. Cutting inward weakens the seam allowance.

If there are two or three notches together, cut them as one across the top, as shown in the diagram.

All construction markings must be transferred from the pattern piece to the fabric. Some of the marking can be done while cutting, as it is in mass production. Slash into the seam allowance, no more than ⅛ inch, to mark such places as: center lines; fold lines; pleat lines; end of darts; the point at the top of the sleeve that matches the shoulder line; points on collar that match shoulder line and center front; and any other points that can be marked at the edge of a fabric piece. Use the point of the scissors and be careful not to cut more than ⅛ inch so as not to weaken the seam.

For those markings in the body of the garment, several methods can be used. In mass production, a marking drill is used to mark dots in the fabric. In very inexpensive clothing, holes are punched in the fabric to mark details. This method is used because it is speedy, even though it damages the fabric and makes alterations difficult—perhaps even impossible. In custom work, a tool that holds two pieces of marking chalk and works very much like a punch may be used to mark dots on the fabric.

The tracing wheel and dressmaker's carbon paper are easy to use and very accurate. Select the lightest color tracing paper that will show on the fabric. Fold the paper with the waxed sides together. Slip the paper into position with the waxed side of the paper against the wrong side of the fabric—see the picture on the following page. One part of the paper is under the fabric and the other part

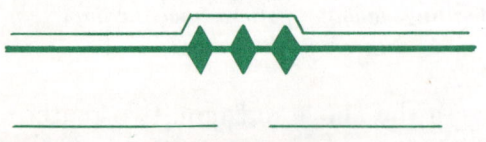

Cutting notches.

284

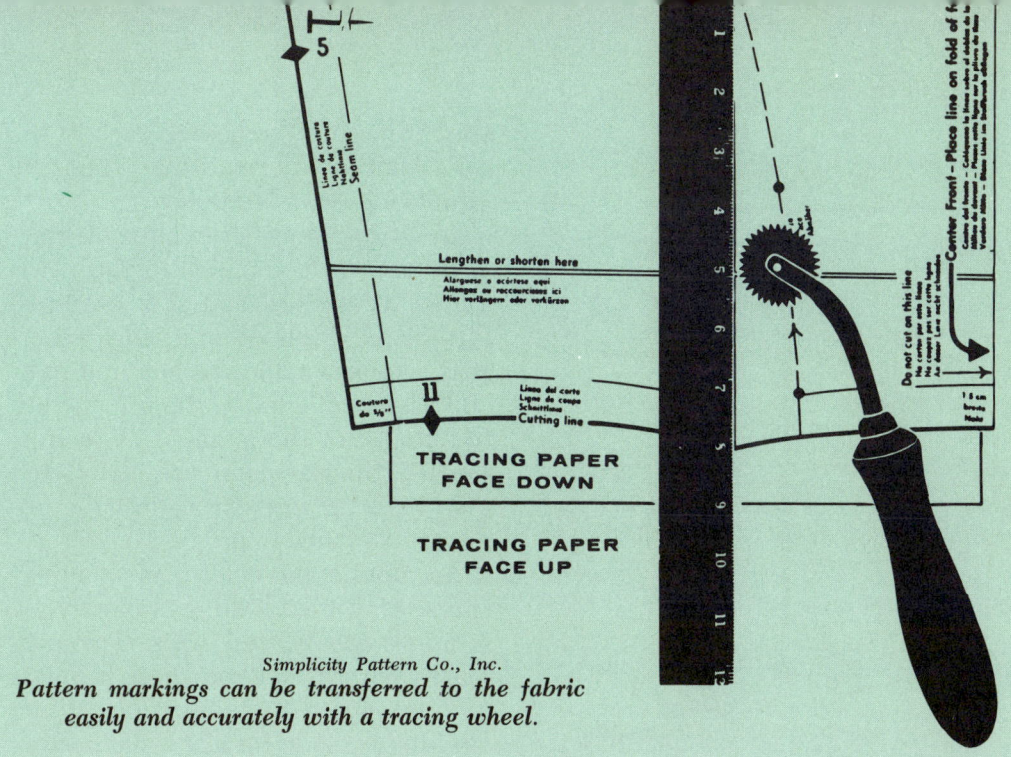

Pattern markings can be transferred to the fabric easily and accurately with a tracing wheel.
Simplicity Pattern Co., Inc.

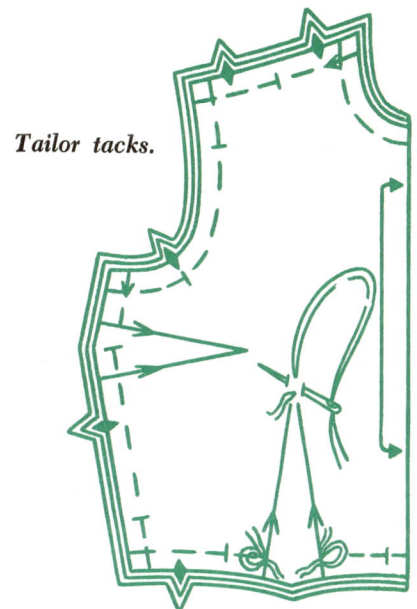

Tailor tacks.

is between the top layer of the fabric and the pattern. Work on a hard surface and trace the markings with a tracing wheel. Go over the lines only once, with firm pressure. Use a ruler to get lines straight. Avoid using this method on sheer fabric where you will be able to see the markings on the right side of the fabric.

Thread markings—tailor tacks—are accurate, safe, and have the added advantage of marking on the right and wrong side of the fabric at the same time. Embroidery thread or darning cotton holds better than regular sewing thread. Use two strands, doubled, in the needle.

Take a small stitch through all layers at each marking point. This stitch should be taken in the same direction as the line you are marking. Leave about an inch of thread at both ends of the stitch. If there is a series of markings, continue making stitches on the markings until the series is completed. Be sure to leave at least two inches of thread between markings. Cut the threads between the markings to remove the pattern.

Basic Skills for Clothing Construction

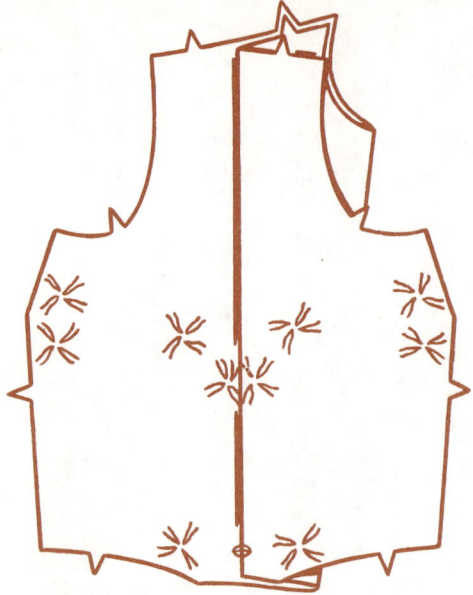

Separate the pieces and cut threads.

Carefully separate the layers of fabric and clip the threads between the layers.

Assembling a Garment

In mass production, a garment is progressively assembled by a series of successive steps, with a special operator or handler for each step. Often individual small items—such as collars or cuffs—are left attached to each other through several steps in production—perhaps applying trim, sewing together, turning, and pressing. They may be broken apart only to be reconnected as additional pieces are added; for example, a band to a collar. The chain may not be finally broken until a unit is completely finished or attached to a larger unit.

For speed and ease of handling, the work is kept flat as long as possible. Crosswise seams are stitched first; then, lengthwise seams. For example, the sleeve may be set into the armhole; then the underarm seam is sewn; the bodice front is joined to the skirt front and the bodice back to the skirt back at the waistline; then the entire side seam is stitched.

In custom and better dressmaking, each unit is completed before it is added to another unit. For example, the sleeve itself is finished—underarm seam sewn and the hem put in or cuff attached—before it is attached to the bodice of the garment. As a rule, the lengthwise seams are completed first, then the crosswise—just the opposite of factory production.

As mentioned before, in commercial sewing the clothing is merely assembled in assorted sizes. The ultimate wearer is not known, so fitting is of no concern in production. When clothing is made for a specific person, however, fitting is an important part of production. Two fittings are usually required, perhaps an additional one for complicated details or major fitting problems. The techniques of fitting are discussed in the following chapter.

• FIRST FITTING: Baste the garment together completely. Sections that have no effect on the fit—yokes and center seams, for instance—may be stitched permanently. Interfacings or underlinings should be in place. Check the major alterations on the bodice and skirt. Look for wrinkling and check the following points:

BODICE:	Grain
	Position of seams— shoulder, underarm
	Neckline
	Width of bodice
	Length of sleeves
SKIRT:	Grain
	Width
	Position of seams
WAISTLINE:	Position
	Size

- SECOND FITTING: Stitch all seams, finish the neckline, complete buttonholes, plackets, etc. Baste the sleeves in the armhole and then check the following:

  Position of armhole seam

  Sleeve grain and distribution of ease

  Mark hemline

  Check added items—pockets, collars, etc.

  Check such other details as length of belt, position of carriers, etc.

- COMPLETION: Stitch the sleeves; hem the skirt; sew on buttons, hooks and eyes, snaps; and complete other small details. After a final pressing, the garment is ready for delivery to the customer.

Construction Techniques

In order to establish sewing skills it is necessary to repeat a technique until you can perform it correctly, quickly, and independently. Continued practice, with emphasis on perfection, will result in mastery. A thorough understanding of construction techniques and the ability to perform them accurately are essential factors in training for employment in any aspect of commercial sewing.

- BASIC SEAMS: A seam is formed by stitching together two pieces of fabric. The width of the seam (seam allowance) in clothing varies depending upon the type of fabric used and the type of garment being produced. Inexpensive, poor quality garments usually have narrow seams, whereas the seams are wider in better quality merchandise. Most seams range from ⅜ to ⅝ inches wide, with the more generous seams ¾ or 1 inch. The wider seams wear better and also permit alterations. When sewing, it is most important to take the exact seam allowance designated so that the finished garment will be accurately sized. The type of seam also varies according to the kind of fabric and the type of garment. Following are the basic seams used in clothing construction and the method for making each. Practice sewing each type of seam until you can do it quickly, neatly, and accurately. Always stitch with the grain of the fabric to assure having both ends of the seams meet evenly. Repeat each seam five times, keeping the work connected according to the method described on page 251.

Plain seam is the simplest and most commonly used seam in garment construction. Two pieces of fabric are stitched together on the seam line with right sides together. The edges of the fabric are left unfinished, and the seam may be pressed open or to one side.

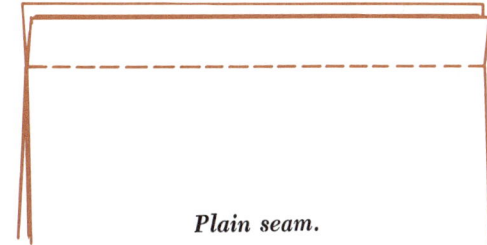

Plain seam.

METHOD: Place fabric under presser foot, with the right sides together.
  —Make a stay (see page 250).
  —Stitch entire length of seam, on the seam line.
  —Keep stitching straight and the same distance from the edge of the fabric.
  —Stay end of seam.

If the fabric ravels, or for a neater appearance, the raw edges of the

Basic Skills for Clothing Construction

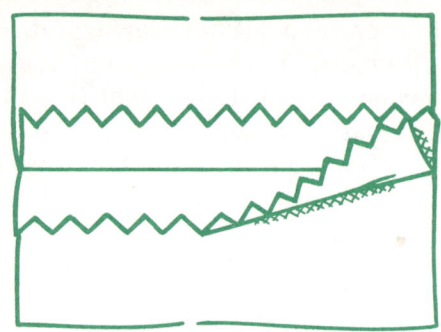

Pinked seam.

seam may be finished in one of the following ways:

- **Pinked:** Stitch a plain seam.
  - —Raw edges may be pinked with a pinking machine—close to the edge—either after the seam is sewn or while the seam is being stitched.
  - —Pinking shears may also be used to pink the edge by hand.
  - —Do not cut off any more of the seam than is necessary to finish the edge.
- **Hemmed:** This seam finish prevents raveling and gives a neat appearance to the inside of a garment. It is especially suitable for light to medium weight fabrics.

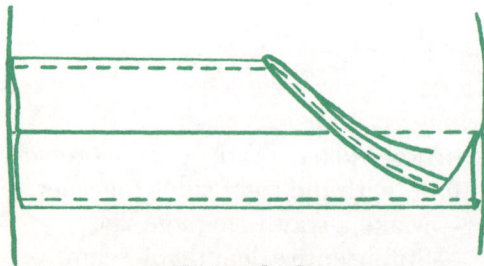

Hemmed edge.

- —Turn raw edge of fabric under ⅛ inch and stitch close to the fold. Be careful not to stretch the fabric.
- —Stitch a plain seam.

- **Bound:** This seam gives a finished appearance to unlined coats and jackets. It is especially suitable for heavy fabrics.

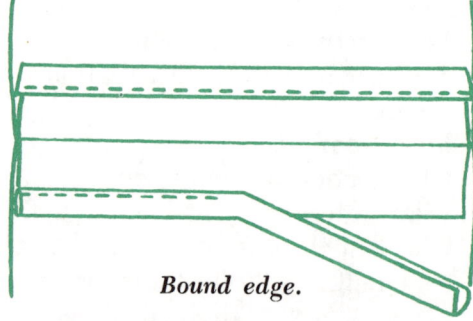

Bound edge.

- —Using the binder attachment, encase the edge of the fabric in either bias or straight tape.
- —Stitch a plain seam.

Top-stitched seam is a variation of the plain seam used for decorative purposes and to give a smooth, flat finish.

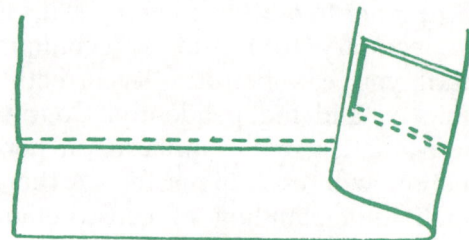

Top stitched seam.

Method: Stitch a plain seam.
- —Turn seam toward one side.
- —On the right side, stitch close to the seam.
- —Two rows of stitching, using double needle, may also be used.
- —Hold the fabric smooth and flat while stitching; avoid puckers.

The *welt seam* is another variation of the plain seam, similar to the top-stitched seam. It is decorative and is often used on heavy fabrics for added strength.

Construction Techniques

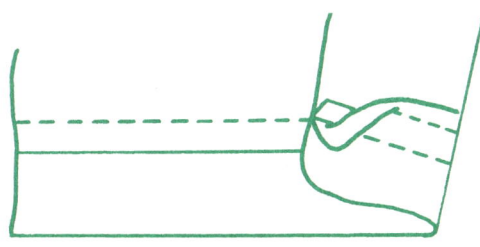

Welt seam.

METHOD: Place fabric under the presser foot with the right sides together and the lower piece extending ¼ inch beyond the top piece.
—Stitch on seam line, staying both ends.
—Open fabric flat and turn seam toward the side, having wider part on top.
—On the right side, top-stitch parallel to the seam line. The top stitching should be ⅜ to ½ inch from the seam line so that the raw edge of the narrow seam will be covered.

The *lapped seam* resembles the top-stitched seam also, but is made with one stitching process instead of two.

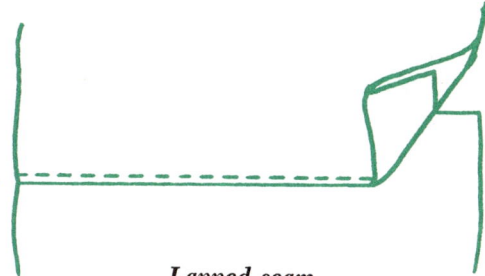

Lapped seam.

METHOD: Turn under the seam allowance on one piece of fabric.
—Lap on top of another piece of fabric, right sides up, raw edges even underneath.
—On the right side, stitch close to the folded edge.

The *tucked seam* is made exactly the same as the lapped seam except the top stitching is ¼ inch from the fold instead of at the fold. The finished seam resembles a tuck.

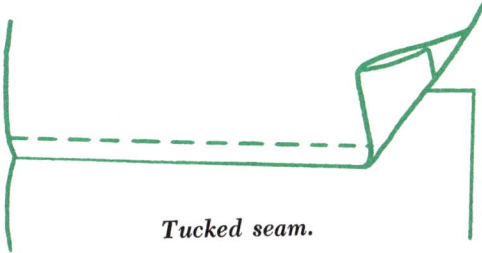

Tucked seam.

Flat-felled seams are used on garments that receive hard wear. The seam is stitched down flat to the fabric and there are no raw edges visible on either side. There are special machines that stitch the flat-felled seam in one operation or the following method may be used.

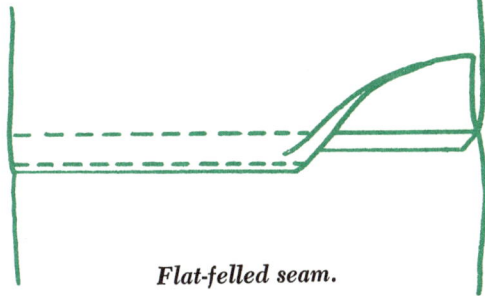

Flat-felled seam.

METHOD: Place fabric under the presser foot with the wrong sides together and the lower piece extending ¼ inch beyond the top piece.
—Stitch on the seam line, staying both ends.
—Open fabric flat and turn seam toward the side, having wider part on top.
—Turn under the edge of the wider seam and stitch flat to the fabric. Stitch on the folded edge.

Basic Skills for Clothing Construction

—Two rows of stitching are visible on the right side of the fabric and only one row on the wrong side. If the opposite effect is desired (only one row of stitching visible on the right side), start the seam with the two right sides of the fabric together.

A *French seam* is used on sheer fabrics to hide the raw edges.

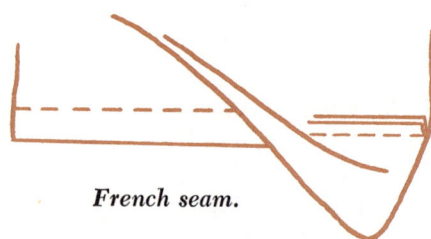
French seam.

METHOD: Place fabric under presser foot with the wrong sides together.
—Stitch seam ⅛ inch from edge or stitch ⅜ inch from edge, trimming to ⅛ inch. The distance from the edge depends upon the designated seam allowance. Stay both ends.
—Turn seam to the inside and stitch ¼ inch from fold. The raw edges will be enclosed in the seam.

A *simulated French seam* looks very much like the French seam when finished and serves the same purpose. It is quicker to make since there is only one stitching instead of two, but it is not as strong as the regulation French seam. Therefore, it should be used only on firm fabrics.

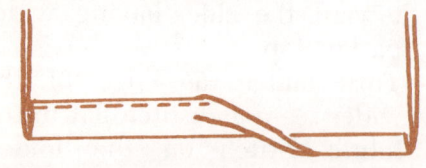
Simulated French seam.

METHOD: Place fabric under the presser foot with the right sides together and the lower piece extending ¼ inch beyond the top piece.
—Turn lower piece of fabric under ¼ inch over the upper piece.
—Turn both pieces over again ¼ inch.
—Stitch the seam, stitching close to the first fold. Stay both ends.

A *corded seam* has covered cording inserted into the seam. It is actually a plain seam with the cording added for decoration.

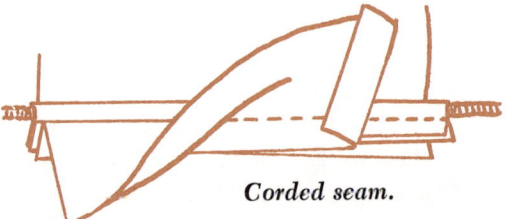
Corded seam.

The cord may be pre-covered or may be covered with bias of matching fabric. To cover cord, cut bias one inch wider than the cord (measure around the cord). Wrap the bias around the cord and stitch close to the cord, using a cording foot on the machine.

METHOD: Place the cording between two layers of fabric right sides together and raw edges even.
—Make a plain seam, using the cording foot so that the stitching will be close to the cord.

A *piped seam* is made the same as the corded seam, using bias fold fabric instead of cording. Lace edgings, ruffling, or other trimmings can be inserted in a seam in the same manner.

Reverse the regulation French seam so that the second stitching is done on the right side, forming a welt that stands up on the outside of the fabric.

Construction Techniques

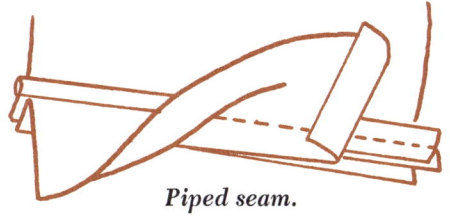
Piped seam.

This seam can be used for slip covers and upholstery instead of the corded seam.

Create Shape and Control Fullness

To create clothing from a flat piece of fabric requires shaping to fit the contours of the human body. There are several ways of doing this—through darts, tucks, pleats, and gathers—each serving a particular purpose. The method used depends upon the kind of fabric, the style of the garment, and the desired effect.

• DARTS: are a stitched fold in the fabric, tapered to a point at one end. They are used to give shape to fabric so that a garment will fit curved areas of the body. Darts may also be used for decorative reasons, in which case they may even be stitched on the outside of the garment.

The dart itself may be either straight or shaped. Straight darts are most commonly used—at shoulder, neckline, bustline, waistline and in sleeves. Shaped darts provide contour under the bustline and over the hipline. Double-pointed darts are used in one-piece garments to taper in toward the waistline and out again over the hipline.

Regardless of the type of dart, the method for stitching is the same. Stitch evenly to a firm, smooth point. Uneven, crooked stitching results in a poor line that is very obvious on the right side of the garment, poor shaping and contour, and perhaps puckers and bulges. Practice making darts until you can stitch a perfect dart that lies smooth and flat.

METHOD: Fold fabric, right sides together, with the markings at the edge of fabric together and the mark at the point of the dart on the fold.

—Stitch the dart, from the markings at edge of fabric to the point.

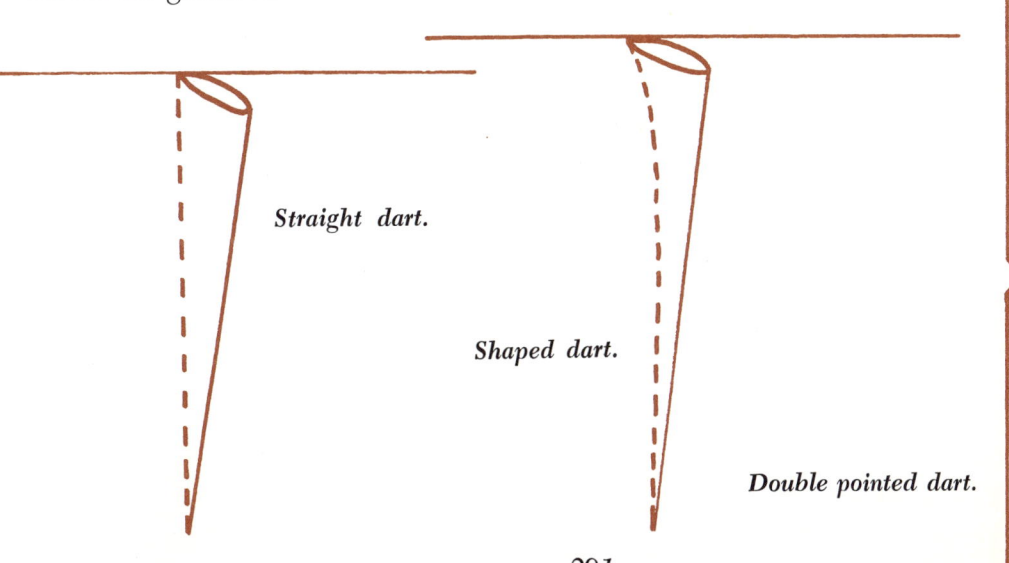
Straight dart.

Shaped dart.

Double pointed dart.

291

Basic Skills for Clothing Construction

——Taper to nothing at the point and stitch the last few stitches along the fold to assure a smooth and flat point.
——To secure the threads, continue stitching a few extra stitches off the fabric.

- TUCKS are also stitched folds in fabric but, unlike darts, the stitching is parallel to the fold for the entire length. They may vary in size from as narrow as $1/16$ inch (pin tuck) to an inch or more, depending upon the effect desired. They serve both a decorative and useful purpose. Sewn on the right side, rows of tucks become part of the design of the garment. Tucks can hold fullness in place if stitched their entire length or release fullness if stitched only part way.

A tucking attachment may be used to space rows of tucks evenly and to assure stitching them all the same width. Tucks may also be sewn easily without an attachment.

METHOD: Fold fabric according to markings. Be sure the fold is straight.
——Stitch an even distance from the fold, according to markings or specifications.

A *dart tuck* is just what the word implies—a combination between a dart and a tuck.

Dart tuck.

Unlike the tuck, the stitching is not parallel to the fold, but tapered to a point like the dart. The point, however, is close to the edge of the fabric. You might describe a dart tuck as an upside down dart. It has two purposes—provide shape and release fullness—and is often used at the waistline.

- PLEATS: are also folds in fabric that create fullness in a garment. They may be stitched down, pressed flat, or unpressed. They may occur singly, like the vent pleat that gives walking room at the lower edge of a skirt; in groups, like the unpressed pleats in-

Stitched tuck.

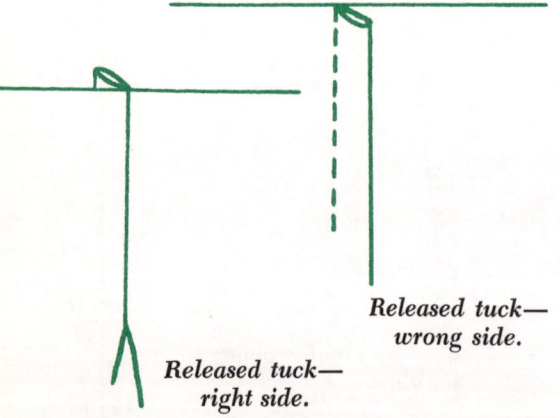

Released tuck— right side.

Released tuck— wrong side.

Construction Techniques

stead of darts for fullness at the waistline of a straight skirt; or the entire garment may be pleated as in an all-around pleated skirt.

Stitched-down pleats require careful handling when stitching so that the fabric does not move out of position causing uneven pleats or bulges. Practice stitching each type of pleat until you can do it expertly.

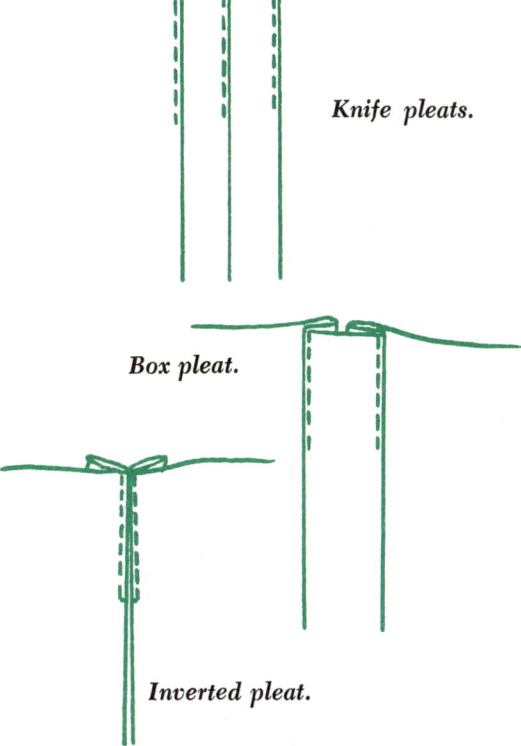

Knife pleats.

Box pleat.

Inverted pleat.

METHOD: Fold the fabric according to the markings.

Knife pleats—all turn in one direction.

Box pleats—folded edges turn in opposite directions, away from each other.

Inverted pleats—folded edges turn toward each other, just the reverse of the box pleat.

—Stitch close to the fold, holding fabric firmly to avoid shifting.
—Stitch as far as the markings indicate, stitching from the top down.
—Keep the folds straight and the pleats even and flat.

• GATHERING: creates fullness by using rows of stitching to pull fabric together. It is used primarily on light or medium weight fabrics. Heavy fabrics are too bulky to gather successfully.

Gathering may be done with an attachment or by the following method.

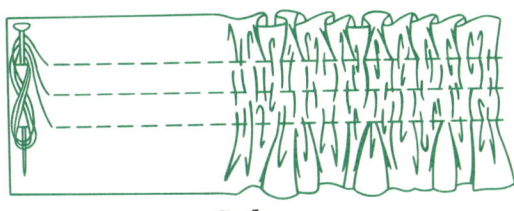

Gathers.

METHOD: Set stitch regulator for a long stitch—6 to 8 stitches per inch.
—Place at least two rows of stitching between the markings where gathers are indicated. If the bottom row is on the seam allowance, the gathering stitches will not be visible on the outside of the finished garment. A third row may be used if the fabric is bulky. Use the toe of the presser foot to guide the stitching.
—Do not stay ends of stitching. Pull threads to under side of fabric.
—Pull up the bobbin threads—carefully so as not to break threads—until gathers are the desired length and fullness is distributed evenly.

293

Basic Skills for Clothing Construction

• SHIRRING: is usually used on sheer or lightweight fabric. It is a form of gathering in which several rows of machine stitching are used not only to create fullness but for decorative reasons as well. As many rows of stitching can be used as desired. They are visible on the outside of the garment, forming a decorative band.

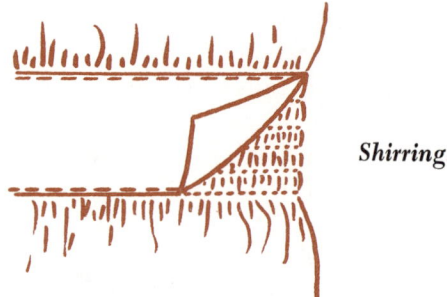

Shirring.

METHOD: Set stitch regulator for a long stitch.
— Stitch as many rows as desired where the markings indicate (may be done with a multiple needle machine).
— Pull threads to the under side of the fabric and secure the threads at one end.
— Pull up the bobbin threads, two at a time, to the desired length and fullness.
— To "stay" the shirring, stitch a piece of fabric—the same size and shape as the shirring band—to the under side. Stitch along the top and bottom rows of shirring stitches.

• EASING is a process by which a longer piece of fabric is stitched to a shorter section without any puckering. The top of the sleeve, for instance, is larger than the armhole to allow room for the arm to move. The back shoulder seam is larger than the front shoulder seam of a dress to allow room for the curve of the back. In both of these cases the larger section must be eased to fit the smaller section and the two sewn without any puckering.

Ease stitching (a large machine stitch) can be used on the seam line of the larger section to pull up the fullness, but it is possible to learn to "ease-in" without the use of any ease stitching. Skillful handling of the fabric is required and practice can help you develop this time-saving skill.

METHOD: Place fabric under the machine with the larger section on top, the shorter section next to the feed dog.
— Stitch a regular seam to the first marking.
— Between markings, where fabric is to be eased, hold lower section firmly but do not stretch it. Ease top section forward without letting puckers form.
— Stitch rest of seam regularly.

Facings and Interfacings

Facings are sewn to the right side of the garment and turned to the wrong side, thus hiding the raw edges. Interfacings may also be used for extra body or reinforcement. They are usually cut the same shape as the facing and inserted between the facing and the outer garment. They may be attached to the wrong side of the garment piece separately or they may be stitched in the seam when attaching the facing.

• FITTED FACING: The method for completing a fitted facing and attaching it to a garment is basically the same wherever a fitted facing is used. First the facing unit itself is completed.

Construction Techniques

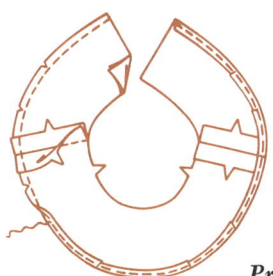

Prepare the facing.

METHOD:
— Join facing pieces together. As in the case of a neck facing, join the front facing to the back facing at the shoulder seams.
— Trim seam and press it open.
— Finish the outer, unnotched edge by turning it under and edge stitching.

Next, attach the facing unit to the garment.

Attach the facing to the garment.

METHOD:
— With right sides together, stitch the facing to the edge to be finished, matching seams and other matching points.
— Trim the seam and clip curves and corners.

Finish the facing.

— Understitch the seam by turning the seam toward the facing and stitching on the facing close to the seam, catching seam and facing only in the stitching.
— Press the facing to the inside.
— Tack to the seams either on a tacking machine or by hand.

• SELF-FACINGS: are cut in one with the garment piece and then folded to the inside to finish an outer edge. Two examples are the hem-facing at the top of a patch pocket and the facing extension of a blouse that buttons down the front or back.

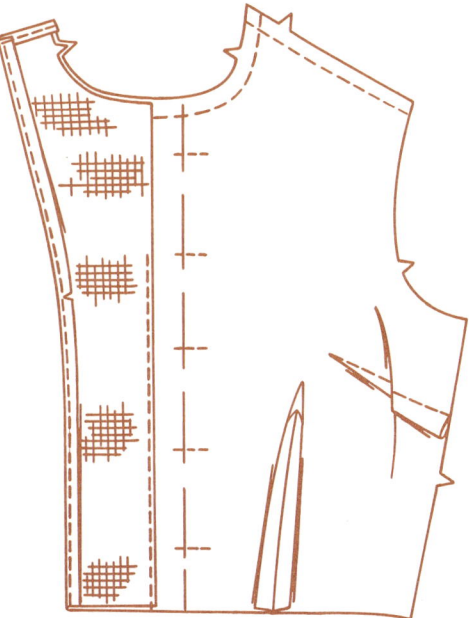

Front facing extension.

METHOD:
— Finish the outer edge of the facing extension by turning under ¼ inch and edge stitching.
— Turn the extension to the outside of the garment along the fold line and stitch raw edges together.

Basic Skills for Clothing Construction

—Trim the seam, clip corners and curves.

—Turn facing to the inside and press. Tack to the seams. In the case of a hem facing, the edge may be left loose, top stitched, or blind stitched in place.

- BIAS FACINGS: are often used around curves, such as neck or armhole edges. Because the bias will stretch, it can be eased around the edge and will conform to the curve. For convenience, rolls of pre-cut bias are available, or the bias strips may be cut from matching fabric. To cut continuous bias strips quickly and easily, use the following method:

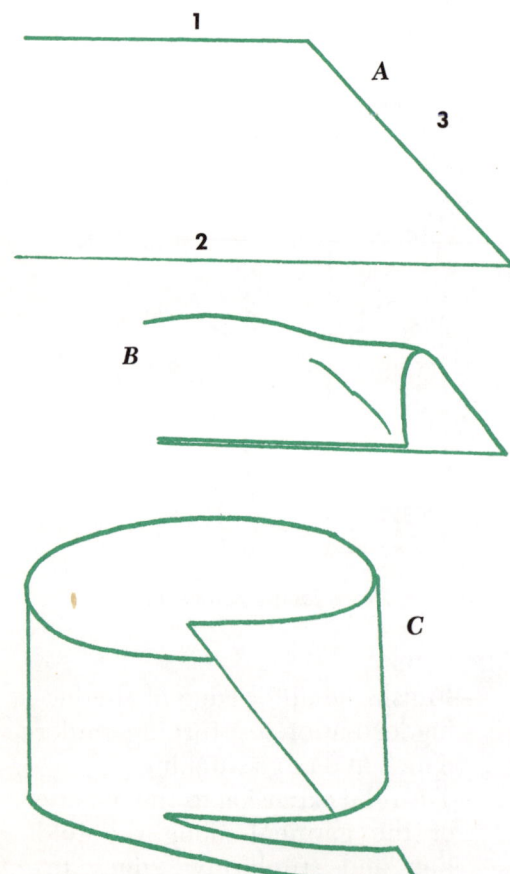

Cutting a continuous bias strip.

METHOD:
—Fold fabric so that the crosswise thread is parallel to the lengthwise thread. (See page 260.) Cut along the fold. The cut edge (3) is the bias.

—With right sides together, stitch a seam along the straight grain edges (1 and 2). The desired width of the bias strip should extend at the end of the seam. See diagram B. Press the seam open.

—Cut the bias strip, using a gauge attached to the scissors as a guide. If desired, mark the width of the strips on the wrong side of the fabric before stitching the ends together. Then cut on the lines.

Bias facings are attached to the garment basically the same as any other facing.

METHOD:
—With right sides together, stitch the bias strip to the edge to be finished. Ease the bias slightly around the curve so that it lies flat.

—Trim the seam and clip curves.

—Press the seam toward the facing.

—Turn the facing to the inside. Turn under the raw edge of the facing and hem in place.

The raw edge of a bias facing is not finished before attaching it to a garment as is the case with a regular facing. Stitching around the edge would stop the "stretch" that is necessary to ease the bias around the curve. If the fabric is not too heavy, a double bias strip may be used to give a neat, even width facing with the least amount of handling.

METHOD:
- Cut bias strips twice the specified width.
- Fold the strips in half lengthwise.
- With right sides together, stitch both raw edges of the bias to the edge to be finished.
- Trim the seam, clip curves, and press the seam toward the facing.
- Turn the facing to the inside. The bottom edge of the facing (the fold) is ready to hem in place.

• DECORATIVE FACINGS are visible on the right side of a garment. They form part of the design and also serve the useful purpose of finishing a raw edge. The method for applying them is the same as the basic facing method with these variations. They are attached to the wrong side of the garment and turned to the outside—just the opposite of a regular facing. Understitching is done on the wrong side which, in this case, is the garment side rather than the facing side. The lower edge of the facing is not finished separately, but after it is attached, it is turned under and stitched to the garment.

Bindings

Bindings also serve two purposes; they finish a raw edge and are decorative. Unlike facings, however, that are visible on only one side of a garment, a binding has the same amount of fabric visible on both sides. Pre-cut, already folded bias binding is available, or the binding may be cut from matching fabric. Cut a bias strip twice as wide as the finished binding plus seam allowance on each edge. Press under the seam allowances, being careful not to stretch the fabric.

Use the binder attachment on the machine to apply the binding quickly, easily, and accurately. Guide the binding into the center of the attachment and stitch; the binding is sewn on in one operation. Practice applying a binding to curved edges—they require more skill than a straight edge—until you are adept at handling the fabric and maintaining a smooth curve.

It is also possible, and sometimes necessary, to apply a binding without an attachment.

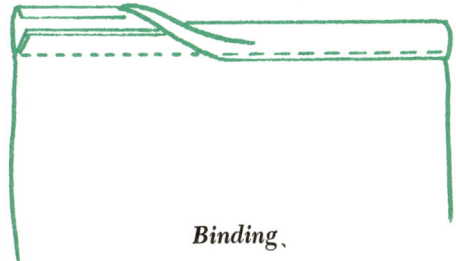

Binding.

METHOD:
- Sew one edge of the binding to the raw edge of the garment.
- Turn under the remaining raw edge of the binding.
- Fold the binding over the raw edges, with the folded edge on the stitching line.
- Stitch in place by hand or machine, as desired.

The binding may be finished on either the right or wrong side. The final result will be neater, however, if machine stitching is done on the right side and hand stitching on the wrong side. The way the binding is to be finished determines how to start. If the final step is to be stitched by machine, start to attach the binding on

Basic Skills for Clothing Construction

the wrong side; if finished by hand, start on the right side.

Collars

There are many different styles of collars but most of them are made basically the same way. They consist of two layers of fabric—an upper collar and an undercollar or facing—and are very often interfaced as well for extra body. The interfacing may be sewn to the undercollar separately or may be stitched in the seam when sewing the collar.

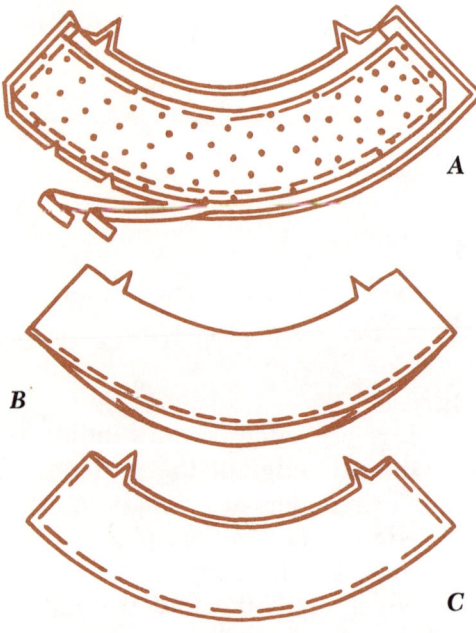

Make a collar.

METHOD:
—Assemble the collar pieces with the two right sides of the collar sections together and the interfacing underneath these two, next to the feed dog. Stitch all three pieces together, leaving the neck edge open.
—Trim the seam and clip corners or curves, depending upon the style of the collar.
—Turn collar right side out, using a collar turner for pointed collars to insure square corners. Smooth the seam with the fingers as you turn it so that the edges will be flat.
—Understitching insures a sharp turned edge. Stitch close to the seam, catching the undercollar and seam only.
—For a collar with corners, stitch the collar sections together first at the bottom edge only—not the ends. Understitch the seam, then stitch the ends; turn the collar.
—Press the collar, keeping the seam on the folded edge.
—Collar may be top stitched, if desired.

The collar may be attached to the garment in a number of ways: with a facing, as is done with Peter Pan or convertible collars; directly onto the neck edge, as a stand-up collar; or onto a neck band and then onto the neck edge, as a tailored shirt collar. Whichever method is used, if the collar is held slightly tight while stitching, it will fit smoothly around the neckline.

• WITH A FACING: There are three different methods for joining the collar with a facing: with a fitted back and front facing, with a front facing extension only (no back facing), and with a bias facing.

METHOD:
—Attach the collar to the neck edge, matching centers and other matching points. NOTE: The undercollar should be against the right side of the garment.

Construction Techniques

— Prepare the facing according to the directions on page 295.
— With right sides together, place the facing on top of the collar, stitch to the neck edge, keeping all raw edges even.
— Complete the facing according to the directions on page 295.

NOTE: With practice, you should be able to stitch both the collar and the facing to the neck edge in one operation. One step rather than two saves time, but it takes practice and skillful handling of fabric to manipulate all three sections at once.

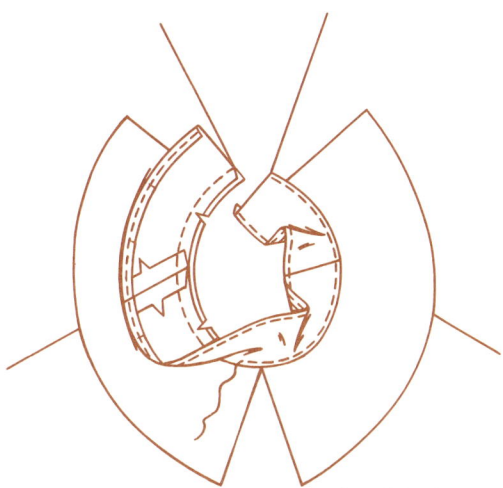

Attaching a collar with a fitted facing.

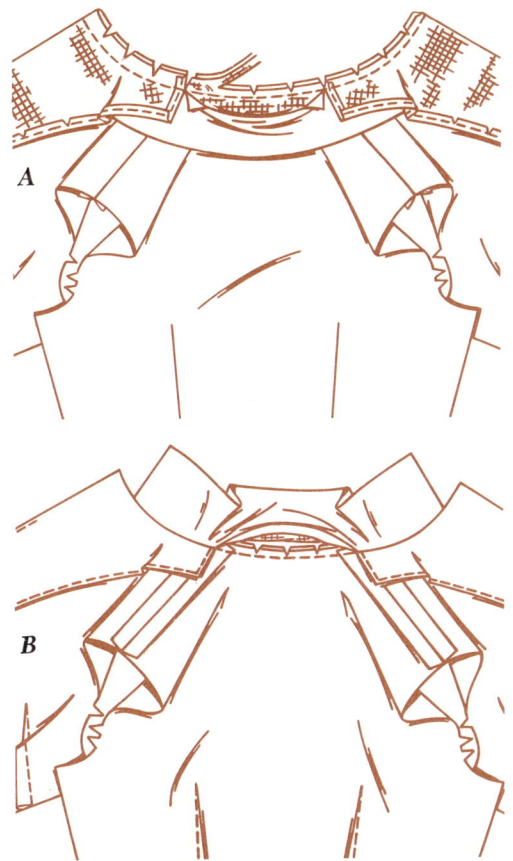

Attaching a collar with a front facing extension.

METHOD:
— Attach both the undercollar and collar to the front edge, but only the undercollar to the back neck edge.
— Clip the collar and undercollar to the seam line at the shoulder line.
— Turn the front facing extension to the outside on top of the collar. The end of the facing should be at the shoulder line.
— Stitch the entire neck seam, keeping all raw edges even. Be careful not to catch the upper collar in the seam across the back.
— Trim the seam, clip curves.
— Turn the facing to the inside. Press the back neck seam upward the collar.
— Turn under the seam allowance of the upper collar across the back neck edge and stitch it to the neck seam.

299

Basic Skills for Clothing Construction

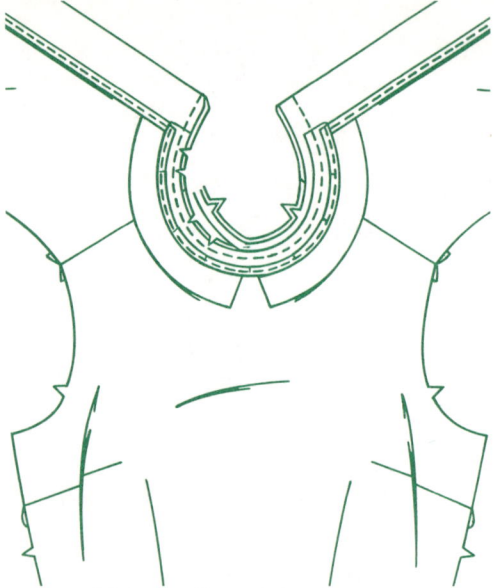

Attaching a collar with a bias facing.

METHOD:
—Attach the entire collar to the neck edge just as in the first method.
—Turn the front facing extension to the outside on top of the collar.
—With right sides together, place a bias strip on top of the collar, extending the bias about ½ inch over the front facings.
—Stitch the neck seam, keeping all raw edges even.
—Complete the facing according to directions on page 296.

• DIRECTLY ONTO THE NECK EDGE: This method is very similar to binding an edge. One edge of the collar is attached to the neck edge. Trim the seam, clip the curve, and press the seam toward the collar. Fold under the seam allowance on the other raw edge of the collar and stitch it to the neck seam.

• ONTO A NECK BAND: In this method, the collar is first attached to a band and then the band is attached to the shirt.

Attaching a collar with a neck band.

METHOD:
—Turn under the seam allowance on the lower curved edge of the neck band.
—With right sides together, place the collar between the neck band and the band facing.
—Stitch around the top curved edge of the band, catching the collar in the seam. Keep all raw edges even.
—Trim seam and clip curves. Press the neck band down.
—Stitch the band facing to the wrong side of the neck edge.
—Trim the seam and clip curves. Press the seam up toward the band.
—Top stitch the turned edge of the band over the seam. Continue the stitching around the entire band, if desired.

Sleeves

In industrial sewing, for greater speed and ease of handling, the sleeve is often attached to the armhole before the underarm seams are closed. After the sleeve is sewn in, the entire side seam—from bottom of sleeve to hem of garment—is then stitched. In custom dressmaking, either method may be used depending upon the style of the garment and the desired appearance. The open seam method is considered the "tailored shirt" method and often uses a flat-felled seam. In the "dress" method the underarm seams are stitched first and a plain seam is used around the armhole. The sleeve that is inserted by the "dress method" is not as bulky under the arm and the garment has a smoother fit.

Join the underarm seam of the sleeve.

When joining the underarm seams of sleeves, it is very easy to make two sleeves for the same armhole if there is no right or wrong side to the fabric. To avoid this, check to see that the notches are on opposite sides, as shown in the drawing.

The top of the sleeve is larger than the armholes to allow extra room for the curve of the arm and for movement. Because of this extra fullness, the sleeve must be eased into the armhole without any puckers. With practice, you should learn to ease the sleeve in to fit the armhole without the use of any ease stitching (see page 294).

METHOD:
—If ease stitching is used, place a row of machine stitching on the seamline around the top of the sleeve. From the underarm edge to the notch use a regular stitch.

Construction Techniques

Then from notch to notch use a long stitch. Pull up the bobbin thread of the ease stitching until the sleeve fits the armhole, distributing the fullness evenly.

—With right sides together and the sleeve uppermost on the machine, stitch the sleeve to the armhole. Start stitching at the underarm seam. Stitch a regular seam to the first marking. Between markings, hold the garment section firmly but do not stretch it. Ease the sleeve section forward without letting puckers form. If ease stitching is used, hold the sleeve on both sides of the presser foot to avoid sewing in any puckers.

—Finish the seam with a regular stitch. Keep the raw edges even.

—If a flat-felled seam is to be used, follow the seam method on page 289.

—Press the seam. If a plain seam, press the sleeve and armhole edges together, from the sleeve side.

Plackets

The placket is an opening in a garment that makes it easier to get it on and off. The slide fastener is a convenient closing for such an opening. It provides a neat, secure finish with no gaps. Although most garments use the slide fastener for closing, other types of placket finishes are also used. A seam may be left open and the raw edges either hemmed or bound. The garment section may be slashed and the raw edge encased in a binding. These plackets may be left open or closed with snaps, hooks and eyes, or

Basic Skills for Clothing Construction

buttons and buttonholes. Such finishes are used in children's clothing, pajamas, pleated skirts, etc.

- HEMMED:

Stitch a narrow hem on the back edge of the opening.

Stitch the seam, stitching across the bottom of the opening also.

Narrowly hem the front edge of the opening.

Lap the front edge over the back edge.

- BOUND:

Bind the back edge of the opening.

Sew a strip of binding to the wrong side of the front edge.

Join the front to the back, stitching across the bottom of the opening also.

Complete the binding on the front edge of the opening.

Lap the front edge over the back edge.

- CONTINUOUS:

Reinforce the point of the slash opening with small stitches.

Spread the slash open so that it is in a straight line.

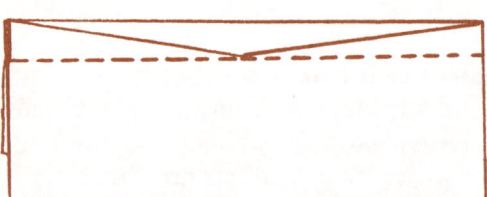

First step in making a continuous lap.

Attach a binding strip to the wrong side of the slash opening. The raw edges are even at each end, but the edges of the opening taper to a point at the end of the slash. The stitching is in a straight line, even with the raw edge of the binding strip, just catching the garment fabric at the point of the slash.

Turn under the remaining raw edge of the binding strip.

Fold the binding over the raw edge and stitch the folded edge to the seam line.

Turn the front edge of the placket to the inside and lap it over the back edge.

Slide fasteners

There is a special zipper machine used for inserting zippers commercially. This job can also be done successfully with a zipper foot on a standard lock-stitch machine. For easier handling, insert the zipper while the garment is still flat; for example, if the zipper goes in the center back seam, insert it before joining the side seams.

With practice, you should be able to insert the zipper easily and accurately without any pinning or basting. To help you learn, however, it may be easier if the opening is basted closed while you work. There are two methods of zipper application—with an overlap and centered.

- LAPPED APPLICATION

Turn under the back edge of the opening ⅛ inch from the seamline.

Stitch this turned edge to the zipper tape, having the zipper face up and the bottom of the zipper even with the lower end of the opening. Stitch from the bottom of the opening to the top. Keep the folded edge close to the teeth of the zipper and the stitching close to the fold.

If the seam is basted closed, turn the zipper face down over the seam. Stitch across the bottom of the zipper

Construction Techniques

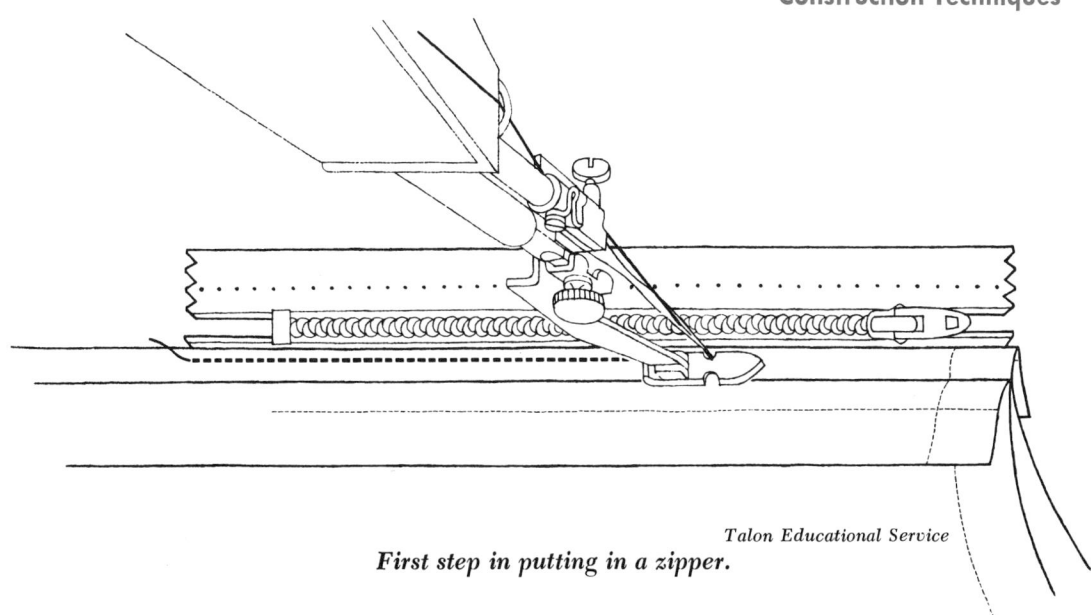

First step in putting in a zipper.

as far as the middle of the zipper tape, turn a square corner, and continue stitching to the top, keeping the stitches in the center of the tape. Remove the basting that holds the opening closed.

If the seam is open, turn under the front edge of the opening on the seam line. Lap the front edge over the zipper, with the folded edge just covering the back stitching.

With the right side up, stitch the front of the opening to the zipper tape. Stitch across the bottom of the opening, turn a square corner, and continue stitching to the top. Keep the folded edge even with the back stitching line. The stitching should

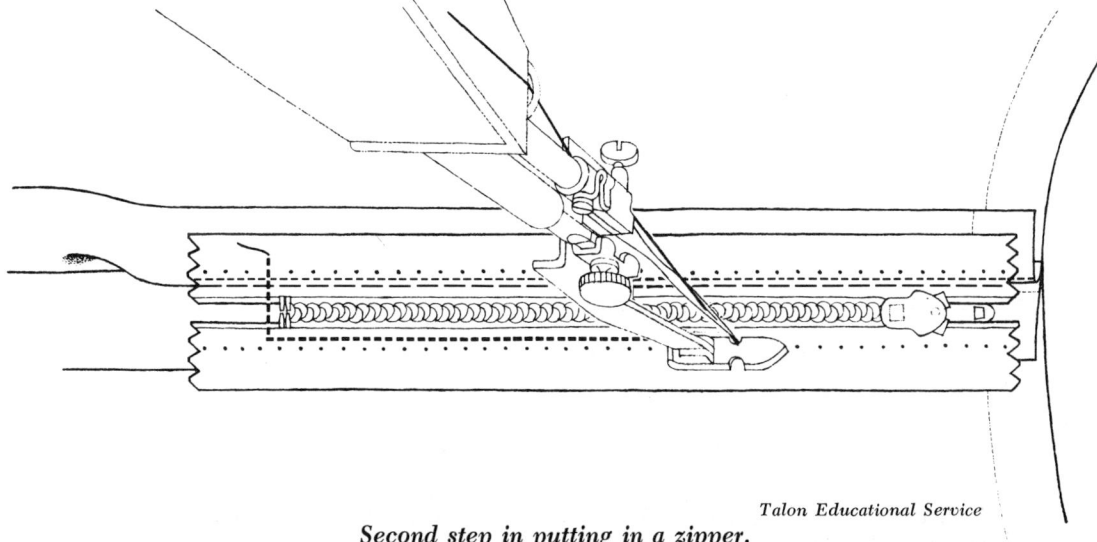

Second step in putting in a zipper.

Basic Skills for Clothing Construction

be approximately ½ inch from the folded edge.

- CENTERED APPLICATION—
  CLOSED SEAM:

Open the zipper and place on the seam face down against the wrong side, with the zipper teeth against the seam line.

Stitch through the center of the zipper tape, from top to bottom of the opening. Keep the zipper teeth against the seam line. Stop with the needle down in the fabric.

Close the zipper. Turn a square corner and stitch across the bottom of the opening.

Turn a square corner and continue stitching to the top, keeping the stitches in the center of the tape.

Remove the basting that holds the opening closed.

- CENTERED APPLICATION—
  OPEN SEAM:

Fold under both seam allowances of the opening.

Open the zipper and place one side under the folded edge with the fold just covering the teeth.

Stitch down, keeping the stitching an even distance from the fold (approximately ¼ inch) and the fold in line with the edge of the zipper teeth. Stop with the needle down in the fabric.

Close the zipper. Turn a square corner and stitch across the bottom of the opening.

Turn a square corner and continue stitching to the top. The folded edges of the opening should meet at the center and the stitching should be an even distance from the center.

Hems

There are many different types of hem finishes—some visible on the right side, some not; most of them done by machine, some not. The type used depends largely upon the fabric and the style of the garment. A hem may be turned by hand and stitched on the standard machine with the regular presser foot or a hemming foot of a hemming attachment may be used. Hemming machines that fold and stitch hems are also available. Regardless of type, the hem should be even in width and lie flat and smooth.

Hem finish—stitched and pinked.

- STITCHED AND PINKED: This type of finish may be used if the hem is not visible when the garment is worn—for example, the bottom of a skirt lining. Place two rows of stitching around the bottom edge. Then pink the edge close to the bottom row of stitching.

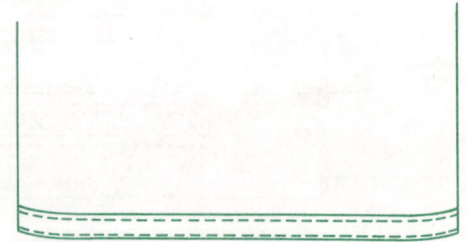

Hem finish— double stitched narrow hem.

- EDGE STITCHED: This hem may be done easily with a hemming attach-

Construction Techniques

ment that folds the hem to any desired width as it feeds the fabric into the machine for stitching. It may also be folded by hand and stitched on a standard machine. The width of the hem may vary from very narrow (¼ inch) up to an inch or more. Turn the edge of the fabric under ¼ inch. Turn the fabric under again to the desired width and stitch in place. If the hem is narrow, stitch close to both edges. The double stitching will give a flatter edge.

Practice making a narrow hem, turning the fabric with the fingers as you sew, until you can stitch a long length at high speed without stopping the machine. To get started, fold the hem under about an inch. Position the fabric in the machine. Hold the first fold between the thumb and middle finger and turn the hem into position with the index finger. Feed the fabric into the machine with the fingers in this position, turning the hem as you stitch.

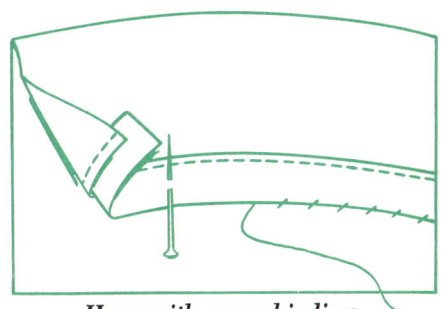

Hem with seam binding.

- WITH SEAM BINDING: A double turned hem finish is not suitable for all fabrics. It is too bulky for heavier fabrics and a ridge would show on the right side at the hemline. For such fabrics, seam binding gives a neat, smooth finish. Lap the seam binding over the raw edge, half on and half off the fabric, and stitch along the edge of the binding. Blind stitch the hem into position by machine or by hand.

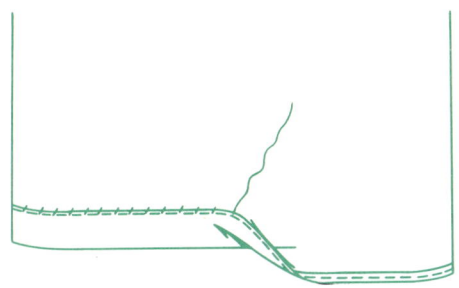

Hem finish—blind stitched.

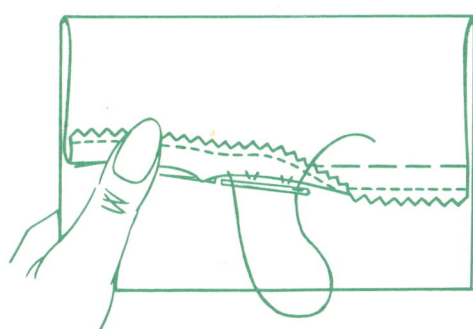

Hand hemming—tailor's hem finish.

- BLIND STITCHED: This type of hem is invisible on the right side of the garment. The first fold of the hem may be edge stitched or not, as desired. The blind stitching may be done on a special machine, with a blind stitch attachment on a standard machine, or by hand.

- TAILOR'S HEM: This type of hem finish can be used on fabrics that do not ravel or on problem fabrics in which a hem is likely to show. It is a hand finish, used in custom dressmaking and tailoring. Pink the edge of the hem and baste it in place about an inch from the edge. Turn the edge back ¼ inch and catch the hem loosely to the garment as shown in the above drawing. Catch just a

Basic Skills for Clothing Construction

thread of the skirt to keep the stitches from showing on the right side. Keep the stitches rather loose. If they are pulled too tight, there will be a ridge on the right side.

In a skirt hem there may be excess fullness that has to be worked in—the more flare to the skirt, the more fullness in the hem. To work in the fullness, stitch around the hem about ¼ inch from the raw edge with a long machine stitch. Pull up the bobbin thread to ease in the fullness until the hem lies flat against the skirt. Then steam the hem to shrink out, or flatten, the fullness, and proceed to finish the hem.

As mentioned before, it is necessary to repeat a technique in order to develop skill. It is also necessary to understand basic techniques thoroughly before advancing to the more difficult ones. If necessary, repeat a project until you understand tech-

To Gain Experience

Organize the classroom as a "shop."

Prepare a job sheet for each project, listing all the construction steps in the order in which they are to be done.

Form an assembly line and assemble the project under commercial conditions, as nearly as possible.

Compare the finished products with commercially-made ones that are similar.

---

niques clearly and can perform them quickly and well. Always keep in mind that speed is important, but accuracy is equally so. The quality of workmanship in the finished product is directly related to the ability of the person who makes it.

Chapter 8

Fitting and Alteration, a Highly Specialized Business

CORRECT FIT is one of the first requirements for being attractively dressed. Beautiful fabric, attractive design, quality construction, and interesting detail work are all important; but the illusion is spoiled if the garment does not fit the wearer to perfection. Ready-made clothing is available in a wide range of sizes for various figure types, but it is cut to fit the ideally proportioned figure in each size range. Most figures do not conform to the ideal proportions. No consideration is given to a high hip, narrow or sloping shoulders, a thick midriff, or any of the other irregularities that most of us have. A person who can purchase a garment that fits perfectly is indeed fortunate. Ready-to-wear clothing cannot be expected to fit as well as a garment that has been custom made. Nearly everyone requires some alteration to the clothes they buy, even though it may be only as minor as straightening the hemline of a skirt or stitching the length of trousers to fit.

Women who do not sew have to pay someone to do any altering that they want done. Even many women who know how to sew turn to the expert for a professional job rather than attempt any but the very simplest alterations themselves. Most traditional stores that deal with ready-to-wear clothing, with the exception perhaps of self-service and large discount houses, offer alteration service for the convenience of their customers. In the alteration department of large department stores, fitters suggest the alterations that are needed, determine whether or not the alteration can be made, then fit and pin the garment for the customers. Seamstresses in the workroom do the actual sewing. In smaller independent or specialty shops, one person may be responsible for both the fitting and the sewing. Many women work independently doing dressmaking or alterations in their own homes. Such a business offers the woman with a family an opportunity to supplement her income in her free time without leaving the home. There is a big demand for this service, so women who do alterations well and are good at customer relations can have as much work as they want or have time for.

Fitting and Alteration

Skill and Understanding Required

Fitting and altering ready-made clothing involves specialized techniques and requires even more skill of a certain kind than making clothes.

- To become expert in this type of work, it is important that a person like to sew and have ability in sewing.
- A thorough knowledge of construction is required for alteration work; therefore it is necessary to study clothing construction in greater depth than the regular high school clothing course offers.
- Precision performance of sewing skills is imperative. The familiar adage, "Practice makes perfect," applies.
- Of equal importance is an understanding of principles that explain why clothes are made the way they are. What purpose does each construction detail serve? Why are specific techniques used? What can be done and what is impossible? What makes specific techniques suitable in one instance and not in another? In other words, knowing the "what's," "why's," and "how's" is necessary to understand fully what is involved in fitting and altering.

Judging What Can Be Done

It is necessary first to know *what* to look for when fitting a garment. In general, the well-fitted garment appears to be comfortable—neither too large nor too small. It fits smoothly, hangs straight, and all structural lines conform to the lines of the body. There is no excess fullness, yet there is sufficient ease to allow for movement without pull or strain. Carefully examine the garment *on the person* to determine whether or not there are any unusual fitting problems and what is causing them. Be thorough, but avoid being too critical. Perhaps some extra fullness or a dropped shoulder line are part of the design. (Specific items to be checked are discussed later in the chapter.)

If there are any fitting problems, it is important to know what corrections can be made and how to make them in the neatest, easiest way. (Specific problems and alteration methods are also discussed later in the chapter.) It is equally important to know what not to attempt. The kind and amount of alteration possible on ready-made clothing depends upon the cut of the garment and how it was made. Some alterations should be avoided; others are just not possible. Little adjustment can be made if the darts or seams have been clipped or trimmed.

However, skimpy hems and narrow seams do not allow much room to lengthen or enlarge a garment. Very little can be done for a garment that is too narrow across the back or too tight across the upper arm. Even if the problem can be corrected, the appearance of the garment is spoiled if the original stitching lines or pressing creases have permanently marked the fabric. Consider the effect of the alteration on the style of the garment and avoid any alteration that spoils the proportion or design.

These are a few of the conditions to consider before determining if the garment can be altered properly.

It may also be necessary to decide whether or not it is worthwhile to alter the garment at all.

Skill and Understanding Required

- Is the alteration relatively easy, such as shortening or straightening the hem? Then there is no problem —of course, the change is worth making.
- Is it more difficult or complicated, involving perhaps the shoulder, armhole, or neckline? Are there several alterations involved? Does making one correction mean making several related alterations?
- Avoid attempting too much. If a dress is too large, for instance, it may be necessary to remake almost the entire garment. How much will the alteration cost? In cases such as these it may not be worthwhile to make the alterations.
- Is there a chance of disappointment in the results? It may be possible to let out a dress that is too small, but will the dress still look skimpy? If too many alterations are necessary or if there is any chance that the results will not be completely satisfactory, it may be wise to suggest that a customer make another selection rather than proceed with the alterations.

"How-to" Points

Whether working in clothing construction or with ready-made clothing, *alteration techniques* are basically the same. The step-by-step procedures may differ somewhat. If a front shoulder seam needs to be raised, a custom dressmaker at the first fitting will probably rip the basted seam first and then repin it correctly. A fitter of ready-made clothing instead, will pin out the excess material in the form of a dart along the shoulder seam rather than rip the seam first. To rip the seam involves releasing the armhole and perhaps even the neckline seam. Whereas the pinning can be done quickly with little delay or inconvenience to the customer. Even for an alteration such as letting out a seam, where obviously no pinning can be done until the seam is released, the fitter may merely write instructions on a work order and do everything else later. At times it may be necessary to rip at once but, for the convenience of the customer, pin only, whenever possible.

A fitter in all probability sees the customer only once. She pin-fits the garment, the alteration is completed, and the garment is ready. If the fitter thinks that a basted fitting is necessary for extensive or complicated alterations, she may ask the customer to return. Usually, however, except for special work such as wedding gowns, there is no opportunity to check the alteration. On the other hand, a custom dressmaker always has a second and sometimes even a third fitting for the clothes she makes. You can see how imperative it is that the professional fitter know her job and be very sure of what she does.

Each fitting problem has its own solution, but there are some basic principles that can serve as guides.
- Avoid *overfitting* or finding too many faults. Correct the most obvious problems first; when they are corrected, other minor faults may have disappeared.
- Be *grain conscious*. If the grain is not straight, here is an easy formula to remember: to raise the slant, make a deeper seam above it; to lower the slant, release a seam above it.

Fitting and Alteration

- It is easier to make a garment smaller than larger. Whatever the adjustment, avoid making a drastic change at any one place. Distribute the amount to be taken in evenly and make several small changes.
- Wrinkles help locate a fitting problem. Follow the wrinkles to the "pointed end" where they originate; that is where an adjustment is needed.
- Follow this general procedure for most alterations:

   —Pin the correction.
   —Mark the pinned line on the wrong side.
   —Remove pins.
   —Rip whatever is necessary.
   —Re-pin corrected line, matching markings.
   —Baste, stitch, press.
   —Complete related alterations.

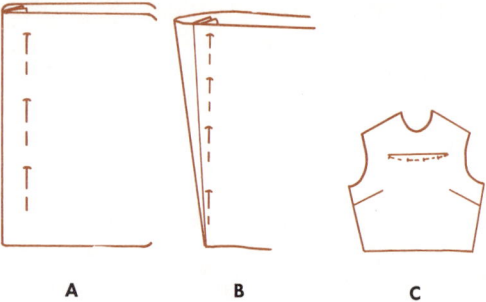

A. Grasp the seam and pin a tuck. B. Pin up extra fullness along dart. C. Pin a tuck across garment to remove excess fullness or length.

There are two pinning methods used in fitting: lap and pin flat; or hold up the fabric and pin. The "lap" method makes it easy to visualize the final results because the garment has a more finished appearance. It is most useful when the straightness of the seamline is involved. You can see immediately whether or not the seam is straight.

With the lap method, the pins should be placed at right angles to the fold.

Lap one side over the other and pin flat.

The "hold-up" method is more easily used in most fitting situations.

With the hold-up method the pins should be placed close together in the same direction as the fold. They indicate the new stitching line in most cases.

Since all fitting is done with the garment right side out, it is necessary to mark the corrected line on the wrong side before removing the pins. If the fabric was *lapped* and pinned flat, slip baste the fold from the right side.

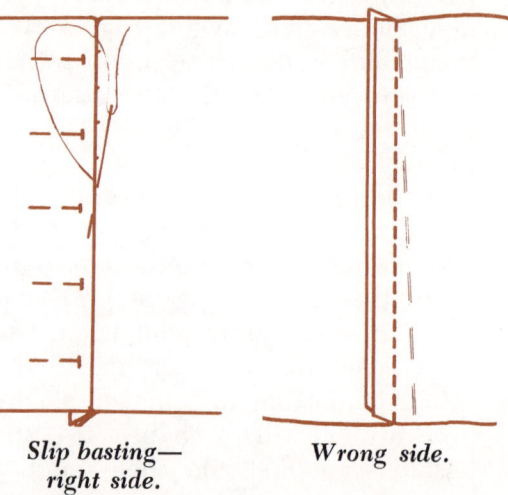

Slip basting— right side. *Wrong side.*

When the pins are removed, the slip stitch will mark a new stitching line on the wrong side.

If the alteration was not pinned flat, the correction can be transferred to the wrong side with pins, chalk, or thread markings. If equal amounts are pinned on both sides of an existing seam or dart, it is necessary to mark only one side. If unequal amounts, or an entirely new line, both sides must be marked.

• TO MARK WITH CHALK: Turn the garment wrong side out. Hold the fabric taut on both sides of the pins and place chalk marks along the pinned line.

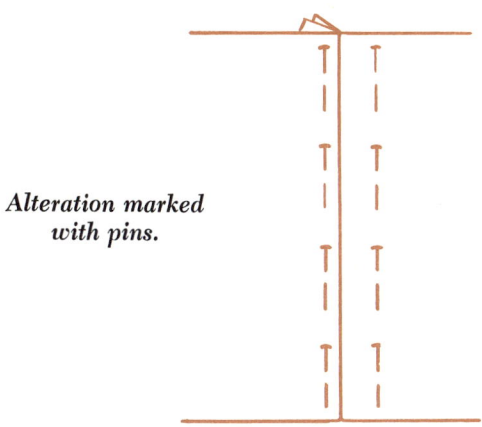

Alteration marked with pins.

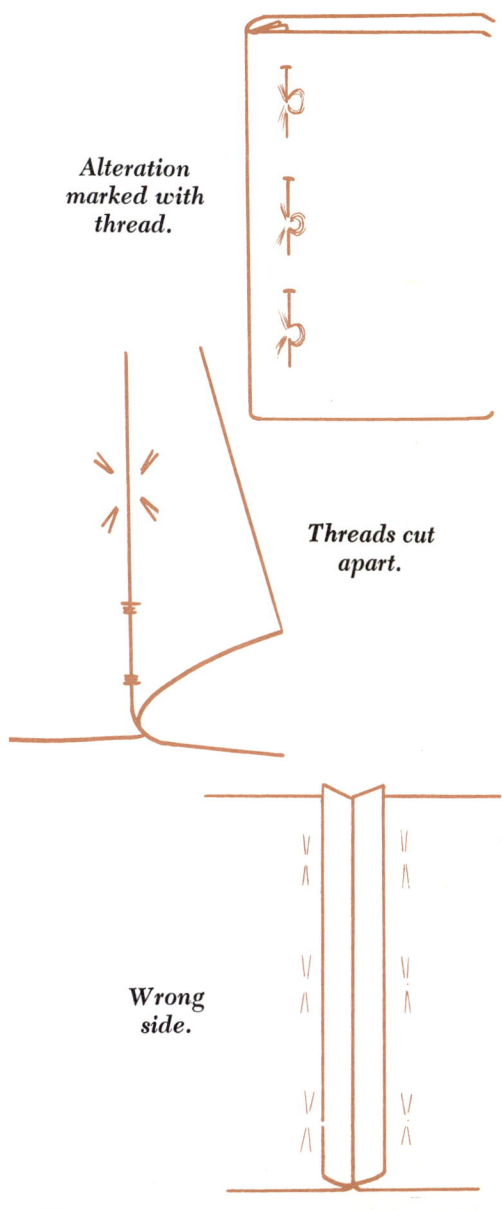

Alteration marked with thread.

Threads cut apart.

Wrong side.

• TO MARK WITH PINS: As you remove the pins, carefully release the underneath layers of fabric, but replace the pin in the top layer on the new stitching line. If it is necessary to mark both sides, place a row of pins on the underneath side, catching only one layer of the fabric. Then proceed to release the other pins, using them to mark the top layer.

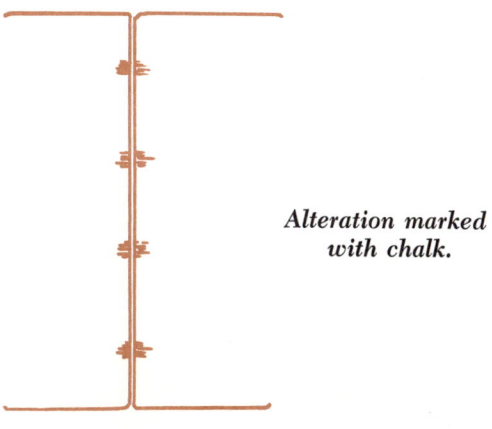

Alteration marked with chalk.

• TO MARK WITH THREAD: Place tailor tacks along the pinned line. Remove the pins. Carefully separate the layers of fabric and clip the threads.

FITTING TECHNIQUES

The following sections outline specific fitting problems and how to correct them. *The information is written for serving ready-made clothing customers,* but with slight variations in procedure the techniques also apply to clothing construction.

Skirt Alterations

The skirt is the simplest part of the garment to fit or alter because, in most cases, only straight lines are involved. NOTE: The information in this section applies to separate skirts as well as to the skirt part of a dress.

Guidelines for Proper Fit

POSITION OF GRAIN:
- Horizontal grain parallel to the floor.
- Vertical grain perpendicular to the floor except when the skirt is cut on the bias.

POSITION OF SEAMS:
- Center seams straight down the center of the body.
- Side seams perpendicular to the floor without veering to the front or the back.
- Side seams located on a straight line from the shoulder to the ankle bone, visible from neither the front nor the back.
- Waistline seam around natural waistline.

FIT AT THE WAISTLINE:
- Snug enough to be comfortable, but not too tight.
- No horizontal wrinkling.

FIT AT THE HIPLINE:
Slim skirt:
- Hang straight without cupping in the rear or swinging out at the side or front.
- Smooth at the hipline.
- Enough ease to allow for freedom of movement. If you are able to pick up at least ½ inch on each side, there is enough ease room. Another test for ease is to lift the skirt at the hipline. If it falls back into place, there is enough ease. If it has to be tugged down into place, it is too snug.
- No horizontal wrinkling between the waist and the hipline.
- Darts ending just above the high point of the hips.

Pleated skirt:
- Pleats hang straight, do not break open.

Full skirt:
- Fullness evenly distributed.

THE HEMLINE:
- Even distance from the floor.
- Attractive length in keeping with the prevailing fashion.

Correcting Fitting Problems

POSITION OF GRAIN:

If a garment was cut off-grain, it is not possible to alter it satisfactorily so that it will fit correctly and the grain will also be perfect. If, however, a fitting problem causes the garment to hang off-grain, it is possible to correct the position of the grain by correcting the fitting problem.

Correcting Fitting Problems

If the horizontal grain is not parallel to the floor, it may be corrected by raising or lowering the skirt piece at the side, whichever is necessary.

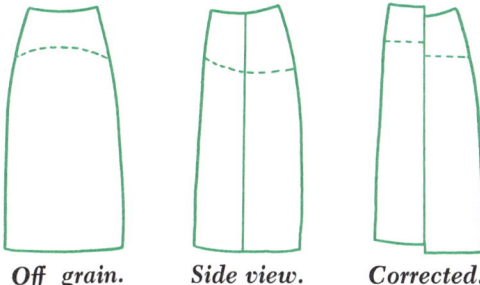

Off grain.   Side view.   Corrected.

METHOD:

—Rip side seam. The hem and waistline seam must be released first.
—Raise skirt piece as far as necessary to straighten the grain.
—Re-pin seam. Stitch and press.
—Adjust and restitch the hem and waistline.

When the vertical grain is not perpendicular to the floor, it usually means that the horizontal grain is also out of position. Again the correction may be made by raising the skirt piece at the side seam. If the vertical grain veers toward the right, raise the left side of that skirt piece.

METHOD:

—Same as used to correct the horizontal grain.

If the vertical grain is still not perpendicular to the floor, further correction is needed. It may be necessary to take a smaller seam—usually below the hipline—on one side of the skirt piece and take a larger seam allowance on the other side. For instance, if the vertical grain veers to the right in the front skirt piece, let out the right side seam of the skirt front below the hip line, raise the left side seam, and take a wider seam allowance on the left front. Use the original seam line in the skirt back piece.

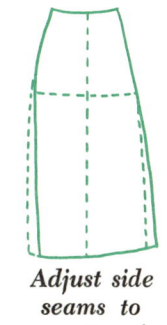

Adjust side seams to correct grain.

METHOD:

—Rip right side seam below the hip line. The hem must be released first.
—Permit the skirt front to swing to the left until the grain falls straight.
—Re-pin right side seam, turning the back under on the original seam allowance and lapping the back over the front only as far as necessary to keep the seam straight. Raw edges will not be even. The front seam allowance will be narrow.
—Rip entire left side seam. The waistline seam *and* hem must both be released.
—Raise skirt piece as far as necessary to straighten the grain.

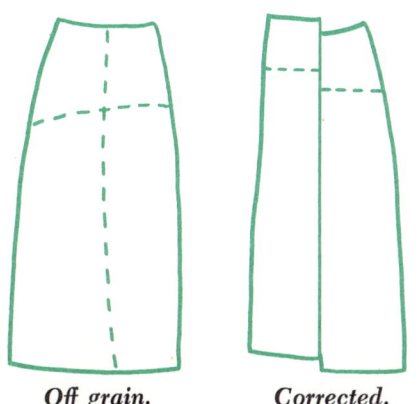

Off grain.   Corrected.

Fitting and Alteration

—Re-pin left side seam, turning the back under on the original seam allowance and lapping the back over the front as far as necessary to make the seam straight and maintain straight grain. Raw edges will not be even. The front seam allowance will be wider than the original seam.

—Stitch side seams and press.

—Adjust and restitch waistline seam and hem.

—NOTE: These directions apply when the vertical grain veers to the right. Reverse sides if the grain veers to the left.

The position of the grain is relatively easy to alter in the first fitting of a garment you are *making,* but is a much more complex alteration in a ready-made garment. Then the waistline seam or waistband, the hem, and perhaps a side opening are all involved. The result is that the skirt has to be almost completely remade. Whether or not the grain can be corrected will depend upon the width of the hem and the width of the side seam allowances. Will there be any hem allowance after raising the side? Is there enough seam allowance to let out one side seam far enough to correct the grain?

Position of Seams

If the center seam, either front or back, does not hang straight down the center of the body, it can be corrected in the same way that vertical grain was handled.

If side seams curve, the correction can usually be made at the waistline seam. If the lower part of the seam veers forward, lift the center back of the skirt at the waistline. This will draw the side seam back into line. Reverse the procedure if the seam veers toward the back.

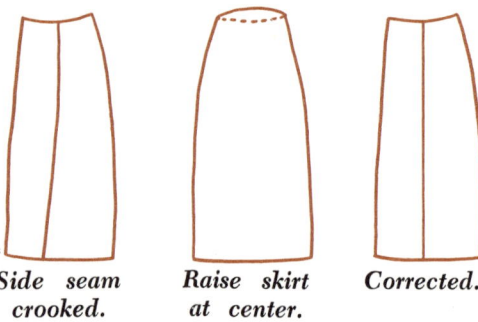

Side seam crooked. *Raise skirt at center.* *Corrected.*

METHOD:

—Pin a dart across the skirt at the waistline. Take up the amount necessary at the center to straighten the side seams. Taper to nothing at each side.

—Release the hem across the back and re-mark it so that it can be straightened.

—Open the waistline seam or remove the waistband across the back.

—Ease the extra material up into the waistline seam or the waistband.

—Restitch waistline seam. Trim excess material.

—Replace hem.

—It may also be necessary to re-pin the side seams. Follow the method used to straighten vertical grain.

If the skirt is attached to a bodice, and the wearer has a very full bust, the side seam may veer to the front because the bodice front is too short for the full figure. Lengthening the bodice across the front will correct the problem. NOTE: This adjustment

Position of Seams

may not be possible, depending upon the width of the waistline seam.

METHOD:
- —Open the waistline seam across the front.
- —Let the skirt drop into position until the side seams are back in a straight line.
- —Re-pin the waistline seam. Later, when stitching this, reinforce it with straight seam tape, since the bodice seam allowance will be very narrow.
- —Check the hemline after the waistline seam is re-pinned and adjust the hem if necessary.

A side seam that is not perpendicular to the waistline seam indicates that one section of the skirt is too narrow for the figure at the waistline, even though the skirt as a whole may fit comfortably. Usually the seam curves toward the front, meaning that the front skirt section is too narrow. This may be corrected by letting out the front and taking in the back at the waistline until the side seam is brought into line.

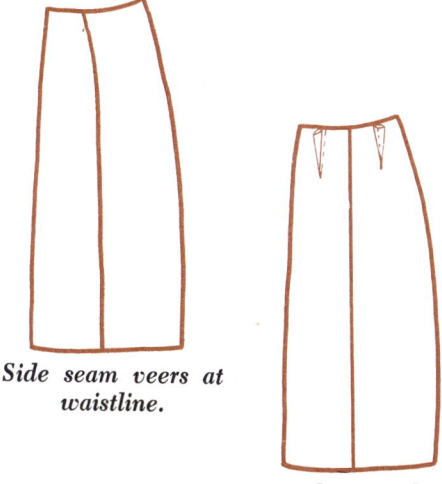

Side seam veers at waistline.

Corrected.

METHOD:
- —Open waistline seam or remove waistband.
- —Release side seams between waistline and hipline.
- —Re-pin the seams, turning under a larger seam on the back and lapping it over the front only far enough to straighten it. NOTE: This method is preferable, but will work only if the seam allowance is wide enough to permit letting out the front seam.
- —When more straightening is needed than the width of the seam allowance permits, let out the front darts, each the same amount, until the side seam is straight.
- —Take in the back darts—each the same amount—until the waistline again fits comfortably. To maintain straight lines and even spacing of the back darts, part of the excess width may also be taken up in the center back seam, tapering it from the waistline to the hipline.
- —If the skirt is attached to a bodice, change the seams and darts in the bodice to match the skirt.
- —Restitch the waistline seam or replace the waistband.

A side seam may hang straight, but be located either too far to the front or the back. If the seam allowance is wide enough, the seam can be relocated. The result will be uneven seam widths. For example, if the seam is located too far front, it will be necessary to take a deeper seam on the back side piece and a narrower seam allowance on the front. In that way

Fitting and Alteration

the seam can be moved farther toward the back.

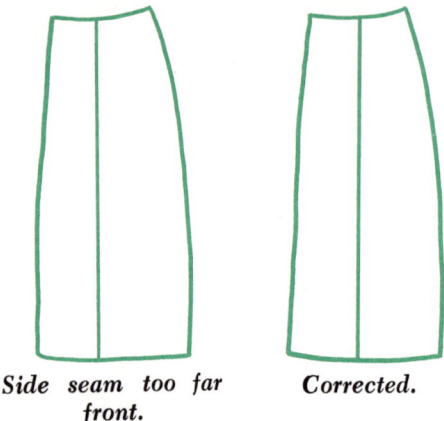

Side seam too far front.   Corrected.

METHOD:
- Release the hem and waistline seam across the side seams.
- Remove the slide fastener, if necessary.
- Rip the side seams.
- Re-pin the seams, locating them on a straight line from the shoulder to the ankle. Restitch and press.
- Insert the slide fastener.
- Restitch the waistline seam and hem.

If the waistline seam is not around the natural waistline, one of two things is indicated. If it is a separate skirt, the waistband may be too loose to hold the skirt in place at the waistline. As a result, the skirt slips down so the waistband seam comes below the waistline. The skirt will have to be taken in. This alteration is discussed in the next section dealing with fit at the waistline. If the skirt is attached to a bodice, however, the fault is probably in the bodice length. Altering this is discussed on page 327.

Fit at the Waistline

If the size of the waistline has to be changed, make the major part of the alteration in either the darts, pleats, gathers, or center seams rather than the side seams. In that way you can keep the grain in the right position on the figure and may avoid having to remove a slide fastener. *Be sure* to keep the side seams straight and in the proper position on the figure as you work.

If the waistline is too loose, divide the amount to be altered equally among the darts or pleats and seams. If the skirt has six darts and a center seam, a difference of ⅛ inch on each will alter the waistline almost 2 inches.

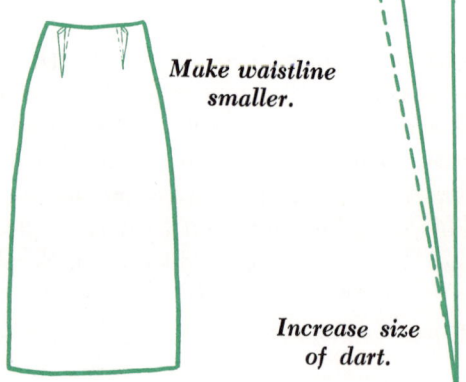

Make waistline smaller.

Increase size of dart.

METHOD:
- pin each dart and center seam deeper until the waistline is as snug as desired.
- Release the waistline seam or remove the waistband.
- Restitch the darts and seams, tapering gradually to the original stitching.
- Make the same alteration in the bodice darts and seams if working with a dress.
- Restitch the waistline seam or replace the waistband.

Fit at the Waistline

—For a princess line dress, take in the darts and seams an equal amount at the waistline. Then taper them gradually to 2 or 3 inches both above and below the waistline.

If you have to take in the waistline of a dress just a small amount, it may be possible to ease it in. To do this, cut a strip of straight seam tape to fit the waist measurement. Pin; then stitch the tape to the waistline seam, easing in the extra fullness.

If the waistline is too snug, it will be necessary first to check the garment carefully to be sure it is possible to make the alteration. Is there enough lap to make the waistband larger? Are there darts, pleats, or gathers that can be released? Examine the wrong side thoroughly. Manufacturers often use different methods for marking construction details. A small hole or slash might make alterations impossible. Are the seams wide enough that they can be let out? Have the seams and darts been clipped at the waistline for smooth fit? Does the clipping interfere with letting out the seams?

METHOD:

—Release the waistline seam or remove the waistband.
—Let out each dart and seam or release pleats or gathers. Distribute the extra amount needed equally until the waistline is comfortable.
—Fit the waistband, marking where the ends will meet when it is comfortable.
—Restitch darts and seams.
—Make the same alteration on the *bodice* darts and seams, if working with a dress.
—Restitch the waistline seam or replace the waistband.
—For a princess line dress, let out the darts and seams an even amount at the waistline. Then taper them gradually to 2 or 3 inches both above and below the waistline.

It is also possible to increase the size of the waistline by raising the skirt. Think of the skirt as a cone.

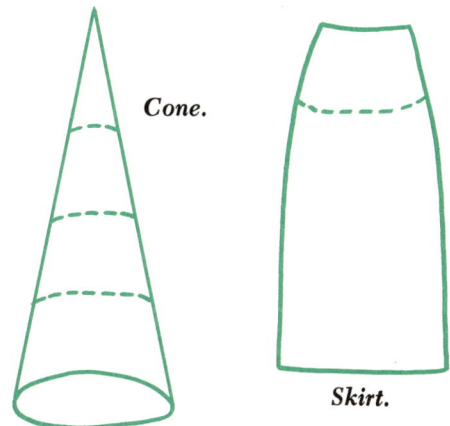

Cone.

Skirt.

The circumference of a cone is larger as the cone widens. In the same way, a skirt that has even a very slight flare is larger below the waistline. Cut off the top of the skirt and the waistline automatically becomes larger.

Before raising the skirt to obtain the extra size needed, however, there are certain things to consider:

• Raising the skirt also shortens it. Can the skirt be shorter? Is there enough hem allowance to lengthen it again if necessary?
• If you are working with a dress, can the bodice be made larger to match the skirt?

Fitting and Alteration

• Is there enough lap to make the waistband larger?

If you can answer "Yes" to these questions, then it is possible to raise the skirt to make the waistline larger.

METHOD:

—Pin a tuck around the top of the skirt, indicating the amount to raise the waistline. Make note of the amount the skirt must be lengthened, if necessary.
—Check that the darts are the proper length. If they need to be lengthened, refer to the section dealing with *fit at the hipline* on page 320.
—Release the waistline seam or remove the waistband.
—Remove the slide fastener.
—From the top of the skirt, cut the amount to be raised.
—Restitch the waistline and insert the slide fastener.
—Lengthen skirt, if necessary.

Horizontal wrinkling at the front waistline, when both the waistline and the hipline fit comfortably, indicates that the skirt is too snug directly below the waist. A prominent hip bone or a large stomach may cause the figure to curve outward quickly rather than gradually. To obtain the needed width over the abdomen, re-shape the front darts.

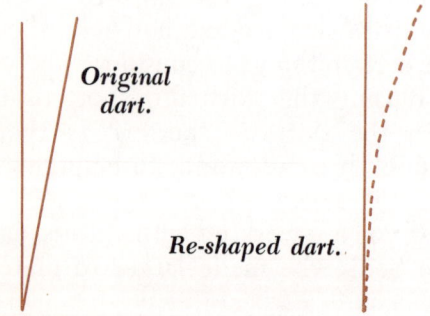

Original dart.

Re-shaped dart.

METHOD:

—Release the waistline seam across the front.
—Restitch the darts, keeping the same width at the waistline but curving them toward the point rather than stitching them in a straight line.
—Remove the original dart stitching. Press.
—Restitch the waistline seam.

Horizontal wrinkling across the back only indicates that the skirt is too long between the waistline and the hipline. Sway-back posture is usually the cause. (Many people have this deep arch just above the hips in back.)

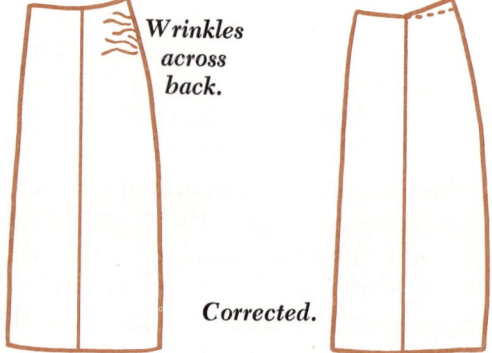

Wrinkles across back.

Corrected.

To remove the wrinkles, it is necessary to eliminate the excess length by lifting the center-back at the waistline. Use the same method as that for correcting the curved side seam by lifting the back. Refer to page 314.

Fit at the Hipline

If the size of the skirt has to be changed at the hipline, the alteration is made at the side seams. NOTE: Unless the figure is irregular, always make the same alteration on both sides. *Be sure* to keep the side seams

Fit at the Hipline

in a straight line from the hipline to the hem, and keep the grain lines straight.

When the skirt is too tight at the hipline, the skirt rides up and there are horizontal folds where the skirt strains around the hipline. If the side seams are wide enough to let out, the skirt can be made larger. If the side seams are skimpy, there is very little that can be done with a slim skirt, but it is possible to raise a flared skirt at the waistline to make it larger, depending upon the length of the skirt.

METHOD:

- Release the hem across side seams.
- Remove the slide fastener, if necessary.
- Rip the side seams almost to the waistline. Do not change the width of the seam at the waistline.
- Re-pin the seam to fit by turning the front under and lapping it over the back. NOTE: The new seam will be narrower than the original one.
- Pin a smooth curve between the waist and the hip. Keep the new seam parallel to the original one, from the hipline to the hem.
- Restitch the seams. Press.
- Insert the slide fastener and make the hem.

When the skirt is too large at the hipline, take in the side seams. The *method* is the same as that followed to make the skirt larger, except that you pin in a deeper seam rather than letting out the seam. Neither is it necessary to rip the side seams first. *Be sure* to keep a smooth line between the waist and the hip as well as a straight line to the hemline.

When the skirt cups at the rear, the skirt is too narrow across the back.

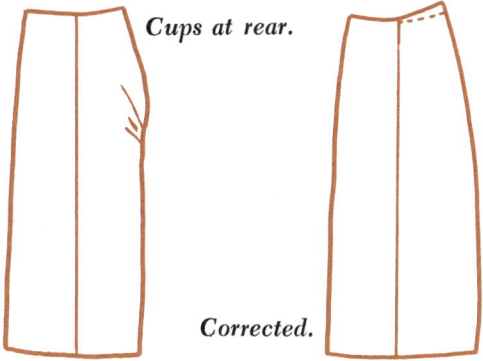

Cups at rear.

Corrected.

Let out the back side seams (refer to page 315) and lift the center back at the waistline (refer to page 314). Then the skirt will hang straight again.

When the skirt swings out at the hemline, check the side seams. If they are not straight, adjusting them may pull the skirt back into place so it hangs straight again. To adjust the side seam, refer to page 314.

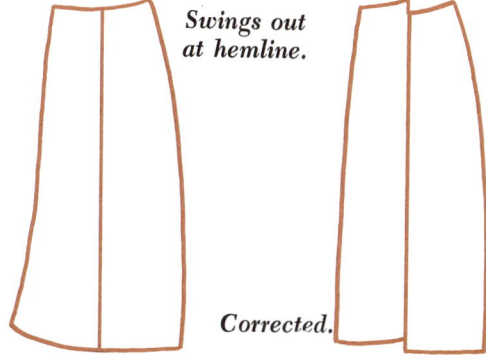

Swings out at hemline.

Corrected.

If the side seams are straight, however, the difficulty is at the waistline. Raise or lower the waistline seam where necessary until the skirt falls back into place. For example, if the

Fitting and Alteration

skirt swings out at the center, raise the side seams at the waistline and the skirt will hang straight. To change the waistline seam, follow the method on page 313.

If the back darts are not the correct length, they can be altered very easily. It is possible to lengthen a dart without any ripping. To shorten a dart, only the stitching at the point must be removed. It is not necessary, in either case, to open the dart completely.

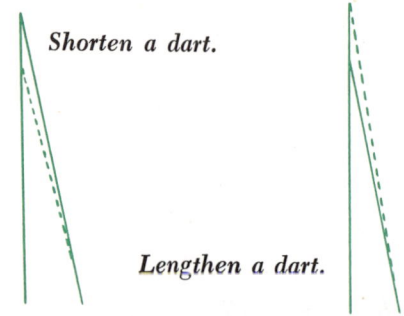

Shorten a dart.

Lengthen a dart.

METHOD:

—Mark the exact point where the dart should end.
—Restitch the darts, slanting from the original stitching to the newly located point.
—If the dart was shortened, remove the original stitching at the point. Press.

If pleats break open or slant, instead of hanging straight, it may mean that the skirt is too narrow or that the top of the pleat needs to be lifted. The easiest way to *increase the size* of an all-around pleated skirt, either pressed or stitched down, is to raise it at the waistline. For the method, refer to page 318.

In the case of a single pleat such as in the back of a slim skirt, raising the

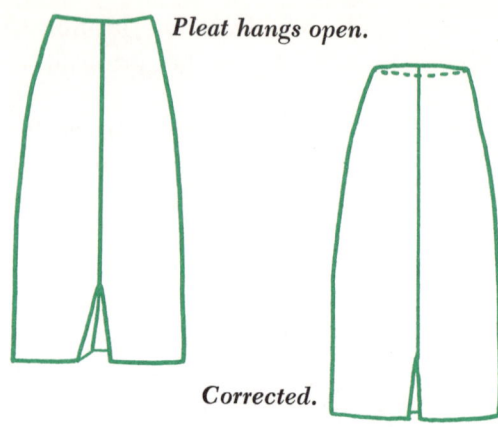

Pleat hangs open.

Corrected.

waistline seam at the top of the pleat will cause it to fall back into line. For the method, refer to page 314.

The Hemline

Adjusting the hem is probably the most frequently made alteration, and the easiest. Shortening a skirt presents no problems. Whether or not a skirt can be lengthened, however, depends upon whether or not there is enough hem to let down. It may be necessary to use hem facing if the entire hem must be lowered. Another consideration—if the hem is let down, will the crease of the original hem remain? Pressing permanently creases some fabrics, making it impossible to steam out the original hemline.

To shorten a skirt, it is possible to mark the new length without having first to release the hem.

METHOD:

—Mark the new length.
—Release the hem and remove the tape.
—Press the lower skirt to remove the crease.
—Trim the hem to even width, if necessary.
—Re-hem and press.

Bodice Alterations

To lengthen a skirt, it will be necessary to release the hem before marking the new length. Otherwise, follow the same method as for shortening. NOTE: Straightening a crooked hem can be done the same way.

If the crease of the original hem is difficult to remove, try one of the following:
- Test the fabric to make sure it will not water spot. If it doesn't, dampen the crease with a wet sponge. Let dry and then steam.
- Again, test the fabric first to make sure it will not water spot. Dampen it with a vinegar and water solution. Then steam it.
- Steam it. Rub the crease with nylon net while still damp. Resteam.

Optical "straightening." Even though a skirt may measure exactly the same distance from the floor, optical illusion often causes the back to look longer than the front. In this case the hem should be corrected so that it looks even from the floor.

BODICE OR SHELL ALTERATIONS

The upper part of a garment is more difficult to fit and alter than the skirt. The areas involved—neckline, shoulder, armhole, sleeve, bustline, and midriff—are more complicated than the straight lines of the skirt. NOTE: The information in this section can apply to a separate blouse or shell, to the bodice of a dress, and, in most cases, even to a coat or jacket.

Guidelines for Proper Fit

POSITION OF GRAIN:
- Horizontal grain parallel to the floor around the bustline and upper arm.
- Vertical grain perpendicular to the floor down both the center front and the center back.
- Vertical grain in a straight line from tip of the shoulder to elbow of the sleeve.

POSITION OF SEAMS:
- Shoulder seam along the top of the shoulder—should not be seen from either the front or the back.
- Underarm seam (directly under the arm) perpendicular to the floor—should be inconspicuous from both the front and the back.
- Armhole seam at the edge of the shoulder—should fall straight down, not at an angle, from the tip of the shoulder both front and back.
- Waistline seam around natural waistline, completely hidden by a narrow belt.

POSITION OF DARTS:
- Underarm darts point to the fullest part of the bust. Each should end about 1 inch from the point of the bust.
- Front waistline darts end ½ to 2 inches below the fullest part of the bust, depending upon the figure. The lower the dart, the looser the fit.
- Sleeve darts at the elbow when the arm is bent.

GENERAL FIT:
- Loose enough to allow for comfort and ease of movement, but not so loose that it hangs.
- Fits smoothly without pulling, straining, binding or wrinkling.

NECKLINE:
- Fits smoothly and lies close to

Fitting and Alteration

the body—whether it is normal, wide, or low.
— Neither gaps nor chokes.
— Collar fits close to the neck.

SHOULDER AREA:

— No wrinkling between neckline and armhole.
— No wrinkling between shoulder and bustline.
— No wrinkling across the back below the neckline.

MIDRIFF AREA:

— No diagonal wrinkling between the bustline and the underarm seam.
— No horizontal wrinkling.

ARMHOLE:

— Comfortable, neither too loose nor binding when arm is in natural position.
— Allows for moderate movement.
— No wrinkling or pulling.

SLEEVE:

— Hangs straight from the shoulder without any twisting or pulling. Short sleeve should not stand out from the arm.
— Wide enough that it does not bind nor strain when the arm is bent.
— Sleeve length is attractive and comfortable. A full length sleeve should cover the wrist bone when the arm is bent.

Correcting Fitting Problems

POSITION OF GRAIN:

— Just as in the case of the skirt, the position of the grain is relatively easy to alter in the first fitting of any garment you are making, but is much more complex in a ready-made garment. Because the bodice has to be almost completely remade, it might be advisable to make another selection, if possible, rather than choosing an off-grain bodice.

If the horizontal grain lines are not parallel to the floor, an adjustment must be made either at the shoulder seam or at the underarm dart. When working with a ready-made garment, the simpler alteration is to change the depth of the underarm dart—increase it to raise the grain, decrease it to drop the grain. Then you will not become involved with the armholes and sleeves as you would if you changed the shoulder seams.

Whether or not you can correct the grain, however, will depend upon the length of the bodice. Increasing the depth of the underarm dart and raising the shoulder seam will both shorten the bodice at the side. Is the bodice long enough at the side to permit shortening? If not, is the waistline seam wide enough that the bodice can be returned to the correct length?

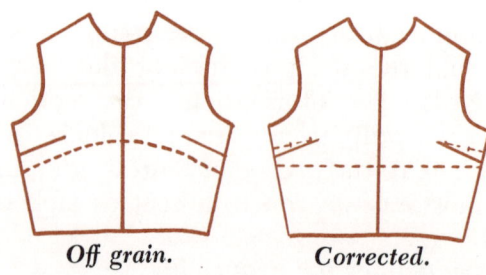

Off grain.   *Corrected.*

METHOD:

— Pin the underarm darts deeper until the grain is corrected.
— Check the bodice length. Mark

Correcting Fitting Problems

the amount to be lengthened, if necessary.
—Release the underarm seam and the waistline seam across the side seams.
—Remove the slide fastener, if necessary.
—Restitch darts and press.
—Restitch side seams. Front and back will not be even at the waistline.
—Restitch the waistline seam, adjusting length.
—Insert the slide fastener.

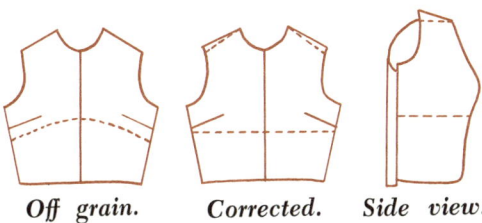

Off grain.   Corrected.   Side view.

METHOD:

—Re-pin the shoulder seam, raising it at the armhole the amount necessary to correct the grain. Perhaps only the front or back seam needs to be raised, not both. If so, pin a deeper seam on one only; keep the original seamline on the other.
—Check the bodice length. Mark the amount to be lengthened, if necessary.
—Remove the sleeve or armhole finishing.
—Release side seams if only one seam allowance was raised. If both front and back were raised, it is not necessary to adjust the side seam.
—Remove the slide fastener, if necessary.
—Re-pin side seams, raising the one necessary to correspond to the raised shoulder seam.
—Restitch side seams and press.
—Restore the armhole to original size by trimming under the arm.
—Insert the sleeve or refinish the armhole edge.
—Restitch the waistline seam, adjusting length if necessary, and insert the slide fastener.

If the vertical grain is not perpendicular to the floor, a correction may be made at the shoulder seam. If the grain veers toward the right front, take a deeper left front shoulder seam. Follow the same method as used to correct the horizontal grain.

In working with ready-made garments, it may be easier to make the correction at the side seams, if possible. Then you will not become involved with neckline, armhole, and sleeves. If the grain veers to the right front, let out the right front side seam and take a wider seam allowance on the left front.

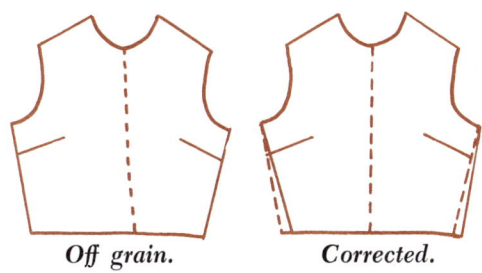

Off grain.   Corrected.

METHOD:

—Release the waistline seam across the front.
—Remove the slide fastener, if necessary.
—Rip the right side seam from about 1 inch below the armhole to the waistline.

Fitting and Alteration

- Swing the bodice toward the left until the grain falls straight.
- Re-pin, turning the back under on the original seam allowance and lapping it over the front just far enough to keep the seam straight. The raw edges will not be even. The front seam allowance will be narrow.
- Rip the left side seam.
- Re-pin, turning the back under on the original seam allowance and lapping it over the front as far as necessary to make the seam straight and keep the grain straight. The raw edges will not be even. The front seam allowance will be wider than the original seam.
- Restitch side seams and press.
- Restitch the waistline seam and insert the slide fastener.

NOTE: These directions apply when the vertical grain veers toward the right. Reverse sides if the grain veers to the left.

If the horizontal grain is not parallel to the floor around the upper arm, either raise or lower the sleeve at the side of armhole—whichever is necessary to straighten the grain line.

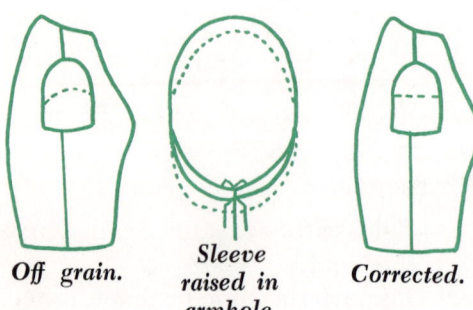

Off grain.   Sleeve raised in armhole.   Corrected.

METHOD:

- Rip the sleeve from the armhole except across the very top.
- Slide the sleeve up or down to straighten the grain. Pin it in place at the center front and center back of the armhole.
- Finish pinning the sleeve to the armhole, adjusting the ease as necessary. Because the sleeve was raised or lowered, the raw edges under the arm may no longer be even.
- Restitch the armhole seam, stitching on the original bodice seamline. If the sleeve seam extends beyond the bodice under the arm, trim the excess material.

If the vertical grain is not in a straight line from the tip of the shoulder to the elbow, it can be corrected by moving the top of the sleeve either forward or back in the armhole.

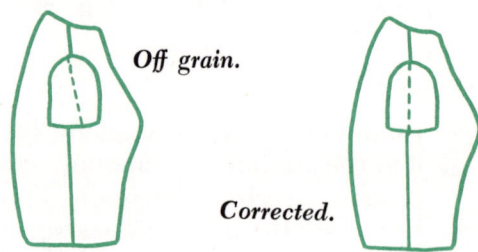

Off grain.   Corrected.

METHOD:

- Release the sleeve across the top from the center front to the center back of the armhole.
- Move the sleeve forward or back until the grain is straight. Pin in place at the top of the shoulder.
- Finish pinning the sleeve to the armhole, adjusting the ease as necessary.
- Restitch the armhole seam.

POSITION OF SEAMS:

If the shoulder seam is not at the top of the shoulder, it can be relocated so that it is not noticeable from either the front or the back. If the seam is too far to the front, move it back by releasing some of the front shoulder seam allowance and taking a deeper back seam allowance. Reverse the process to move the seam forward.

This alteration is very easy when making a dress, but becomes quite complex in ready-made clothes because both sleeve or armhole finishes and neckline finish or collar are affected.

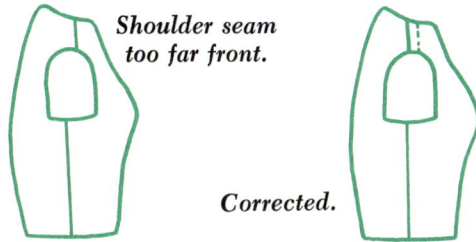

Shoulder seam too far front.

Corrected.

METHOD:

—Release the neck finish across the shoulder seams.
—Release the sleeve or armhole finish across the shoulder seams.
—Rip the shoulder seam.
—Re-pin the shoulder seam by turning the back under more than the original seam allowance and lapping it over the front just far enough that the seam lies flat at the top of the shoulder.
—Restitch the shoulder seam and press.
—Replace neck and armhole finishes.

This method can also be used to adjust a shoulder seam that does not lie flat.

If the underarm seam is not perpendicular to the floor, it can be corrected by adjusting both the side seams and the waistline darts. If the seam veers to the front, take a deeper back side seam and let out the front side seam. If more straightening is needed, it may be possible to let out the front waistline darts and take in the back ones. Keep in mind, however, the purpose of the darts—to create shape so that the garment will fit the curves of the body. The wider the dart, the more shape is created. Whether or not you can increase or decrease the darts depends upon the figure.

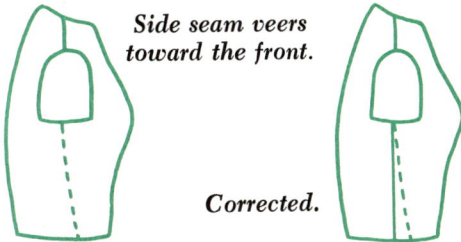

Side seam veers toward the front.

Corrected.

METHOD:

—Release the waistline seam across front.
—Remove the slide fastener, if necessary.
—Rip side seams only as far as necessary.
—Re-pin the seam by turning one under more than the original seam allowance and lapping it over the other just far enough so that the seam is straight.
—Release front darts as far as necessary to straighten the side seam.
—Increase the width of back darts until waistline is the correct size.
—Restitch the waistline seam.
—Replace the slide fastener.

If the underarm seam is located too far to the front or the back, it can be

325

Fitting and Alteration

relocated only if the seam allowance is wide enough.

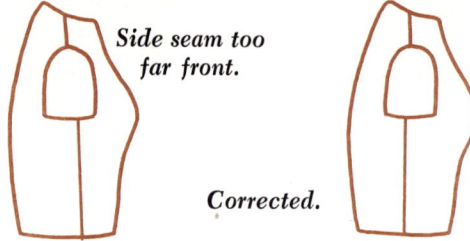

Side seam too far front.

Corrected.

METHOD:
— Release the armhole seam across the underarm seam.
— Release the waistline seam across underarm seam.
— Remove the slide fastener, if necessary.
— Rip the side seam.
— Re-pin the side seam by turning one under more than the original seam allowance and lapping it over the other just far enough to relocate the seam in the proper position.
— Restitch the seam and press.
— Restitch the waistline and armhole seams and insert the slide fastener.

If the armhole seam is not at the edge of the shoulder, the sleeve will have to be moved either in or out on the shoulder. Whether or not the sleeve can be moved out farther will depend upon the width of the armhole seam. With normal seam allowance, the most the shoulder can be lengthened is ¼ to ⅜ inch, unless there are both front and back shoulder darts that can also be let out.

METHOD:
— Release the sleeve across the top from the center front to the center back of the armhole.

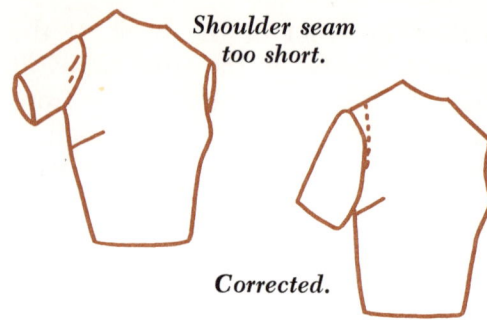

Shoulder seam too short.

Corrected.

— Re-pin the sleeve, moving it out on the shoulder as far as necessary. Do not change the seam allowance of the sleeve, and keep at least ¼ inch seam allowance on the bodice.
— Check that the armhole seam falls straight down from the edge of the shoulder, both front and back.
— Check for straight grain.
— Restitch the armhole seam.

When the shoulder line is too long, the sleeve can easily be moved farther in on the shoulder or shoulder darts can be inserted in both the front and back.

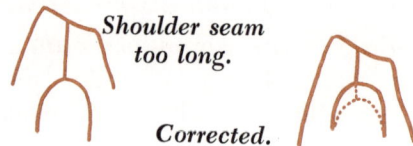

Shoulder seam too long.

Corrected.

METHOD:
— Mark a new armhole seam on the bodice. Start at the edge of the shoulder and taper back gradually to the original seamline. Be sure the line is straight down from the shoulder, both front and back.
— Release the sleeve across the top of the armhole as far as the newly marked seamline.

Correcting Fitting Problems

—Re-pin the sleeve to the newly marked armhole seam. Follow the original seamline of the sleeve and maintain straight grain.
—Restitch the armhole seam.
—Trim away the excess material from the bodice.

This method can also be used when the armhole seam needs to be straightened.

By inserting shoulder darts, it is possible to shorten the shoulder line without disturbing the sleeves. If there are already shoulder darts, it may be possible to make them deeper.

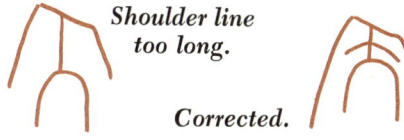

Shoulder line too long.

Corrected.

METHOD:

—Pin a dart in both front and back bodice at the center of the shoulder. Make the dart as deep as necessary to raise the armhole seam to the proper position.
—Release the shoulder seam across the pinned darts.
—Stitch darts and press.
—Restitch the shoulder seam.

If the waistline seam is not around the natural waistline, the fault is in the length of the bodice. If the bodice is too long, it can easily be shortened.

METHOD:

—Place a tape measure around the natural waistline.
—Mark the natural waistline by placing a row of pins around the bottom of the tape measure.
—Release waistline seam where necessary.
—Remove the slide fastener, if necessary.
—If the bodice is shortened very much, it may also be necessary to take it in at the waistline to match the skirt. Refer to the section dealing with fit at the waistline, page 316.
—Re-pin the bodice and skirt on the new bodice waistline seam. Use the original skirt-waistline seam.
—Check the hem length and re-mark if necessary.
—Restitch the waistline seam and insert the slide fastener.

If the bodice is too short, very little can be done to lengthen it unless there is a wide seam allowance at the

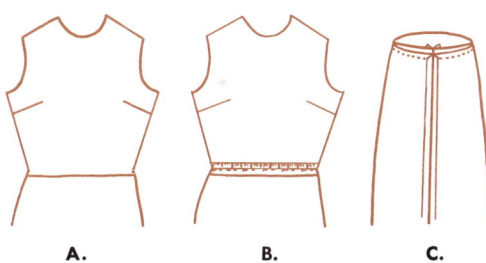

A. Waistline seam below natural waistline. B. Mark natural waistline. C. Deeper bodice seam.

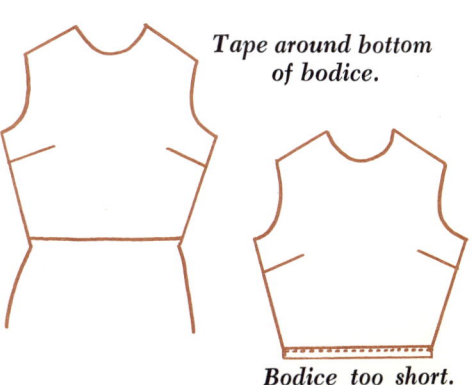

Tape around bottom of bodice.

Bodice too short.

327

Fitting and Alteration

waistline. With normal seam allowance it can be lengthened only as much as ⅜ inch.

METHOD:

—Remove the slide fastener.
—Release the waistline seam.
—Stitch straight seam tape to the waistline edge of the bodice, lapping it ¼ inch over the edge of the fabric.
—Re-pin the bodice and skirt, placing the seam allowance of the skirt at the top edge of the seam binding on the bodice.
—Check the seamline by placing a tape measure around the waistline. The seamline should be completely hidden. Adjust if necessary.
—Restitch the waistline seam and insert the slide fastener.

Positions of Darts

If the underarm darts do not point to the fullest part of the bust, they are not giving shaping where needed and should be relocated.

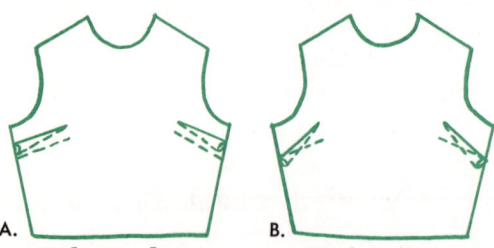

A. *Relocate dart.*   B. *Reslant dart.*

METHOD:

—Mark the correct position for the underarm dart.
—Release the underarm seam across the dart.
—Remove the original dart.
—Mark a new dart, the same length and width as the original, in the correct position. The dart may be completely raised or lowered (A) or merely reslanted (B) as shown in illustration.
—Stitch the newly located dart. Press.
—Restitch the underarm seam.

If the darts are not the correct length, they can easily be lengthened or shortened. Follow the method used to change the length of the darts in the skirt. Refer to page 320.

If the sleeve darts are not at the elbow when the arm is bent, they too are not giving shaping where needed and should be relocated. Follow the same method used to raise or lower the underarm darts.

General Fit

The amount of fullness in the bodice is, in part, a matter of personal preference. Some people like their clothes to fit rather snugly, while others prefer a looser fit. It is also a matter of design. For instance, a dress with dolman sleeves allows for much more ease than one with regular set-in sleeves. A dress with tucks at the waistline allows for fullness through the midriff, whereas darts at the waistline are used for a smooth fit.

Making the bodice larger or smaller is a common, simple alteration. The side seams can usually be let out or taken in easily. The amount you can let out a seam, of course, depends upon the width of the seam allowance. With normal seam allowance, the most you can gain is ⅜ inch, which amounts to 1½ inches total around the bodice. Some adjustment may be made at the darts if the bodice needs to be altered through the midriff or waistline. For *method*, refer to the section dealing with increasing the size of the waistline, page 317. Keep in mind, however, that darts *create* shaping, so changing the width of a dart can cause other fitting problems. If the figure is slim, you might be able to let out darts, but if you take them in you create too much shaping for the slim figure. The result is a poor fit. Just the opposite is true if the figure is full. Let out darts and you lose some shaping. The result again may be poor fit.

The bodice should fit smoothly without any wrinkling. Wrinkles are an indication of a fitting problem and the need for an alteration. Of course, they do help the fitter locate the difficulty. For example, if there is wrinkling from the neckline to the underarm, the problem is at the neckline. Correct the problem and the wrinkles disappear.

Causes of wrinkles and how to eliminate them will be discussed for each area of the bodice.

Neckline

If the neckline is too high, it can be cut lower.

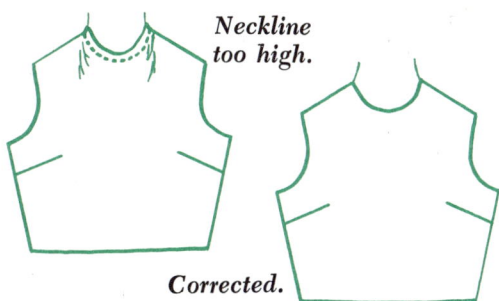

Neckline too high.

Corrected.

METHOD:

—Mark the proper position with a row of pins or with a chalk line.

—If fitting a dress you are *making,* use the marked line as the new seam allowance and trim the excess fabric.

—If working with a ready-made garment:

Remove the collar and neck finish.

Fit the collar and facing to the new seam allowance.

Restitch the neckline seam.

If the neckline feels snug, but is in the proper position, let out the shoulder seams just enough to relieve the strain.

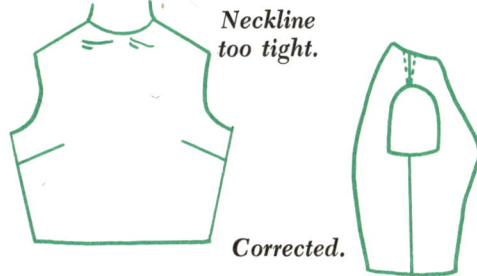

Neckline too tight.

Corrected.

METHOD:

—Release the neckline seam across the shoulder seams.
—Let out the shoulder seam at the neckline, tapering gradually to the original seam line at the armhole.
—Adjust the facing and collar to match the neckline.
—Restitch the neckline seam.

If the neckline is too large, it can be made to fit by taking a deeper shoulder seam.

METHOD:

—Pin the shoulder seam to as deep a point as necessary for the neckline to fit close to the neck. Taper

Fitting and Alteration

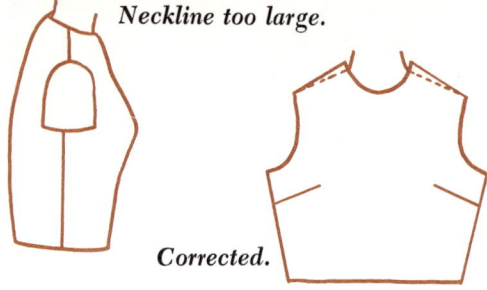

Neckline too large.

Corrected.

to the original seam line at the armhole.
—Release the neckline seam as far as necessary.
—Rip the shoulder seam.
—Re-pin shoulder seams on the new seam lines.
—Stitch and press.
—Adjust facing shoulder seams to match. If there is a collar, make it smaller to fit the new neckline.
—Restitch the neckline seam.

If the neckline gaps in the front, the extra fullness can be taken up by moving the front shoulder toward the armholes.

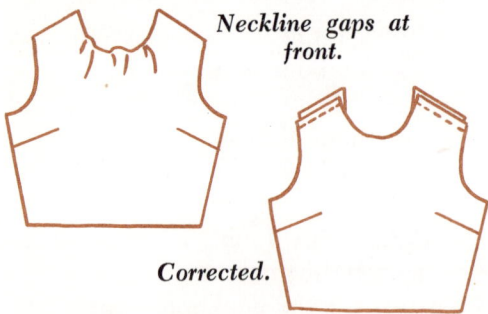

Neckline gaps at front.

Corrected.

METHOD:

—Release the neckline seam across the shoulder line.
—Release the sleeve or armhole finish across the shoulder line.
—Rip the shoulder seam.
—Smooth the front shoulder seams toward the armhole; re-pin. Be careful to keep the center front straight. The ends of the shoulder seams will not be even at either the neckline or the armhole.
—Restitch shoulder seams. Press.
—Restitch the neckline seam, adjusting the curve at the shoulder.
—Trim excess from the front armhole at the shoulder.
—Restitch the sleeve or armhole finish.

If the neckline gaps in the back, the extra fullness can be taken up by making small darts at the neckline.

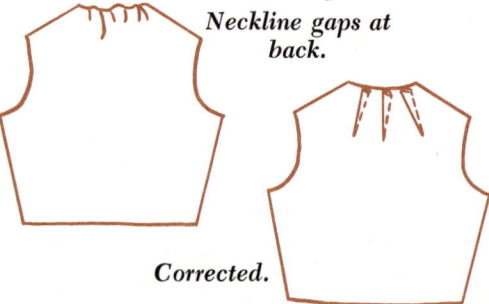

Neckline gaps at back.

Corrected.

METHOD:

—Pin the excess fullness into darts of even width.
—Release the neckline seam across the back.
—Stitch darts and press.
—Adjust the neck finish to fit the new neckline.
—Restitch the neckline seam.

If a collar stands away from the neck, either the collar is too long or the neckline is too large. We have already discussed how to make the neckline smaller. It follows that if the size of the neckline is changed, the collar must also be adjusted accordingly.

Shoulder Area

If there are diagonal wrinkles from the neckline to the underarm, un-

Shoulder Area

usually sloping shoulders are the reason. To eliminate the wrinkling, take a deeper shoulder seam at the armhole. Inserting a small shoulder pad may also improve the shoulder line. If the wrinkling is in the front only, adjust the front shoulder seam, but do not change the back.

shoulder seam will determine whether or not it can be let out.

Wrinkles—armhole toward bustline.

Corrected.

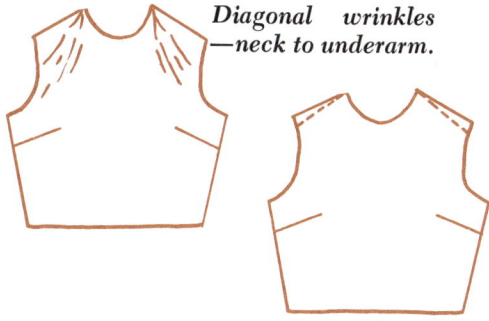

Diagonal wrinkles —neck to underarm.

METHOD:

—Pin the shoulder seam to as deep a point as necessary at the armhole to eliminate the wrinkling. Taper gradually to the original seam line at the neck.
—Release the armhole seam as far as necessary.
—Rip the shoulder seam.
—Restitch on the new line; press.
—Since this alteration makes the armhole smaller, adjust the sleeve or armhole facing accordingly. Take a deeper seam in the facing or mark a new seamline across the cap of the sleeve, lowering it the same amount the shoulder was lowered.
—Restitch the armhole seam.

If there is wrinkling from the top of the armhole toward the bustline, very square shoulders are the cause. The wrinkles can be eliminated by taking a deeper shoulder seam at the neck end or by releasing the shoulder seam at the armhole edge. The width of the

METHOD:

—Smooth wrinkles out of the front and back upwards at the neckline. Pin a new seamline, tapering to the original line at the armhole.
—Mark a new neckline seam in the correct position.
—Release neckline and shoulder seams as far as necessary.
—Restitch the shoulder seam on the new line and press.
—Restitch the neckline on the marked line.

If the shoulder seam is wide enough that it can be let out, use this method to eliminate the wrinkles.

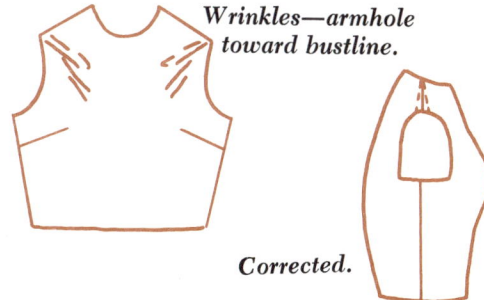

Wrinkles—armhole toward bustline.

Corrected.

METHOD:

—Release the armhole seam across the shoulder.
—Release the shoulder seam to

within about 1 inch from the neck edge.
—Re-pin the shoulder seam, taking a narrow seam allowance at the armhole to eliminate wrinkles. Taper gradually to the original seam allowance at the neckline.
—Restitch the shoulder seam and press.
—Since this alteration makes the armhole larger, adjust the facing or sleeve accordingly. Let out the seam in the facing or mark a new seam allowance across the cap of the sleeve, raising it the same amount the shoulder was let out.
—Restitch the armhole seam.

Wrinkles across the base of the neck indicate a very straight back or very erect posture. The back bodice is too long in the shoulder area and the wrinkles can be eliminated by removing the extra length.

—Release the shoulder seam.
—Mark a corrected shoulder and neck seamline beginning with the original seam at the armhole and enough lower at the neck edge to remove the extra length from the bodice.
—Re-pin the front and back bodice at the shoulders. Raw edges will not be even. Use the original seamline of the bodice front and the corrected seamline of bodice back.
—Restitch the shoulder seam and press.
—Restitch the neckline seam. Trim excess material.

Wrinkling from the shoulder blades across the back to the armhole indicates rounded shoulders. The wrinkles can be removed by taking a deeper shoulder seam at the armhole of the back only. Follow the same method used to eliminate wrinkles from neckline to underarm, page 331, but adjust only the back shoulder seam.

Midriff Area

Diagonal wrinkles from the bustline toward the side seam often occur when the figure has a larger than average bust. Increasing the width of the underarm or waistline darts—perhaps both—will create more shaping for the full bust and eliminate the wrinkling. Keep in mind that, when you make the underarm dart deeper, you also shorten the bodice at the side seam. Is there enough length to adjust it to fit? If you make the waistline darts wider, you may also have to adjust the side seams so that the waistline will fit properly.

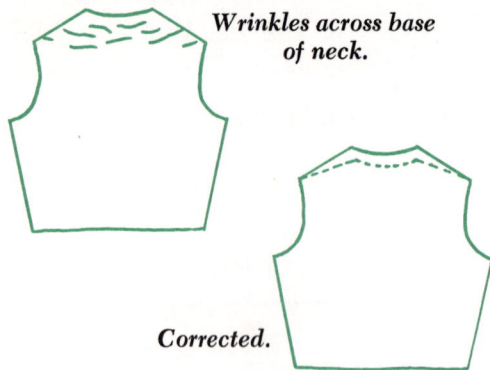

Wrinkles across base of neck.

Corrected.

METHOD:

—Pin a tuck across the center back, raising the bodice back the amount necessary to eliminate the wrinkling. Taper to nothing at the shoulder edge of the armhole.
—Release the neckline seam.

Midriff Area

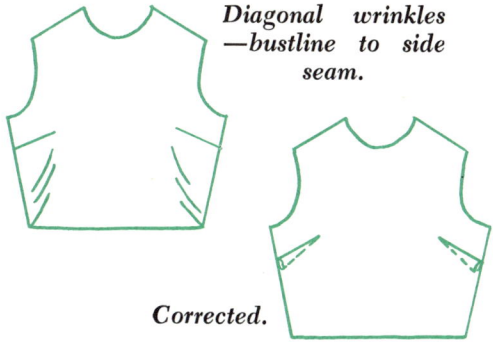

Diagonal wrinkles —bustline to side seam.

Corrected.

Follow the method used to straighten the horizontal grain. Refer to page 322.

If the figure has a low bust, waistline darts may cause the garment to draw across the bustline.

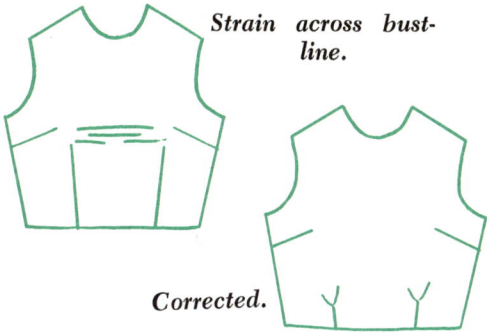

Strain across bustline.

Corrected.

To eliminate the strain, remove the darts and replace them with tucks, pleats, or gathers that allow for more fullness and ease of fit.

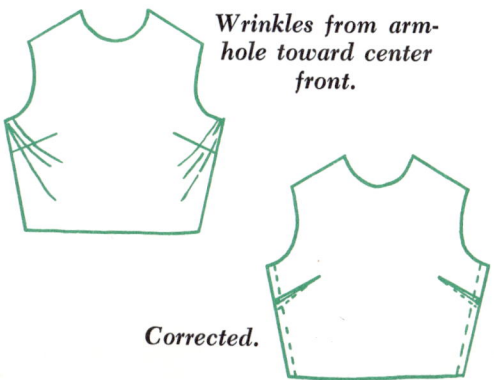

Wrinkles from armhole toward center front.

Corrected.

Wrinkles from the armhole toward the center front indicate that the garment is too full through the bustline.

To correct this problem, reverse the procedure used for the full figure. First, make the underarm dart smaller. This eliminates some shaping that is not needed. Then, to remove the remaining excess material, take a deeper side seam on the front bodice only. Use the original back side seam allowance.

If the figure has a high bust, the fullness under the bustline needs to be lifted and pulled back.

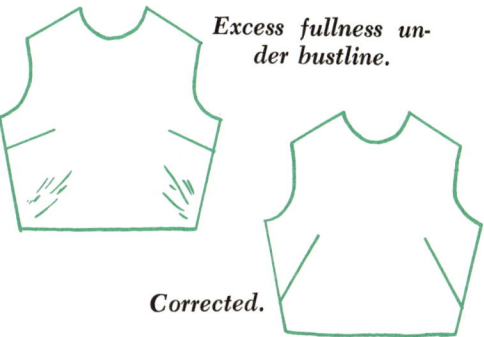

Excess fullness under bustline.

Corrected.

Relocating the underarm dart so that it slants upward from the underarm seam toward the point of the bust improves the fit by eliminating surplus fullness and smoothing the midriff. For the method, refer to page 328.

Horizontal folds of fabric above the waistline are an indication that the bodice is too long. To eliminate the ripples, remove the excess length by shortening the bodice.

Follow the method described on page 327. NOTE: It may be easier to eliminate the excess material by first pinning a tuck, as deep as necessary, around the bodice above the waistline.

Fitting and Alteration

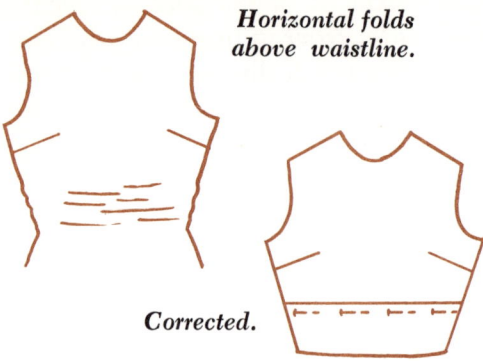

Horizontal folds above waistline.

Corrected.

A bulge across the back of the bodice is quite common for the person with an unusually straight back or when a person is short-waisted in the back. Again, the bodice is too long and the bulge can be eliminated by removing the extra length. Perhaps merely shortening the bodice across the back at the waistline seam will remedy the situation. It may be necessary, however, to lower the entire bodice back.

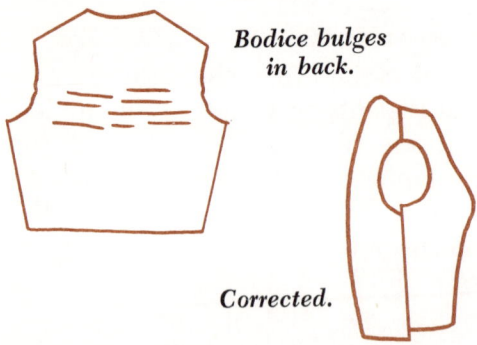

Bodice bulges in back.

Corrected.

METHOD:
— Pin a tuck across the back bodice to as deep a point as necessary to eliminate the excess length.
— Release the armhole seam across the underarm seam.
— Release the waistline seam across the back.
— Release the side seams.

— Remove the slide fastener, if necessary.
— Lower the bodice back as far as necessary to eliminate the excess length and re-pin the side seams. Raw edges will not be even at either the armhole or the waistline.
— Lengthen waistline darts if necessary.
— Mark the new waistline seam.
— Stitch side seams.
— Restitch the armhole and waistline seams.
— Insert the slide fastener.

Armhole and Sleeve

If the armhole is too tight, it can be enlarged by letting out the underarm seam in both the bodice and sleeve or by stitching a deeper armhole seam under the arm.

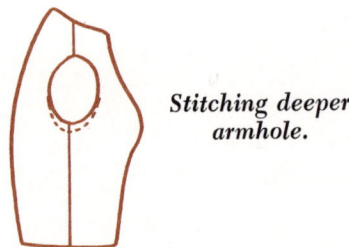

Stitching deeper armhole.

As the stitching is lowered, the armhole circle becomes bigger. After stitching the new seam, trim the excess material under the arm.

If the sleeve is also too tight, continue to let out the underarm seam the entire length of the sleeve.

If the armhole is too large, the bodice will sag just below the armpit. To make the armhole smaller, take a deeper underarm seam in both the bodice and sleeve.

If the sleeve is also too loose, continue to take in the underarm seam the entire length of the sleeve.

Armhole and Sleeve

If a person is round shouldered and/or has a larger than average bust, it is possible that there will be *excess fullness at either the front or back armhole,* but not at both. In this case make the correction by smoothing the bodice up toward the neckline; then take up the extra fullness with a shoulder dart.

of the sleeve is too short. This occurs when the person has very square shoulders and/or large arm muscles. Letting out the top of the sleeve cap may eliminate the wrinkling if the difficulty is only slight. Refer to page 331 for the correction for square shoulders.

Excess fullness at armhole.

Corrected.

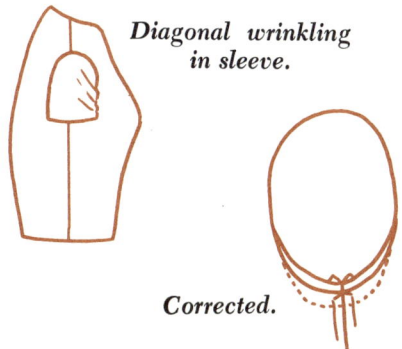

Diagonal wrinkling in sleeve.

Corrected.

METHOD:
— Rip the armhole seam as far as necessary.
— Rip the shoulder seam to within about 1 or 2 inches of the neckline.
— Smooth the bodice up toward the neck until ripples at the armhole disappear.
— Pin a shoulder dart as wide as necessary to eliminate the extra fullness.
— Re-pin the shoulder seam.
— Stitch the dart and shoulder seam. Press.
— Restitch the armhole seam.

If the sleeve twists in the armhole, check the grain. If it is not straight, correct the grain and the sleeve will hang straight. For the method, refer to page 324.

Wrinkles from the top of the sleeve to the underarm indicate that the cap

It may be necessary, however, to raise the sleeve in the armhole to obtain the extra length needed in the sleeve cap. Refer to page 324 for this method.

Square shoulders may also cause the *lower edge of a short sleeve to stand out from the arm.*

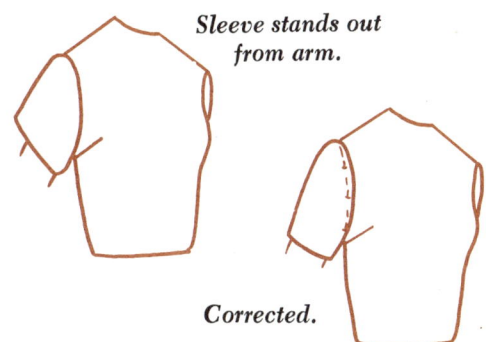

Sleeve stands out from arm.

Corrected.

Again, it will be necessary to raise the sleeve at the bottom of the armhole (refer to page 324); then the sleeve will hang straight again.

Horizontal wrinkles across the

Fitting and Alteration

sleeve at the armhole indicate that the cap of the sleeve is too narrow. Perhaps the armhole seam is not in the proper position. If it has to be let out, refer to page 326. It may be necessary to let out the sleeve seam allowance also in this case, to get extra width. If the sleeve is very tight across the heavy part of the arm, however, there is very little that can be done.

If the sleeve is either too short or too long, the length can be adjusted at the hem. Lengthening, of course, depends upon the width of the hem. An exception is the tailored shirt sleeve. If it is too long, it will be easier to remove the sleeve from the arm hole, recut the top of the sleeve eliminating the excess length, then reset the sleeve in the armhole. If it is too short, there is little that can be done to this type of sleeve.

Keep in mind that the length of the sleeve is part of the design of the garment and should not be changed drastically.

To gain experience

In class, work with a partner—each working on the *other's garments.*

Gain practice in fitting by making a basic dress for your partner. She does the same for you.

Each student bring to class a recent dress purchase. Examine your partner's garment critically according to the GUIDELINES FOR PROPER FIT *outlined in this chapter.*

Are there any fitting difficulties?

If so, determine the cause or causes of the trouble.

Determine whether or not they can be corrected.

Determine the easiest and best method for correcting the faults.

List any related alterations *that are involved.*

Proceed to fit and alter the garment.

The classroom may be organized as a workroom or shop in which the faculty and staff of the school can have alteration work done.

- *Discuss personal skills needed to serve the public.*

- *Set up a schedule of prices to be charged.*

As you develop skill, you may have an opportunity to earn money on your own by doing simple alterations for your friends, family, or neighbors.

Bibliography

Chapter 1: YOU IN THE WORLD OF WORK

McLean, Beth Bailey and Paris, Jeanne. *The Young Woman In Business.* Ames, Iowa: The Iowa State University Press, 1962

Tolman, Ruth. *Guide to Beauty, Charm, Poise.* New York: Milady Publishing Co., 1963

Whitcomb, H. and Lang, R. *Charm.* New York: McGraw Hill Book Co., 1964

Zapoleon, Marguerite W. *Girls and Their Futures.* Chicago, Ill.: Science Research Associates, Inc., 1962

American Women, Report of the President's Commission on the Status of Women. Washington, D. C.: U. S. Government Printing Office, 1963

Handbook on Women Workers. U. S. Department of Labor, Women's Bureau. Washington, D. C.: U. S. Government Printing Office, 1965

Future Jobs for High School Girls. U. S. Department of Labor, Women's Bureau. Washington, D. C.: U. S. Government Printing Office, 1966

Labor Laws Affecting Women (by state). U. S. Department of Labor, Women's Bureau. Washington, D. C.: U. S. Government Printing Office, annual

Your Social Security. U. S. Department of Health, Education, and Welfare. Washington, D. C.: U. S. Government Printing Office, 1966

Federal Labor Laws and Programs. U. S. Department of Labor. Washington, D. C.: U. S. Government Printing Office, 1964

FILMS AND FILMSTRIPS

"Getting and Keeping Your First Job" Guidance Associates
   A two-part filmstrip. Part I presents criteria for evaluating job opportunities. Part II explores personal relationships on the job and job performance. 2 color filmstrips (Part I—67 frames, 14 min.; Part II—64 frames, 14 min.), 2 l.p. records.

"Your Job Interview" Guidance Associates
   Explores job interview techniques, shows how the employer evaluates applicant. 2 color filmstrips (I—65 frames, 14 min.; II—72 frames, 15 min.), 2 l.p. records.

"How to Apply For a Job" Award Records and Film Co.
   Color filmstrip and l.p. record

"How to Be a Better Employee" Award Records and Film Co.
   Color filmstrip and l.p. record

Opportunities in Clothing

"I Want a Job" Forum Films
> Depicts good and poor interviews. Color, sound film, 22 min.

"Getting a Job" Encyclopedia Britannica Films
> Explores leads open in search of a job and how to use the many aids for job hunters. Black and white, sound film, 16 min.

Chapter 2: A PLACE FOR YOU IN THE CLOTHING FIELD

Fried, Eleanor L. *Is The Fashion Business Your Business?* New York: Fairchild Publications, Inc., 1961

The Fashion Group, Inc. *Your Future in the Fashion World.* New York: Richards Rosen Press, Inc., 1963

Jarnow, Jeannette A. and Judell, Beatrice. *Inside the Fashion Business.* New York: John Wiley and Sons, Inc., 1965

Kaplan, Albert A. and de Mille, Margaret. *Careers in Department Store Merchandising.* New York: H. Z. Walck, 1962

Home Economics Has a Career for You in Textiles and Clothing. Washington, D. C.: American Home Economics Association, 1963

Merchandising As a Career. Chicago, Illinois: The Institute for Research, 1965

1966–67 Occupational Outlook Handbook. U. S. Department of Labor. Washington, D. C.: U. S. Government Printing Office.

FILM

"Fashion Means Business" March of Time
> Color, sound film, 17 min. Operation of the fashion industry.

Chapter 3: THE COLOR, LINE, AND DESIGN STORY IN FASHION

Chambers, Bernice G. *Color and Design.* Englewood Cliffs, New Jersey: Prentice-Hall Inc., 1965

Chambers, Helen G. and Moulton, Verna. *Clothing Selection.* Philadelphia, Pa.: J. B. Lippincott Co., 1961

Erwin, Mabel D. and Kinchen, Lila A. *Clothing for Moderns.* 3rd edition. New York: The Macmillan Co., 1964

McJimsey, Harriet T. *Art in Clothing Selection.* New York: Harper and Row Publishers, Inc., 1963

FILMS AND FILMSTRIPS

"Discovering Color" Film Associates of California
> Color, sound, 15 min.

"Discovering Line" Film Associates of California
> Color, sound, 17 min.

"Discovering Perspective" Film Associates of California
   Color, sound, 14 min.

"Discovering Texture" Film Associates of California
   Color, sound, 17 min.

"Line in Your Wardrobe"
   Color, 68 frames

"Color Keying in Art and Living" Encyclopedia Britannica
   A Study of color relationships applied to aspects of everyday life.
   Color, 10 min.

Chapter 4: THE FABRIC STORY TODAY AND TOMORROW

Cowan, Mary I. *Introduction to Textiles.* New York: Appleton-Century-Crofts, 1962

Denny, Grace G. *Fabrics.* 8th edition. Philadelphia, Pa.: J. B. Lippincott Co., 1962

Hollen, Norma and Saddler, Jane. *Textiles.* New York: Macmillan Co., 1964

Klapper, Marvin. *Fabric Almanac.* New York: Fairchild Publications, 1966

Labarthe, Jules. *Textiles, Origin to Usage.* New York: Macmillan Co., 1964

Linton, George E. *Applied Basic Textiles.* New York: Meredith Press, 1966

Linton, George E. *The Modern Textile Dictionary.* New York: Meredith Press, 1962

Lyle, Dorothy S. *Focus on Fabrics.* National Institute of Dry Cleaning, Silver Springs, Maryland, 1964

Potter, M. David and Corbman, Bernard P. *Fiber to Fabric.* 3rd edition. New York: McGraw Hill Book Co., 1959

Stout, Evelyn B. *Introduction to Textiles.* 2nd edition. New York: John Wiley and Sons, Inc., 1965

Wingate, Isabel B. *Textile Fabrics and Their Selection.* 5th edition. Englewood Cliffs, New Jersey, 1964

Wingate, Isabel B., Gillespie, Karen R., and Addison, Betty G. *Know Your Merchandise.* 3rd edition. New York: McGraw Hill Book Co., 1964

U. S. Department of Agriculture. *Consumers All, The Yearbook of Agriculture 1965.* Washington, D. C.: U. S. Government Printing Office, 1965

American Fabrics Magazine, Editors. *Encyclopedia of Textiles.* Englewood Cliffs, New Jersey: Prentice-Hall, Inc., 1960

A Dictionary of Textile Terms. Dan River Mills, Inc., New York, 1964

Fibers For Contemporary Fabrics. Celanese Fibers Marketing Co. New York, 1967

Textile Fibers and Their Properties. Burlington Industries, Inc. Greensboro, North Carolina

Textile Handbook. American Home Economics Association. Washington, D. C. 1966

Opportunities in Clothing

FILMS AND FILMSTRIPS

"Cotton, Nature's Wonder Fiber" National Cotton Council
   Color, sound film, 28 min.

"Only Silk is Silk" Modern Talking Picture Service
   Color, sound film, 17 min.

"Design X–1099" Modern Talking Picture Service
   Color, sound film, 27 min.

"Facts About Fabrics"
   Sound, 26 min.

"Wool, From Sheep to Clothing" Wool Education Center
   Sound, 11 min.

"The Romantic Story of Man and Wool" Pendleton Woolen Mills
   Sound, color

"Textile Fiber Personalities" J. C. Penney Co.
   Color filmstrip, 38 frames

"Care of Textiles" J. C. Penney Co.
   Color filmstrip, 38 frames

"Printing and Finishing of Fabrics" Cranston Print Works Co.
   Color filmstrip, 9 min.

SUGGESTED SOURCES OF INFORMATION

Trade Associations

Cotton: The National Cotton Council of America
P. O. Box 12285, Memphis, Tenn. 38112

Linen: Linen Trade Association
45 E. 17th St., New York 10003
The Irish Linen Guild
1270 Avenue of the Americas
New York, N. Y. 10002

Man-Made Fibers: Man-Made Fiber Producers Association, Inc.
350 Fifth Ave., New York, N. Y. 10001

Silk: International Silk Association
489 Fifth Ave., New York, N. Y. 10017

Wool: The Wool Bureau
16 West 46th St., New York, N. Y. 10019

Home Laundry Division of the Association of Home Appliance Manufacturers
   20 North Wacker Drive, Chicago, Illinois 60606

Bibliography

American Institute of Laundering
  Joliet, Illinois

National Institute of Drycleaning
  Silver Springs, Maryland

American Association of Textile Technology
  100 West 55th St., New York, N. Y. 10019

Chapter 5: MERCHANDISING CLOTHING—A FASCINATION BUSINESS

Logan, William B. and Moon, Helen M. *Facts About Merchandise.* Englewood Cliffs, New Jersey: Prentice-Hall Inc., 1967

Picken, Mary Brooks. *The Fashion Dictionary.* New York: Funk and Wagnalls Co., 1957

Richert, G. Henry, Meyer, Warren G., and Haines, Peter G., *Retailing Principles and Practices.* 4th edition. New York: McGraw Hill Book Co., 1962

Robinson, O. Preston, Robinson, Christine H., and Zeiss, George W. *Successful Retail Salesmanship.* 3rd edition. Englewood Cliffs, New Jersey, 1961

Wingate, Isabel B., Gillespie, Karen R., and Addison, Betty G. *Know Your Merchandise.* 3rd edition. New York: McGraw Hill Book Co., 1964

Wingate, John W. and Nolan, Carroll A. *Fundamentals of Selling.* 7th edition. Cincinnati, Ohio: Southwestern Publishing Co., 1959

Wingate, John W. and Weiner, J. Dana. *Retail Merchandising.* 6th edition Cincinnati, Ohio: Southwestern Publishing Co., 1963

Films and Filmstrips

"The Importance of Selling" Encyclopedia Britannica Films
  Role of selling in the modern economy. 20 min.

"The Face in the Mirror" Jim Handy
  Little things that impress customers. 24 min.

"It's the Little Things That Count" Bates Mfg. Co.
  Effective ways to gain the buyer's confidence. 30 min.

"Your Retail Store" Key Productions
  42 frames, black and white

"The Right Approach" International Films Bureau
  Welcoming the customer. 9 min.

"Terry Takes a Tip" Talon
  Selling techniques in women's ready-to-wear. 20 min.

"Selling Your Personality" Business Education Films
  The right and wrong way of selling. 11 min.

Opportunities in Clothing

"Challenge Across the Counter"   National Cash Register Co.
    152 frames, recording

"Department Store Cash Register Procedure"   National Cash Register Co.
    Part I—2 filmstrips, recording. (1) Your Cash Register (66 frames); (2) Cash-Take Transaction (74 frames)
    Part II—2 filmstrips, recording. (1) Transactions Requiring Sales Slips (71 frames); (2) When You Go to the Selling Floor (82 frames).

Suggested Sources of Information

Associations:

American Retail Federation
1145 Nineteenth St. N. W.
Washington, D. C. 20036

Women's Apparel Chains Association
11 East 26th St.
New York, N. Y. 10010

National Retail Merchants Association
100 West 31st St.
New York, N. Y. 10001

Periodicals:

Journal of Retailing
New York University
100 Washington Square East
New York, N. Y.

Department Store Economist
Chilton Company
Chestnut and 56th St.
Philadelphia, Pa. 19139

Stores
National Retail Merchants Assoc.
100 West 31st St.
New York, N. Y.

Department Store Journal
25 West 45th St.
New York, N. Y. 10036

Women's Wear Daily
Fairchild Publications, Inc.
7 East 12th St.
New York, N. Y. 10003

Chapter 6: INDUSTRIAL SEWING—THE TOOL FOR MASS PRODUCTION

Arnold, Pauline and White, Percival. *Clothes and Cloth.* New York: Holiday House, 1961

Kogos, Frederick. *Apparel Engineering and Needle Trades Handbook.* Fred'k. Kogos Publishing Co. 1140 Broadway, New York. 1960

Seams and Stitches. Union Special Machine. Chicago, Illinois

Silverman, Julia E. *Power Machine Sewing.* New York: Richard R. Smith. 1942

Singer Machine Manuals—31–15, Lockstitch Machine; 271W1, Buttonhole; 331K4, Tailoring Machine; 460/14, Overedger; and 175, Single Thread Chain Stitch.

Bibliography

Film

"The Inheritance" Amalgamated Clothing Workers

Suggested Sources of Information

Periodicals:

Women's Wear Daily
Fairchild Publications, Inc.
7 East 12th St.
New York, N. Y. 10003

The Bobbin Magazine
Needle Trades Publishing Corporation
1120 Shop Road
P.O. Box 527
Columbia, South Carolina 29202

Chapter 7: BASIC SKILLS FOR CLOTHING CONSTRUCTION

Erwin, Mabel D. and Kinchen, Lila A. *Clothing for Moderns.* 3rd edition. New York: The Macmillan Co. 1964

Better Homes and Gardens. *Professional Sewing Tips.* New York: Meredith Press, 1966

Better Homes and Gardens. *Sewing Book.* New York: Meredith Publishing Company, 1961

Singer Sewing Library. *How To Do Dressmaker Tailoring.* New York: The Singer Company, 1961

McCall's Step-by-Step Sewing Book. New York: McCall Corporation, 1966

Simplicity Sewing Book. New York: Simplicity Pattern Co., Inc.

Vogue Sewing Book. New York: The Butterick Company, Inc.

Chapter 8: FITTING AND ALTERATION—A HIGHLY SPECIALIZED BUSINESS

Erwin, Mabel D. and Kinchen, Lila A. *Clothing for Moderns.* 3rd edition. New York: The Macmillan Co. 1964

Better Homes and Gardens. *Sewing Casual Clothes.* New York: Meredith Press, 1966

Better Homes and Gardens. *Pattern Adjustments.* New York: Meredith Press, 1966

Better Homes and Gardens. *Sewing Book.* New York: Meredith Publishing Company, 1961

U. S. Department of Agriculture. *Fitting Coats and Suits.* Washington, D. C., U. S. Government Printing Office, 1963

Singer Sewing Library. *How to Measure, Alter, and Fit.* New York: The Singer Co., 1960

Singer Sewing Library. *How to Mend and Refit.* New York: The Singer Co., 1961

Opportunities in Clothing

The name and address of suppliers of the films and other supplementary materials mentioned in the previous lists are given below:

Associated Films, Inc.	347 Madison Ave. New York, N. Y. 10017
Award Record and Film Co.	1000 E. Colorado Pasadena, Calif. 91106
Coronet Films	Coronet Bldg. Chicago, Illinois 60601
Encyclopedia Britannica Films, Inc.	1150 Wilmette Ave. Wilmette, Illinois 60091
Guidance Associates	Pleasantville, New York 10570
Key Productions	Available through: Stanley Bowmar Co., Inc. 12 Cleveland St. Valhalla, New York 10595
Modern Talking Picture Service, Inc.	1212 Avenue of the Americas New York, N. Y. 10036
American Home Economics Assoc.	1600 Twentieth Street, N. W. Washington, D. C. 20009
U. S. Government Printing Office	Superintendent of Documents Washington, D. C. 20402
The Butterick Company, Inc.	161 Sixth Avenue New York, N. Y. 10013
Celanese Fibers Marketing Co.	Consumer Relations Department 522 Fifth Avenue New York, N. Y. 10036
Dan River Mills	111 West 40th Street New York, N. Y. 10018
McCall Corporation	230 Park Avenue New York, N. Y. 10017
Simplicity Pattern Co., Inc.	200 Madison Avenue New York, N. Y. 10016
Film Associates of California	6736 Selma Avenue Hollywood, Calif. 90028
National Cash Register Co.	355 Fleet Street Pittsburgh, Pa. 15220

INDEX

A

A-line skirt, 204
Absences from work, 27
Accessories, 221–225
Accordion pleats, 204
Acetate
  definition of, 115
  characteristics of, 116, 117
  advantages and disadvantages, 116
  hints for handling, 117
Achromatic, 50
Acrilan, 121
Acrylic fibers
  sources of, 121
  characteristics of, 122
  hints for handling, 123
Acrylonitrile, 121
Advancement
  sewing machine operator, 39
  salespeople, 34
  stock clerk, 36
Advertised merchandise, selling, 172
After-image, 53
"All Wool," 99
Alpaca hair, 99
Alteration
  basting, 268
  fitting stage, 200
  "How-to" points, 309–311
  judging, 308, 309
  lines, 276, 278, 279
Alterations
  marking, pins, chalk, thread, 311
  procedure, 310
Altering, 41
Amalgamated Clothing Workers of America, The (see *Unions*)
"Analagous," 50
Angora sweaters, 207
Apparel industry, 231
Application, job
  sample form, 16, 17
  simple, 20–26
Assemblers, 253
Authorization of the customer's charge, 176

B

Balance, formal, informal, 72, 73
  of color (see *Color*)
Band, 272
Bandeau bra, 215
Basic skill in clothing construction
  Chapter 7, 258–307
Basket weave (see *Plain weave*)
Basting (see *Stitching*)
Bed jackets, 219
Bell skirts, 204
Better Business Bureau, 14, 15
Bias
  cut slip, 217
  definition, 260
  faced collar, 300
  facings, 296, 297
  seam, 229
Binding, 272, 297, 298
Blazer, 204
Blended yarns, 129
Blondes and colors, 58
Blouses, 205, 207; care of, 206
Bobbin
  helpful hints, 242
  winder adjustment, 247
  winding, 242
Bodice or shell
  alteration, 321–336
  armhole; tight, loose, fullness, wrinkles, 334–336
  darts; underarm, length, sleeve, 328
  fitting in construction, 200
  general fit, 328, 329
  grain; horizontal, vertical, 322–324
  guidelines for proper fit, 321–332
  midriff wrinkles; bustline-side seam armhole-center front, horizontal fold, 332–334
  neckline; high, snug, loose, gaps, 329, 330
  seams; shoulder, underarm, armhole, waistline, 324–327
  shoulder wrinkles; neckline-underarm, armhole-bustline, base of neck, across back, 330–332
  sleeve; tight, loose, twist, length, 334–336
Bolero, 204
Bonding fibers, 130
Boning (girdles), 212
Bonus, 21
Bouclé yarns (see *Yarns*)
Bound placket, 302
Box pleats, 204, 293
Bras, 214–217
Briefs, 212
Brunettes and colors, 58
Bulking, 261
Bust, small, large, 81
Buttonhole, 199, 263
Buttonholer, 233
Buttonholes, 199
Buttons (coat), 202
Buying, 158

C

Cafeteria, 21
Camel's hair, 98
Carbon paper, dressmakers', 264
Cardigan jacket (suit), 203, 204
Care of
  blouse, 206, 207
  bra, 217
  girdle, 214
  hosiery, 221
  shoes, 223
  stock, 188
  sweater, 208, 209
  swim wear, 211
  wool, 97
Career girl, The real, 27–29
Cashmere, 98
Cash register receipt and detail tape, 175, 176, 177
Cash sale returns, 183
Cellulose acetate, 115
Center back, front, 276
Center of interest, 78
Chain stitch (see *Stitching*)
Chain stores, 154, 155
Chanel type (suit), 204
Charge sale, 176; return, 183
Check your selling I.Q., 169
Chemical term, 118
Child-labor, 24
"Chroma," 50
Chrysalis, 104
Circle chart, 239; skirts, 204
"Classic," 45
Clean finish, 271; machine, 248
Clip, 271
Closed seam (see *Seams*)
Cloth, 85
Clothes brush, 267
Clothing maintenance, 83
  packaging, 181, 182
  repair, 41
Coats, 201–202, 207
  all-weather, 201
C.O.D. (see *Sales transaction*)
Collars, 298–300
Color
  adjacent, 53
  complementary, 55
  advancing, 51
  appearance, 57
  balance, 56
  combinations of, 55
  complementary, 50
  contrasts, 52, 53
  cool, 49
  emotions associated with, 60

345

Index

Color (cont.)
  emphasis, 78
  fundamentals of, 46, 47
  harmony, 54
  hue, 49
  intensity, 49, 52
  intermediate, 48
  language, 49, 50
  light and dark, 51
  moods, 50, 59
  nature of, 59
  new, 46
  personality, 52
  primary, 48, 53
  pure, 55
  related, 50
  secondary, 48
  shade, 49, 56
  size relationship, 51
  value, 49
  wave length, 48
  wheel, 48, 49
"Combed cotton," 89
Commissions and production, 180
Companion items, 172
Comparison shopper, 36, 37
Complaints, 183
Complementary merchandise, 172
Construction
  lines, 65
  markings, 279, 284
  shape and fullness, 291–294
  techniques, 287–306
Continuous placket, 302
Contour bra, 215
Convenience items, 172
Corded seam (see *Seams*)
Cords, thread, 261
Corselet, all in one, 212, 213
Corset, 213
Costume, 204
Cotton
  advantages and disadvantages, 91
  characteristics, 90
  "classing," 89
  hints for handling cotton, 92
  processing, 89
  shrinkage labeling, 91
  sources of, 88
  testing, 90
  thread, 261
Credit union, 21
Creslan, 121
Crewel (needles), 265
Current look, 43
Customer, consultant help, 152, 153
  services, 160, 183
  suitability for, 194
Cutter, 252, 253
Cutting
  line, 276
  machine, 263
  marking, 284–286
  mass production, 279
  process, 279–286
  suggestions, 284

D

Dacron, 123
Darts, 291, 292
de Chardonnet, Count Hilaire, 109
Decorative facing, 297; lines, 68
Denier hosiery, 219
Department stores, 155, 156
  advantages of, 156
de Réaumur, René A., 109
Design, 72
Direct printing, 146
Discharge printing, 146

Discount, privileges, 21;
  stores, 157, 158
Disposable clothes, 149
Distribution or Marketing, 151–153
Dirndl skirt, 204
Divided skirt, 204
Double complementary colors, 54
Douppioni silk (see *Silk*)
Dresses
  afternoon, 197
  babydoll, 195, 196
  basic, 195
  blouson, 195, 196
  coat, 195, 196
  chemise, 44
  cocktail, 197
  daytime, 195
  dinner, 197
  empire, 195
  formal, 197
  morning, 195
  princess, 195, 196
  sack, 44
  sheath, 195
  shift, 44, 195
  shirt waist, 195
  skimmer, 195
  smock, 195
  tent, 195
Dressmakers, 39–42; price
  samples, 40, 41
Drill, marking, 284
"Dry goods," store, 153
Durable press (see *Pressing*)
Dusters, 218
Dye and dye finishes, 145
  (also see *Synthetic dyes*)

E

Ease, 271
Easing, 294
Edge stitching (see *Stitching*)
Electric scissors, 263
Embossing (finishes), 145
Emery bag, 265
Empress Josephine (French Empire), 44
Empire waistline, 43
Employers' techniques with applicant, 15
Employment
  agencies' fees, 15
  agency, 12, 14
  as a sewing machine operator, 38
Epaulets, 44
Equal Employment Opportunity, 24
Equal Pay Act, 24
Experts' guide, The, 194

F

Fabrics
  bras, 214, 215
  blouse, 205, 206
  characteristics, 83
  charts, 226
  coat, 201
  crepe, 128
  deep-pile, 140
  finishes, 142–150
  folding chart, 280
  girdle, 212
  gloves, 223
  history of, 83
  hosiery, 219
  labeling, 86, 87
  lounge wear, 218
  panties, 218
  pattern requirements, 226
  preparation of, 279

Fabrics (cont.)
  quality, 131
  shoes, 221
  shorts and slacks, 209
  skirts, 204
  sleepwear, 218
  slips, 217
  straighten, 279
  suits, 202
  swim wear, 210
Face shapes, 68
Facing
  definition, 272
  fitted, 294, 295, 299
"Fad," 45
Fair Labor Standards Act, 24
"Fashion"
  cycle, 45
  defined, 43, 194
Fasteners, 229
Features and color, 57
Federal
  Income tax, 22
  Old-Age and Survivors Insurance, 22
  Trade Commission, 87
  Wage and Hour Law, 23
Fees, employment agency, 15
Felting, 129
Fibers
  content, 85
  dope, 109
  groups, 86
  man-made, 109–110
  natural, 88–109
  yarn, 126–129, 225
Figure fashion analysis, 79
Filament
  description, 109
  yarn, 126
Filling knit, 137
Finishes; appearance, performance, 144–147
First fitting, 286
Fitting
  a highly specialized business, Chapter 8, 307–336
  blouse, 206
  bra, 216
  coat, 202
  correcting problems, 312, 321
  girdle, 214
  gloves, 225
  hosiery, 220
  in construction, 40, 200
  panties, 218
  second, 287
  shoes, 223
  skirt, 205
    full, 312
  slip, 217
  shorts and slacks, 210
  swim wear, 211
  techniques, 312–336
Fitting-room pointers, 171
Flared skirt, 204
Flax, 93
Flat-felled seam (see *Seam*)
Flat pinning, 310
Foam lamination, 130
Fold line
  definition, 276, 280
Foot treadle adjustment, 248
Form finisher, 266
Formal (symmetrical) balance (see *Balance*)
Fortrel, 123
Foundation garments, 212–217
French seams (see *Seams*)
Fringe benefits, 21, 22
Full slip, 217

Index

G

Garment construction
  assembling, 286, 287
  completion, 287
  manufacturing plant conditions, 38
  packaging, 256
  production steps, 252–257
  quality, 255
Garter belt, 212
Gathering, 293
Generic groups, 87
Gift merchandise, 172; wrapping, 182
Girdles, 212–214
Glass fiber clothing, 149
Gloves, 223–225
Golden section, 74
Gored skirt, 204
Go-together selling pointers, 172
Gowns, sleepwear, 218
Grading (see *Layer*)
Graduation, 78
Grain
  crosswise, 259
  importance of, 309
  lengthwise, 259
  line, 276
  off grain, 260
  of garment, 198
  perfect, 279
  position of, 312–314
  true, 259
Granny gown, sleepwear, 218
Grass-bleaching linen, 93
Gray goods, 142
Greige goods, 142
Gross income, 22
Group hospital and life insurance, 21

H

Hair
  colors and clothing, 58
  fibers, 98
Half sizes, 199; slip, 217
Handbags, 224
Handbook on Women Workers, 24
Handling complaints, 182, 183
Hand sewer, 39
Health form, 18
Heavy duty thread, 229
Heel styles (shoes), 222
Hems
  coats, 202
  edge stitched, 304, 305
  qualities, 199
  skirts, 205
Hemmed plackets, 302; seam, 288
Helpful hints for customer relationships, 164
"High fashion," 46
Hips, 82
History of fashion, 43
Hold-up pinning, 310
Homespun weave (see *Plain weave*)
Honesty (employee), 28
Hosiery
  full-fashioned, 219
  gauge, 219
  higher denier, 219
  irregular, 220
  lower denier, 219
  measuring, 264
  needle count, 219
  plain knit, 219
  seamless, 219
Hostess gowns, 218
Housecoat, 218
Household furnishings, 41, 42
How clothes are made, 126–142
How colors affect each other, 52, 53
Hue (see *Color*)

I

Impression, first, 46
Independent store, 153, 154
Industrial sewing, 37, 231–257; sewing machine, 41
Informal (asymmetrical) balance (see *Balance*)
Inspection chart, 254
Inspectors, 254
Insulation, 147
Intensity, 49, 52
Interfacing, 227, 228, 272
Interlining, 228, 272
Intermediate color (see *Color*)
International Ladies Garment Workers Union (see *Unions*)
Interstate commerce, 23
Inventories, 192
Inventory sheet, 191
Inverted pleats, 204, 293
Iron, hand, 266
Iron-on interfacing, 227
Iron-on seam binding, 229

J

Jacquard, Joseph Marie, 136
Jacquard weave, 136
Job
  application, 13, 14
  attitude, 10
  availability in production, 38
  experience in the sewing operation, 38, 39
  hunting, 11
  interviewing, answering questions, qualifications, 11
  requirements (special), 11
  security, 23
Junior (size), 199

K

Knee lever adjustment, 247, 248
Knife pleats, 204, 293
Knitted fabrics, 136, 141
  double, 137
  filling, 137
Knowing Your Merchandise, 193, 194
Kodel, 123

L

Laminated fabrics, 140
Language of color, 49, 50
  fashion, 45
  sewing, 268
Lanolin, 97
Lapel, collar (coat), 202
Lapped seam (see *Seams*)
Lapped (slide fasteners), 302, 303
Lappet weave, 135
Lap pinning, 310
Lastex, 212
Laundering
  acetate, 117
  acrylics, 123
  cotton, 92
  durable press, 149
  knit fabrics, 141
  laminated fabrics, 140
  linen, 95
  nylon, 120, 121
  pile fabrics, 139
  polyester, 124
  pre-lined fabrics, 140
  rayon, 114, 115
  silk, 108
Laundering (cont.)
  stretch fabrics, 141
  wash-and-wear, 148
  wool, 102
Layaway (see *Sales transactions*)
Layer, 271
Lay-offs, 23
"Learn More About" acetate, 115
  acrylic fibers, 123
  appearance finishes, 146, 147
  cellulosic fibers, 117
  control of a power-driven machine, 235, 236
  cotton, 89
  employment opportunities, 42
  fabric construction, 138
  fabric finishes, 144, 148
  linen, 94
  machine adjustments, 245
  nylon, 119
  polyester fibers, 123
  rayon, 113
  silk, 106
  the sewing machine, 248
  thread the machine, 239, 240
  wool, 100
  yarns, 127, 129
Leather (coats), 201
Leno weave (see *Plain weave*)
Letter of application, 15
Line
  combination, 64
  curved, 61
  diagonal, 62
  horizontal, 62
    examples, 67
  I.T.Y.V., 68, 69
  transitional, 62
  vertical, 62, 67
    examples, 67
  wavy chart, 239
Linen
  advantages and disadvantages, 95
  characteristics, 94, 95
  hints for handling, 95
  labeling, 93, 94
  line, 94
  production of, 92, 93
  retting, 93
  sources of, 92
Lingerie, 217–221
Lining
  fabrics, 228, 272
  coat lining, 202
Llama hair, 99
Local wage tax, 22
Locating workers, 14
Location lines, 276
Lockstitch sewing machine, 239
Long-leg panty girdle, 212
Longline bra, 215
Lounge wear, 218
Loyalty as personal asset, 28
Lycra, 125

M

Machine spreader, 252
Mail-order houses, 158
Man-made fibers, 86, 109–126
Mark-downs, 187
Marketing, direct-indirect, 151
Markers, 252
Matching points, 276
Materials, 85, 259–268
Measurements, taking, 272, 275
Mechanical stretch weave, 138
Mechanics of selling, 174–192
Medical department, 21
Medium of expression, 72

347

Index

Merchandise
  arrangement, 187, 188
  handling of a sale, 176
  inspection, 185
  receiving; entering, preparing for sale, distributing, returning, 34, 35
  records, 189
Merchandising, 30–37, 152
Mercerized cotton thread, 229
Mercerizing, 90, 144
"Merry Widow" (corselet), 213
Mesh knit hosiery, 219
Military influence on fashion, 44, 45
Milium treatment, 147
Minimum wage, 23
Misses (size), 199
Modacrylics, 122
Mode, 46
Mohair, 99
Molecular chain, 118
"Monochromatic," 50
Monofilament yarn, 110
Moods and color, 50, 59
Mothproofing, 147
Multifilament yarn, 110
Multiple needle machine, 233

N

Nap, 145, 226, 260
Napping, 144, 145
Natural
  dyes, 145
  fibers, 84, 86, 88
  flair, 46
  order of color, 56
Neckline, 68; fit, 200
Necks, 81
Needle
  board, 267
  count, hosiery, 219
  replacement, 246
Needles
  machine, hand, 265
  crewel, 265
  sharps, 265
Negligee, 218, 219
Negroes and color, 58, 59
Net income, 22
Newton, Sir Issac, 47
"Non-personal selling," 159
Non-woven interfacing, 227
Notch, 271, 276, 284
Notions, 229
Number of colors per outfit, 56
Nylon
  characteristics of, 120
  hints for handling, 120, 121
  sources of, 119

O

Off grain, 260
Oil the machine, 248, 249
"One way" fabric, 281
On-the-job training, 11, 27, 37
Operation, sewing machine, 235, 236
Oppositional lines, 62
Opposition (see *Graduation*), 77, 78
Optical illusions, 65–67
Original creation, 40
Orlon, 121
Outer garment (coats), 202
Outline, figure impressions, 64
Out-of-scale, 76
Overcoat (styling), 202
Overfitting, 309
Overtime, 23

P

Padded bra, 215, 216
Paid holidays, 21
Panel and seams (girdles), 212
Paneled slip, 217
Panties, 218
Panty girdle, 212
Pajamas, 218
Paper clothing, 149
Parts, sewing machine, 235
  thread control, 239
Pattern
  commercial, 276–279
  cutting, commercial, 282–284
  figure and size chart, 274, 275
  markings chart, 277
  matching, 199
  measurements, 273
  pinning, 281, 282
  placement, 281–284
  size, 226, 272
  type, 272
Pay check, The, 22
Pea jacket, 204
Peignoir (see *Negligee*)
Pension plan, 21
Personal
  interview, 19
  approach to selling, 164
  hygiene, 234, 235
  manner and actions, 20
  qualifications of stock clerk, 35
  references, 11
Personality and color, 52
Petticoats, 217
Piece-dyed, 145
Pigments, 48
Pile, 145; weaving, 134, 135
Pin-basting (stitching), 268
Pin cushion, 265
Pinked seam, 288; hem, 304
Pinking shears, 262
Pins, 265
Pin tuck, 292
Piped seam, 290
Plain knit
  hosiery, 219
  seam, 287, 288
  weave, 131–133
Plackets, 301, 302
Planning of sales promotional events, 152
Plant facilities, 24
Pleated skirt, 204, 312
Pleats, 292, 293
Power
  of color, the, 59
  of line, 65–67
Print fabrics and scale, 76
Point presser, 267
Polyester fiber, 86, 123, 124
Polymer, 118
Polymerization, 118
Polyurethane fiber, 124, 125
Pounding block, 268
Power stretch, 138
Pre-inventory sales, 192
Pre-lined (bonded fabrics), 140, 141
Preparatory finishes, 142–144
Preparing merchandise, 185
Press cloth, 266
Pressers, 255
Pressing
  acetate, 117
  cotton, 92
  durable, 148, 149
  knit fabrics, 141
  laminated fabrics, 140
  linen, 95
  nylon, 121

Pressing (cont.)
  pile fabrics, 139
  pre-lined fabrics, 140
  rayon, 115
  silk, 108
  stretch fabrics, 141
  wash-and-wear, 149
  wool, 103
Press mit, 268
Pressure on material, regulation, 245, 246
Pre-teen (size), 199
Price tag, 175, 186, 187
Principles, color use, 54–57
Principles of design, 72–79
Printing (finishes), 145, 146
Prism, 47
Problem figures, 40
Production card, 180
Production
  chart (garment), 253
  cut-backs, 23
Professional look, 162; manner, 161
Profit-sharing, 21
Promotional, 31
Proportion, 74
Proportional patterns, 279
Pucker, 271
Puff iron, 266
Pullover sweater, 208

Q

Quiz yourself on your work habits, 27

R

Raincoat (styling), 202
Rainwear shoe styles, 222
Ratine yarns, 128
Rayon
  advantages and disadvantages, 114
  characteristics of, 113, 114
  cuprammonium, 111, 112
  definition of, 115
  hints for handling, 114
  production of, 112
  source, 111
Ready-to-wear, 195–204
Receipt of transaction, 180
Receiving clerk, 185
Red-heads and color, 58
Reflection of color, 58
Regenerated fiber, 111
Regular length panty girdle, 212
Reinforce, 270, 271
Related
  color, 50
  merchandise from other departments, 172
  sewing, 41, 42
Released tuck, 292
Repair sewing, 39
Reprocessed wool, 99
Resume, sample, 11–13
Retail Wholesale and Department Store Union (see *Union*)
Retail Clerks International Association (see *Unions*)
Retailing, 151
Returns, 182, 183
Reused wool, 99
Rhythm
  definition, 76–78
  of lines, 63
Rib weave (see *Plain weave*)
Ripping, 251
Roving strand, 127
Ruler, 264

Index

S

Safety rules
  bobbin winder, 247
  corner stitching, 239
  general, 235
  machine operation, 236
  oiling the machine, 248
  replacing the needle, 246
  sewing, 234, 251
  straight stitch, 237
  threading, 241
  under threading, 243
Salary, 20, 21
Sale, recording, 175–180
Salesmanship techniques, 163–173
Sale merchandise display, 188
Salesperson, 30–34
Sales
  slip, 175, 177, 179
  transactions, 174
Sample maker, 39, 40
Sateen fabric, 134
Satin weave, 131, 134
Scale, 76
Scissors, 262, 263
Scouring wool, 97
Screen printing, 146
Scutching linen, 93
Seam allowance, 276, 283; binding, 229, 305; roll, 267
Seams
  basic, 287
  bound, 288
  closed, 304
  coats, 202
  corded, 290
  flat-felled, 289
  French, 290
  lapped, 289
  piped, 290
  open, 204
  skirts, 205
  top-stitched, 288
  tucked, 289
  welt, 288, 289
  width, 198, 199
  woven edge, 229
Seam stitching
  helpful hints, 250
  width, 287
Section production
  (see *Step production*)
"Section work," 249
Selecting colors for an individual, 57
Self-facings, 295, 296
Selling, "non-personal," "personal," 159
Selvage, 259
Semi-skilled vocation, sewing, 233
Send transaction, 176; sales slip, 178
Sericin, 104
Sericulture, 104
Sewing
  acetate, 117
  acrylics, 123
  cotton, 92
  custom, 39
  department, 254
  durable press, 149
  fabrics, 83
  knit fabrics, 141
  laminated fabrics, 140
  linen, 95
  machine operator, 37
  nylon, 121
  operation, 37
  pile fabrics, 139

Sewing (cont.)
  polyester, 124
  pre-lined fabrics, 140, 141
  rayon, 115
  services, 39–42
  silk, 108
  stretch fabrics, 141, 142
  wash-and-wear, 149
  wool, 103
Sewing machine rate, 231
Shapes in fashion, 64
  needles, 265
Shaped dart, 291
Shears, 262
Shearing finishes, 145
Sheath (skirts), 204
Shirring, 294
Shoes, 221–223
Shorts and slacks, 209, 210
Shoulders, rounded, 81
Sick leave, 21
Silicone resins, 147
Silk
  advantages and disadvantages, 107
  characteristics, 106
  doupioni, 105
  hints for handling, 108
  labeling, 106
  production of, 104
  reeled, 104, 105
  sources, 103
  spun, 105
  thread, 229
Size, clothing
  blouse, 206
  bra, 216
  coats, 202
  cup, 216
  girdle, 213
  gloves, 225
  hosiery, 220
  lounge wear, 219
  panties, 218
  patterns, 199–200
  shoes, 222, 223
  shorts and slacks, 210
  skirt, 205
  sleepwear, 218
  slip, 217
  sweater, 208
Sizing (finishes), 144
Skilled jobs, 39
Skills in fitting and altering, 308
Skipped stitches, 247
Skirt alterations
  hemline; shorten, lengthen, optically straight, 320, 321
  hipline fit; snug, loose, cups, hemline, dart length, pleats open, 318–320
  grain; off grain, horizontal, vertical, 312–314
  guide lines for proper fit, 312
  seams: center, side, waistline, 314–316
  waistline fit; loose, snug, horizontal wrinkles, 316–318
Skirts
  fit, 200, 312
  length, 44, 45
  quality details, 204, 205
Skirt marker, 264
Slash, 271
Sleepwear, 218
Sleeve board, 267
Sleeves
  fit, 200
  industrial sewing, 300, 301
Slide fasteners, 199, 205, 302, 304
Slim skirt (fitting), 312
Slips, 217

Slub yarns, 128
Small scale production, 40
Social Security, 11, 22
Socks, 219
Soft pleats, 204
Space division, 70, 71
Spandex, 124, 138, 212, 214
Special interest merchandise, 172
Specialty shops, 155
Spectrum, 47
Split complementary colors, 55
Sponge ironing, 267
Sportswear, 209–211
Special laws for women, 24
State Employment Office, 14
Stain-resistant, 147
Standard of living, 38
Staple fibers, 85
State Employment Service, 14
Status and prestige, 25, 26
Stay stitching (see *Stitching*)
Steam press, 266
Step production, 37
Stitching, 198, 268
  backstitch, 250, 269
  basting, 268
  blind, 270
    hem, 305
  catch, 270
  chain, 269
  charts, 236
  continuous, 251
  correction, 246
  curved, 239
  directional, 269
  ease, 269
  edge, 269
  incorrect feeding, 246
  gathering, 269
  lock, 269
  loop, 246
  padded, 270
  practice charts, 238
  stay, 269
  straight, 236, 237
  tack, 270
  top, 269
  turning corners, 237
  under, 269
Stock
  automation, 176
  card, 189, 190
  clerk, 34–36
  control, 31, 152, 185, 187
  counts, 190–192
  dyed goods, 145
  handling, 187, 188
  rooms, 36
Stockings, 219
Stores image, 160
Store maintenance, 159
Store, The, 153–162
Straight
  cut slip, 217
  dart, 291
  grain and pattern grain, 282
  lines, 60, 61
Strapless bra, 215
Stretch
  degree of, 138
  direction of, 138
  fabrics, 141, 142
  hosiery, 219
  weaves, 138
  yarn, 128
Style
  bras, 215, 216
  contrasted with fashion, 194
  definition of, 46
  shorts and slacks, 209

349

Index

Style (cont.)
　slips, 217
　swim wear, 210
Styling
　coats, 201
　girdles, 212, 213
　gloves, 223, 225
　hosiery, 219
　lounge wear, 218
　panties, 218
　skirts, 204
　shoes, 222, 224
　sleepwear, 218
　suits, 202–204
Suede (coats), 201
Sueding (finishes), 145
Suits
　dressmaker, 202, 203
　ensemble, 203, 204
　slack, 203, 204
Sunburst (radiation rhythm), 77
Swagger coat (styling), 202
Sweat shop, 25
Sweaters; blend, cardigan,
　cashmere, 207–209
Swim wear, 210–211
Symbolism of color, 60
Synthetic
　dyes, 145
　fabrics (coats), 201
　fibers, 85, 117–119, 186
　sweaters, 207
　thread, 229, 261

T

Tack Stitching (see *Stitching*)
Taffeta weave (see *Plain weave*)
Tailoring (underlining), 228
Tailor tacks, 285
Tailored
　robes, 218
　skirt, 301
　slip, 217
　suits, 202–204
Tailor's
　chalk, 264
　ham, 268
　hem, 305
Tally sheet, 181
Tape measure, 263
Teen bra, 215; size, 199
Temperature and color, 51
Terylene, 123
Testing laboratories, 183
Textile, definition of, 85
Textile Fiber Products Labeling
　Act of 1958, 87
Texture of the fabric, 52
Thimble, 266
Thread
　breakage, 247
　changing, 241, 242
　count, 131
　physical properties, 260
　size, 261
　tension, 244, 245
　treated, 261
　types, 229
　weight, 261
Threading procedure, 240
Throwing (silk), 105

Time payment (see *Sales transactions*)
Tint, 49, 56
Tools and equipment
　cutting, 262, 263
　marking garments, 264
　measuring, 263, 264
　pressing, 266–268
　sewing, 265
Topcoat (styling), 202
Top stitching (see *Stitching*)
Tow (linen), 94
Tracing, paper, 284, 285
　wheel, 264, 284
Trench coat (styling), 202
Triacetate, 117
Triad, 55
Tricot, 137
Trim, 270
Trimmers, 255; trimmings, 229
Tucks, 292
Tucked seam (see *Seams*)
Tussah silk, 105
Tuxedo coat (styling), 202
Twice-knit (see *Knitting double*)
Twill weave (see *Weave*)
Two-way stretch girdle, 212

U

Underlining, 228, 272
Understitching (see *Stitching*)
Under threading, 242–244
Unemployment Compensation, 23
Unions, 25
Unit control system, 189
United Garment Workers of America
　(see *Unions*)
Upper threading 240–242

V

Variety stores, 155
Vertical figure divisions, 75
Vicuna hair, 99
"Virgin Wool," 99
Viscose rayon, 111, 112
Vocational-technical courses, 11
Vogue, 46
Voucher, 180
Vycron, 123

W

Waistband (skirt), 205
Waistline
　fit, 200
　girdle, 212
　placement, 75
Warp knit, 137
Wash-and-wear, 148
Water-repellent, 147
Weave
　core spun, 138
　double, 136
　figure, 135
　pile, 139
　rib, 133
　twill, 131, 133, 139
　weft, 130, 137
Weaving pattern, 131
Weft knit, 137
Weighting (silk), 106

Welt seam (see *Seams*)
"What do I want to do?" 10
Where to apply for a job, 13, 14
Wild silk (see *Tussah silk*)
Withholding tax, 22
Women's Bureau of the U. S.
　Department of Labor, 24
Women's fashion center, 39
Women's sizes, 199
Women, working statistics, 9
Wool
　advantages and disadvantages, 102
　characteristics of, 100
　cleaning, 102
　fulling, 98
　insulating quality, 101
　labeling wool, 99
　mothproof, 102
　processing, 96, 97
　sources, 95, 96
　sweaters, 207
　testing, 100
Wool Products Labeling Act
　of 1939, 99
Woolen yarns, 97
Work area
　certificate of condition, 11
　habits, safety, 234, 235
　of the cash register, 181
　of salesperson, 152
Work
　conditions, 25
　of the sewing machine operator,
　　38
　of the stock clerk, 35
　married women, 10
　standards, 23–25
　world of, 38
Workman's compensation, 23
Worsted yarn, 97
Woven interfacing, 227
Wrap-around skirt, 204
Wrapping or sacking, 181, 182
Wrinkle resistance, 147
Wrinkle-resistant cotton, 91
Wrinkles, avoiding, 310

Y

Yarn
　bouclé, 128
　bulk, 128
　classification, 129, 145
　combination, 129
　into fabrics, 129
　monofilament, 110
　multifilament, 110
　ply, 129
　ratine, 128
　shantung, 128
　simple, 129
　S and Z twist, 128
　slab, 128
　spun, 126
　swivel, 135
　warp, 130
Yard goods, 225–229
Yardstick, 264

Z

Zefran, 121
Zipper, 229